Entrepreneurship: globalization, innovation and development

Entrepreneurship: globalization, innovation and development

Elizabeth Chell

THOMSON

LEARNING

Australia • Canada • Mexico • Singapore • Spain • United Kingdom • United States

THOMSON

LEARNING

Entrepreneurship: globalization, innovation and development

Copyright © 2001 Elizabeth Chell

The Thomson Learning logo is a registered trademark used herein under licence.

For more information, contact Thomson Learning, Berkshire House. 168–173 High Holborn, London, WC1V 7AA or visit us on the World Wide Web at: http://www.thomsonlearning.com.

Britsh Library Cataloguing-in-Publication Data
A catalogue record for this book is available from the British Library

ISBN 1-86152-318-1

First edition published 2001 by Thomson Learning

Typeset by Leech Design, Cumbria
Printed in the UK by TJ International, Padstow, Cornwall
Project management Genesys Editorial Limited

Contents

Acknowledgements

The writing of this book has been much slower than I would have liked. I owe a debt of gratitude to a number of people for helping me in my endeavours. First and foremost are friends and especial mention should be made of Sandra Morris, who has been unstinting in her support. I would also like to thank those research students and research associates who have helped me gather primary data which I have used illustratively throughout the book. In particular I thank Dr Susan Baines (Newcastle University), Dr Luke Pittaway (Lancaster Univerity) and Dr Paul Tracey (Oxford University). I also thank Dr Mohd Ezani Mat Hassan for personal permission to quote material from his thesis, *Quality Management in Malaysian Organizations*. I am grateful to Professor John Burgoyne for personal permission to quote material from his paper "Learning: conceptual, practical and theoretical issues" presented at the British Academy of Management Conference, Nottingham, September 1998. I am ever thankful for secretarial support from the School of Management, Newcastle University, in particular in the production of tables and figures. I thank Malcolm Hart onetime owner-director of Gill Air for his entertaining account of the turnround process and for the entertaining workshop he presented to my masters students. I also thank him for permission to make reference to the case of Gill Air in this text. I am also extremely grateful to the many owner-managers and entrepreneurs whom I have interviewed over the years. They are too numerous to mention but truly without the knowledge I gained from those fascinating encounters this book could not have been written. I would also like to acknowledge the support of the ESRC, the University of Newcastle, the Tyneside TEC and the NEBS Management for research grants which have enabled me and others to foster the development of ideas and understanding of the workings of entrepreneurially led ventures. In particular I would like to mention Mr Ian Forster and Dr Sally Messenger for their unwavering confidence in my ability to develop further the research aspirations of the NEBS Management. I hope that I continue to fulfil those aspirations.

Finally I would like to make the following acknowledgements for permission to reproduce material:

Human Resource Development in Small to Medium Sized Enterprises, Department of Employment Research Paper No 88, p38, Fig 5 (adapted); Crown copyright is reproduced with the permission of the Controller of Her Majesty's Stationery Office;

Influences on team-role behaviour, adapted from Figure 3.1 What Underlies Team Role Behaviour? in R. M. Belbin (1983), *Team Roles at Work*, Butterworth Heinemann, p.28, reprinted by permission of Butterworth

Heinemann Publishers, a division of Reed Educational & Professional Publishing, Ltd.

An adaptation of Table 3.1 The Nine Team Roles from R. M. Belbin (1983), *Team Roles at Work*, Butterworth Heinemann, p.22, reprinted by permission of Butterworth Heinemann Publishers, a division of Reed Educational & Professional Publishing, Ltd.

Table 5.1 A thin line can separate some allowable weaknesses from unacceptable behaviour in R. M. Belbin (1983), *Team Roles at Work*, Butterworth Heinemann, p. 51, reprinted by permission of Butterworth Heinemann Publishers, a division of Reed Educational & Professional Publishing, Ltd.

Contrasting features between personnel management/IR and HRM based on Figure 2.2 'Twenty-seven points of difference', in J. Storey *Developments in the Management of Human Resources*, p.35, reprinted by permission of Blackwell Publishers.

A Suggested Model of the Strategic Human Resource Management of Employers in the Entrepreneurial Firm, based on Figure 1.1 in J. Storey (ed) (1989), *New Perspectives on Human Resource Management*, p7, reprinted by permission of Routledge.

The Five Stage Model for Small Business Growth, reprinted from *Long Range Planning*, 20, 3, p.48, 1987, with permission from Elsevier Science.

Rows 1–13 of Table 6.2 How 'global' are the top transnational corporations? Plus the *Notes* at the end of the Table, reprinted by permission of Paul Chapman (a Sage Publications Company) and the author; from Peter Dicken (1998) *Global Shift*. pp 194–5; © Peter Dicken, 1998.

Factors associated with group innovation theory and their impact on the innovation cycle, based on Figure 3, p. 326 of M.A. West (1990), 'The social psychology of innovation in groups', in West, M.A. and Farr, J.L. (Eds), *Innovation and Creativity at Work* 1990 © John Wiley & Sons Ltd. Reproduced by permission of John Wiley & Sons Ltd.

A model of the antecedent influences which lead to enhanced business performance, based on R.G.McGrath, I.C. McMillan and S. Venkataraman (1995). 'Defining the development of competence: a strategic process paradigm'. *Strategic Management Journal*, 16, pp 251–275. 1995 © John Wiley & Sons Ltd. Reproduced by permission of John Wiley & Sons Ltd.

Various Kinds of Strategies from the Deliberate to the Mostly Emergent, based on H. Mintzberg and J.A. Walters, (1985). 'Of strategies, deliberate and emergent', *Strategic Management Journal*, 6, p. 270, 1985 © John Wiley & Sons Ltd. Reproduced by permission of John Wiley & Sons Ltd.

Entrepreneurship & Regional Development, 10, 2, 125, Table 2. 'Forms of Business Ownership by Business Turnover', from E. Chell and S. Baines 'Does gender affect business performance?' © Taylor & Francis Ltd. (Http://www.tandf.co.uk/journals). Reproduced by permission of Taylor and Francis Ltd.

Martha Mazvevski and Mark F. Peterson (1997), 'Societal Values, Social Interpretation and Multinational Teams', in C. Skromme Granrose and S. Oskamp (eds), *Cross-Cultural Work Groups*, Sage Publications, Inc. pp. 68–71. © 1997 by Sage Publications, Inc. Reprinted by permission of Sage Publications Ltd.

Dedication

To my dear mother, Madge Chell, née Parkin of Hartshead, Liversedge, the county of Yorkshire and in memory of a dear father, James Leonard Chell of Heckmondwike, the county of Yorkshire, 21 May 1922 – 24 August 1987, for all you have both given me.

Preface

This study of entrepreneurship and enterprise, begun in 1998, has taken two years to produce, during which time there has been a heightened awareness within the British Government of the need for greater enterprise by business and commerce, and by the universities. There is, however, no political message in this book in the sense of the 'party political'; it is coincidental that the politico-economic thrust towards developing an enterprise culture and the direction that my studies have taken concur. Rather I was pondering how such issues as business development, the management process and the drive for business to become globally competitive articulated with entrepreneurialism. Resolving that set of issues became a particular purpose in the execution of this book.

Furthermore, throughout the 1990s, it was very apparent that the small to medium-sized enterprise (SME) and the multinational corporation (MNC) were being encouraged to think 'globally', that is, to consider their international competitiveness and where they were positioned in the marketplace. Such international pressures on businesses and economies are reshaping the syllabi in business schools. Innovation, change and business venturing are key processes driving the development of business. This climate provided a focus in defining what the student of enterprise would need to know. However the book addresses a much wider audience than that of the embryonic entrepreneur. It approaches the subject from a multi-disciplinary perspective; broaching subjects which deal with the geography of entrepreneurship, the psychology of the entrepreneur, learning styles and training needs to the design, development and professional management of enterprise. Whilst it has breadth of coverage, and one hopes depth, it was never intended to be a leading edge research monograph. Students who wish to pursue advanced research in entrepreneurship will find useful ideas which they will need to extend through the usual painstaking research processes.

In sum, this book aims to meet the needs of students who wish to take business management modules in entrepreneurship and enterprise. Such people will be the managers and entrepreneurs of tomorrow. Arguably, they need to be better equipped to understand the global context of enterprise, the nature of entrepreneurial behaviour in all its manifestations and the various ways in which enterprise can be managed.

Probably the real beginning of this book dates from 1997 when I sketched out a detailed plan. There were to be a number of themes that I wanted to weave into the text. I wanted very much to get away from the idea that entrepreneurship meant small business and business founding; such a focus was, in my opinion, too restrictive. Further, in developing a curriculum for entrepreneurship I wanted to see what ideas could be gleaned and developed from the mainstream literature. However, given the subject matter of enterprise, it seemed to me important to attempt to meld entrepreneurship theory and practice. The only way to achieve this in a text was to use real case study material by way of concrete illustration of ideas. Much of the theory of entrepreneurship has emanated from the US. However, not only for this reason did it seem crucial to broaden the coverage beyond the shores of the British Isles and examine the various themes relating to the development of entrepreneurship and enterprise as far across the globe as possible. I was, of course, acutely aware of the importance of cultural difference and trust that the reader will understand that one can only write within the limitations of one's own knowledge, understanding and cultural perspective on entrepreneurship. Having said that, I have endeavoured to use a wide variety of case material and knowledge from other parts of the world in the hope that this will make the book both interesting and relevant to the cosmopolitan citizens of the 21st century.

The use of vignettes, case studies and exercises as appropriate also addresses another issue: that of different students' learning styles. The student and the lecturer will be able to use the book experientially using the text as a source of material for tutorials, theory and research. The book is designed so as to enable its use by students at different levels and practitioners with different experience and background. The text is intended to be read both by undergraduates with little experience who will be more reliant on the one text with its illustrative material and postgraduate/post experience students who are perhaps reading a part time MBA or Msc in Entrepreneurship and who will appreciate the opportunity to generate their own materials by following the experiential route. Practitioners will I hope find the broad sweep of the subject matter of considerable interest. I am thinking particularly of people who are engaged in developing regional economic policies, addressing training and development issues, and whose concerns may be to raise awareness of the importance of enterprise in their community. Indeed, perhaps the text will help higher education establishments and the business community take a step towards each other, providing issues for constructive dialogue and debate.

In realizing these themes in the text, no attempt has been made to run each strand through every chapter but they do emerge, hopefully in a balanced way, across the text as a whole. The theme of culture, national and organizational culture is a particularly difficult thread to deal with. It is impossible for a person from one culture to write a book that reflects multicultural perspectives. To deal with this issue I have discussed in chapter 1 the nature of culture and how it impacts on behaviour. Further, I have used case study material throughout the book from different national cultures. It is hoped that this will be sufficient for classes of students from different races to be able to work with and debate the possible impact of this important factor on entrepreneurial behaviour in their country.

Chapter 1 discusses the nature of organizational structure and culture. Entrepreneurs can design the organization which will facilitate or hinder entrepreneurial activity. An awareness of such structural issues is rarely addressed in entrepreneurship courses. Furthermore, organizations are not situated 'in vacuuo', they are contextually embedded and an important part of that context is culture. The nature of cultural difference is explored, as is the phenomena of organizational cultures. Some practical implications for management and enterprise of handling cultural issues are explored. Chapter 2 continues to pursue the theme of culture and context by switching the focus to that of environmental infrastructural issues. In this chapter it becomes evident that the role of the nation-state and of world trade are just two aspects of the political economy which shape the environment for enterprise. Moreover, it is argued that crucially the environment for firms includes other firms. Hence the interrelationship between firms is extensively explored. The practical implications comprise the subcontracting relationship and the development of the small firm network. Finally the chapter addresses the issue of global competitiveness, the need for managers of firms aspiring to be globally competitive to think innovatively and manage change effectively. Chapter 3 shifts the focus again by examining the different legal forms of business and some of the issues of new venture creation. This contrasts with the previous chapter in that the emphasis is primarily on small scale, and the different ways of getting started. A major theme is the issue of planning, and the sources of help and advice are those aspects which vary according to country and location. As a counterbalance to small scale, the final section of the chapter considers the nature of corporate venturing. There are many research-based practical suggestions and considerations made throughout this chapter.

The theme of the next five chapters is entrepreneurial behaviour. Chapter 4 addresses the issue of the nature of the entrepreneurial personality. Many people believe that entrepreneurs are different but it has been extremely difficult for researchers to identify in what respects they differ from other managers, other occupational groups or the general population. In this chapter, the importance of context and type of business are emphasized as having a bearing on the type of person who will put their stamp on a business. The different types of business owner/entrepreneur, definitional issues and the importance of business aspirations as they affect the business process are discussed and illustrated. Some of the latest theoretical thinking on the nature of the entrepreneur is broached. The topic covered in chapter 5 – individual and organizational learning – is particularly important in the context of the small to medium-sized business. Entrepreneurs and business owners tend to learn through concrete experience and on a 'need to know' basis. Business schools, in the UK at least, have tended to address the needs of corporate business and not those of the entrepreneur or the SME. This chapter examines the nature and process of learning from both a theoretical and practitioner perspective. The uses of different types of knowledge and learning are illustrated through particular examples.

If any behaviour is constant in business life it is the taking of decisions. This behaviour is examined in chapter 6. Issues such as the decision makers' intention, their cognitive style (that is, the different ways in which people may approach a decision) and the tensions which may arise and need to be managed, are addressed. The chapter moves on to consider problem solving in relation to decision taking. Decisions are often taken in the context of a crisis, therefore such a situation is illustrated and some lessons drawn. The chapter moves on to consider how decisions are framed, the issue of risk in decision making and the problem of 'escalation'. The next chapter – chapter 7 – pursues issues of motivation and control in respect of enterprise. The issues covered include the reasons why someone might wish to be self-employed, unemployment, the decision to found one's own business, the cross cutting effects of culture and the process of motivation and control. The process is complex; it encompasses performance, business outcomes and reward issues, issues of comparative behaviour, equity and the role of entrepreneur on patterns of motivation. Finally the chapter examines the small-firm-network structure as a system which affects particular kinds of motivation and control such as cooperation, flexibility and the achievement of quality standards. Finally, under the theme of entrepreneurial behaviour, the question of gender and whether it affects business performance is considered in chapter 8. The increasing presence of women in the labour market and changes in the role of women in society are approached from a British perspective. It is recognized that gender is an issue where cultural values are deep-seated and vary across countries. Thus the chapter approaches issues of gender and business performance from the British context and illustrates them by actual case examples. There is scope for students to research the issues from their own cultural perspective. The chapter moves on to consider issues of family and business. Here there is less reluctance to cross cultural boundaries. Some problems associated with the family business are addressed and illuminated through case study material. The chapter concludes with a brief examination of interrole issues and succession problems in the family firm.

Whilst the theme of entrepreneurial behaviour continues throughout the next three chapters the particular theme being addressed is that of the team management of enterprise. Thus chapter 9 considers the nature of the leadership of enterprise: the roles of leader and manager are compared and what has been labelled a 'charismatic' or 'transformational' style of leadership is discussed. This chapter indicates that there are discernable differences in approach and style between entrepreneurs and managers of business. Chapter 10 takes up the challenge of the 'economics of individualism' and examines a raft of issues in respect of the team development and management of enterprise. It shows the interdependency between entrepreneur/owner manager and the team, the nature of group dynamics and development, some of the problems of team behaviour and the possible benefits of teams working effectively together. The latter may be enhanced by the phenomenon of developing a 'collective mind' and 'heedful interrelating'. Issues of multiculturalism in teams and team building and development conclude this chapter. Innovation and creativity, which form the subject matter of chapter 11, are fundamental entrepreneurial behaviours, yet to be effective they necessarily occur in a team context. The nurturing of innovation, the types of strategies which may be adopted and the support for scientific innovations are all elements of this chapter.

The next four chapters go some way towards the issue of taking entrepreneurship education and training seriously by considering how an enterprise can be professionally managed. Chapter 12 starts with the development of enterprise. Enterprises may be designed to suit particular purposes and certainly it is demonstrated that some organizational forms lend themselves to the expression of enterpreneurial behaviour. The chapter picks up the theme of possible design faults and how these may be addressed; in particular the networked form of enterprise is discussed in its various manifestations. The next section of the chapter examines the stages of enterprise development, problems that typify these stages and some of the issues as perceived by the owner-manager. The chapter concludes with a detailed examination of factors which affect the growth of enterprise. Although the term 'strategy' has entered into discussion in earlier chapters, in chapter 13 it is given fuller treatment. It has been said that 'strategy' is a term used by business school professors and adopted by corporate leaders, but has little currency for the business owner-manager or entrepreneur. This chapter sets out to prove otherwise. It attempts to show how fundamental strategic thinking is, and that it is far from incidental to the success of an enterprise. A wide range of possible entrepreneurial strategies and tactics is identified and the importance of strategy for competitive positioning is addressed. Chapter 14 attempts to close another gap; on the one hand, there is the human resource manager (HRM) specialist who tends to apply HRM theory to the large firm, and on the other hand, the small firm owner-manager who does not have the resources to employ an HRM. Yet, as highlighted in this chapter, selecting and retaining the right staff, equipping them and updating them with the right skills, is fundamental to effective firm performance. The chapter also addresses the issue of trade unionism and the small firm, albeit from a British perspective. The chapter concludes with a consideration of national policies towards industrial regeneration and the importance of human resource management practice in enterprise. The theme of the professional management of enterprise is developed in chapter 15 by a consideration of the nature of quality and firm performance. The process of quality management, strategies for delivering quality standards and the adoption of BS5750/1SO9000 are discussed and illustrated. The chapter concludes with the issue of developing a quality culture and is accompanied by a case study from Malaysia.

The final theme and chapter considers the nature of the so called 'new economy' and more speculatively, the future of enterprise. Inevitably the importance of the information technology revolution is discussed in this chapter given that the twin concepts of 'informationalism' or knowledge management and 'globalization' are fundamental to the nature of the new economy. The chapter discusses the geography of this new industrial space, the pivotal role of global cities and the emergence of the 'electronic cottage'. Finally the chapter returns to the issue of technological innovation and the role of science in development of economies. This is illustrated by a case study of 'Silicon Valley'. The chapter concludes by summarizing some of the insights developed in earlier chapters.

Elizabeth Chell
Walwick, Northumberland
June 2000

Explanatory note

Chapter notes are given at the end of the book. They are keyed to the text with superscript numbers, e.g.[2]. Subsidiary references to the same note are given in the form 'Smith 1996 (see note 5): p. 123' indicating that the full reference for 'Smith 1995' is given at note 5 for that chapter (if a note for another chapter is meant, the chapter number will also be given: 'Smith 1996 (see note 5, chapter 6): p.123'). The page number, if given refers to the book so referenced, not this book.

List of figures

List of tables

Part 1
Culture and Context

CHAPTER 1

Structure and culture

There are many issues that have hindered the development of entrepreneurship as a discipline, one of which is its relationship with organizational behaviour and the base disciplines (economics, sociology and psychology) that comprise 'management'. One focus of these studies of organizational form (size, structure) has enabled an understanding to be developed of the nature of different types of organization. But the issue of size of organization has become 'sensitive'. In Europe, for example, the proportion of small to medium-sized enterprises is 95 per cent of the stock of all firms.[1] Yet management education has focused on the large corporation as the primary source of knowledge on MBA and other education programmes. In this chapter, the issue of diversity of organization form is illustrated. Furthermore, such diversity is not only illustrated in respect of shape (structure) and size, but also in the wide differences in organization culture and management style. Finally, the importance of these issues for behaviour within organizations and their performance is addressed.

Designing structure

The arbitrageur who goes to market with his or her goods in order to sell them at a profit has an enterprise but very little by way of organizational form. Similarly, the man who works from his garage has minimal organization and administration. But once the business grows and he needs premises and to recruit and employ others, there is a requirement for some kind of order. Even the 'skunk works' has a form – often in relation to a larger organization – a management style and a distinct culture. In this innovative type of business the structure is consciously designed with the purpose of facilitating creative and innovative thinking. There is, it would seem, a close relation between the purposes, the means of achieving them (strategy) and organizational structure.

In the virginal business venture, the business plan defines the shape and nature of the business. The goals are identified, the resources and means by which they are to be achieved set out and acted upon. For the emergent enterprise such activity reflects an 'action plan', often only loosely based around a business plan, from which the emergent strategy and organization are co-created. To a very large extent therefore the founder or founding team consciously designs the structure of their virginal enterprise. But what principles is this design based on? Indeed, to what extent do founders consider alternative forms? What mental models do they contemplate? What design principles have they at their disposal? These issues are broached in the next section as the idea of organizational design is introduced.

The nature and development of organization structure

A strategic decision on the part of management is usually ensued by the development of plans to achieve the strategic goal effectively and efficiently. This defines the intention; that the goals are intended to be realized i.e. brought about, and with the minimum waste or effort. The strategic goals may involve the pursuit of new business opportunities and have implications for the tasks to be performed and skills required, the need to create a new department or even separate business. Hence, the strategic decision has implications for the subsequent design configuration of the organization.

Mintzberg[2] pointed out that there are five different ways of looking at how organizations function:

- **the flow of formal authority** – this may be centralized around the organization's 'hub' or decentralized to its various sub-units
- **the flow of regulated activity** – in the different functional areas of an organization this will reflect closely the form of organization, the nature of the business and sector differences
- **the flow of informal communication** – which tends to be unrelated to the formal structure as signified, for example by an organizational chart
- **the set of work constellations** – the nature of work groupings and teams and the way they work across functional 'boundaries'
- **the flow of ad hoc decision processes** – which not only reflects the 'top down' or 'bottom up' form of governance but also the political nature of organizational decision making.

Different organizational structures differ on these five dimensions. The result is that of organizational complexity. For example, the small business (employing up to 20 people) has centralized power and authority with a very short hierarchy. Businesses in process, batch or the production of one-off products or services, will regulate the flow of their activity differently and this will have design implications. All organizations operate at an informal level though in the small firm where it is possible for all staff to know each other this may have greater predominance. The greater the informality the greater the flexibility of operations. It is this design feature which enables the firm to be responsive. Moreover, informality can breed a creative culture giving individuals greater freedom to bring to bear their own skills and interpretation of the task. Further, people cluster in peer groups in order to get the work done, these groups are not related to the formal hierarchy. However, not all small firms exhibit precisely these design and behavioural features. There is what might be termed a paradox of control particularly in the owner-managed firm. The small firm owner-manager who wishes to maintain a semblance of total centralized control ensures that the direction and speed of the organization as a vehicle for business production are controlled but this may stifle individual creativity, commitment and thereby the growth and development of the enterprise. Finally, decisions taken show ad hoc patterns of influence not merely along the vertical dimension, but diagonally, bringing in people from different parts of the organization. When these five different ways of functioning are taken together it is clear that organizational processes are complex and difficult to map with any precision.

Mintzberg argues further that there are in fact only five types of organization. They are:

- the simple structure
- the machine bureaucracy
- the professional bureaucracy
- the divisionalized form
- the adhocracy.

Arguably, of the above there are only two types – the organic, virginal structure exemplified in the simple entrepreneurial firm and the adhocracy and the mechanistic bureaucratic structure exemplified in the two types of bureaucracy: machine and professional, and the so called divisionalized form[3]. To these may be added:

- the matrix structure
- the networked organizational structure
- the team organization
- the virtual organization or Internet company.

According to Mintzberg there are five elements to any organizational structure: the strategic apex, the operating core, the middle line, the technostructure and the support staff. The differential balancing of these elements produce each of his five types. Thus, he argues, the **simple structure** is based around direct supervision (i.e. the decisions and whims of the owner-manager) in which the strategic apex is the key part; the **machine bureaucracy** is based on the standardization of work processes in which the technostructure (i.e. analysts whose job it is to affect the work of others) is pivotal; the **professional bureaucracy** is based on the standardization of skills in which the operating core (i.e. those employees who perform the basic work related directly to the production of goods or services) is the focal aspect; the **divisionalized form** is based on the standardization of outputs, in which the middle line (i.e. middle management) is the core; the **adhocracy** is based on mutual adjustment (coordination by means of informal communication) and in which the support staff – sometimes with the operating core – is the crucial element. Thus, Mintzberg's five structures form a useful start point for consideration of organizational design principles.

Arguably organizational structures evolve from the **simple form**. This assumes an owner-manager who wishes to grow their business and can successfully marshal resources to achieve the intended level of growth on a fairly continuous basis[4]. Continuous development is based on strategic decisions which, as argued above, have implications for the shape, that is, the design and structure, of an organization. The principles of design include **division of labour** – the degree of job specialization, **standardization** – specifying the work content, the work output and the requisite skills, **supervision** – the means for coordination of work effort, which raises the issue of span of control and administration – the principle of command and control through the mechanisms of formal authority and hierarchy. All such aspects of organizational design have quite far reaching implications for management and in particular the management of the 'human resource'.

Box 1.1: Overall Production Limited

Bill Overall has considerable experience in the apparel industry. In its heyday in the 1950s and early 1960s he had managed a large clothing firm located in the clothing belt around Leeds-Manchester (UK). However, the industry became uncompetitive, there was more sourcing abroad and Bill was given the task of closing down the factory and making hundreds of workers redundant.

Twenty years later, he owned and managed his own small workwear business. He employed ten people and his wife came in to do the books. The business catered for a niche market, producing workwear in batches to supply particular customer orders. He was well networked in the industry and there was a steady flow of work and a full order book. But he had no intention of expanding the business. It wasn't lack of experience, quite the contrary, he never wanted the experience of making someone redundant again.

Different people have different reasons for settling on a particular size threshold for the company they have created.

New developments that require specialized labour involve either training and developing existing staff or recruiting new employees with the requisite skills and experience. Standardization tends to mean a 'detached' examination of jobs, the measurement of inputs and outputs and a clear notion of what is acceptable performance. Employees cannot be expected to perform their jobs well unless there are such notions, which are communicated to them clearly. Moreover, the maintenance of quality is intimately bound up in the ability to distinguish between standards of performance being achieved on all such measures.

The effects of poor design

Deficient structure and/or lack of principles

Mintzberg discusses at some length the problems with the five organizational designs identified above. The **simple structure**, he suggests, has too great a dependence on the 'strategic head': such centralization of control in effect means that employees must understand and accept the management style of

Box 1.2: TSL Informatics

Tom Lester is a technically very competent guy who had set up a small software development company on a science park located next to a Northern England university. He busied himself doing deals around potential developments with a Scandinavian based firm. The intention sounded fine, it would mean business development and growth (if it came to fruition) and there was certainly room in the facility for expansion.

The problem was that Tom never discussed his plans openly, he kept his cards close to his chest. His 'right hand man', Mary Rodrigues, had the crucial management role of human resource planning. It was also her job to trouble shoot, to hire and fire, but most importantly to develop a structure for the business which fitted the plan. She made a point of extracting whatever information she could from Tom in this regard.

It was not difficult to identify some of the problems which were developing from this lack of communication. Although Mary was loyal to Tom his reluctance to discuss matters led to an ineffective working relationship. Some of the consequences were that people's jobs were not clearly defined and there was an uncomfortable role overlap. Friction occurred where people were finding the lack of clarity around their precise responsibilities irritating. There were also some underlying worries about the viability of the business and their confidence in their boss, Tom, and the management generally, was waning.

the 'boss' if they are to be valued and wish to stay with the company. The lack of formality and degree of role overlap can present problems for employees who can tolerate only low levels of ambiguity. To avoid 'role interference', mutual adjustment needs to be well developed and understood. This is likely to demand high levels of interpersonal competence and management capability in order to achieve a smooth running operation.

However, manufacturing firms work efficiently and effectively under a system of operational controls, where jobs are clearly specified and tasks and functions are well integrated. Many small manufacturing firms have found that by adopting ISO9000 they can make themselves more attractive as a supplier to a larger corporation,[5] which in turn helps assure their viability.

Bureaucratic structures all have the potential to stifle innovation and creativity. This is particularly true of the **machine bureaucracy** – in particular the routinization of tasks. In addition, the classic machine bureaucracy tends to be obsessed with control and as the name suggests presents a highly mechanistic view of the management process.[6] Machine bureaucracies are conflict ridden due to both vertical and horizontal cross cutting divisions: 'The problem is not to develop an open atmosphere where people can talk things out, but to enforce a closed, tightly controlled one where the work can get done despite them.'[7] In today's climate of globalization and internationalization of business the machine bureaucracy presents a dinosaurian image of the organization which is unable to adapt to and deal effectively with changed external circumstances.[8]

The **professional bureaucracy** has a different set of characteristics, chief amongst these being the dominance of highly autonomous professionals at the operating core who control their own work. It typifies public sector organizations, especially in medicine and education. Traditionally the notions of 'strategic direction' are built around individuals and there is a lack of controls outside those of the profession. This individualism tends to promote the *prima donna* and presents difficulties of dealing with incompetence. Although it operates on a largely democratic basis, decision making tends to be via committees and as such is unwieldy and inflexible. Attempts to exert controls over such professional bureaucracies have resulted in the development of the technostructure and middle management at the expense of the operating core, diverting resources away from the primary task and wresting control from the professionals. Such measures inevitably cause resentment, affect morale and do not necessarily result in the desired increases in efficiency and effectiveness.

Experiments and strategic changes made by successive governments in the UK in order to 'privatize' different parts (for example those which are readily hived off such as catering and cleaning) of these public sector organizations has yielded modest but not undisputed successes. Other attempts to create an internal market within the health service intended, amongst other objectives, to increase the organization's efficiency and achieve higher standards, through the application of competitive pressure. Arguably, however, the emphasis towards increased managerialism and a reduction in the power of the professional has resulted in irreversible changes in organizational structure and culture.

The **divisionalized form** is typical of the large (usually multinational) corporation. This structure comprises a strategic apex usually known as 'headquarters' (HQ) and a number of divisions each of which have their own structure – usually that of the machine bureaucracy. The autonomy of the divisions is highly circumscribed by the role of HQ in monitoring performance. However, this decentralization is largely illusory because HQ manages the strategic portfolio, allocates financial resources, designs the performance control system, appoints managers to the divisions, monitors behaviour and provides support services. The rationale for this form is to capture market diversity, and divisionalization tends to encourage further diversification. Like the machine bureaucracy it operates in largely stable but not very dynamic environments. The problems this form presents include HQ usurping divisional powers by centralizing product-market decisions. Its general managers have less autonomy than the owner-manager of a private business despite the amount of training and development. It tends to protect vulnerable parts of its operation, and its control systems encourage steady improvements in financial performance but tend to discourage entrepreneurialism. This form not only has financial and economic consequences but its actions can also have social consequences, some of which may be considered to be irresponsible, for example damage to the environment. The tendency for increased bureaucratization of form may also be perceived as a burden on society which requires looser, more competitive structures. Despite its size, power may effectively be concentrated in very few hands. The need to develop countervailing powers through trade unionism and government has long been recognized. Finally, this form does not appear to work effectively outside the private sector.

The **adhocracy** is a highly organic structure which facilitates innovation. The organization houses formally trained specialists who tend to be grouped in teams. In order to avoid the stifling effects of bureaucracy, the adhocracy pays little attention to the classical principles of management and contrasts markedly with the professional bureaucracy, which also employs trained specialists. An important difference is that standardization does not feature, the primary purpose is to create new knowledge and novel solutions to problems. In order to achieve this, specialists work in multidisciplinary project teams. Managers tend to be part of the specialist teams. Rather than supervise, they tend to liaise, facilitate, negotiate and coordinate. Power is decentralized and there is no true strategic apex, strategy is likely to be implicit in the decisions made and not consciously formulated. Instead, senior managerial roles involve handling conflict, channelling aggression, monitoring projects and, importantly, external liaison. Environments for these firms are complex and dynamic. The research and development (R&D) firm which produces customized solutions is typically an **entrepreneurial adhocracy**. At VSW Scientific Instruments Ltd[9] the owner-manager acted both in a sales capacity and as a catalyst stimulating innovation in the project teams set up to produce customized solutions to clients' problems.

The adhocracy as an organizational form may have a short life, it is a youthful structure where there are pressures to bureaucratize. However, the adhocracy is an important organizational form in the present global competitive arena because of its enhanced ability to innovate and refresh itself. It is essentially a democratic structure, although the high degree of ambiguity and fluidity which typifies it requires considerable tolerance. The internal environment tends to be highly politicized. Other problems which arise are of managing productivity and efficiency. The latter arises from a low competence at carrying out the mundane, the high cost of communication and the management of unbalanced workloads. However, if the adhocracy can resist the pressure to bureaucratize, it will continue to function as a source of innovation and creative solutions to problems. It is the latter which is rather more in demand than the standardized, off-the-shelf solution of 'yesteryear'.

The adhocracy may be the organizational form of today but it is not the only one. Others have now developed to achieve high levels of innovation. These are the **matrix**, the **team** and the **networked** structures. Apart from their ability to innovate they have other crucial characteristics in common as identified by Kanter (see note 8): they stimulate and empower people; they are progressive in their human resource management practices; they take an integrative approach to problem-solving. Matrix structures comprise permanent cross functional teams and as such are **multi-functional**. They have both a project manager and a functional head. They can be found in all sectors of industry and commerce; in the public and the private sectors. They can also be found in multinational companies (MNCs), where they give the added advantage of accommodating cross-cultural differences. They have other potential advantages too, including the ability to meet special programme or project needs, flexibility, closer attention to customer service, greater accountability, improved decision making and problem solving (because the team is closer to the issues) and improved organizational decision making.

There has been a strong movement away from the idea that individuals, whether they be leaders or the owner-manager, make decisions. Increased democratization of the organization has resulted in team-organization.

Teams[10] may be permanent or temporary and are brought together primarily for the purposes of lateral integration and problem-solving. They have the added advantages of increased effectiveness, competitiveness, improved communication and cooperation.[11] They are also common in innovating, entrepreneurial companies.[12] Some of the potential but not insurmountable problems are time spent in meetings and the pressure of conflicting loyalties.

The networked organization structure is another modern variant which gives competitive advantage through reduced overheads and increased efficiency. The structure comprises a sparse central core with outside linkages to essential business services. The relationships may be contractually based or through strategic alliances. The result is a **virtual organization**. Benetton was one of the earliest and best known examples of this structure. Virtual organizations of this kind have been facilitated by advances in information technology that enable them to function effectively across geographical distances. Key jobs for management are the coordination of the 'system', although the complexities of such a system are a potential disadvantage.

The rise of e-commerce, the role of information technology and in particular, the internet, have produced the company of the future today. The excitement and phenomenal valuing of as yet (at the time of writing) unprofitable dotcom companies is a consequence of their estimated enormous potential, once established, to reach global markets. This type of company also has the advantages of a minimal organizational structure such as low space requirements (a single office or back bedroom may be sufficient for start up purposes) and a flat organizational structure. Other infrastructure is dictated by computer equipment and telephone lines. It is too early to make definitive statements about these companies as they are too new to be well researched and understood. Yet one feature which is emerging is the extent to which they are well networked externally to other actual or potential dotcom entrepreneurs, business angels and likely investors.

> First Tuesday, a club where venture capitalists meet entrepreneurs, started in October 1998 as a networking group for 50 friends and contacts. Today firsttuesday.com has 30,000 registered users and hosts monthly meetings in 16 British and European cities. First Tuesday has an estimated flotation value of £50 million, and (Julie) Meyer hopes it will go public.[13]

Whatever the structure all organizations are open systems whose 'boundaries' are porous to environmental influence. This in particular is true of the organization's culture.

Organizational metaphors

Another approach to understanding the nature of organizations is the use of the metaphor. The metaphor enables us to ask 'what is an organization *like*?' The answer may be, like a 'well oiled machine', 'the *Marie Celeste*', 'an onion', etc. Metaphors are not intended to be taken literally, rather they are linguistic devices which enable us to understand one construction through the medium of another.[14]

The purpose of using a metaphor is to encapsulate some crucial aspect of the phenomenon being explained. So, for example, to describe an organization as 'a well oiled machine' suggests that, like an engine, its parts fit well together but also, being 'oiled' it is clearly well maintained so that it can also be adduced that it runs smoothly and achieves its purposes. Hence a brief phrase – a metaphor – sums up the nature of a particular type of organization.

Metaphors also indicate 'what is seen' and from what perspective. To describe an organization as a 'well oiled machine' is a positive image, whereas to attribute its origins to the Dickensian era or, more extremely, to the age of the Brontosaurus, is to make a strong statement about the antiquated or outmoded practices of an organization.[15]

The use of the term 'bureaucracy' to indicate red tape (another metaphor), mechanical efficiency, impersonal service and so on, is also being used as a metaphor. It is apposite. A not infrequent complaint of small firms' owner-managers (notably in the UK) is aimed at the bureaucracy of government – there is too much regulation, meaning red tape and paperwork which creates demands on the owner-manager's time and results in delays and inefficiencies.

The irrationality of the rational bureaucratic model has been highlighted in a number of ways.[16] The idea of a bureaucracy is the 'impersonal application of a system of rules', but whose rules, why are they valued, are there any alternatives which might also be useful and therefore valuable? Such an attempt by bureaucracies to present an impersonal face in the name of efficiency has given rise to other criticisms. For example, Morgan[17] has used the metaphor 'psychic prison' to suggest the dark, irrational side of such organizational forms. He describes it in Freudian terms, indicating a repressed 'anal' form of sexuality.

> We should be alert to the hidden meaning of the close regulation and supervision of human activity, the relentless planning and scheduling of work, and the emphasis on productivity, rule following, discipline, duty and obedience. The bureaucracy is a mechanistic form of organization but an anal one, too.
>
> Morgan, 1996 (see note 17)

Certainly there are studies of 'neurotic organizations' where, for example, a psychiatric model has been applied for the purposes of understanding dysfunctional styles of management.[18] In the following case study,[19] there are features which exemplify both Morgan's 'psychic prison' and the Kets de Vries-Miller **compulsive** management style.[20]

Box 1.3: Electro-Diesel Inc

Electro-Diesel Inc was, on paper at least, a highly successful small business. It employed 15 people and in 2000 had a turnover of £1 million. Mr Binder had bought the company in 1990 and was the majority shareholder/managing director. He had expanded the business out of the marine industry into diesel engines generally and his customer base reflected this. The company's markets were both national and international.

The company structure included a works manager and an office manager, Miss Piece, whom Mr Binder regarded as his 'right hand person'. Mr Binder was formal – the relationship between himself and his right hand person was not on first name terms – controlling and showed a low level of trust.

Miss Piece's job had developed from that of the traditional secretary into one in which she assumed a wide range of duties. She had, for example, recently redesigned the company's administrative procedures. This was a huge task and included much of the detail for the company's ISO9000 certification and health and safety policy. Mr Binder's primary role was managing the strategic direction of the company, but he also had an overseeing and controlling role.

Whilst Miss Piece claimed (in Mr Binder's presence), to have considerable autonomy in her job, this was not borne out. For example, although she was responsible for the recruitment of non-technical staff, it became clear that Mr Binder was heavily involved. He approved the shortlist and the interviews were conducted jointly. Furthermore, when it came to the design of the ISO9000 system it transpired that Mr Binder had 'got the system designed round us ... everybody adheres to it so traceability is no problem'. This gave Mr Binder the ability to monitor staff more closely and a greater degree of control.

Mr Binder was able to pay above average wages and this helped compensate for his difficult and, at times, oppressive management style. However, the foreseeable problems for this company are finding a successor and taking the company to the next stage of its development. Employees have not been allowed to think for themselves therefore much of the talent, energy and creativity has been rechannelled into doing what the boss wants. It does, however, raise the question of what constitutes effective working relationships. From Mr Binder's perspective the relationships were very effective. However, it had served to create a dependence which in the longer term was likely to become dysfunctional.

Culture

An individual's behaviour reflects their management style, whereas the way of doing and being of a company is said to reflect the organization's culture. The study of culture has been thought important due to the global competitive milieu in which firms operate. The notion of 'culture' is complex.[21] The key question is whether culture is a phenomenon which is integrated into a social system and is thereby symbolic, or whether it is an ideational phenomenon distinct from the social system and is thereby a structural variable.[22] This distinction can be summarized as something which organizations *have* (a structural variable) or something which organizations *are* (a symbolic metaphor). Organizations have technology, a workforce, markets, suppliers and so on; they also have an annual rate of turnover, of absenteeism, motivation and a level of job satisfaction. These are all factors which may be measured and are subject to change. To suggest that culture is just another variable like satisfaction or motivation suggests that it too can be readily changed and manipulated. Alternatively, where culture is used in a metaphoric sense organizations are imbued with culture which is the expression of deeply held beliefs and values, patterns of thinking, feeling and being which permeate social and organizational life experiences.

Whichever approach is selected, understanding the culture of an organization is important to management, leadership and employees. If it is something the organization has, then to understand it is in large part to be able to control it by means of manipulation. However, if the organization *is* its culture then understanding it is an essential prerequisite for management, whilst attempting to change it is likely to prove problematic.

Structure and culture differentiated

In general, 'structure' refers to the conditions in which people go about their business. Work and play can be conditioned, that is, structured, by roles and relationships of people within a social situation. Such roles and relationships may be viewed as legitimate in a formal setting or casual (perhaps non-legitimate) in informal settings. Organizations are structured in these ways. Thus organization structure may be thought of as a system of roles and associated tasks, reporting relationships and communications that link the work of role occupants. The formal structure is the official structure of an organization whereas informal structure is the set of unofficial relationships amongst members.

A number of writers have attempted to relate culture to organizational structure. It was clear from the analysis of Mintzberg that structure had implications for the way things were done in the particular organizational type. Charles Handy (see chapter 9) makes the same point. By using metaphors he suggests that a centralized power culture (such as Mintzberg's simple structure) can be visualized as a 'web', bureaucracies are 'role cultures', the matrix, a 'task culture' and the individualistic person culture (Mintzberg's adhocracy) may be characterized as a 'cluster' (see Table 1.1).

According to Handy, power is centralized in a 'power culture', there are few procedures, to progress an employee has to understand the unspoken rules and expectations, in particular what the 'boss' wants! People who are comfortable in this culture feel a strong sense of commitment, if they do not 'fit

Table **1.1** Handy's analysis of the relationship between structure and culture

Cultural form	Organizational form
POWER	WEB
ROLE	BUREAUCRACY
TASK	MATRIX
PERSON	CLUSTER
	Source: Handy 1995 (see note 14, chapter 9)

in', then they are likely to feel intense dissatisfaction. This implies that human resource management in the small or medium-sized enterprise is likely to be an issue. The role culture is typical of a bureaucracy. It is suitable for people whose preferred way of working involves structure and routine. Problems occur through external interventions which are designed to make a bureaucracy something it is not – a responsive adaptable organization equipped to deal with change and external turbulence (for example, government quangos, NHS trusts, public utilities). This serves largely to destabilize: roles are challenged and reshaped, rules are broken, a degree of chaos and extreme job dissatisfaction may ensue.

A **task culture** is project based and power is distributed. There is primarily the adoption of a matrix arrangement to create cross-functional teams (see above). This tends to reduce hierarchy, to give opportunity to empower and to reduce routine. The implications are that such a culture needs to be effectively managed if it is to work at all, it requires interpersonal skills, HRM capability and the efficient utilization and control of resources.

A **person culture** is organized around individuals, for example a small firm of professionals ('boffins' and science based firms, lawyers, consultancy firms, R&D units). Such individuals tend to be like-minded. People's personal aims and ambitions are closely tied to the organization's goals and purposes.

In this analysis culture is to organizations just like meaning is to writing: organizational culture is that intangible way of being which emanates from the juxtaposition of structure and process and ways of doing. Gurus like John Harvey Jones, Tom Peters and Rosabeth Moss Kanter place considerable importance on getting the culture right. This suggests that, by manipulating the structure, process and artefacts of culture it is possible to change how it is manifested and expressed. Harvey-Jones[23] turned round ICI and in so doing changed the company's culture.

Management has often viewed 'culture' in more restrictive ways, for example:

- as **commitment to goals and values** – this has particular implications for how the manager motivates and leads
- as a **recipe for success**, for example the company turnround or 'search for excellence' – the management implications primarily concern the strategy they are to put in place and the kinds of organizational changes they envisage such as changes in structure and design
- as **a means of exercising control** – culture is about socialization, the effects of informal organization on the firm and its performance.

If organization structure is the computer 'hard wiring' then culture is the software. According to Geert Hofstede,[24] patterns of thinking, feeling and acting are behaviours which arise from a person's mental programs or **software of the mind**; a customary term for such mental software is **culture**.

Layers of culture

Culture has its roots in human societies. The study of culture has been traditionally the province of anthropologists. Their work has shown that there are many historical influences on the values and beliefs which form the basis of a society. They include nationhood and ethnicity (one's sense of belonging and identity), religion (spiritual beliefs and sense of purpose in life and death), linguistic affiliation (use of language for expression, the ordering and making sense of the world), gender (sexual identity), generation (the sense of separation of grandparents, parents and offspring), social class (that which affects educational and other life opportunities), and work (occupation, professional or other allegiances, and so on). But what possible mechanisms enable the creation of a **business culture**? Clearly, economic, organizational and business behaviour impact society and its culture through the dominance of institutionalized attitudes and practices. Networking and support structures which help embed a business within a community all shape interactively the culture within and outside the firm. And so gaining an understanding of how culture has developed and how it manifests itself enables us to understand, for example, differences in business practice.

Drawing on cultural anthropology, Geert Hofstede has pointed out that within any society people face a number of common problems; he asserts that how these are dealt with form the basis of cultural difference. Table 1.2 lists these 'common problems': they formed the basis of his measure of cultural variation between nations.[25]

Table **1.2** Dimensions of national culture

POWER DISTANCE	How a society deals with the issue of authority relations
INDIVIDUALISM	How a society deals with the relationship between the individual and society
GENDER	The society's concepts of masculinity and femininity
UNCERTAINTY	A society's ways of dealing with uncertainty.
SHORT TERM – LONG TERM	The balance of a society's values towards the past, present and future

Source: Hofstede 1980 (note 25) and Hofstede 1991 (note 26)

Power may be manifested in different ways but fundamentally the question is how long or short are the hierarchies of authority relations? It is apparent in Western industrialized societies that within organizations, hierarchies are being flattened, there is a movement towards increased participation and democracy. There has been a burgeoning of the middle class, of a 'meritocracy' and a '*nouveaux riches*' of 'fat cats' and millionaire entrepreneurs. These apparent changes may all have served to shorten power differences within society. Western cultures have also tended to be highly individualistic, with personal competitiveness valued highly and consequently poor team players. Whilst this emphasis is being switched gradually, in many nations in the Far East, Japan and Africa there has long been a strong sense of the importance of the collective. How societies deal with question of gender difference also varies, some draw very clear distinctions between the role of the sexes (for example Moslem communities and the Japanese), whereas other societies blur these distinctions. Fear is a strong motivator and where societies have historically suffered invasion and had difficulties protecting their borders, there tends to be a high degree of regulation and control in order to protect against possible conflict and associated feelings of uncertainty.

The four dimensions of national cultural variation form 16 possible combinations. Hofstede, using data from more than 50 countries, was able to sort them into 13 clusters. These clusters, based on a particular combination of the four dimensions, he suggested indicated the countries' national cultural identity.

At a later stage a fifth dimension of culture was added. This new dimension was termed **short term – long term orientation** and concerned the ethical values of Confucianism.[26] A short term perspective concerns a past and present focus on more static values such as unqualified respect for traditions, for social and status obligations (e.g. one's 'elders and betters'), small savings and investments, concern with 'face' and possessing the truth. A long term perspective, on the other hand, focuses on the future, hence the values associated with this are more dynamic, for example they include the adaptation of traditions to contemporary contexts, qualified respect for social and status obligations, thrift, large savings and investments, perseverance, subordination and concern with virtue (rather than truth).[27]

National culture is thus treated in a **macro** sense, as a wider **sociocultural** force. But how might this impact organizations, and more particularly entrepreneurship? If national culture is immanent then there is the potential for considerable influence of culture in a **micro** sense, as an internal dynamic force impacting organizational members and their activities. This suggests that there are shared values and common understandings within organizations which are influenced by culture. As shown in Figure 1.1 the effects of culture impact symbolically at three levels:

Figure **1.1** Domains of organizational culture

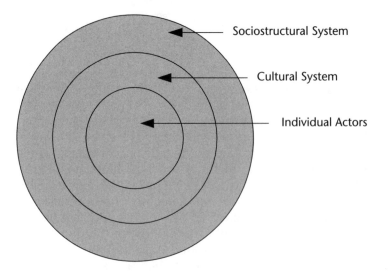

Sociostructural System

Cultural System

Individual Actors

Table **1.3** Organizational culture attributes

Entrepreneurial	vs	Administrative
external		internal focus
task		social/status
risk		safety
individuality		conformity
group		individual rewards
collective		individual decision making
decentralized		centralized decision making
adhocery		planning
innovation		stability
competition		cooperation
simple		complex organization
informal		formal procedures
commitment to the mission		commitment to the organization
knowledge valued		procedures valued

- a **sociostructural system** of formal structures, strategies, policies and management processes
- a **cultural system** of shared and meaningful symbols manifest in myths, ideology and artefacts
- **individual actors** with their particular endowments, experience and personality.[28]

This suggests that, notwithstanding the holistic nature of culture, there are dimensions which will form a particular permutation and influence the manifestation of organization culture. Table 1.3 presents a set of 14 such attributes.

These attributes can be organized as shown in the table to suggest an entrepreneurial profile. Moreover the dimensions appear to be consistent with Hofstede's[29] six organizational cultural dimensions. Here it is also possible to arrange them in such a way as to show the contrasting entrepreneurial and administrative dimensions (see Table 1.4).

An organization's culture reflects its entrepreneurial orientation. However, organizations need also to be sensitive to local culture, especially where their strategic aim is globalization. The following case gives an example of how a small local fast food chain was able to compete with a global giant, McDonald's.

Table **1.4** Organizational culture dimensions

Entrepreneurial		Administrative
Results	v	Process orientation
Job	v	Employee orientation
Parochial	v	Professional interest
Open	v	Closed system
Loose	v	Tight control
Pragmatic	v	Normative orientation

Source: Hofstede *et al.* 1990

Culture as a means of identifying and solving business problems

The case of Jollibee shows how sensitivity to culture can help solve a particular company's problems. In this section the focus will be on spheres of cultural influence and how they can affect management practice. According to Schneider and Barsoux[30] there are five spheres of cultural influence: regional, industrial, professional, functional and corporate. The challenge is understanding the complexity of such cultural influences and working out a strategy and tactics for managing them.

Regional cultures have evolved due to geography (for example the cultures of New York may be compared with that of California), history (for instance that of East and West Germany), politics (for example Northern Ireland or the island of Saint Martin in the Lesser Antilles), economics (for example Central and Eastern Europe – centralized, socialized and collectivized systems), language (Brittany and Wales still retain their own languages) and religion (such as the Roman Catholic south and the Protestant north of Europe). Other regional differences may be due to urban-rural differences (for instance the

Box 1.4: The Jollibee Fast Food Chain[31]

In 1981, McDonald's started to open stores in Manila, the Philippines. Jollibee was a small local 11 store chain which was now being confronted by the competitive forces of a global giant. Jollibee rose to the challenge. It benchmarked itself against McDonald's on quality, service and costs. This improved Jollibee's operating systems and enabled it to establish a network of some 65 domestic stores by 1990.

However, Jollibee did not simply copy McDonald's, it innovated. Jollibee recognized that a problem with McDonald's strategy was that it did not incorporate local tastes. Jollibee offered a more tailored menu which included sweet hamburgers, a new chicken dish and a noodle dish for children. This consumer sensitive menu earned the loyalty of existing customers and allowed the company to expand its fast food operation.

Scottish Highlands in comparison with Fifeshire). Other regional locations can give competitive advantage (for example Silicon Valley, California).

Exercise
Identify your own set of regional cultural differences

Industry cultures are known almost intuitively, for example most people would suggest that there are cultural differences between construction and consulting, (due for example to working practices, the balance between labour and professional managers, etc), retailing and pharmaceuticals (service and customer orientation compared with science base and long term invest-ment orientation). Clearly it is important to be able to recognize and analyse the differences. Some companies have attempted successfully to cross indus-try cultures, for example, retailers such as Sainsbury's and Marks and Spencer's have moved into the financial services sector. However, there is con-siderable scope for greater industry transformation as a consequence of the rapid development of the life science industry. The genetic modification of seeds is now bringing diverse industries like agriculture and pharmaceuticals closer together. Not only can crops be designed for their higher nutritional value they can also be designed for higher medicinal value. Hence pharma-ceutical companies are already encroaching on the chemical and agricultural industries. However, this may become even more extensive as delivery vehi-cles for medicines proliferate (for example, soaps, cosmetics, foods and bev-erages). Firms such as Procter and Gamble are now looking to build strategic alliances with cosmetics companies such as L'Oreal.[32] Table 1.5 shows pre-dicted transformations in industries as a consequence of the life science rev-olution.

One reason for industry differences is said to be due to differences in the 'task environments' which affect the way decisions are made (see Table 1.3).

Table **1.5** Projected industry transformations as a consequence of the development of the life science industry

Already involved	Becoming involved	Soon to be involved
chemicals	environmental	robotics
pharmaceuticals	mining	household appliances
agriculture	energy	internet communications
food processing	cosmetics	information services
mutual funds	supermarkets	media
law firms	pharmacies	
	military	
	computer hardware	
	and software	
Source: Enriquez and Goldberg 2000 (see note 32): p.100		

For example decision making can vary according to the degree of actual and perceived risk and the time it takes to know the consequences of a particular decision. Thus in the biotechnology industry there are high risks due to uncertainties associated with product development and a slow rate of feedback because it may take years to develop a particular product. This may be compared with retailing where the degree of risk is low, but the speed of feedback high.

Other reasons for industry differences may concern the following.

- **Product market characteristics.** In some industries sharing information in order to arrive at agreed standards is thought to be important (for example the major utilities – water, electricity, gas – the computer software industry), whereas in others (for example pharmaceuticals) secrecy has typically been the norm.
- **Degree of regulation.** Protected environments mean little competition and do not encourage a customer-orientation (for example the telecommunications industry is now changing as a consequence of increased competition).
- **Technology.** This can have a major impact on labour intensity and working practices (as in process, for example chemicals, and small batch, for example engineering, industries). Technology may also be affected by government policy, for instance the deregulation of the transport industries such as bus and trains.
- **Sources of competitive advantage.** Typically some industries value efficiency over customer satisfaction or place more importance on developing the human resource as in knowledge intensive industries such as consulting.

Other elements of industry culture include that of the professional culture, which behaviourally has the effect of empowering employees to make judgements. Such judgemental capability comes from intensive training, supervision and socialization, for example law firms, hospitals and universities. Also there are recognized differences in what constitutes appropriate behaviour, for instance doctors are cautious and non-aggressive, whereas lawyers are trained to develop an adversarial stance.

Functional cultures are associated with industry and firm difference. The marketing function has a different way of working to the production function, for example. This can lead to clashes, as employees identify with their own functional grouping. Friction, stereotyping and a lack of cooperation can ensue. In some contexts putting together cross functional teams may be one way of breaking down such barriers (see above). There are also national differences in respect of the valuing of different functions, for example the engineer is more highly valued in France than in the UK where the accountant is more highly regarded.

The evidence for the existence of a corporate culture can be seen when two companies in the same industry attempt to merge. Different sets of behaviour and practices, values and beliefs, and underlying assumptions are apparent. But what are the reasons for such differences? Corporate culture derives from the influence of the founder (or turnaround leader), unique company history, and stage of development.

- **The role of the founder** is clearly important, as evidenced by the roles played by Anita Roddick in conceiving of the highly successful cosmetic franchise, The Body Shop, Richard Branson and the development of the Virgin conglomerate, and Bill Gates and the global firm Microsoft.
- **The strength of a leader** to change company culture, for example in the case of John Harvey-Jones, once head of ICI, who through considerable restructuring was able to create an innovative, competitive and renewed international organization.[33]
- **The administrative heritage** of a company comprises its operating procedures, routines, policies, etc which reinforce certain ways of working, values and beliefs, and determine what practices become the norm and are accepted.
- **The stages of development** (for example start up, established, professionally managed) are important, though opinions vary as to how many stages there may be and the ease with which they can be identified. They are important for diagnostic reasons as different problems tend to arise at different stages.[34]
- **The nature of the product or service.** Differences in product and customer orientation may be due, in part, to the monopolistic situation enjoyed by the company as, for example in telecommunications and transport industries before deregulation. Other examples include industries which traditionally have an ethos of care, for example funeral services, nursing homes and veterinary practices.

It has been suggested that corporate culture may be so strong in a multinational (MNC) that is has an homogenizing effect.[35] However, Hofstede's classic work which involved IBM suggests that this may be only a surface resemblance. National cultural differences persist despite being confronted by a strong corporate culture (see the case of Jollibee competing with McDonald's).

How does corporate culture manifest itself?

Trompenaars[36] takes the view that 'culture is the way in which a group of people solves problems'.[37] However, when familiarizing oneself with a culture one usually starts with outer appearances – dress, language, food – before recognizing customs and habits, then perhaps values and beliefs. Trompenaars uses a different basis for describing cultural differences (see Table 1.6).

His approach is different from that of Hofstede, he has addressed the problem of how cultural difference impacts on management practice, in particular at international levels, where it may affect decision making and negotiations between companies. Trompenaars' approach is pragmatic; he sees culture as being a complex system of meaning which is implicit in a people's ways of doing and being. To understand a particular culture is to understand how people think; how 'they actively select, interpret, choose and

Table **1.6** The basis of cultural differences between peoples

Relationships with people		Attitudes to time	Attitudes to the environment
Universalism vs particularism	Rules vs relationships	Past vs future orientation	Focus of good or ill
Individualism vs collectivism	Individual vs group		
Neutral vs emotional	Expression of feelings		
Specific vs diffuse	Range of involvement		
Achievement vs ascription	How status is accorded		

Source: Trompenaars 1993 (see note 36)

create their environments'.[38] For example how do people decide what is the right thing to do? Do they invoke a rule (or a principle) or do they tend to value the particular relationship rather more? In business, this is likely to affect what a contract means to each party, how a business trip is organized and whether HQ is regarded as more important that one's operating base. In international business there may be greater representation from collectivist cultures. In such cultures, to be unaccompanied suggests a lack of power and status. To what extent is it acceptable to show one's feelings in a particular culture? This may be done through tone of voice, the style of communication, deliberate choice of language, and so on.

Deal and Kennedy[39] concentrate on the symbolic meaning of organizational culture. Culture, they suggest, manifests itself through the following.

- **Expression** – how what is valued is expressed, for example by the use of slogans and mission statements as in the cases of Price-Waterhouse 'Strive for Perfection', or Chubb Insurance 'Underwriting Excellence'.
- **Unspoken rules** – for example in respect of how you are expected to behave and how you are expected to dress.
- **How control is exercised** – for example as evidenced in the importance of committees and the degree of individual autonomy.
- **The physical appearance of the company** – such as smart new buildings, tidiness and office layout.
- **Symbolism** – what, for example, symbolizes a person's status and how the organization is presented to the outside world (such as its concern for ethical or environmental issues), presenting symbolically what is important through standards, placing emphasis on quality and so on.
- **Rites and rituals** – that is ceremonial observance. Events are ritualized in order to emphasize the extent to which they matter. This may include recognizing and rewarding success. Ceremonies are ritualized events – 'culture on display'.
- **Play** – this has the useful function of bonding, helping resolve conflict, facilitating cooperation, sharing and enhancing vision.

This genre of management texts suggests that despite the fundamental importance of core values a culture can be manipulated by management through changing the symbols and other manifestations. One critic suggests that it is just such attempts at formulaic approaches which undermine the value of management knowledge. Newman[40] suggests this approach is too simplistic. Newman's alternative analysis identifies three types of culture: **traditional**, **competitive** and the **transformational**.

The traditional culture is organized around 'hierarchy'. Hierarchies Newman suggests are gendered, in so far as women tend to occupy the lower grades and tiers of work and there is a strong differentiation into 'women's work' and 'men's work'.[41] The competitive culture gives a particular meaning to what counts as competitive behaviour. For example it is 'hard, macho and cowboy', it involves working long hours and power lies where the action is. Many of the ways of doing are 'go-getting, insurgent, ruthless and tough'. Women of course can join in if they can 'prove' that they can deliver. The transformational culture concerns the so called 'new managerialism'. The idea is to build a strong culture around missions and vision, underpinned by a set of guiding principles. Such culture recognizes the value of people and attempts to empower staff. It places greater emphasis on communications and related skills and a new style of managing which is participative, where there is greater equality and partnership, operating within a flattened hierarchy of structured relations. This remodelling of cultural variation raises some exceedingly interesting issues, not least of which in an owner-managed enterprise is how a female owner-manager might want to structure relationships.

Conclusions

This chapter illustrates the fact that organizations vary considerably. An obvious way of considering this variation is to examine structure. One conclusion which is emerging from this analysis is that structure and entrepreneurial behaviour are linked. There are apparently many constraints on the large bureaucratic form which detract from its ability to be flexible, responsive and innovative. Rather this type of organization is designed to work according to a set of rules, routinely and deliberately. Of the basic forms the simple structure and the adhocracy lend themselves to entrepreneurial behaviour. However these forms tend to be small. As a company grows its leadership will want to remain competitive and in order to be so, to retain the entrepreneurial flair that enabled it to achieve its present position and size. There are other organizational designs which enable the company to retain flexibility, innovativeness and responsiveness to the market place. These structures include the matrix, networked, team and virtual organizational designs. Hence organizational shape, form and design is necessary (but not sufficient) to accomplish entrepreneurial goals. Further it is apparent that there are 'design deficiencies' of the various organizational forms that suggest potential problems which may be anticipated and addressed by the company's executive management.

Organizations can be described analytically as above, however they can also be described holistically. The so-called 'organizational metaphor' is a way of describing what organizations are like. One of the more incisive metaphors is that of the 'psychic prison'. This draws on the idea that people's knowledge and understanding is limited by their thoughts, illusions and exposure to experience, etc and that people become trapped by unconscious processes thus limiting their comprehension of events.

> People in everyday life are trapped by illusions, hence the way they understand reality is limited and flawed. By appreciating this and by making a determined effort to see beyond the superficial, people have an ability to free themselves from imperfect ways of seeing. However ... many of us often resist or ridicule efforts at enlightenment, preferring to remain in the dark rather than to risk exposure to a new world and its threat to the old ways.[42]

Management style within such organizations can be dysfunctional, although one might ask ineffective, from whose point of view?

Just as management style is to an individual's behaviour so the way of doing and being of an organization is to its culture. Culture is not yet another variable which the organization *has*, it is in a more holistic and metaphoric sense what the organization *is*. Culture derives from the deeply held, shared values of organizational members which affect how it goes about its business. There does however appear to be a relation between type of structure and the nature of culture, but that is only a part of what needs to be understood in order to apprehend the nature of culture. There is clearly a complex relationship between internal organization culture and the local, regional or national culture. Organizational boundaries are porous to some extent in that employees bring with them values, beliefs and attitudes yet large corporates are able to maintain that corporate identity across national boundaries. However this is the crux of the matter. Hofstede found that the values and beliefs of IBM employees varied across national boundaries enabling him to classify national cultures. McDonald's is a highly successful global fast food franchising concern yet Jollibee was able to compete on its home territory because it understood and modified its strategy to accommodate, the local culture.

Hence whatever the size of organization, understanding culture can help management solve its problems. Moreover there seem to be specific aspects of the 'recipe' which enable the company to address the issue of how it might be more effective, more successful and more entrepreneurial. Some researchers are very clear on the relationship between organizational culture and success when they argue that:

> Although strategy, market presence and technology are clearly important, highly successful firms have capitalized on the power that resides in developing and managing a unique corporate culture. This power resides in the ability of a strong, unique culture to reduce collective uncertainties (i.e. facilitate a common interpretation system for members), create social order (i.e. make clear to members what is expected), create continuity (i.e. perpetuate

key values and norms across generations of members), create collective identity and commitment (i.e. bind members together), and elucidate a vision of the future (i.e. energize forward movement).[43]

Organization culture is fundamental to understanding organizational achievement and successful performance. The culture gives the firm its identity and whilst each is necessarily unique there are features which the more successful performers have in common. It is knowledge and understanding that shapes the beliefs and values of the firm as corporate entity – large or small – which ultimately shape its culture. It is with this knowledge that the remainder of this book is concerned.

CHAPTER 2

'Glocalization'

Over the past 40 years in particular, major transformations have taken place in the world economy. This suggests the importance of external factors – political, physical, locational, spatial, temporal and so forth – in influencing firm behaviour. In this chapter, the focus shifts from the cultural milieu to the world stage. Governments continue to use the rhetoric of competition (when cooperation might be the more appropriate means of achieving much sought after societal ends emanating from national wealth). Firms – large or small – are exhorted to widen their horizons and become 'global'. But what does it mean to be a 'global' company? Can small firms as well as large conglomerates be globally competitive? Furthermore, taking full consideration of cultural factors, how can firms be both globally integrated and locally responsive? It is the aim of this chapter to address these questions.

Environments

Organizational environment is said to be all those elements which exist outside the organization's boundaries that have potential to affect the organization. 'Organization' may be considered to be the **firm**[1] whose business objectives define its operations internally and its relations to outside bodies with a view to the furtherance of its enterprise.

Firms are embedded in a local milieu and networked within a socio-economic environment. Hence the firm is not an independent entity but an organization having interdependencies and externalized interconnections which enable it to carry out its purposes. The business and its organization are part of a system which includes various transformational, technological and economic processes, the outcome of which is the realization of surplus value or profit.

Thus the internal environment of an enterprise is concerned with specificities of organization for the explicit purpose of achieving its business goals. Moreover, organizations are open-systems, that is, the 'boundaries' are porous, materials and resources are absorbed, processed and delivered. All bodies outside this organization are part of the external environment of the firm.

The role of the nation-state

Taking a global perspective it is clear that business environments are highly variable. The globe is not only divided geographically into land masses – continents – but it is further divided politically into nation-states of which there are an increasing number, currently about 170. The nation-state may be thought of as a container of distinctive business practices and a regulator of economic activities within its boundaries.[2]

Hence Porter (see note 27) considers that nation-states have enormous influence on the competitive strengths of firms located there. However, he tends to downplay the role of government and emphasizes:

- **factor conditions**, in particular infrastructure, including transport and communications but also human resource endowments, especially knowledge and skills
- **demand conditions** primarily from the home market
- **related and supporting industries** stressing the importance of suppliers, the processes of innovation and upgrading
- **firm strategy, structure and rivalry**, placing emphasis on the way firms are managed, normative and attitudinal factors, standards of achievement and the need for intense rivalry.

Secondary factors, according to Porter, are the role of chance, which may create new entrepreneurs and that of government.

Porter's 'diamond' has been much criticized, firstly for its reductionism – reducing an otherwise highly complex set of contextual factors down to four – secondly, it underplays the role of the state and thirdly it ignores the role of transnational business.

States compete in order to enhance their international trading position and to capture a larger share of the gains of trade, although, clearly, nations do not compete in the same way as behoves a business.[3] Nations operate within a politico-economic ideology or system. Western governments in the 1980s tended to espouse a market-ideological view, especially in the US (under Reagan) and the UK (under Thatcher). This has been superseded by a 'market rational/regulatory' approach.[4] However, a number of countries, especially in the Soviet-led system to the close of the 1980s, adopted a plan-ideological dogma in which the State owned and controlled most of the economic units. This is evolving into a planned rational/developmental system in which an increasing proportion of firms is privately owned but where the State continues to intervene by setting explicit national economic and social goals.

Some of the effects of economic transformations by State planned economies in Eastern and Central Europe are discussed in a commentary by Richard Scase.[5] He points out that market reforms have not necessarily increased the level of entrepreneurial activity in Eastern and Central Europe. Rather 'proprietorship' is in evidence. Small business owners have carved out niches for trading purposes. They were able to reap sufficient profits from trade to achieve a satisfactory standard of living but they appeared to have no long term aspirations for capital accumulation. Thus small business proprietorship offered opportunities for personal economic survival and psychological benefits such as autonomy but left the socio-political and economic transformations largely untouched.

Clearly the political system is fundamentally important to firm behaviour and performance, but so too is the physical infrastructure. Good roads and rail networks, seaports, airports and telecommunications systems are crucial, as is a sound banking and financial system. Further, governments also determine trade policies, fixing tariffs on imports and through fiscal and monetary policies, controlling the money supply, interest rates and the 'price' of exports. This power to organize its internal affairs gives each state national sovereignty.

Tariffs or duties levied on imported goods is clearly a barrier to trade. Restrictions on trade are not thought to be in a nation's interest and so since the Second World War (1947 to be precise), there has been the development of an international institutional framework for promoting free trade, by the regulation and reduction of tariff barriers. This framework, known as the GATT (General Agreement on Tariffs and Trade) initially had 23 signatories but now its successor the WTO (World Trade Organization) has about 124 member countries and covers more than 90 per cent of world trade. The WTO takes a 'rule-oriented' approach to multilateral trade cooperation. Such rules are non-discriminatory – they must apply to all countries. A second important rule is that imported goods must receive the same treatment as domestic goods. However there is still fierce disagreement between nations over a number of issues and there are perceptions between developing and developed nations in respect of the implementation of agreements, let alone the need to make progress in instituting new arrangements.

It is not surprising that the global system might appropriately be thought of as dynamic if not volatile. However, in order to explain the processes of internationalization and globalization, it is necessary to consider that governments have influence over foreign investment policy. Such policy can be either outward or inward. Governments can place restrictions on outward investment, for example by insisting that proposed overseas investments be approved or by regulating the export of capital. Most governments, however, compete for inward investment and may have developed a set of policies to control it. These policies include:

- screening mechanisms
- regulatory mechanisms to control the operations of foreign firms
- restrictions on the transfer of capital and methods of taxing corporate profits
- measures to stimulate overseas investment.

Whilst there are some national differences towards foreign direct investment (FDI) these are less marked than they were in the past. Indeed, there have been attempts to agree a framework for the regulation of FDI though as yet little progress has been made.

Box 2.1 Foreign direct investment in UK regions

Manufacturing gross value added (GVA) by UK and foreign owned companies

£ millions   GO REGION/COUNTRY

	UK	NE	NW	M	Y&H	EM	WM	E	L	SE	SW	EN	W	SC	NI
Foreign 1994	4172	277	350	108	211	170	655	386	257	625	268	3307	286	512	68
1995	5340	410	477	124	333	262	750	470	305	730	217	4078	390	793	79
1996	5859	377	493	134	333	327	949	569	369	728	277	4557	539	658	104
1997	6478	369	555	146	245	500	1000	566	450	862	451	5145	539	682	112
Average (94-97)	5462	358	469	128	280	315	839	498	345	736	303	4272	438	661	91
UK 1994	9518	348	1317	176	1061	875	1004	804	690	1093	669	8037	505	725	251
1995	11428	453	1678	205	1147	1048	1153	908	868	1292	881	9634	690	846	258
1996	11977	608	1738	185	1279	1058	1330	906	789	1231	959	10083	595	980	318
1997	13579	774	1833	217	1487	1162	1482	1035	849	1286	977	11102	888	1212	378
Average (94-97)	11626	546	1642	196	1244	1036	1242	913	799	1225	872	9714	670	914	301

Source: Annual Census Of Production/Annual Business Inquiry, ONS

The North East is the UK's smallest region in terms of population (c. 3 million) and contribution to GDP (c.3 per cent). The government office (GO) has focused on attracting industries that build on the region' s traditional competitive advantage, especially in manufacturing. The region has been most successful at attracting investment from the Far East, with more limited success on US investment, which accounted for 50 per cent of investment in the UK last year. Inward investment in the region has been focused around the following key sectors:

automotive   life sciences
electronics   microelectronics
chemicals   food and drink
call centres/services   engineering

Inward investors are attracted to the North East because of the competitively priced property, good quality of life, strong partnerships between organizations involved in fostering economic development in the region, the supply chain infrastructure and regional assistance grants. There are a number of weaknesses which undermine the competitive advantages, including a lack of skilled labour, shortage of modern premises (particularly for service sector operations) and some important gaps in the training programme. There is also a danger that the region may lose out on inward investment in low cost manufacturing to Eastern Europe and knowledge based investment to Cambridge/Oxford.

Governments, of course, have their domestic policies which vary between the development of incentives for business such as capital grants and loans, tax concessions, etc, through state regulation of national industrial activity. As regards the latter, there has been a trend towards deregulation of certain industries including transport, finance and telecommunications and the stimulation of competition within such industrial sectors. The overall aim is to facilitate the national competitiveness of industry and to progress the development of new (future) industries in knowledge and the life sciences.

Nation-states having their distinctive politico-economic systems and national culture[6] are organizing themselves in regional blocs for trade and economic purposes. International economic integration is still an espoused ideal towards which some nations are moving faster than others. The most advanced regional trade bloc is that of the European Union (EU). However, there is a hierarchy of measures to be agreed for any trading bloc in order that it can be said to have achieved true economic union. These measures are:

- free trade in which trade restrictions between member countries have been removed
- customs union where an external trades policy is adopted by all members
- common market which allows the free movement of all factors of production
- economic union through which broader economic policies are harmonized.

The development of such regional trading blocs gives the advantages of size, the idea is to create a 'virtuous circle of growth'. There are social provisions to protect weaker member states,[7] however, there are sensitive issues, in particular those of adopting a common currency and relinquishing national sovereignty on a range of economic issues.

Other regional trading blocs have been developed but not to the extent of the EU. For example an agreement was forged between the US and Canada in 1988/9 – the CUSFTA.[8] This was superseded by the North American Free Trade Agreement (NAFTA) which included free trade with Mexico. There have been a number of concerns raised over this agreement, not least of which is the employment implications for the US. There are clearer advantages for Mexico both in terms of attracting inward investment from its wealthier and more economically advanced neighbour and securing access to US and Canadian markets. As yet this agreement has not gone beyond that of free trade aspirations, there is no customs union. A third example of a free trade area is the AFTA (Asia Free Trade Area) which has been superseded by the APEC (Asian-Pacific Economic Policy Forum). This was formed in 1989 and includes East and South East Asia, Australia, New Zealand, Chile and Canada, the US and Mexico. Whilst the member countries are diverse, politically the relationship enables the US to signal its commitment to Asia, in particular the fast developing market in China. It is also in Japan's interests to develop such relationships including that with the US. Malaysia has a different agenda and wishes to preserve 'Asianness'; this would mean excluding the North American countries, Australia and New Zealand. It would also enable them to protect themselves against the possible domination of such developed economies.

The transnational corporation

If nations are so powerful to control their internal affairs to what extent does the transnational corporation (TNC) threaten their autonomy? 'A transnational corporation is a firm which has the power to coordinate and control operations in more than one country even if it does not own them.'[9]

TNCs have the ability to control different aspects of a production chain over a widely dispersed geographical area, taking advantage of geographical differences in the factors of production and of national policies and (of particular concern to a nation) the ability to switch investments between locations. The removal of investment by the German multi-national firm Siemans from the North East of England in the mid-1990s and a similar move by the German car manufacturer BMW primarily from the West Midland based Rover plant in the UK in 1999 have caused both political and economic repercussions. In the latter case the enormous interdependency of a plethora of small subcontracting firms threatened the livelihoods of thousands of workers beyond the gates of the Rover plant at Longbridge. Hence governments have the right to fear the power of the TNC and as a matter of policy need to balance their power by the development of indigenous new economic activity.

Clearly, however, firms internationalize because there are advantages in so doing. They need to be able to outcompete indigenous firms and here size can be an advantage. After satisfying the home market, a firm tends to look overseas to capture new markets. But the TNC goes beyond the idea of exporting surplus home production to that of producing commodities overseas. There are three types of advantage of so doing: they include ownership-specific advantages such as knowledge, skills or competencies which the firm has a proprietary right to use, size conferring negotiating strength, market power and/or better access to finance; locational advantages arising from markets, resources, production costs, political conditions and/or cultural and linguistic affinities; and internalized market advantages primarily to reduce the uncertainty, get a return on research and development (R&D) expenditure and retain know-how within its own bounds.[10]

There is no linear sequence of activities which a firm must demonstrate or have experienced before it becomes global. The pattern – domestic market—license or export—establish sales outlet in overseas market—establish production facility in overseas market – is not a necessary one. Indeed firms are being encouraged to move very quickly into a global strategic position. And with the advantages of the internet, this is fast becoming a realistic strategy. For the smaller firm, however, having a well defined niche, a depth of understanding of the competition and a sound financial base are essential prerequisites. This must be backed up by a far-sighted, competent management team.

But do globalizing firms reflect their origins? How many truly global firms are there? It is beyond the scope of this chapter to give a definitive answer to this question, however, others have attempted an answer. Dicken argues that TNCs are not 'placeless'; by examining the geographical extent of the top 100 corporations he was able to derive an index of their transnationality.[11] This index was based on their foreign sales, foreign held assets and foreign employment. It showed, for example that the top 13 corporations have an index greater than 75 and that without exception they originate from small countries (such as Switzerland, the UK, the Netherlands, Belgium and Canada) – see Table 2.1 below.

Table **2.1** The top 13 transnational corporations measured against an index of 'globalization'

| Ra | Ri | Index | Company | Country | Industry | Foreign share of | |
						Assets	Employment
60	1	92.3	Thomson Corp.	Canada	Publishing and printing	95.7	88.7
71	2	92.2	Solvay	Belgium	Chemicals	92.8	89.5
50	3	91.4	RTZ	UK	Mining	–	96.9
17	4	90.5	Roche Holdings	Switzerland	Pharmaceuticals	90.4	82.9
42	5	88.8	Sandoz	Switzerland	Pharmaceuticals	–	85.1
15	6	88.4	ABB	Switzerland	Electrical equipment	85.2	93.7
52	7	87.3	Electrolux	Sweden	Electronics	–	82.8
13	8	86.5	Nestlé	Switzerland	Food	65.6	96.9
24	9	85.0	Philips	The Netherlands	Electronics	87.7	83.0
23	10	84.5	Unilever	UK/The Netherlands	Food	77.5	89.9
58	11	80.2	Glaxo-Wellcome	UK	Pharmaceuticals	75.2	75.0
93	12	79.3	Akzo	The Netherlands	Chemicals	71.0	73.4
61	13	78.6	Seagram	Canada	Beverages	76.9	–

Key
Ra – Rank by total foreign assets.
Ri – index of transnationality. Represents the average of foreign assets to toal assets, foreign sales to total sales and foreign employment to total employment.

Based on Dicken 1998 (see note 2): pp.194–5

However, when looking at the majority of TNCs, the home base tends to dominate as the parent company makes executive decisions in order to control its international operations. Thus, for example Fiat is an Italian company, McDonald's is American, Siemans is German and Nissan is Japanese primarily because nationally-based characteristics tend to persist. This is largely because the TNC has evolved through a complex process of 'embedding in which the cognitive, social, political and economic characteristics of the national home base play a dominant part.'[12]

Organization-environment relationship

Understanding the factors that shape the environment is important but do firms behave so analytically? Rationality is bounded. There are constraints on the information available to the decision taker at any one time and so deci-

Box 2.2: The characteristics of industry-environments

Dynamic	concerns the rate of industry change
Uncertain	pertains to the predictability of industry events
Complex	the number of different relevant attributes in the industry
Resource scarce	the extent to which the industry is lean in respect of needed resources
Homogenous	the similarity of competitors in respect of size, resources, strategies and costs
Interconnected	the extent to which events or components of the industry are organized and interrelated

sions are always made in a climate of relative risk and uncertainty. The environment can be a crucial determinant of a firm's survival.[13] The greater the competition, the lower the firm's likely profitability. However, environments vary across industry sectors. Smith *et al.*[14] summarize the characteristics of such environments along six dimensions, as shown in Box 2.2 above.

These six dimensions are used to describe three generic industry environments: emerging growth, mature and fragmented.

● **Emerging growth environments** are dynamic, uncertain, complex and resource rich, heterogeneous and low on interconnectedness. Such an environment is typical for firms with high rates of innovation, such as new technology small businesses.
● **Mature industry environments** are less dynamic, more predictable, less complex and highly homogenous; interconnectedness is high as competitors tend to know each other. Resources are scarce. This presents an unattractive picture to potential new entrants.
● **Fragmented industry environments** are characterized primarily by no one firm having a dominant market share. The clothing industry in the UK is highly fragmented. The environment is moderately dynamic and uncertain, moderately well resourced and is characterized by considerable complexity of competition. Firms often face geographically distinct market segments where the rules of competition and degree of interconnectedness vary. They have characteristics which are typical of both the mature and emerging industry environments.

The perceived environment

The shaping of the environment for small business development is one of considerable concern at political and economic levels.[15] Setting up any business involves taking risks and the nature of the environment – resource rich or not, turbulent or stable, opportunity plentiful or not and so on – can facilitate or inhibit small firm growth and development. Comparative analysis of small firm environments across countries highlights constraints, difficulties and 'best practice', which help economic development agencies, at local regional and national levels, address small firm development needs. Globally, national politico-economic conditions and determinants of cultural difference vary. Thus simply to contrast western and eastern economies is exceedingly crude. Within the West there are important variations and with the opening up of Eastern Europe to a capitalist market economy approach, understanding these differences is critically important.

A study by Krzysztof Obloj and Lars Kolvereid[16] compared and contrasted the environments and cultures of three countries – Great Britain, Norway and Poland. Their measures, however, were of the *perceived* environment. They examined possible differences in labour, capital, customers, the economy, stability and hostility. On their measures of these items, they found significant differences between business owner perceptions between countries, though not always as strongly as might have been expected. Perceptions of course are shaped by expectations thus perceptions are relative and in one sense difficult to compare. For example Polish business owners did not perceive their environment to be exceptionally scarce in resources, hostile or unstable. Great Britain was the country with the greatest variety of support services, which contrasted in particular with Norway where support services were perceived to be limited. Further, Polish owner-managers differed from their Norwegians and British counterparts on reasons for start up. They particularly wished to achieve a higher position in society, to have more influence in the community, to be respected by friends, to increase the status and prestige of the family and to have higher earnings. Interestingly the Polish owner-managers were also more highly educated than the British or Norwegians. Education in the West has largely ignored the small business sector as providing career options for young people. Degree programmes in business have been largely geared towards large business. This attitude is slowly changing with the realization that large business alone cannot deal with the problem of unemployment.

National environments do not by any means tell the whole story. There is considerable regional variation within countries which affects new firm formation and regional prosperity.[17] Regions vary in terms of their labour market characteristics (for example skills shortages, existence of particular skills, need to reskill to attract new business into the local economy), the availability of capital for investment purposes, the size of the local population and potential local customer base, the nature of the regional economy – for example the North East of England is characterized as a branchplant economy, reliant on inward investment and undergoing considerable industrial regeneration. Even more intangible are regional and local attitudes towards self employment and business venturing.

In the UK, Barclays Bank has attempted to capture regional variation in entrepreneurial activity.[18] It developed an 'entrepreneurial index' which it used to survey the counties of England and Wales. This showed Cambridgeshire to be top of the league, followed by the other southern counties of Buckinghamshire (2), Devon (3), Berkshire (4) and Kent (5). Counties with a low proportion of entrepreneurs and featuring at the bottom of the table were Oxfordshire (40), Hertfordshire (41), Lincolnshire (42), Hampshire (43), Mid, South and West Glamorgan (44) and Humberside (45).

UK economic policy includes provision of a networked small business advisory service which currently comprises 'one-stop-shops' known as the Business Links. However, within any region there are other small business development agencies and advisors. Ironically, however, in the Tyneside (North East) region (ranked 38 on the Barclays Entrepreneurial Index) the number of economic development agents and small business advisors is inversely proportional to the rate of small firm start up and entrepreneurial activity generally. Some of the key factors which make Cambridgeshire a vibrant entrepreneurial area in contrast to Tyneside and the North East generally are known. They include, for example, communications links to London and to large corporate headquarters, well developed relations between the university science base and industry fostering business spin-offs and a positive attitude towards entrepreneuring. Given such evidence of regional disparities it behoves economic development agencies locally and governments nationally to address questions of the underlying factors which have created such variation in order to address below average levels of entrepreneuring by creating a facilitating climate and raising the level of entrepreneurship nationwide.

Webs of enterprise

The environment for any firm is importantly that of other firms. Other firms comprise suppliers, customers and service providers making up a complex web of interrelationships. Large corporations, as has already been argued, may dominate an industrial sector within a particular regional economy. Their presence influences the nature and existence locally of other (usually small) firms. Indeed whatever the precise structure of the corporate conglomerate the development of a satellite of small firms around it will be evident.

Four types of corporate conglomerate have been identified, namely, the 'multinational', the 'international', the 'classic global' and the 'complex global'.

- The **multinational organization** (MNC) is typified by expanding European companies. It is, essentially, a decentralized federation of overseas national businesses. Each national business has a high degree of autonomy and a predominantly 'local' orientation. It can respond to local needs but it is unable to achieve scale economies and any internal flow of knowledge is also reduced.
- The **international organizational form** emerged in the 1950s and 1960s primarily in the US. This type of corporation is formally controlled and coordinated by headquarters which transmits information and know-how to its subsidiaries. It is less responsive to local needs that the MNC.
- The **classic global corporation** was developed by Ford and Rockefeller in the 1900s. Overseas subsidiaries have little autonomy to develop their own products or strategies. However, this type of corporation does achieve effi-

ciencies due to economies of scale. But local market conditions and local learning is largely ignored.

- The **complex global model** has an integrated network structure with flexible coordinating processes. Overseas operations are an integral part of a network of flows of knowledge, information, products, resources and so on. Units are thus highly interdependent and knowledge is both developed and shared worldwide.

Clearly from such diverse structures different strategies emerge which have implications for the local milieu of the business economic unit. Where the focus is 'multidomestic', that is the corporation as it were holds a portfolio of businesses, its strategy will reflect the competitive conditions prevailing in each country. In effect, it will develop a series of domestic strategies. In contrast the global-oriented corporation must develop a strategy which integrates its activities on a worldwide basis whilst maintaining some country perspective. There will inevitably be tensions between globalizing and localizing pressures. Whatever balance is achieved the predominantly global and the portfolio business corporation must be both globally aware (for example of competitors' investments strategies, technology bases, costs, sources of supply and energy) and locally responsive to differences in market structure and consumer demands.

Corporate headquarters and R&D functions tend to be located in the home country, close to big city activity where there are good communications and social and cultural activities. Production is organized differently. There are a number of patterns.

- **Globally concentrated production** – concentrated in a single location or plant and then exported to world markets through the corporation's marketing and sales networks.
- **Host market production** – where production is located in and oriented to the host market. This is a case of replicating the home production unit within the overseas market.
- **Product specialization for a global or regional market** – production is organized to serve a large market (such as the European Union). An internal market is created around a production system in which items are fabricated, transported and assembled elsewhere in the system for sale to the entire regional market. European car production tends to operate along these lines.
- **Transnational vertical integration of production** – involves the production of semi-finished product in different manufacturing plants. Hence different parts of the corporation's production system are located in different parts of the world. There is no connection between where the item is produced and its final market destination. The rapid increase in the use of offshore production facilities (for example in clothing and textiles) has arisen due to the low wage costs of labour in developing countries, the fact that standardization of the production process enables the use of unskilled labour and government factors in export policies create advantages.

In addition to the above there are other arrangements of economic units which affect the local milieu of the firm. The *intra*national location of production units should not be forgotten. Economies like that of North Eastern England (see earlier discussion) comprises a 'branchplant economy'. Branch plants are usually located in areas of high unemployment and where there are regional incentives.

A further development is that of the international strategic alliance. This is collaboration on a global scale and enables a firm to achieve a specific goal which it could not otherwise achieve alone. Only some of the participants' business activities are involved. The majority of corporate strategic alliances occur between North American, European and Japanese corporations. They may take the form of cooperation in R&D (for example in the 'life sciences' and pharmaceuticals industries), joint manufacturing (e.g. Honda and Leyland, BMW and Rover cars) and joint bidding consortia (e.g. telecommunications).

An additional organizational form which has also become more prevalent is that of the network structure. A network is a system of structured relationships between or among firms each playing a part in the business goal of product or service delivery. The network has arisen as a strategy to achieve global competitiveness. This has been particularly apparent in Europe and less so in some areas, for example the United States.[19] Such differences in the geographical spread of networks has led to considerable research on the rise of industrial districts in, for example the Emilia-Romagna district in Italy and the absence of such well developed network structures in the United Kingdom. Political arguments for change comprise the failure of capitalism, the collapse of US hegemony and delayering of organizations to increase efficiency and the failure of organizational structure to convert from rigid to more flexible adaptive structures. The most convincing argument is that advantage occurs from **flexible production**[20] (see Box 2.3).

One reason why the small firm network is less prevalent in the UK and the US may be the existence and strength of the franchised business.[21] An interesting contrast between the franchised form and the small firm network is the adoption of Tayloristic principles in the former, for example McDonald's. The cultural differences between northern and southern Europe might give some clues for the development of an explanation as to why the management of control is handled very differently.

The increased incidence of externalized production chains means that a higher proportion of various operations are outsourced and performed by independent firms, in other words, they are subcontracted. Box 2.4 summarizes the major elements of a subcontracting relationship.

The advantages of subcontracting include:

- avoiding investment in new plant
- flexibility in coping with fluctuations in capacity
- externalizing risk and the costs of the operation.

The costs to the subcontractor are:

Box 2.3: Advantages of flexible production

- Greater responsiveness to changing and fragmented markets because small suppliers have more direct information.
- Small units have more widely skilled personnel who can be redeployed more quickly.
- Information technology reduces transaction delays and costs when the small firm searches for the best supplier. This offsets any advantage that the large firm might have had through centralized purchasing or in-house suppliers.
- Technological changes make the production of small runs and changes in products more feasible. This results in the greater variety of product, which appeals to the customer.
- Effort is more directly related to reward in the small firm and there are more chances of achieving ownership status.
- Non-specialized tasks in smaller organizations reduce the separation between concept and execution – the gap introduced by Taylorism (see chapter 9) and put into practice by Ford.

- bearing the risk, being expendable and lacking countervailing power where the subcontractor is a small firm
- having a high proportion of subcontracted work so reducing the firm's freedom of movement strategically (for example to develop new products)
- creating a dependent relationship.

The benefits to the subcontractor may however outweigh the costs. These include:

- access to otherwise unattainable markets
- the continuity of orders
- the possible injection of capital.

There is increasing use of international subcontracting due to low transportation costs.

The subcontracting form of a networked firm may comprise as many as three tiers of subcontractors. Such firms tend to develop dependent relationships with the contractor who may be their main (or even only) customer. A very high proportion of the vehicle manufacture industry uses this form (for example up to 50 per cent vehicle assembly at General Motors and 30 per cent in Japanese vehicle manufacturers).[22] The dependency relationship is highly variable. For example subcontractors in Japan are relatively independent of the large firm they supply. There tends to be greater collaboration in determining prices, design and sharing information. Also contracts now tend to be large modules rather than single items and payment arrives earlier. Some large organizations, for example the UK High Street retailer, strictly control their relations with their suppliers, setting standards and conditions for production and delivery largely on their own terms. Quality standards (BS5750 and ISO 9000) have had a similar controlling effect, enabling the large organization to control carefully the quality of its supplies.[23]

The small-firm network (SFN) comprises firms which on average employ ten people.[24] The network can comprise as many as six layers, as shown in

Box 2.4: Major elements of the subcontracting relationship

Technical aspects of production

- Subcontracting **processes** }
- Subcontracting **components**}   Industrial subcontracting
- Subcontracting **entire products**   Commercial subcontracting

Nature of the principal firm

- Producer firm (both industrial and commercial subcontracting)
- Retailing/wholesaling firm (commercial subcontracting)

Type of subcontracting (motivation of principal firm)

- Speciality subcontracting
- Cost-saving subcontracting
- Complementary or intermittent subcontracting

Types of relationship between principal firm and subcontractor

- Time period may be long term, short term, single batch
- Principal may provide some or all materials or components
- Principal may provide detailed design or specification
- Principal may provide finance, e.g. loan capital
- Principal may provide machinery and equipment
- Principal may provide technical and/or general assistance and advice
- Principal is invariably responsible for all marketing arrangements

Geographical scale

- Within border, i.e. domestic subcontracting
- Crossborder, i.e. international subcontracting

Source: Dicken 1998 (see note 2): p.231

Figure 2.1 below. This structure ensures that the producers procure raw materials, are supplied with semi-fabricated parts and business services sell on their product to distributors from whence its final destination is the customer. On the face of it this appears to be a complex structure which evolves because of the value of sharing information and the efficiencies which accrue resourcing strategies.

The difference in dependency relations between different structures is shown in Figure 2.2. Marks and Spencer plc follows the model of the 'capitalist ideal' very closely. Power resides in the organization, which controls both suppliers and customers. However, in the SFN model at the broad waistband both customers and suppliers have choices. This distributes power and creates the conditions for cooperation. Under these conditions a firm cannot afford to deceive; this in effect moderates any tendency towards malfeasance and the ability to maximize self-interest. Furthermore other, arguably more positive, reasons for this structure's effectiveness are that it provides greater flexibility, stimulates innovation and maximizes sector-wide problem-solving.[25]

Figure **2.1** The subcontracting model of small firms networks

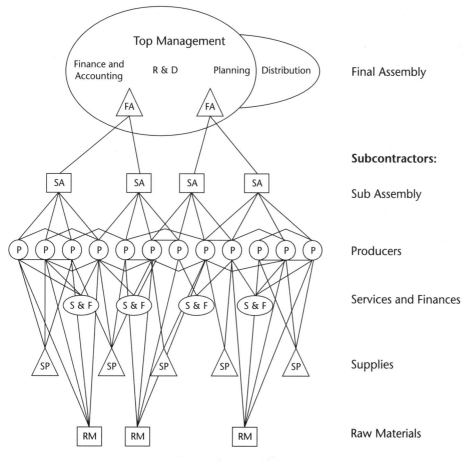

Source: Perrow 1992 (see note 19): p.458

But what is the 'glue' that binds such organizations together? In one sense there is none, in another the structural conditions not only encourage cooperation but also foster trust. For example:

- sharing and discussing information on issues of mutual interests – markets, technologies etc
- similarity of processes and techniques that facilitate the evaluation of another's behaviour
- experience of being helped by another firm
- long term relationships even though contacts may be intermittent
- little difference among firms in respect of their size, power or strategic position
- rotation of leadership, representing a collection of firms
- similar financial rewards to the firms and the employees within them
- firms *collectively* experience the economic advantages of increased sales and profits

Figure **2.2** Dependency and independency networks

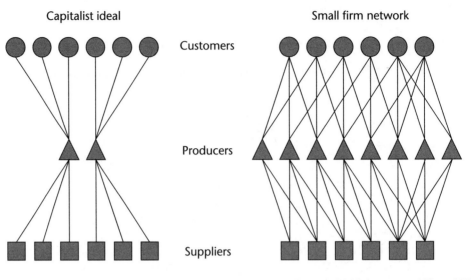

Source: Perrow 1992 (see note 19): p.457

● the binding effects of similarities in fate, generated by trade or professional associations, economic agencies, trades unions and so on.

This analysis underlines the importance of *cooperation* between firms within an overall *competitive framework* engineered in large measure by politic-economic policies of nation-states. This theme of competitiveness is re-visited below.

Competitiveness

Being sensitive to its situation and the constraining and facilitating aspects of the environment is important for any firm. But this is not to develop a 'sense of place', rather it is to develop both a tacit knowledge and a basis for making informed judgements about the future goals and strategic direction of the enterprise. This knowledge will enable the firm to position itself strategically and decide how it should best deploy its resources to gain competitive advantage. Since his first volume *Competitive Strategy*, Michael Porter[26] has devoted his intellectual energies to the task of enabling firms to understand the competitive environment in which they are operating. A subsequent volume *The Competitive Advantage of Nations*[27] has addressed the broader issue of how the firm can compete globally and internationally and what may be deduced about the particular competitive advantages that a nation offers its industries. It may be argued that such knowledge is only of importance to dominant firms in a nation's key industries. However, as we shall see, the adoption of globalization strategies is possible for the small to medium-sized business and, furthermore, being innovative, changing or developing new industry and 'getting in first' are just the kind of tactics that the successful global company needs to adopt.

Fundamental to Porter's argument is that all firms need to understand the forces of competition (see Figure 2.3 and earlier discussion). The strength of each of these forces depends on the underlying structure of the particular industry. Hence every industry is unique and is affected by a particular configuration of competitive forces. A nation provides a better environment for competing in some nations rather than others. Secondly, firms must position themselves within the industry. Positioning is about recognizing the firm's competitive advantage. Firms can compete either by achieving a cost advantage (lower cost) or by differentiating the product in the market place by adding value, improving its quality and so on. The former strategy results in increased efficiency and productivity and the latter higher revenues per unit. The more competitive a nation's industry the more prosperous the nation. Thirdly, the firm must decide on its competitive scope. Scope includes the range of products, distribution channels, types of buyers and geographical areas it will sell to. Industries are segmented and a firm may choose to compete in a particular segment. This provides another strategic choice for the firm. These three aspects of competition combine to produce four generic strategies (see Figure 2.4). The worst strategic error a firm can make is to 'get stuck in the middle' or attempt all the strategies, for example the British and Spanish ship building industry.

Each firm performs discrete activities that may be grouped into a logical sequence forming the **value chain**. At each stage of the value chain the firm seeks to add value and thus compete with its rivals. In this way firms may realize competitive advantage essentially by conceiving of new ways to conduct activities, employing new procedures or new technologies or utilizing

Figure **2.3** The five competitive forces that determine industry competition

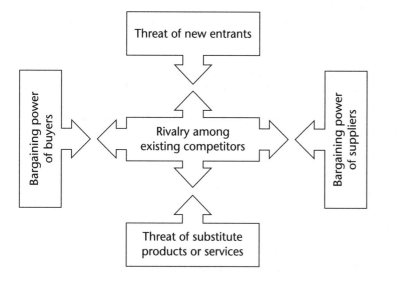

Source: Porter 1990 (see note 27): p.35

Figure **2.4** Four generic competitive strategies in ship building

		COMPETITIVE ADVANTAGE	
		Lower cost	Differentiation
COMPETITIVE SCOPE	Broad target	**Cost leadership** e.g. Korea offers good quality of vessels at lower prices (and lower costs)	**Differentiation** e.g. Japan offers premium quality vessels at premium prices
	Narrow target	**Cost focus** e.g. China offers simple standard vessels at even lower prices and costs than the Koreans	**Focused differentiation** e.g. Scandinavia offers specialized types of ship-icebreakers – which command high prices

Source: Porter 1990 (see note 27): p.39

different inputs. Whilst these activities may be discrete, they are also linked and interdependent. Thus, quality, efficiency and effectiveness are achieved by the way the value chain is conceived and managed. Key aspects of managing the value chain are:

● coordination of operations
● careful management of linkages to produce efficiencies and manage advantageous trade-offs
● managing the value chain as a system
● seeing the value chain as part of the value system within the industry
● managing external dependencies
● creating value for the buyer
● gaining cost-advantage throughout the value chain
● considering the competitive scope of the firm *vis à vis* its rivals.

The main way of gaining competitive advantage is by innovating. The most typical ways of achieving this are:

● technological change
● new or shifting buyer needs
● the emergence of a new industry segment
● shifting inputs costs or availability
● changes in government regulations.

A further important way of gaining competitive advantage is by early exploitation of an opportunity. This is because early movers:

● reap economies of scale

- reduce costs through cumulative learning
- establish brand names and customer relationships before direct competition develops
- have the widest choice of distribution channels
- identify the best locations and sites from which to operate
- obtain the best sources of raw materials and supplies.

When reading literature on new business creation, the issue of **sustained entrepreneurial performance** is rarely addressed. Porter, on the other hand, addresses one aspect of this by considering the issue of a firm being able to sustain its competitive advantage. This is done by the firm:

- identifying higher-order advantages (e.g. skills and capabilities) which potential rivals find more difficult to duplicate
- proliferating its advantages and not relying on a single advantage
- constant improvement and upgrading
- spotting industry changes, moving early to exploit them and thereby cutting off the competition
- being prepared to destroy old advantages in order to create new ones
- being prepared to change.

The above are the fundamentals of competitive behaviour which any firm must consider if it is to compete effectively in global or international markets. But how does the firm develop the capability to compete on a truly global, worldwide stage? As discussed in an earlier section of this chapter, some international competition is **multidomestic**, that is, the firm competes on a country-by-country basis, identifying the advantages that are largely confined to each country in which they compete. At the extreme, firms which, arguably, compete globally do so by combining domestic competitive advantages with additional advantages that accrue from competing in many countries. Such advantages include economies of scale, the ability to serve multinational customers and a transferable brand reputation.

It has to be said that, given the existence of national boundaries, national cultural differences and the concentration of a firm's assets in the 'home-base', from an international business management perspective it remains controversial as to whether any business can be termed 'global', indeed, whether 'globalization' is a meaningful concept. However, this is not to deny the utility of internationalization strategies or business goals, which include the desire to offer a product or service within worldwide markets and in that sense to have a worldwide presence and a claim to be called a 'global company'. Some industries and their products or services may lend themselves more readily to this, for example confectionery, pharmaceuticals and computer software. However, if a fundamental criterion of the global firm is the distribution of its asset base across the world (and not just its product or service), then it would seem that the networked firm is the new global business form. Thus, the current debate about the nature of globalization is unresolved. However, whether ultimately it is considered to be more appropriate to label strategies as being 'international' rather than 'global' remains to be seen. With this caveat made, the next section considers some of the implications of 'global competitiveness' or what some may prefer to term 'international competitiveness' behaviour.

Some implications of global competitiveness: the need for innovative thinking and the management of change

Achieving global competitiveness is also a matter of strategic thinking at the firm level. Getting the strategy right may involve developing the management team and instigating fundamental change within the organization. Rosabeth Moss Kanter[28] has concerned herself with the issues of competitiveness and the development of innovative styles of management practice.[29] In the *Change Masters*, for instance, she contrasts two ways of thinking which she terms **segmentalism** and **integrative thinking**. Segmentalism, as the name suggests, concerns the compartmentalization of actions, events and problems. Each aspect is isolated, independent of context and connections. It is quite likely that this way of thinking will be reflected in the organizational structure, the walling off of separate departments, minimal exchanges and a lack of cooperation. Such a culture stifles innovation.[30] In integrative cultures the reverse is the case: 'They aggregate problems, so as to re-create a unity that provides more insight into required action. This helps make possible the creative leap of insight that redefines a problem so that novel solutions can emerge.'[31]

Incentives for change and organizational transformation

There is no one route to change and development: a company may be small and entrepreneurially led in any field or it may be a division of a corporate, multi-national company. Essentially the key is having the right culture, which in this instance means the way things are done. In Box 2.5 below a list of behaviours is identified which typify the low growth, low innovating company. It is clearly important however also to identify the appropriate characteristics of the successful innovating company. These are presented in Box 2.6.

The looseness of the organization structure frees up employees to act and take responsibility for their actions. The very environment of uncertainty associated with innovation creates opportunities and challenges. A commitment to problem-solving along with rising to challenges results in the empowerment of employees. This is discharged due to the relative lack of interference from senior management (hence freedom to act) and the low levels of formalization which give the scope to tackle jobs in the most appropriate ways seen fit. Senior management's role tends to be to set the bigger picture and the broad assignments to be addressed and to allow others to define these and take responsibility for delivery. The matrix structure means that few people act entirely on their own. Typically, cross-functional teams

Box 2.5: Rules for stifling change[32]

1. Regard any new idea from below with suspicion.
2. Insist that people who need your approval to act first go through several other levels of management to get their signatures.
3. Ask departments or individuals to challenge and criticize each other's proposals.
4. Express any criticisms freely and withhold your praise.
5. Treat identification of problems as signs of failure, to discourage people from letting you know when something in their area isn't working.
6. Control everything carefully.
7. Make decisions to reorganize or change policies in secret and spring them on people unexpectedly.
8. Make sure that requests for information are fully justified and make sure that it is not given out to managers freely.
9. Assign to lower-level managers responsibility for figuring out how to cut back, lay off, move people around, or otherwise implement threatening decisions you have made. And get them to do it quickly.
10. Never forget that you, the higher-ups, already know everything important about this business.

Box 2.6: The characteristics of successful highly innovative companies

Treatment of employees	Sound employee relations policies and practices, egalitarian systems, accountability coupled with responsibility.
Flexible structure	Matrix organization, lack of formality, flattened hierarchy.
Organization culture	Culture consciousness, emphasis on freedom, looseness and creativity, youthfulness, change viewed as an opportunity not a threat, common focus.
Virtuous circle	Growth and development attracts able and committed individuals who take pride in their company and give enhanced performance.

are formed to address particular problems/opportunities. This serves to create interdependencies and as such is **integrative**, to adopt Kanter's terminology.[33] Indeed, Kanter goes further when she says: '... [to] produce innovation, more complexity is essential; more relationships, more sources of information, more angles on the problem, more ways to pull in human and material resources, more freedom to walk around and across the organization.'[34]

It is, of course, people who innovate and this is why getting the management of people and the culture right is so fundamentally important. To operate at these high levels of creativity and innovation people need to feel committed, to belong and to take pride in their company. Success tends to inculcate further successes and this also engenders confidence in the competence of the leadership to deliver those further successes. Employees also have more self confidence due to the supportive culture, which makes them feel important. Sources of new ideas are looked for inside the company. This people-centred environment creates a culture of pride coupled with a culture of change. Further, the rewards tend to be contingent rather than material, that is the conditions which management have inculcated serve to reward employees as well as promote innovation.

No one has suggested that innovation and the management of change is easy. Kanter addresses some of the difficulties of what she terms 'swimming in newstreams'.[35] Newstream activities may be contrasted with those in the 'mainstream' on criteria of evaluation, historical base and experience and sunk costs. Thus to be effective management must know which stream it is swimming in. Newstreams, being about the fast development of new and innovative projects, are likely to have an uncertain and bumpy ride and therefore require:

- committed and visionary leadership
- 'patient money'
- planning flexibility.

Mainstream practice in organizations, however, pursues certainty, short term 'results' and control through planning. In these respects, newstream needs and mainstream management are at loggerheads. Newstream initiatives also breed intensity – both emotional and knowledge. The nature of the teamwork requirement goes beyond cooperation to a level of shared understanding at cognitive and technical levels. This requirement implies a high degree of compatibility amongst personnel, sound communications and overlapping capability. The idea that innovative teams can go their own way may be motivating for the team but can cause resentment in a company that is operating the two systems. Thus being able to separate out the teams perhaps into smaller operating divisions helps reduce the problem. This also facilitates the separation of style and procedures. Clearly, whilst bureaucratization stifles innovation, too much laxity can lead to inefficiency, there is a need for an appropriate balance between funding levels and project management. Throwing abundant resources at a project too quickly is likely to lead to inefficiency, whereas multistage resourcing will ensure managed progress.

There are clearly considerable organizational and management development and training implications of commitment to newstream activity. In some organizations where both cultures are in evidence Kanter suggests that 'the post-entrepreneurial manager will be adept at both styles, switching strokes to fit the situation'. How feasible this is is perhaps a moot point. However, newstream culture does challenge the mainstream approach and loosens traditional hierarchical authority, respect for bureaucracy, corporate identification and career dependence.

Strategies for achieving world class standards

In a later volume, Kanter identifies the following set of questions.

- How does globalization change the requirements for business and individual success, in small as well as large companies, in domestic as well as international pursuits? What kinds of companies are best prepared to take advantage of opportunities in the global economy? What kinds of leadership skills must be cultivated?

- As companies reinvent themselves and pursue international markets, how do changes in business affect people as managers, workers, consumers, voters and community residents?
- What is the meaning of 'community' in a global economy? Do communities matter and to whom? Can the spirit of community be restored and people reengaged in meaningful civic action to ensure a strong economy and high quality of life?
- How can cities and regions attract and hold the best companies and the best jobs? How can they harness global forces for local advantage? How can they be masters, not victims, of change?[36]

Kanter's message is that everyone is affected by global trends, including small businesses. Regional economies are important because they are not constrained by boundaries; they are better defined and more socially coherent. Nations, as pointed out by Hofstede,[37] are artificial constructs of socio-political processes. Regions are more likely to contain stable social groupings and associated local cultures. They have the potential for regionally based businesses to be global as well as local. However, to be global as well as local depends on perspective, the global business has wide horizons, the standards of quality to which it aspires are simply world class, such standards cannot fail to meet local needs! Such competitive standards are arrived at through the bringing together of world class resources in: **concepts, competence** and **connections.** These three Cs cover all crucial aspects of business venturing, that is **thinking** (for example the ability to innovate continuously, to conceptualize one's product or service in high profile market imagery, for example Phileas Fogg snack foods), **making** (the ability to meet high process-quality standards, to deliver cost-effective production etc) and **trading** (for example to make connections and to network effectively with the right people at the right time). These three Cs, Kanter argues, are the basis of business excellence. Thus, world class companies are more **entrepreneurial**, continuously seeking better ideas (concepts), investing in customer-driven innovation; **learning oriented**, searching for more and better ideas and opportunities, creating high standards of performance and investing in their employees' knowledge and skills; and **collaborative**, valuing relationships and partnerships. Kanter[38] argues that the three Cs make for a virtuous cycle which works in the following way.

- Strong partners offer each other access to the best and latest concepts.
- Network membership forces learning, which creates a gradual convergence of competence.
- Powerful connections open doors to still more introductions to powerful people.

It is the cosmopolitans who act in these ways, who make themselves attractive local partners and create conditions which require more cosmopolitan leaders with boundary crossing skills. 'The actions of cosmopolitans to move concepts around the world reinforce the power of customers, wherever they are, to demand the world's best.'[39]

Conclusions

New economies are emerging which are increasingly networked on a global scale.[40] They are global because their core activities of production, marketing and circulation are organized globally. In this chapter the focus has been on environmental factors that have fostered such developments. Key to the environment, however, are economic structures, in particular other firms. Nation-states are also important as repositories of business practices. Moreover, they also set the economic-political framework in which businesses may operate. However, the development of global oligopolies has posed some threats for governments. Securing foreign investments in industrial developments is attractive, for the restructuring of regional economies and areas of high unemployment. However, large transnational corporations have the power to withdraw investment and it is this power which governments should rightly respect if not fear. With little evidence of other benefits accruing in a region – for example the development of transferable skills – it behoves political leaders to refocus attention on the development of entrepreneurial skills for the regeneration of the industrial base, thus reducing reliance of foreign direct investment.

Whilst the focus in this chapter has been on the more tangible aspects of the environment, it has been made clear that local, national and corporate culture are also important determinants of business behaviour. Political ideologies and deeply held attitudes and values are evident from comparative work between market and planned economies. Further it was also shown how regional disparities occur within nations. This is often the result of an historical inheritance – the 'branchplant economy' of the North East of England being just one example.

The new global economy is also shaped in part by complex interdependencies between firms. These have resulted from the organization of transnational corporations, subcontracting arrangements and network structures. Interdependencies have implications for firm behaviour, especially the obligations and responsibilities of firms towards each other. However, whilst national boundaries and cultures persist and firm assets are predominantly located in the 'home-base' there is a basis for challenging the concept of the global enterprise. The key to the future is whether the dominant organizational form will become the networked organizational form, with a world-wide distribution of assets. With only one advanced regional trading bloc – the European Union – and many political obstacles to free trade such changes are unlikely to happen speedily.

Finally, consideration was given to what management needs to do to address both the competitive and 'global' imperatives. Again the internal culture can be one which appropriately supports change and organizational development, the argument being that only by being innovative (i.e. leading edge) will companies compete effectively on a local, national or international stage. Given increased pressures to globalize, standards of performance need to be matched at that level if the company is to hold its own. Offering products and services which can compete globally will also assure success in local markets. In this way, it may be argued that companies can be both globally and locally competitive: they can be 'glocal'!

CHAPTER 3

Business form and new venture creation

A new business venture may arise for any number of reasons; it may be a private enterprise of an individual or group of business partners/acquaintances or it may be a potential spin off from an existing corporate organization. The reasons why people set up their own business vary. The factors are known as 'push' or 'pull' factors. **Push** factors include unemployment and redundancy and social marginalization. **Pull** factors include having a good idea, wanting to be your own boss, desiring independence. On the other hand, the management of an existing corporate venture may be looking for ways to refresh and reinvigorate the business, there may be a corporate sense of the need to maintain the company's position at the cutting edge of innovation, or to establish a lead on the competition through research and development and the commercial testing of the potential of new ideas.

But whatever the motivation, all new businesses must be based on a good idea. This 'good idea' must be a realistic, viable proposition, that is, (a) there must be evidence of a need in the market place for the good or service and (b) the founder/inventor/director must have the skills and competencies to deliver.

This chapter commences with a consideration of the legal form of business, a matter which is likely to be of particular concern to the private owner-manager. It goes on to consider some of the key issues and considerations in founding a business. Fundamental to this is the business plan and the continued planning process. In contrast to business founding, the chapter concludes with a discussion of the process of corporate venturing. First there is a need to clarify the differences in the legal form of business.

Legal form

Founding a business is for some thought to be the *sine qua non* of entrepreneurship though by far the larger proportion of people who found businesses intend merely to make a livelihood for themselves, they are not entrepreneurial in the sense of wishing to grow a business, employ others or accumulate capital, rather they wish to maintain a lifestyle. The business founder may be a **sole trader**, s/he may enter into a business **partnership** with one or more people or they may set up a **limited company**.

KEY CONCEPT 3.1
Sole trader

A **sole trader** is an individual trading on his or her own, not as a company, corporation or partnership.[1]

The sole trader is typically an **arbitrageur** – the person who produces a good or service and sells it on at a profit. Examples of sole traders are craftspeople (potters, jewellers), tradespeople (plumbers, electricians) and dealers, that is, someone who produces nothing but buys and sells goods for a profit (such as, antique dealers, second hand book dealers, art dealers, etc).

KEY CONCEPT 3.2
Partnership

A **partnership** is a form of business association or company in which the partners are fully responsible for the partnership's liabilities.[2]

Business partnerships often arise quite serendipitously. Mike Murray was employed as a manager in a company which produced paper and paints for house interior decoration. His neighbour had spent his working life as a manager in the clothing industry.[3] The two business men got together and set up a company producing bridal wear; the company grew fast, exceeded its business planned projections and became a limited company. As it happened the business partnership did not survive as long as the business! Another example of a partnership is the solicitor's firm, which typically is headed by partners who may employ other solicitors within the firm.[4] There are many businesses in the business services sector which are partnerships. There are however advantages of changing the status of a business from a partnership to a limited liability company: it is not unknown in a partnership for one partner to abscond when the business runs into difficulties perhaps by incurring a bad debt or through mismanagement by one of the partners.

KEY CONCEPT 3.3
Limited company

A **limited company** is one in which the liability of the shareholder in the company is limited by legal statute to the amount of capital he or she has subscribed in the event of the company's failure.

In the UK once a limited company has been established and registered the ownership must put their company accounts on public record annually otherwise they are liable to be fined.

KEY CONCEPT 3.4
Public limited company

A **public limited company** (plc) is one whose shares are quoted and dealt with on the Stock Exchange. A private company may become a public company by 'going public', usually with the advice of the issuing house or merchant bank.

Founding a business

Financing the venture

Money and resources are needed to start a business and the amount of money depends on the particular business and the sector it is in. In general manufacturing tends to have higher set up costs than service sector businesses. A high proportion of new start ups set up with less than £7000. The primary source of funds is that of the business founder(s). However, where loans are taken out from banks the founder usually has to offer collateral to secure the loan. This security may be the family home. The founder will also be able to use their savings and/or obtain some grant support (for example from economic support agencies such as Business Link in the UK). Other options of financing the venture are debt financing or equity financing.

Debt financing means to borrow money in order to finance the business. The sources of funds may be (and often are) from family or friends, alternatively the prospective owner may be able to obtain a loan from a local High Street bank[5] (see Box 3.1), more rarely from the Business Link, a finance company or a 'business angel'. The sum borrowed must be repaid at a later date usually specified by the party or parties concerned. However, in evaluating the decision to make a loan, it certainly is not true that '[the] bank manager gains little from the success of the business but stands to lose a lot if it fails.'[6] There are bank charges (at business rates) on the company account and as the business grows clearly more money will go through the account.

In 1976, when Anita Roddick wanted to open a second shop she went back to the bank to raise the money.

> I got the same brusque treatment as before. I only wanted to borrow £4000, but the answer was no. I had no track record. I had only been trading for a few months ... I should wait for at least another year .... I had no intention of waiting that long before I opened a second shop. I had to find someone willing to invest in me .... it was ... Ian McGlinn ... he said he would lend me £4000

Box 3.1: Financing The Body Shop

'Before I could make any further progress I needed to raise some money. Gordon and I had calculated I would need about £4000 to get the business started, but I thought that as we could use the hotel for collateral there would be no problem. Unfortunately I went about it the wrong way. I made an appointment to see the bank manager and turned up wearing a Bob Dylan T-shirt with Samantha on my hip and Justine clinging on to my jeans. It just did not occur to me that I should be anything other than my normal self. I was enthusiastic and I gabbled on about my great idea, flinging all this information about how I had discovered these natural ingredients when I was travelling and I'd got this great name, The Body Shop and all I needed was £4000 to get it started … . When I had finished he (the bank manager) leaned back in his chair and said that he wasn't going to lend me any money because we were too much in debt already … .

'I was ready to give up, but Gordon is more tenacious than I am. "We will get the money" he said, "but we are going to have to play them at their own game." He told me to go out and buy a business suit and got an accountant friend to draw up an impressive-looking "business plan", with projected profit and loss figures and a lot of gobbledegook, all bound in a plastic folder.

'A week later we went back to the same bank for an interview with the same bank manager. We were both dressed in suits. Gordon handed over our little presentation, the bank manager flipped through it for a couple of minutes and then authorized a loan of £4000, just like that, using the hotel as collateral. I was relieved – but I was angry too, that I had been turned down the first time. After all, I was the same person with the same idea. It was clear to me that bank managers did not want to deal with mothers and babies … .'[7]

in return for a half share of the business … When the company went public in 1984 his stake was worth £4 million; it is now worth in excess of £140 million …[8]

Equity financing comprises funds invested in exchange for a share in the ownership of the company. This is a less desirable option to many small business venturers because they do not want to lose overall control.

A **venture capital firm** invests in new or expanding businesses with high earning and growth possibilities. They want businesses with a potential high rate of return; they often give information, advice and assistance in return.

Choice of business form

Starting a new business from scratch

The advantage of starting a business from scratch is that the founder can develop it in a way that suits them. The founder is solely responsible for the business' success. The disadvantages are the time taken to get established and to make the business profitable. The difficulties stem from the lack of an established customer base and the many mistakes that the founder is likely to make at the outset. No matter how much planning is done, a start up is risky. There is no guarantee that the idea will work. It is not unusual for would-be founders to attempt a number of different business start ups before they hit on the idea that enables them to make a successful business launch. Not all business owners stick with the one industrial sector as did Henri Strzelecki,[9] examples of significant side steps include moves from fish processing to the hotel and hospitality industry, timber and also trucking into boutique wine production, paint to bridal wear, property to bread production.[10]

Buying an existing business

Buying an existing business is one way of reducing the risk. There is a shorter time to get started and usually an existing track record, i.e. good will. The new business may already have systems in place thus alleviating the business owner of having to start such systems from scratch. Potential disadvantages are: the purchaser usually has to pay for 'goodwill', there may be 'ill will', the systems may be poor, outdated systems and technology may be being used. This is likely to suggest a turnround situation to the astute business person. 'Joe'[11] bought into a bakery business which he had discovered was stagnating. Within six months he had rationalized production lines, expanded the customer base and begun planned investment in plant and equipment.

Buying a franchise

Franchising has become 'big business'.

KEY CONCEPT 3.5
Franchising

Franchising is the arrangement by which the owner of a product or service allows others to purchase the right to distribute the product or service with help from the owner.

Lack of business experience and technical knowledge would appear to be sufficient reason for a person to decide not to go into business for themselves. However, there is another route which can be taken, that of franchising. The franchised business has become a popular option, it reduces the risk to the owner-manager of a start up situation and means they are relieved of weighty decisions in respect of profiling the business and its products, advertising, pricing, management style and many other dimensions of business practice. All these are taken care of by the franchiser. What the franchisee loses in this deal is independence and this may be too high a price to pay for many business owners. Another high cost is the monthly payment to be made to the franchiser, it can vary from 2 to 12 per cent of sales.

The business person who is considering purchasing a franchise should investigate it thoroughly beforehand. Critically important is what assistance the franchiser will be providing in terms of location, set up costs, securing credit, training of staff. They should also check the documentation from a legal point of view. Reliance on the franchiser does not cover all eventualities. For example Robert and his wife bought into a print/copyshop franchise. Neither had served any time in the printing industry and so they had no technical knowledge of printing equipment and machinery. When problems

Box 3.2: How many franchised businesses do you know?

Here are a few well known names: what are the main features of the franchised business?

Company	Characteristics
McDonald's Prontaprint Mrs Field's Cookies DynoRod The Body Shop	*Standardization of the product or service, company image, style and presentation ... It has been argued that some franchised companies such as McDonald's are good examples of the practice of scientific management.* *What do you think?*
Your suggestions:	

occurred in the print room this proved to be a major constraint on future business growth.

Setting up a business incubator

Business incubators are often referred to as 'managed workspaces'. They often have government backing and are intended to increase job generation and business development/start up. They provide shared office space, management support services and management advice. Science parks linked to a university provide a model for the incubator unit for science-based enterprise and technology transfer from the academic department. Examples are the Business and Science Park Enscede, The Netherlands which is adjacent to the University of Twente and St John's Innovation Centre, Cambridge, UK which is a short distance from the University.[12]

Spinning-off a business venture

'Spin-offs' are businesses which owe their existence to another organization.

KEY CONCEPT 3.6
Spin-offs

A spin-off is an independent company producing a product or service similar to that produced by the entrepreneur's former employer.

Some highly innovative companies purposively incubate and then spin-off companies. However, there are other cases where the impetus is the employee's frustration. The individual leaves and takes valuable expertise with them, setting up a rival concern which could have been part of the larger corporation! Given the highly competitive environment, it could be seen as a failure of management were this to occur.[13]

Setting up a global business

Many new firms start with the idea of going global immediately. There is considerable growth potential for businesses overseas, for example in Eastern Europe, the former Soviet Union, China and the Far Eastern 'Tiger' economies. New technology and changing market forces will lead to an increase in global start ups in the next decade. The risks associated with this kind of venture are high for the obvious reasons but the potential gains if the venture is successful are also high. Other current examples are internet companies. E-commerce enables firms to establish a global network very quickly.

Sources of help and advice

In the UK Business Link provides a 'one-stop-shop' of advice and support to help the new business founder. It also helps with the training and development of the founder (e.g. business planning and marketing – usually one day's duration). It provides grant aid (in 1998 this was £500 plus a loan option of £1000). It can provide useful contacts. It also has an arrangement with a major High Street bank which may offer the business founder free banking facilities in the first 12 months of operation. In some regions of the UK there is a plethora of advisory agencies to help people set up their own business. The North East of England, for example, is particularly well endowed. However, it has to be remembered that advice does not sell goods or services. The real problem in such regions is the size of the market, the paucity of well connected distribution channels and deeply embedded cultural attitudes.

The business founder, of course, can use and develop his or her own network of useful contacts and is encouraged to do so. Becoming a member of a formal business network may be one way of establishing such links.

The business plan

As was apparent from the case of The Body Shop (see Box 3.1), preparing a business plan can be very important if start up funds are being sought. However, the business plan is also important because it forces the business founder to think through the issues and problems associated with starting a business. The business plan may be thought of within the broader context of a longer term planning process which commences with the owner-manager addressing their personal objectives in setting up the business, proceeds through a SWOT analysis for setting business objectives, deciding on the strategies and tactics to be adopted, examining the operating needs of the business and developing budgets to meet these needs.[14] It is no longer unusual for a founder to decide at the outset on the size to which they are prepared to grow the business or at what stage or age they will disengage, sell the business on and possibly retire. Some venture capitalists will enable the founder to put a business plan together on this basis.

Business plans are not all the same but there are some key elements which generally are addressed (see Box 3.3).

Box 3.3: The business plan – fundamental questions

- What is the mission or purpose of the business venture?
- What do I need to know about the industry, including suppliers and market?
- Am I to work on my own or employ others – if so, how many personnel, with what skills, functioning in what capacity?
- What financial information do I need, where are the sources of finance to come from and how is the finance to be used?
- What are my plans for producing the good or service?
- What policies do I need to develop, for example for extending credit?
- Are there any legal matters I need to consider in order to protect my interests and those of the business?
- What are the critical risks I am going to have to face?
- What does the SWOT analysis tell me about the strengths, weaknesses, opportunities and threats facing the germinal business?

A comprehensive format for a business plan would look something like the following (see Table 3.1). Clearly, for an entirely new start up, self-employed person or microbusiness, the business plan is likely to be simpler and not include all the elements listed. As such a business plan can vary in length from 10 to 50 pages, but the norm would average around 15.

It is quite usual to preface documents such as the business plan with a concise executive summary. This is the part of the document which is likely to be read first and entice the prospective investor to read further or not. It must therefore include all the important elements, perhaps one of the more important being professionalism. However, for a new startup estimating the costs, size of potential market and likely revenue, is difficult. No one should be under any illusion that they will get it right! The likelihood is that the prospective owner-manager will underestimate costs and overestimate the market and likely revenues, though just occasionally the market can be underestimated and with it likely demand. Attempting to meet such a demand in the short term can be just as problematic.

Most new starts go into business areas which are familiar to them. This, however, presents a greater problem for women whose work experience is likely to be less than that of their male counterparts. Other difficulties which need to be addressed through the business plan are the need to be able to communicate clearly the technical aspects of product production. This becomes even more pertinent when dealing with science-based/new technology innovations. The market needs to be confident that the technical aspects of the product are sound, whereas what the investor also needs to be confident of is

Table **3.1** Outline of a business plan

1. **Overview/summary**
   Purpose of plan
   How much finance is required, and what it is for
   Brief description of business and its market
   Highlights of financial projections

2. **The company and its industry**
   Purpose of company
   History of company
   Past successes of company
   Discussion of industry

3. **The products/services**
   Description of products/services and applications
   Distinctive competences or uniqueness of product/service
   Technologies and skills required in the business
   Licence/patent rights
   Future potential

4. **Markets**
   Customers
   Competitors (strengths and weaknesses)
   Market segments
   Market size and growth
   Estimated market share
   Customer buying patterns
   Critical product/service characteristics or uniqueness
   Special market characteristics
   Competitor response

5. **Marketing**
   Market positioning – critical product/service characteristics or uniqueness in relation to competitors
   Pricing policy
   Selling/distribution policy
   Advertising and promotion
   Product/service support policy
   Interest shown by prospective customers

6. **Design and development (if appropriate)**
   Stage of development
   Difficulties and risks
   Product/service improvements
   Product/service developments in future

Table 3.1 continued

7. Manufacturing and operations
Premises location
Other facilities
Production/service capacity
Sources of supply of key materials or workforce
Use of subcontractors
Nature of productive process – machinery and critical points

8. Management
Owners/directors and other key management
Expertise and track record (detail CVs as an appendix)
Key management compensation
Summary of planned staff numbers and recruitment plans
Training policies
Consultants and advisors

9. Financing requirements
Funds required and timing
Deal on offer
Anticipated gearing
Exit routes for investors

10. Financial highlights, risks and assumptions
Highlights of financial plan (sales, profit, return on capital, net worth, etc)
Commentary on financial plan
Risks and how they will be tackled

11. Detailed financial plan (quarterly for three to five years)
Profit and loss
Contribution and break-even analysis
Cash-flow analysis (monthly in first year)
Sensitivity analysis
Balance-sheets (annual only)

12. Items frequently included in appendices
Technical data on products
Details on patents, etc
Consultants' reports on products or markets
Order and enquiry status
CVs of key managers
Organization charts
Audited accounts
Names of accountants, solicitors and bankers

Source: Dewhurst and Burns 1993 (see note 6): p.138–9

a market need, that the product has commercial potential. Technological developments can 'lie on the shelf' for years before the time is right for their commercial exploitation – the fax machine being a good example.

There is a great deal of library/desk work which can be done when preparing the business plan, particularly in respect of potential markets and likely competition. It can surprise one to find that there are owner-managers who do not know who their competitors are! For the new technology-based business however, there will be a need to develop business plans at each of the critical stages in product development.[15] The investment requirements of the potential business enterprise will change as development moves from working prototype through 'first saleable product' to 'establishing a product range'.[16] Being first in the field may mean little or no competition but this is unlikely to last especially where there are protracted periods needed in order to get the product to market. Patenting then becomes an issue, as does defending the patent. Hence in the design and development section of the business plan the potential investor needs sufficient detailed information to be convinced that the project is viable and that the risks involved can be assessed. A case will also need to be made for investment in modifications to existing products especially where the competition has become stronger both technically and strategically.

Shifting from an idea to actual production is a major step and the investor will also need to be assured about the new production facilities, control over management processes and achieving quality standards. This also includes the need to identify any subcontracting of work and how it would be handled, where the premises are likely to be located, their potential (for example a prime site) or problems which are foreseeable. There clearly is a temptation not to remark on such problems, to gloss over difficulties in order to present a convincing watertight case to the potential investor. Whether that would fool anyone in the short term is debatable and even if it did, whether it would prove to have been wise in the longer term is equally doubtful. Besides, an unwillingness to discuss the pros and cons of one's venture may only demonstrate an inability to think a project through and convince the investor that the proposer lacks management capability or nouse.

Once the investor is convinced that the *idea* is of interest they need to be equally sure that the management of the venture will be carried out competently. Some may go as far as the belief of separating the idea from its implementation; that is, that the inventor is unlikely to be the best person to take the idea forward to the production stage.[17] But where the business plan is addressing the production plan, how production is to be carried through and by whom is an important area for detailed description. The proposer may already have identified key personnel – they may be people with whom they have worked before – their capabilities, backed up by an appended *curriculum vitae*, should be included.

Finally, the budgets and financial requirements of the prospective business should be presented. Such arrangements are various; use of one's own funds plus a bank loan is the most common arrangement, but where bank loans are not forthcoming many small or micro-business owners seek loans from family and close friends. Where a project requires large amounts of initial investment capital the issue of share ownership becomes important. How much of the business is the founder willing to 'give away'? The case of The Body Shop shows how easily this can be done. At the commencement of a venture no one really knows its growth potential: Anita Roddick for the need of £4000 'gave away' 50 per cent of what has become a multi-million pound business. New businesses in e-commerce appear to demonstrate that kind of potential as the following anecdote demonstrates.

> Sir Michael Bett ... stood to make £1.5 million this week from his shares in an internet company.
>
> This was the value of Sir Michael's 1.15 per cent share in Just2clicks.com, which this week floated on the London Stock Exchange's Alternative Investment Market.
>
> Just2clicks.com operates business to business websites in electrical power, air freight, pulp and paper and road transport industries.
>
> The company's chief executive is Karl Watkins, a prominent businessman, who has an 11.6 per cent stake worth more than £15 million. Sir Michael is chairman. Entrepreneur Luke Johnson's stake was valued at £13 million and Labour politician Alan Donnelly's at £1.8 million. Mr Donnelly invested £1250 on December 20 1999, shortly after standing down as party leader in the European Parliament.
>
> According to *The Times,* there are no companies comparable to Just2clicks.com in the UK. A similar company, Vertical.Net, exists in the US, valued at $7.7 billion (£4.4 billion). It operates 56 industry websites and has a joint venture with British Telecom.[18]

Clearly any financial plan for a new business must include detail about the risks involved and the assumptions being made. There may – as in the case of Just2clicks.com – be a consortium of investors. This reduces the risks that a single individual would face and is not unusual where a company is preparing for the next stage of its development – flotation. But whatever the stage there are still risks to be borne. Investors are particularly interested in estimates of cash-flow, sales forecasts, projected profit and loss and break even analysis. Such information enables the nature of the risk to be assessed. Beyond this the potential investor needs to be confident that the owner-manager can deliver a thriving business and motivate staff to perform well. Beyond systematic analysis and assessment many investors rely on 'gut-feel' and are backing their own judgement that the venture will yield at least the expected return.

The founding of a business is a process not an event. At some point the resources are gathered, a site has been found and the business commences; the first customer is identified, the first product sold. However, the business plan is only the beginning of a need to think through and plan strategy, operations, procurement, sales etc, at the venture creation stage many owner-managers may shun a formal planning process. 'Back of an envelope' calculations are not unknown. Formal meetings may seem irrelevant as everyone knows everyone else. However, meeting customers' orders and needs to a standard requires the development of appropriate systems and so an awareness of planning is inevitable.

Business planning

At each stage of the business' development, the owner-manager may ask him or herself 'where is the business at?' Such questioning signals the need to take stock and consider what choices are open to them and what actions to authorize next. However, few people make decisions entirely on the basis of gut feeling and intuition, some degree of planning appears to be necessary for business management and development to take place efficiently and effectively. Does planning and the formality of the planning process exist principally in the large firm environment? To what extent and how, might the owner-manager of the small firm plan?

Planning is a fundamental **management** process. Planning is necessary whether a person is managing their own (small) business or whether they are employed to manage a wholly owned concern or new venture spin-off. So what is planning?

Planning may be thought of not merely in terms of maintaining stability over

---

KEY CONCEPT 3.7
Planning

Planning is the process of setting objectives and determining what should be done to accomplish them.

---

operations, but as a measure for staying ahead of the competition. The arguments for planning are reasonably compelling even in the small business. There it is important for the owner-manager to make their strategic plans (their vision) explicit and to carry employees along with them. The vision or strategy needs to be operationalized so that employees can work towards achieving the owner-manager's objectives.

As outlined in chapter 2, all organizations – large or small – face competitive pressures on all fronts from both the external and the internal environments. Planning offers advantages which enable managements to deal with such challenges (see Box 3.4).

The language of planning

The idea of a vision and the time scale over which a plan is being conceived are fundamental. However, once the business ceases to be very small planning

Box 3.4: The advantages of planning

Focus and flexibility
Focus is about knowing what business you are in and what as a business you do best. This includes knowing your customers and how to serve them well.

Improves performance
Planning helps improve a business' performance because: it is results oriented, it focuses on priorities, it concerns the best use of resources and it is about problem solving – in relation to threats and opportunities.

Improved coordination
Theoretically objectives can be considered to be hierarchically organized in a means-end chain – what is a strategic objective at one level may be translated into a set of tactics at another level for its eventual achievement. The better coordinated the objectives both vertically and horizontally, the more efficiently and effectively will the organization run.

Improved control
If objectives are clearly defined then it becomes clear what needs to be done to achieve those objectives. This makes the evaluation of performance more effective as it becomes clear when things miss the target what corrective measures need to be taken.

Time management
The job of management is largely unstructured and there are pressures to deal with the immediate rather than the important. Planning helps the owner-manager decide what is important and how to allocate time to their many commitments so that the strategically important, longer term issues do not get overlooked.

will occur at different levels and to different time scales. All such plans need some sense of overall direction which is generally communicated from senior levels (the owner-manager who may now have the title of 'managing director') and creates the structure within which other plans are conceived and operationalized. Thus a **strategic plan** is a comprehensive plan that reflects the longer term needs and direction of the organization, whilst **operational plans** are plans of limited scope that address those activities and resources required to implement strategic plans, for example production, financial, marketing and human resource management plans.

Such plans are not the same as **policies**. Policies communicate broad guidelines for making decisions and taking action, for example recruitment, smoking and disciplinary policies. Policies identify issues of importance and inform employees how they are expected to behave in respect of that issue. Good policies are communicated to all and are readily understandable.

Procedures describe what actions are to be taken in specific situations. Procedures are precise guidelines which do not permit discretion on the part of the employee. Commonplace examples are the fire drill and other health and safety measures to deal with noxious substances, hazardous waste and physically dangerous environments.

Single-use plans are used only once to meet the exigencies of a unique situation, for example budgets. **Projects** are also single-use plans in that they are plans to accomplish a specific task. Team management to execute projects is an important aspect of the human resource planning associated with this type of plan.

Plans may focus on internal matters and examine ways in which they can be better achieved. Plans may also have an external focus, scanning for opportunities to be exploited and threats to be avoided. Contingency planning is a way of dealing with uncertainty. It concerns anticipating future possibilities through scenario planning. Crucially it concerns the posing of 'what if ... ?' questions.

It is said that entrepreneurs plan insufficiently and this may be a contributory factor in the failure of the business venture. It is argued therefore that all potential and actual owners of a business enterprise need to understand the planning process and to be sufficiently well informed to plan ahead. Historically the typical owner-manager has tended not to have pursued higher levels of education or to take formal business training. Hence there are two possible reasons why owner-managers tend not to plan: they are emotionally unsuited to it – they think and act intuitively and they are simply unaware of the various tools which would enable them to plan systematically. Such tools include forecasting, scenario planning, benchmarking, participation and the use of staff planners (see Box 3.5).

Box 3.5: Planning tools

- A **forecast** is the process of making assumptions about the future. There are economic, qualitative, quantitative forecasts. The degree of sophistication varies.
- **Scenario planning** involves identifying possible futures and developing plans for dealing with them.
- **Benchmarking** uses external comparisons to evaluate business performance better and identify possible actions for the future.
- **Participative planning** is a process for involving as many people as possible in the planning process. This achieves understanding, acceptance and commitment (usually).
- **Staff planners** are employed to take responsibility for leading and coordinating the planning system. Their role is advisory. But they may help line managers in preparing plans, developing special plans, gathering important information needed to develop a plan, assisting in communicating the plan to others and monitoring an extant plan and suggesting specific changes.

Corporate venturing

Corporate venturing (sometimes referred to an **intrapreneuring**) involves an activity which is entirely new to an existing organization and which is initiated and developed internally. Usually it involves a higher risk of failure and greater uncertainty than the company's core business. It will be managed separately and is undertaken as part of the company's innovativeness and competitiveness strategy with a view to developing new products and capturing new markets. It is fundamentally different from the extension of existing product lines; it requires new management thinking and style, a change in corporate culture with, in particular, high demonstrated commitment to the new venture and a willingness to learn fast. The new management style needs to be entrepreneurial rather than traditional otherwise there is a risk that the venture will fail.[19]

Kanter[20] has famously addressed the need for American corporations to innovate, to transform themselves into globally competitive entrepreneurial organizations. The need to do so occurs when the corporation begins to stagnate at what is known as the 'maturity stage'. Recognizing this and the dangers it entails means the need by senior management to revise the corporate strategic plan, developing new goals which only a new venture can deliver. But there are other important reasons. Existing managers need new challenges and there is also a need to develop the future management. Other reasons such as the need to survive and to provide employment may be apparent, the latter perhaps more so for UK and Japanese corporations than American.[21]

Occasionally a company develops new technology that suggests a new business opportunity, but the development would take the company into new unexplored markets. This is high risk and the company may not be ready to pursue such a strategy. Rather than pursue an *internal* business development an alternative strategy is to spin the business off, taking an equity (but not necessarily a controlling share) in the new technology business. Such an option is best pursued when it would not make corporate sense to make the internal changes necessary to house the new technology based enterprise.

The importance of senior management's attitude and approach to new venture creation cannot be overemphasized. It requires a change in corporate culture engendering a supportive climate which is not controlling. This in itself provides a considerable challenge to traditional management. In sum the challenges are:

- Creating a venturesome climate and a pervasive commitment to venturing
- Selecting the business development strategy, i.e. the strategy that drives the venturing effort
- Defining and using venture selection methods
- Managing disappointment.[22]

The objective to be borne in mind by all management is how to create a profitable new business within the existing corporation.

Creating a venturesome climate involves nurturing enthusiasm and demonstrated commitment. Such commitment needs to be sustained over time and it must be clear that senior management's attention lies with the new development. Table 3.2 identifies ten tactics to be deployed by senior management in order to steer a successful course for the creation of the new venture.

Selecting the appropriate business development strategy is clearly important. It may be **revolutionary** (radical) or **evolutionary** (incremental). Revolutionary strategies are of the Schumpeterian type, which build on new transformational innovations and are high risk. Guidelines in this situation include the following.

Table **3.2** Strategies to facilitate corporate venturing

1.	Insist that the entire division pursues new-business development.
2.	Don't assume the firm must offer specific, extrinsic rewards for new-business activities
3.	Demonstrate significant and visible personal commitment.
4.	Sustain the commitment over a long period.
5.	Assign very good people to the new business.
6.	Assign the necessary resources to the new business.
7.	Develop an in-depth knowledge of customers and markets.
8.	Build organizational confidence.
9.	Empower the creators of the new business.
10.	Build momentum.

Source: Block and MacMillan 1993 (see note 19): p37

- The need to focus on carefully chosen key technologies in which the company can achieve and retain leadership.
- The need to commercialize evolving technology early and aggressively. This enables the company to test the new product and learn by mistakes before those mistakes develop into possibly expensive failures. It also needs to reduce market uncertainty, develop its own know-how with respect to the product, identify and learn about the distribution network for the product and ensure customer know-how. Early training obviates the need to spend huge amounts of cash years in advance of a revenue stream, in other words the problem often referred to as **cash burn** is avoided.
- The need to get a working prototype out quickly which a multifunctional back up team can then use to 'reconfigure' the industry.
- The need to develop new technologies in support of new product development. It is critically important, to identify the pace-forcing technology in order to gain a commanding lead. Once selected, the core technology will force related technologies to keep up whilst giving the venture the lead it needs to establish itself as the dominant technology.

Evolutionary new business development strategies are less risky, involving extending existing know-how into new products or services and/or new markets. Over time the company can become highly diversified, developing its knowledge of new markets. Clearly a major advantage of this strategy is being able to use and apply existing know-how. As the technology is already familiar there is less resistance by distributors and customers, thus increasing the probability of success. However, the huge returns which can come from a radical, industry transforming venture are unlikely to materialize. Moreover, existing competitors will be able to counter the advances of the new evolutionary venture and as such the enterprise is unlikely to gain a strong proprietary position. The advantages to the radical innovator tend to be the converse of those for the evolutionary venture. In particular existing competitors tend to be left behind as their existing know-how ceases be of any use, enabling the new venture to steal a march on them.

Defining and using venture selection criteria is the means by which senior management judges whether new venture ideas are worthy of further support. They include

- whether the proposed new venture fits strategically into the types of markets, technology and products it wishes to focus on
- the size limit that may be placed on the ventures that may be supported
- the market position to be achieved
- the amount of investment the company is willing to make in the new enterprise
- its financial performance
- the time horizon within which the new company will become a profitable concern
- the degree of risk the parent company is willing to take
- the degree of consistency with the parent company's corporate values
- the feasibility of the new venture achieving a strong proprietary position etc and
- the potential impact the new venture may have on the parent's reputation.

Whilst not all criteria may be selected some are clearly critically important, such as strategic fit, ability to confer a competitive advantage and to achieve a high rate of return on capital invested. There do appear to be differences in the criteria used in this screening process between those companies which back successful and unsuccessful new venture developments. For example the existence of a 'product champion' is not a sufficient reason for going ahead with a new venture. A study by MacMillan found that:

> The companies with unsuccessful venturing programs generally required that fully developed business plans be submitted to management committees, which, after much deliberation, handed down a decision, generally negative, with little explanation. To a venture's proponents, the process was akin to dealing with the Delphic oracle: the basic selection criteria emerged only over time and after the rejection of many seemingly viable ideas.[23]

Given the amount of time, excitement and energy which goes into such processes it seems only reasonable to give proper feedback and if the answer is 'no', not to hide behind a committee in order to give it.

Managing disappointment is clearly difficult and needs to be handled sensitively. For example if a venture fails and company support is withdrawn, senior management needs to be clear whether the failure was due to bad management or bad luck. A feature of entrepreneurialism is the ability to turn failure into success. A major setback with a new venture on this basis should be examined carefully to see what, if anything, can be learnt. Sometimes in that process a new opportunity emerges which enables the situation to be salvaged. Managing the process of new venture creation can also be done best by setting milestones or targets to be achieved. If the team fails to hit one of the targets a review might examine how the new venture may be redirected in order to get back on track. This is much more encouraging than a stop/go mentality would engender. Sometimes it is inevitable that a failing venture must be terminated. The quick 'removal of the sticking plaster' approach is important. This prevents floundering around. It also encourages personal engagement by senior management to give the reasons why the venture is to be shut down and to emphasize that it is the business, not the personnel, that has failed.

Senior management clearly has a number of responsibilities in managing the process of birth of a new venture. These include deciding what strategic goals will drive the engine of that venture, developing a climate for generation and evaluation of business ideas and designing and launching the venture. Guidelines are helpful for evaluating the venture opportunity's economic potential. Such guidelines need to take account of the nature of the technology, the level of investment needed in new technology, the nature of the innovation – radical or evolutionary – asset intensity and the known entry barriers to the industry in question. On this basis a realistic estimate can be made of:

- breakeven period
- gross margins
- after-tax profit potential
- nature and number of required investments
- asset intensity
- product differentiation
- impact on overall corporate performance
- impact on the corporation's existing customers and business
- impact on the firm's competitive advantage.

Having established whether the new venture is feasible and will yield a return further issues include the need to put together a venture management team. Critical roles are:

- **technical innovator** (the individual who generated and developed the innovative idea)
- **venture manager** (the intrapreneur responsible for progressing the new venture project)
- **product champion** (the promoter of the new venture idea within the corporation)
- **chief executive or division manager** (the person with executive authority and control over allocation of resources to the fledgling/proposed new venture)
- **executive champion** (the incumbent of a senior position within the parent company who facilitates the process of venture development by

removing obstacles and developing policies to enable the venture to capture much needed resources).

The team will need to perform effectively and be evaluated on the basis of results, commitments, early successes and team spirit. Whilst there appears to be no correlation between venture performance and compensation of the venture management team, incentives to attract and retain the right calibre of person is important. It is not unusual therefore for senior management to devise incentive schemes, which may include generous bonuses. Arrangements however can vary enormously and are likely to be tailored to the particular case.

Other important considerations for the corporate management are where the venture may be suitably located within the corporation. Block and MacMillan suggest six possibilities.

- **Assigning the project to a line manager.** This places the new venture within a corporate division and exposes it to operations expertise but the new venture may disrupt present business activity and as such can generate conflict.
- **Creating a separate section in an operating division.** The line manager responsible for the venture will be able to gather a team around them, whilst being able to draw on the organization's considerable expertise. Initially however the venture may detract from the division's overall performance and be subject to internal politics and bureaucracy.
- **Assign the venture to the R&D department.** The venture manager can assemble a team to help launch the venture. Situated as it is it will be able to draw on technological expertise, however it will lack access to marketing and business expertise.
- **The venture manager reports to a senior staff position.** This reduces the intrusion into existing operations but by the same token there is little exposure to operations expertise.
- **The venture manager reports to a new venture division.** This enables the venture manager to have direct access to senior corporate management. It enables a focus on the venture's development to be maintained with intrusions from other corporate operations minimized. However the converse of this strategy is that the venture is removed from the corporation's mainstream, as such it has to compete for resources and it becomes a highly visible target for removal.
- **The venture manager reports directly to the CEO.** The venture is assured maximum political protection, with the cooperation and resourcing that goes with a privileged position. Ironically this may make the venture more difficult to evaluate and development may proceed to a point where failure has become costly. With privilege comes jealousy and this may be difficult to manage, particularly if the venture is less successful than had been hoped or expected.

The factors governing the decision regarding location will depend on a number of factors, including the political one of the extent to which there is general acceptance of the venture, the corporate experience of venturing, the need for the venture to succeed, overall corporate performance, corporate structure, size of the venture, stage of the venture's development and its anticipated future location. Certainly there are ways in which the venture can be protected from organizational antagonism. All such factors will need to be carefully weighed before a decision on venture location is made.

Conclusions

Business start up and new venture creation are exciting activities which need to be carefully understood and managed. Indeed, as this chapter has shown, there is no one legal form, no single strategy to be pursued nor is there one type of business venture that may be adopted. Furthermore, founding one's own business appears to be fundamentally different from intrapreneuring or internal new venture creation. There are, however, for both processes support structures, different strategic options and management tools and techniques for guiding and directing the process towards a successful outcome. Just some of these tools are outlined in this chapter, however fundamental to and perhaps the key to both is business planning.

Exercise
Compare and contrast business founding and corporate venturing. Faced with the personal decision of which course to pursue, what would be your choice?

Part 2
Entrepreneurial Behaviour

CHAPTER 4

Personality: type of company, type of person

People often ask me to explain Microsoft's success. They want to know the secret of getting from a two-man, shoestring operation to a company with more than 21 000 employees and more than $8 billion a year in sales. Of course, there's no simple answer and luck has played a role, but I think the most important element was our original vision.

We thought we saw beyond that Intel 8080 chip and then acted on it. We believed that there would be computers every-where because computing power would be cheap and great new software would take advantage of it. We set up shop betting on cheap computer power and producing software when nobody else was … . We got there first and our early success gave us the chance to hire more and more smart people. We built up a world-wide sales force and used the revenue it generated to fund new products. But from the beginning, we set off down a road that was headed in the right direction.[1]

Introduction

The idea of an entrepreneurial personality has enjoyed a chequered history rather like that of leadership.[2] Perhaps this is not surprising for the owner-manager, the entrepreneur, the chief executive officer are indeed leaders. However, in this chapter it is assumed that the owner-manager/entrepreneur is a leader but is not discussed in terms of leadership qualities. Instead past and current approaches to understanding the entrepreneurial personality are reviewed and illustrated with small vignettes and stories. Importantly how-ever, the chapter commences with some considerations in respect of the type of company founded and/or managed. This raises issues for the type of person who might carry out such activities.

The next section of the chapter examines various 'typologies' of entrepre-neurs. It raises two important scientific questions: 'what exactly is a typol-ogy?' and 'is it possible to classify people rigorously into "types"?' Traits and types often go together so the chapter explores what single traits and what profile might be associated with the 'entrepreneur'. As the chapter develops further by discussing definitions and process issues it is intended that the complexity of the investigation of an entrepreneurial personality becomes evident. Hence the chapter concludes with a discussion of current influences and future developments on research which seeks to deepen the understanding of the nature of this particular socio-economic being.

Type of company

The owner-managed and directed business is a different proposition to that of the limited company where shareholder interests and public image are major influencing factors in boardroom decisions and debate. Indeed, the owner-managed business has been said to reflect the personality of its owner, that individual who conceived the business idea, gathered together the resources and founded the business according to their vision and predilections.[3] The extent to which such an individual impresses their particular stamp on the company has engaged the minds of academics and to some extent the business community. There are certainly heads of owner-managed businesses who are high profile – locally, regionally, nationally and internationally.

Exercise
As an exercise, try composing your own list of 'household names' – how many are locally, nationally or internationally known people?

But is it *really* down to a single individual? Even in the smallest of businesses, does the owner-manager not rely on others? Is it fair that one person may get all the credit for what was after all a team effort?

These questions are the imponderables. There is no single answer that fits all businesses; it certainly would appear that it does depend on any number of factors which configure the particular business. However, the smaller the size, the more likely that the business will reflect the aspirations and vision of the owner-manager.[4]

So how does one become an owner-manager?

There are three obvious routes to becoming an owner-manager: inheritance, buying or founding. Inheritance of a business is often associated with the family business. The owner-manager of such a business has decided that it is time to disengage, retire or set up another business. The immediate issue is thus one of succession. In the well planned business the likely successor will have been identified and groomed for the managing director's role, though in many small businesses there is not an obvious successor. There may be no family member who wishes to take over. The retiring head must then consider other options, for example a strategic alliance which gives the retiree a stake in the new business, outright sale of the business, or bringing someone in as managing director with the option of them having a shareholding stake in it. In these circumstances it is clear that planning for succession is a sensible strategic move on the part of the owner-manager.

Buying a business is also an option for the would-be owner-manager. It may

Box 4.1: Michael's Cookie Business

Michael, like so many entrepreneurs, started his entrepreneurial career at school and had seriously wanted to set up his own business since the age of 18. He didn't settle down easily at college. After six months of a three year degree programme he jacked it in and went overseas. This was an unsuccessful move; he broke his arm, returned and did a one year business studies course. He got a short term job in Tourism which took him to the USA where he promoted a sport and leisure activity of his country. He went back home with $10,000 in the bank. These were the funds he needed to get started in business on his own.

Michael tried a couple of ideas which didn't work before embarking on a successful business venture. He took his inspiration from Mrs Field's Cookies. His problem was that he didn't have the money to set up a hot cookie shop. So he had to 'think of a creative way of doing it'. He made the cookies himself, very large, put them in jars and distributed them to existing retail outlets. Now after 11 years and overcoming not a few difficulties on the way, he (and his brother, whom he brought into the business after an early crisis) has built up the business to that of a successful small business. He employs 45 staff and uses 28 self-employed distributors. He exports the product and has two companies overseas. He aims at a young market and has developed the profile and image of the company to reflect this. This includes factory tours which are fun and educational, allowing the kids to eat 'as much as they can'. His aspirations are to produce the world's biggest cookie and to franchise his concept worldwide, but in particular 'to break back into the American market'. But more than this Michael 'wants to be a global person; that's what appeals about the global market, I want to be in it, not just stuck down here ... aware only of what's going on in this country'.

also be, of course, that they are adding to their portfolio of owned businesses by this route. Another possibility is that of buying into an existing franchise. Buying a business is clearly a different proposition to that of inheriting or founding. There are a number of considerations, not least of which is *what business?* Usually a would-be business owner will identify a business in a sector with which they have prior experience and a degree of technical knowledge which gives them a tacit understanding of how doing business in that particular sector works. It has been suggested that one of the reasons why women owner-managers appear to perform less well than their male counterparts on measures of business growth is that they have less experience and knowledge of their chosen sector. However, there is a range of arguments in respect of this complex issue. This is explained more fully in chapter 8 but a briefing position is outlined in Box 4.2.

Lack of business experience and technical knowledge would appear to be sufficient reason for a person to decide not to go into business for themselves. However, there is another route which can be taken, that of franchising. The franchised business has become a popular option, it reduces the risk to the owner-manager of a start up situation and means they are relieved of weighty decisions in respect of profiling the business and its products, advertising, pricing, management style and many other dimensions of business practice. All these are taken care of by the franchiser. What the franchisee loses in this deal is independence and this may be too high a price to pay for many business owners.

Box 4.2: Gender and business performance

There is equivocal evidence as to whether gender impacts on business performance at all. Those people who believe they have evidence that gender does affect business performance may take different positions. On the one hand, it has been argued that women are different from men. They are less competitive and they lay less store by conventional performance criteria. Success for them is more likely to be viewed in terms of the achievement of their own intrinsic goals – job satisfaction, a cooperative, harmonious working culture, ability to please others by producing quality products, etc. Others argue that women and men are not and never have competed on a level playing field. Most women carry a dual burden which includes primary responsibility for domestic and child caring in the home to be set against the demands of paid employment or running one's own business. Under such circumstances it is unlikely that women can put in the same amount of time and quality of time into their business.[5]

Box 4.3: How many franchised businesses do you know?

Here are a few well known names: what are the main features of the franchised business?

Characteristics? See end of book for answers.[6]

McDonalds's

Prontaprint

Mrs Field's Cookies

DynoRod

The Body Shop

Yo Sushi!

Your suggestions:

The downsizing of companies has left many executives with golden hand-shakes, redundancy payments and the freedom to think through their future. Buying a business is certainly one option, so too is founding. But should the would-be entrepreneur really stick with the same industry sector? This may be a finely balanced decision despite the rhetoric about the need for tacit knowledge. Knowledge is the inalienable resource that is brought to the business and which the owner-manager draws on at all stages of its establishment and further development. In business knowledge comprises technical skill, social and interpersonal skills and encompasses specific domains of business and commercial knowledge, including traditional functional areas. Boyatzis[7] defines specialized knowledge as facts, principles, theories, frameworks or models. However, the world of the entrepreneur is replete with ambiguity which they need to make sense of. In order to make progress they place an interpretation on what may be impressions and treat them as if they are facts. Thus there tends to be a blurring between what is known and interpretations, which are treated as if they are known facts. However, knowing *what* (facts and the relationship between them) and knowing *how* are crucially different. The latter is *capability* and fundamental to competent performance. It assumes the ability to draw upon specialized knowledge in the execution of tasks (such as developing a business plan or producing product to a standard). Such specialized knowledge may include that of the traditional functional disciplines such as marketing, production, finance and human resource management and which enable the entrepreneur to develop the business more effectively.[8]

Box 4.4: Joe's Bakehouse

Joe was a manager who had been employed by large bakery concerns for some 20 years – in fact all his adult working life. He wanted a change; he no longer wanted to work for someone else but to work for himself. He got a job as production manager in a bakery employing 100 people which produced a wide range of low margin, low quality breads and cakes. After six months he did a deal with the owner; he bought a controlling share in the business, negotiated sole control (that is, he did not want any interference in his decisions) and declared his intention to turn the business round. Within the year he had reduced the range of products from x to y, improved the quality of the new product range and invested in new production equipment. He went from strength to strength, innovating by bringing on a new product range, exploring new overseas markets, empowering the workforce and getting them behind him. In this situation Joe drew on all those years of accumulated wisdom and now he channelled it into the business from which he and his employees could profit.

Box 4.5: Richard's 'Healthwise':
From property to hot bread to chilled food!

Richard, at a similar time in life to Joe, had worked for several multinational companies (MNCs) in property development and had found himself temporarily between jobs. He sailed around the world. He did not want to go back to working for another MNC and so decided that he would buy a business. His wife found a small advertisement for a microbusiness producing bread. Richard had no experience in this industry. What Richard did have were entrepreneurial skills which enabled him to take this tiny business and grow it quickly into a 'healthy-eating', chilled-food business producing a range of dishes marketed through supermarket chains. Richard took on a partner who helped finance the business but otherwise left Richard to manage and direct its operations. The business has gone from strength to strength and has achieved a firm foothold in a major supermarket chain across New Zealand.

Type of person

Who is the owner-manager? Does the owner-manager have a particular set of personality characteristics which would increase the likelihood of them setting up in business? Is there a type of person who is more likely to be a business owner? Questions such as these have teased so many minds and inevitably there is no one simple straightforward answer. The quest for finding an answer however is fascinating.

Box 4.6: The Body Shop

Anita Roddick's vision revolutionized the sale of cosmetics on the High Street, by producing products in small sizes and cheaply packaged. With the high profile modern image of the shop, she appealed to the average shopper with perhaps a limited budget to spend on themselves. This change was widesweeping, changing the industry in the Schumperterian sense of innovation. The major High Street stores could not ignore it, they imitated and competed on that basis.[9]

Entrepreneur versus craftsperson

Psychological theory has long distinguished between 'types' and 'traits' as approaches to discussing the nature of personality. 'Types' are very broad categories of the person which often form an initial description but are criticized for their susceptibility to stereotyping. Typologies can be useful for exploratory purposes but do need to be based on true populations and a rigorously valid sampling frame if they are to be of lasting value. Sociologists have combined constellations of characteristics including, for example, demographic and behavioural, from which they have derived a typology. Typical of this approach is the work of Smith (1967), Curran and Stanworth (1973) and Tuck and Hamilton (1993).[10] The fundamental distinction being made is between an 'opportunist' and a 'craftsperson' (or 'artisan').

The **craftsperson** is described as a 'loner' whose social and commercial links are limited, whose trust in external agencies is low, who cherishes their independence and who originates from a modest working class background. In contrast the **opportunist** often has a professional or middle class background, is concerned with market rather than production issues, possesses considerable self-confidence and has outgoing cosmopolitan attitudes. Whilst there is considerable agreement that these two types are distinctly different, the original descriptors are thought to reinforce a stereotype which is not necessarily typical of owner-managers.

A rather different approach is the psychological, for example Chell has suggested adopting the idea of a classification system of business owners. This is based on the principles of hierarchical ordering from the specific to the more general and uses the criterion of 'family resemblance' for categorization purposes.[11] Such a classification system is the first step towards description of a population, by enabling the process of categorization into types. By analogy this system may be compared with biological classification systems, an example of which is given below (see Figure 4.1). An objection which may be raised towards such an approach is that human beings are unique, with unique histories, experiences and personal make-up. Whilst this is undoubtedly true, labelling is a very basic human behaviour which enables people to develop their understanding and make sense of their world.[12]

Figure **4.1** An example of a biological classification system of the order of perching birds, showing a selection of species of the finch family

Order:	**Perching birds (passeriformes)**			
Family:	Finch			
	(Fringillidae)			
Species:	**Chaffinch**	**Green Finch**	**Bull Finch**	**Gold Finch**
	Fringilla coelebs	Chloris chloris	Pyrrhula pyrrhula	Carduelis carduelis

The ideas behind this approach are: (a) to capture the variety within the population of owner-managers, (b) systematically to distinguish different types (and in particular, the entrepreneur) and (c) to be able to develop detailed profiles of the 'species'. The research suggested a superordinate category of business owner (the Order) and four basic level categories (the **genus** or family): the **entrepreneur, quasi-entrepreneur, administrator** and **caretaker**.[13]

Figure **4.2** A typology of business owners analogous to a biological classification system

Order:	**Business owner**			
Family:	Entrepreneur	Quasi-Entrepreneur	Administrator	Caretaker

This typology can be taken a stage further to the subordinate level (or **species**), that is, types of entrepreneur, caretaker and so on. Subsequent research lends some support to this idea. For example, several studies have distinguished between **portfolio, serial** and **single-business** entrepreneurs;[14] the caretakers include the craftsperson, but also other 'lifestyle' businesses, the 'mom and pop' store, the inventor-boffin and the '*petite bourgeoisie*'.[15] However, the typology 'novice' versus 'habitual' entrepreneur[16] cuts across this typology, suggesting (to continue the analogy) a distinction between the fledgling and the mature exemplar of the species.

The 'trait' of entrepreneurship?

The idea that there might exist a single trait which distinguishes the 'entrepreneur' from managers and other populations has been roundly criticized.[17] There have been studies which have suggested that the entrepreneur is a risktaker, a deviant, has a high need for achievement, a strong internal locus of control and a tolerance for ambiguity.[18] Thus there was no agreement as to which characteristic might typify the 'entrepreneur' and there was no conclusive evidence to support any one of this list as being the more likely characteristic.[19]

It seems obvious that if the population of business owners being studied varies from the hairdresser to the owner of a fast growth, new technology business there may not be one trait in common. For example, levels of risk are likely to vary. Given that the future is inherently uncertain, most decisions taken will involve an element of risk. The key question therefore is not whether a person founding a new business, developing a new product or attempting to open a new market is taking a risk, but rather how they handle the risk element.

Box 4.7: Michael and his experience of risk

Then at Christmas sales started to go down ... I suddenly started thinking 'God, sales are going down'. Michael's brother came home from university. He got involved in the business and between them they kept it going over Christmas by going out and selling to new customers.

This crisis led to the realization that the business was vulnerable and to remain viable it needed sound financial management – a skill which Michael did not have but his brother did. This realization was the start of a productive business partnership: 'I found having him was such a bonus because suddenly I had someone who knew the business that I could talk to and we talk about problems and opportunities and so on.' But this was not the only crisis the business faced. Five years later they purchased another business only to discover that the technology did not work and the confectionery product started to go off. One upshot was that they lost their supermarket customer. Michael was not one to be down on his luck for very long. He had the knack of turning a crisis into an opportunity. He changed the marketing strategy overnight and commenced selling this particular confectionery product through schools. It worked. In fact it became a major plank of the company's sales strategy as the brothers vastly increased their product range of confectionery and added factory tours directed at this young market segment.

Entrepreneurial profile

More recent research has suggested that there might be a **profile** of entrepreneurial characteristics. David McClelland[20] attempted to identify the key competencies which are needed for **entrepreneurial success**. The research team identified 12 'successful' and 12 'average' entrepreneurs in each of three types of business (manufacturing, service and marketing or trading), in each of three developing countries (India, Malawi and Ecuador). It should be noted, however, that the term 'entrepreneur' included the 'small business owner-manager'. McClelland and his team devised a method they called the **Behavioral Event Interview**, which requires the respondent to give an account of critical incidents in the life of the business. The resultant tape-recorded interviews were transcribed and coded. A group of 'judges' were then asked to identify the kinds of competencies revealed.

Using this method the research team was able to identify nine competencies which were significantly more characteristic of successful rather than of average owner-managers. They grouped these nine competencies into three categories – **proactivity, achievement orientation** and **commitment to others** (see Table 4.1).

Table **4.1** The nine competencies of successful entrepreneurs

Proactivity	Achievement orientation	Commitment to others
Initiative assertiveness	Ability to see and act on opportunities Efficiency orientation High quality work Systematic planning Monitoring	Commitment to the work contract Importance of business relationships
		Source: McClelland 1987 (see note 20)

This competency based profile is clearly of considerable interest, particularly to trainers and others whose objective is to develop entrepreneurial potential, with enhanced business growth.

An alternative approach is to develop the profile irrespective of the success of the business. Such a model assumes that entrepreneurs do not always succeed and enables the context and outcomes to be distinguished from the entrepreneurial behaviour. In this study, the owner-managers were interviewed about any critical incidents which affected the development of the business. Their strategies and tactics for dealing with them were also noted, as were the consequences of their actions. This analysis enabled natural categories of person characteristics to be identified and attributed to the 'entrepreneurial type'. The resultant profile[21] is given below (see Table 4.2).

The problem of definition

If not all business owners are 'entrepreneurs' then who is an entrepreneur? The difficulties that had been encountered with attempts to identify a single trait using psychometric methods left the question wide open. Some suggested that it was the *wrong* question to ask (e.g. see note 22) and that it would be more fruitful to focus upon what entrepreneurs *do*. For example, they found businesses, don't they? This raised a number of thorny questions, for example is founding a business a necessary prerequisite of being an entrepre-

Table **4.2** The characteristics of a 'prototypical' entrepreneur

Alert to business opportunities
Pursues opportunities regardless of resources currently controlled
Adventurous
An 'ideas person'
Restless/easily bored
High profile image maker
Proactive
Innovative
Thrives on change
Adopts a broad financial strategy

Source: Chell *et al.* 1991 (see note 11): p.76

neur? Further, is not there a relationship between what people do and who they are? Questions such as these helped fuel the debate.

The fundamental problem appeared to be that there were as many definitions of what an entrepreneur is as there were academics researching the problem! This of course took no account of the fact that the lay person also has a view about the nature of entrepreneurs. Whatever definition is taken, certain assumptions are made and the words of a particular language are used to describe and define. Some languages, such as Finnish, only have a word meaning 'entrepreneur', they do not appear to distinguish between types of business owner. This indicates clearly how culture and language shape thought even in the socio-economic sphere.

Defining the 'entrepreneur' is thus a difficult task. To illustrate some of the problems two possible definitions are presented:

Definition A: The Capitalist

- Owns the means of production
- Is able to marshal resources successfully
- Assumes the risk for the sake of profit.

The advantage of this definition is that ownership can arise from buying or inheriting a business as well as founding one, but *is* ownership really a necessary prerequisite of being an entrepreneur? John Stuart Mill in the 19th century described the Lancashire cotton mill owners as being typical capitalists. But we can also see that all owner-managed businesses could be included in this definition; no distinction is actually being drawn between the business owner of the corner shop or of the high technology business.

Definition B: The Opportunist

- Is able to recognize and proactively pursue opportunities for business development and growth
- Is confident that the resourcing of the opportunity will not be a problem.

The advantage of this definition is that ownership is not a prerequisite of entrepreneurship. Furthermore, whilst it is acknowledged that business founding is an entrepreneurial act, neither definition assumes that founding is a necessary condition of entrepreneurship. This definition has such breadth that senior executives of, for example not for profit organizations may also be included.

Exercise
List the pros and cons of each definition and name people who fall within it. What does each definition suggest about the characteristics of entrepreneurs?

If the kernel of entrepreneurial behaviour is the relentless pursuit of opportunities then this would suggest a number of associated characteristics.[22]

- The motivation or intention to create wealth and accumulate capital.
- To be alert to opportunities.[23]
- Alertness to opportunities appears to be associated with the skills of information seeking and networking.[24]
- From the recognition of an opportunity and its positive framing, the ability to imagine or envision its development or exploitation.[25]
- Judgement – knowing which opportunities to pursue.[26]

The process of entrepreneurship

Economic activity concerns trade. The process at firm level is managed strategically (implicitly at least) and operationally by the owner-manager and their team. But how is the process managed to give sustained performance? What motivates the owner-manager to deliver a particular kind and level of performance?

The owner-manager is motivated to achieve a particular outcome for the business. Some will seek growth, others will be content to maintain the business at current levels of size and performance and yet others will be concerned with survival. All such goals are mediated by the need to make a profit. A proportion of the owner-managers, being motivated by wealth creation and the desire to grow their business will be alert to opportunities which they can exploit. The owner-manager brings to this situation their experience, skills, competencies and abilities and critical personality characteristics.

Their experience comprises tacit knowledge and understanding of the industry and their reputation which makes them attractive as someone with whom to do business.[27] Crucial skills include **networking**, which increases the incidence of opportunities, **image making**, which gives profile to the business and makes it attractive for resourcing purposes and **innovation**, which enables them to differentiate the business in the marketplace. Critical personality characteristics comprise **initiative or proactivity** indicated by their alertness to opportunity, **opportunism** characterized by the relentless nature of their opportunity seeking behaviour, imagination and envisioning capability and **judgement** – knowing which opportunities to pursue and which to drop. These person characteristics result in a predictable sequence of behaviours: the pursuit of opportunity, the marshalling of resources in that pursuit and the differentiation of the business in the marketplace. The business owner who behaves in these ways we term an entrepreneur. He or she is rewarded by the level of profit which the business venture achieves.

Survival

The business owner whose aspirations are to ensure that the business survives will behav0e in ways very unlike those of the growth-oriented entrepreneur. S/he may not recognize some situations as opportunities and may even construe them as threats. The environment may be poor and there may be a paucity of resources to draw upon in order to exploit opportunity.

Box 4.8: Self employment in a poor entrepreneurial climate

Don is a sole trader whose core business is to raise funds for voluntary sector organizations and who also does some management consultancy and training. He had been employed in the voluntary sector before being made redundant. He wished to remain in the voluntary sector 'because that's all I've ever done'. Getting started was difficult; his clients were people who would normally have been his employer, he found this psychologically intimidating. Gradually he built up some essential marketing skills. 'I had a notion at the start that there were a number of local market places and I would build up a client portfolio in each but it hasn't worked out that way.' Two years ago Don did a piece of work for a charity based in the West Midlands, but that was the only work that he had from there. He also tried trade fairs and bought a stand for three days, which cost him about £1000 from which he picked up £7000 worth of work. He did not regard that as very successful. He said 'I feel very reactive at times, I don't feel that I have a choice because there's only me and you don't want to turn down work.' The problem, he suggested, was that there was little time to market himself proactively and to think about his business plan. The upshot is that 'at the minute I'm seven and a half grand overdrawn and the bank aren't giving me any more and I'm waiting for a payment from [a client] to bail me out. I'm OK for the next month. Then I have to pick up some more jobs again. So with that level of stress – it's been that way for about three years – and we've managed to keep our heads above water, but it's starting to wear us down a bit'.

Maintenance

The business owner whose aspirations are for maintaining the business at present levels suggests that a deliberate strategy has been put in place to achieve this objective. It also suggests an adequate resource base to maintain current levels of activity. Furthermore, it indicates that sufficient opportunities are

Box 4.9: Bill Overall's workwear firm

Bill Overall had had plenty of experience in the clothing industry. He had managed a large clothing firm in Leeds (UK) in the 1970s. But low cost competition from abroad resulted in closure and Bill was the manager whose unpleasant job it was to make hundreds of workers redundant. It was little consolation that he was one of the last to leave. He started his own business in workwear. By using his extensive network of contacts in the industry he was able to identify a niche and quickly establish a customer base. These conditions enabled him to keep the business at a steady state. He employed a workforce of ten and his wife came in to keep the books. Growing the business was out of the question: 'what, and have to face another recession and worse? No thank you!' This way his life was hassle free; he and his wife had a comfortable standard of living and he was able to provide secure employment for a small but contented workforce.

being recognized and pursued to fill the order book and maintain current levels of activity. This owner-manager has achieved a balance between realizing sufficient income to continue with a desired and comfortable lifestyle and a level of business development with which they can cope. As personalities they tend to prefer routine to hassle and a future which is predictable rather than uncertain.

Growth

Owner-managers have relentlessly pursued and exploited opportunities in order to create wealth. Their ability to recognize and back their judgement of the right opportunities to pursue has paid off. Further, they have been able to

Box 4.10: Richard Branson moves into the record business

Over bacon and eggs at the nearby Riviera Cafe, Branson excitedly sketched out a picture of the empire he was planning to build. It was obvious, he said, that there was money to be made in records. With mail order up and running, his next plan was to start a record label. He did not need to know the difference between *Van der Graaf Generator* and *Blodwyn Pig* in order to spot the business potential for discounting records. But nor was it calculation as to how best to exploit the burgeoning youth market which accounted for Virgin's initial direction. It was not dictated by grand design but by the imperatives of survival. The mail order business had arisen to raise money in order to support *Student*. Branson did not need to share the tastes of his peers to cater for them. One of his skills was to know how to use the knowledge of those around him. He was the enabler, the catalyst who made things happen ... Then came a crisis – a precipitating event – the post office workers went on strike for five weeks. Overnight the flow of cheques dried up. Faced with shelves of records, Richard made an instant decision: Virgin would open a shop ... So brisk was business at the Oxford Street shop that it was decided to open another as soon as possible. However, the record shops proved to be yet another example of Branson gestating an idea in high enthusiasm, executing it in a rush of energy and activity and then growing bored with it, restless for some other challenge or distraction. From this emerged the idea of a recording studio; Virgin would now produce records on its own label.[28]

marshal the required resources and differentiate the business in the market-place.

Clearly in this model the emphasis is on opportunism, it leaves open the question of the relative importance of innovation as a feature of the entre-preneurial process.

Present influences, future development

The complexity of the entrepreneurial process and the need to contextualize behaviours in order to interpret them has tended to sweep aside the tradi-tional trait approach which focused on the identification of a single trait of entrepreneurship to the development of more complex processual models.[29] Other influences include work emanating from economics and organizational psychology. Questions such as how central is innovation to the entrepre-neurial process? have not been resolved.[30] However, the idea of the entrepre-neurial process being essentially innovative derives from Schumpeter, who asserted that the entrepreneur is a dynamic force that disturbs the economic equilibrium through innovation.[31] Innovation is a process which results in new combinations, e.g. in product or process innovation, opening up a new market, capturing a new source of supply or results in the reorganization of an industry. Furthermore, what innovation signifies in organizational and behavioural terms is 'change'. This in itself indicates fundamentally different personality characteristics: from the person who desires change, indeed who 'thrives on change', to the person who finds change a hassle, stressful and who approaches it with caution. Research evidence suggests that the entre-preneur enjoys change whereas the 'caretaker' owner-manager and to some extent the administrator find it to be something of a hassle.[32]

Influences from economic psychology include the work of Shackle[33], in which it is suggested that the entrepreneur perceives the potential of situa-tions and characteristically gambles on their imagination and Kirzner (note 24) whose thesis concerns opportunity identification – alertness to profit opportunities and exploitation of such opportunities requires creative imagi-nation in the face of uncertainty. The entrepreneur is able to spot opportuni-ties which would otherwise be overlooked; Casson (note 27) identifies 'judgement' as being critical – faced with the same situation and the same objectives, Casson argues that different individuals take different decisions. They do so because they perceive the situation differently. The entrepreneur therefore is a person whose judgement differs from that of others; Schultz (see note 33) argues that entrepreneurial behaviour is the ability to operate flexi-bly and turn one's attention to work of economic value. Risk, he suggests, does not distinguish between the entrepreneur and the non-entrepreneur.[34] Further, what these studies indicate in their different ways is the importance of the **cognitive** dimension of personality.

This cognitive approach was evident in the 'Situation-Act Model' devel-oped by Chell (see note 17), Bird's emphasis on the need to focus on inten-tional behaviour and cognitive style[35] and Low and MacMillan's suggestion that opportunities are created and that chances of successfully creating such opportunities are enhanced through the development and advantageous positioning of the business owner in his or her network.[36] Other authors[37] developed such thinking, for example Learned examined the interaction between intention, sensemaking and decision to found, while Boyd and Vozikis built on Bird's work on entrepreneurial intention. They suggested that self-efficacy plays an important role in the development of entrepreneurial intentions and actions. Intentions are structured further by both rational analytic thinking (**goal directed behaviour**) and intuitive/holistic thinking (**envisioning**). They hypothesized that the entrepreneur will pursue business opportunities when self-efficacy is high (i.e. the ability to succeed in realizing their intentions). In addition they will assess the psychological consequences of failure.

There also seems to be a convergence of thinking about which personality characteristics might matter. For example, the ability to recognize and create opportunities repeatedly emerged both in interactionist models and other studies which took a psycho-economic approach, e.g. Busenitz.[38] This may be related to an aspect of the entrepreneurs' behaviour which has received scant attention – that of 'adventurousness'.[39] This appears to be related to 'opportunism', for opportunities do not present themselves without keen attention and activity on the part of the entrepreneur. The seeking of opportunities may thus take the entrepreneur far afield – in search of ideas that they can incorporate into new product lines (e.g. Phileas Fogg snacks), sourcing materials at competitive prices (e.g. where labour is cheap) and opening new markets where risks and uncertainties are high. The notion of 'entrepreneurial intention' has also continued to exert an influence.[40] But running in parallel were other developments, shifting the balance away from trait psychology to a consideration of skills and competencies.[41] Competencies are more attractive because they are evident through proficient performance of tasks and as such have action and organizational performance implications. However the same sort of problem besets the competency research, namely the identification of which competencies – the profile – and being able to demonstrate their implications for person and organizational performance.

Another approach – the **social constructionist** – has arisen from such ideas as the need to 'embed' behaviours in the entrepreneurial process. It was considered that there is a need to reconceptualize the mechanistic approach of interactionists and to recognize the fundamental organicity of the process.[42] Learned's work, already referred to, suggested a transactional model in which 'sense making' was hypothesized to create the link between an entrepreneur's cognitions and the perceived situation. Important theoretical developments in social constructionism have cleared the ground for a new set of questions to be asked about the nature of entrepreneurs and their (fast growth) firms.[43] These questions include, for example how entrepreneurs socially construct time so that different constructions can be shown to contribute to organizational variability in respect of rates of growth,[44] the social construction of space – suggesting differences in horizons and envisioning possibilities of entrepreneurs and entrepreneurial top teams,[45] and the construction of effective interrelating by 'successful' entrepreneurs to achieve enhanced performance.[46] This model of the entrepreneur as an agent within a socio-economic structure suggests the importance of understanding both the person and how they can (and indeed do) make a difference.

CHAPTER 5

Individual learning, organizational learning and learning organizations

There is no single unified theory of learning, yet understanding how people learn, adapt and change is fundamental in a progressive world of global economic and social change. Learning, however, is not solely about learning *what*, that is about 'things' – the concrete reality 'out there' – it is also about learning *how*, that is the processes by which things work whether these be tangible mechanical processes or intangible social processes, it is about learning *why* things occur or happen the way they do, that is, to be able to explain events or occurrences, and it is also about learning *how to learn about* the what and the how. Theories of learning thus raise some fundamental questions about how people manage their lives and develop themselves.

A *laissez faire* view might question the importance of understanding learning in the context of business development and entrepreneurship, so why devote a whole chapter to this topic? The answer is both philosophical and pragmatic. On the one hand, advocates of a *laissez faire* approach could argue that people find their own level, what will be will be. On the other hand, proponents of social progress will always advocate the need to develop the base level of understanding and awareness and that learning is fundamental to fulfilling this societal need. Other arguments have also been put, for example the competitiveness argument: how can a nation compete effectively on the world stage if its individuals *and* its institutions and organizations cannot develop their knowledge base to a competitive level? Further, given a global competitive arena, does any one nation have a choice but to develop its citizens' knowledge and skills base, to enable them to learn?

How do people learn?

There are many theories of learning. Burgoyne[1] in a recent paper lists 12 – to this we may add social learning theory (see Table 5.1).

The **operant conditioning** school has been made famous by the animal experiments – Pavlov's dogs and Skinner's rats and pigeons[2] – which were used to demonstrate its tenets. Operant conditioning assumes the learning of an association between a stimulus and response and reinforcement of appro-

Table **5.1** Learning theories

	School	Process	Product
1.	Operant conditioning	Association	Habit
2.	Trait modification	Learning style	Knowledge skills and attitude change
3.	Information transfer	Memory – Storage and retrieval	Public knowledge/ know-how
4.	Cybernetics	Adaptation	Survival
5.	Social learning	Modelling, imitation	Behaviour modification
6.	Cognitive	Information processing, mental models and maps	Personal knowledge
7.	Humanistic	Growth and discovery	Development
8.	Social influence	Socialization, identification	Identity, self concepts
9.	Psychoanalytic	Dynamic between the conscious and the unconscious	Personal Integration
10.	Post structural	The agency of culture	Traditions
11.	Existential	Choice through action	'Being', meaning
12.	Communities of practice	Apprenticeship	Communal 'knowledge'/ know how
13.	Tacit	Intuition	Performance

Source: Burgoyne 1998 (see note 1)

priate behavioural responses by means of a reward. It has been criticized for its mechanistic approach to learning and is said not to be appropriate in respect of higher forms of learning.

Trait modification assumes that when learning takes place it changes the 'trait profile' of the individual. 'Trait' may include knowledge, skills and attitudes. This theory has particular relevance in the world of training, where considerable work is done to profile people and jobs and effect a match.[3]

Also important in its application to industry is **information transfer**. This approach assumes that knowledge is a 'commodity' that can be acquired, communicated and passed on. Fundamental to this theory is how knowledge is stored, accessed, retrieved and disseminated. It reflects many of the characteristics of the educational process and is assumed also to apply to industrial processes such as technology transfer.

Our understanding of human and organizational behaviour has been advanced by the use of metaphors. The cybernetic approach is one such metaphor and assumes the application of systems theory to individual[4] and organizational learning.[5] When considering individual learning, the person is considered to be the system which takes information from the situation and adapts. Organizational learning will be dealt with in detail in a later section of this chapter.

Social learning theory has taken a number of forms, for example OB Mod[6] and role modelling.[7] Social learning theory, unlike operant conditioning, introduces the idea of 'cognitive processes', that is the ability of people to think about what they are doing. Thus, having thought about the possible consequences of their actions, a person can decide on an alternative course of action. Bandura (see note 7) argues that people are also capable of learning by observing the actions of other people. Imitation has important social and organizational consequences. But people also imagine different scenarios and act them out in their mind; they talk about them outside the immediate situation where action might be required of them. Thus in reflecting on behavioural possibilities, a person also applies their accumulated experience to enable them to decide what to do. Understanding the consequences of their actions also provides a means of self-regulation. They enable the evaluation of own performance against a desired performance level – whether that be one's own standards or an externally imposed or expected standard of performance. Closely allied to this is the **cognitive school**. From this perspective the suggestion is that in thinking about their situation people develop mental models or 'schemata' which they use to plan and regulate their behaviour. Knowledge is very personal and subjective (as in social constructionism) rather than public and objective as in information transfer. Such personalized mental maps are modified due to making sense of one's experience.[8]

The **humanistic school** distinguishes between the emotional and the intellectual aspects of learning. Both need to be pursued in a balanced way if the individual is to reach a fully developed state, in respect of their self fulfilment and moral development.[9]

Social influence theories regard individuals as social constructions. An important consideration is how people perceive their environment, conceptualize and make sense of it. How they perceive the behaviour of others – and themselves – is also fundamental to questions of identity. This includes personality – what am I like? occupation – what skills and attributes do I have which enable me to perform my job – and reputation – how well do I do what I do?

The **psychoanalytic approach** based on the seminal work of Freud and Jung assumes that there is an interplay between the conscious and unconscious which affects the interpretation of experience and hence of learning. It has found expression in developing a person's self awareness in interpersonal situations through, for example transactional analysis and understanding the behaviour of groups.[10]

Structuralism assumes that society and social interaction are regulated by social structures, institutional, legal, political, educational, economic and so on. These structures are assumed to take on, as it were, a tangible form that is be embodied in some way, through legal statute, bureaucratic red tape, parliamentary procedures etc. Post-structuralism, on the other hand, assumes an intangibility of social structuring processes. There is nothing fixed which generates psychological, social and cultural consequences. Experience of social phenomena is temporary; people develop temporary ways of operating in these environments based on perception, experience and interpretation of the here and now. What people learn are assumptions about how things tend to work; it is, to coin a phrase, the 'software of the mind'.[11]

Existentialism[12] turns traditional learning theory on its head. Instead of assuming that thought precedes action, existentialism suggests that actions precede and generate meaning. Also fundamental to this philosophy of being is that people have choices; thus a person can generate new situations through wilful intended behaviour.

Situated learning refers to the collective, local and informal nature of learning which may exist in 'communities of practice'.[13] People occupying marginal positions in a community, for example outsiders or newcomers, gradually learn the collective way of doing things and as such they eventually become incorporated as community members.

Finally, **tacit knowledge** suggests an understanding of situations familiar to the incumbent which he or she may not be able to articulate.[14]

Such theories go far beyond the lay concept of learning – that which takes place essentially in the classroom. However, this broadening of the concept of learning is important for several reasons. First, it reflects an increasingly understood aspect of people's lives, which is that a person's learning continues from cradle to grave. Hence, learning in the classroom context is only a small part of such a lifelong learning process. Secondly, such theories reflect our understanding that learning is not simply about 'facts', it is also about **processes** – how things work, **development** – how a person may develop themselves, by acquiring new depths of understanding and new skills and **attitudes** – learning different and socially acceptable ways of responding and dealing with situations. Indeed, self development may include achieving mature, socially adjusted behaviours and personal awareness to enable the person to achieve self-fulfilment and well-being. It is therefore clear that people may learn a great deal from experience. In the next section therefore the nature of how people may learn from experience is considered.

Experiential learning

Experiential learning stands on the shoulders of several great social scientists and philosophers of the earlier part of the 20th century. They include Piaget, Dewey and Lewin and have been carried forward by Jung, Erikson, Maslow and Rogers.[15] From such work different perspectives and principles have been derived. Based on these traditions there are five contemporary applications of experiential learning theory: widening access policies for minority communities, the poor, developing countries, etc; competence based education, for example the National Vocational Qualifications (NVQ); lifelong learning and career development, for example adult development programmes and continuing education and the University for Industry; experiential education through simulations, on the job training and experiential exercises; and curriculum development – widening the number and type of subjects that may be taught at all levels. Clearly when such a breadth of applications is considered it is understood that experiential learning can profoundly change people's lives.

Experiential learning is holistic in that it combines experience, perception, cognition (thinking) and behaviour. Moreover, it is about a process of learning. Ideas are formed and reformed through experience – a process which permits adaptation. Hence all learning is relearning because no one ever starts from a blank sheet of paper or an empty head, everyone has some concept – however crude – of what it is they are dealing with. Furthermore, experiential learning is about overcoming resistance to new ideas. In this respect learning may be thought of as a 'dialectical process', furthered by the resolution of conflicting views of the world. Hence, learning arises as a result of tension between 'old' and 'new' knowledge. What a person once thought is no longer adequate to explain new experience – that person has doggedly to hang on to those old beliefs or revise them in the light of new experience.

Kolb's model of the learning process has four modes (see Figure 5.1). Each mode describes a different aspect of the learning process and at any of the four points conflict can arise.

Figure **5.1** Kolb's experiential learning cycle

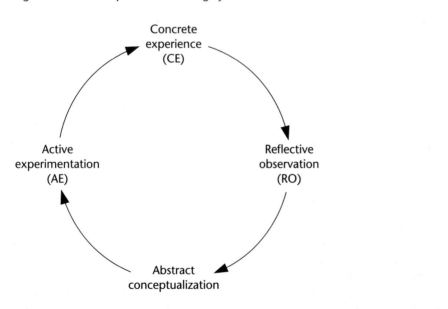

Source: Burgoyne 1998 (see note 1)

A person must be able to involve themselves fully with their (new) experience, reflect upon it from different perspectives, label it in a way which integrates the experience into a theoretical frame and then use it to make decisions and solve problems.

Another way of thinking about this learning cycle is to consider the modes as being two dimensions whose extremes are polar opposites. Hence, one dimension has at its extremes concrete reality and abstract conceptualization and the other dimension has reflective observation at one extreme and active experimentation at the other. From this it has become clear that people have preferred learning styles.

According to Kolb, the whole experiential cycle is involved in learning; learning is not simply the realm of thinking. Learning also involves transactions between the person and their environment, that is, reciprocal influences and as such concerns the complex process of adaptation. The whole person adapts to new circumstances, not just their thoughts or their emotions. Hence, learning encompasses adaptation and when sustained throughout life, development.

Personal development

It is axiomatic that a consideration of 'self development' cannot begin unless there is an adequate notion of what is meant by 'the self'. Notions of 'the self' have a long and distinguished history and it is appropriate to begin with the work of George Mead.[16]

George Mead argued that a person develops their notion of the self through social experience. They learn to develop such a notion in stages. First, they do this by means of game playing as children, taking on the roles of others and assuming appropriate attitudes. Children have no single unified notion of 'self', there are many selves through this role enactment process. Second, people become self-conscious or self-aware as they notice the attitudes of others towards them. To be regularly rebuked 'must mean' they are naughty or worthless. Third, as the child grows up they begin to join organized social groups. Such groups are important because they present elements of an identity and behaviour and attitudes of the group are organized around the particular purposes of the group. The new member assimilates these attitudes, identifying with the group and adopting its social attitudes.

Group identity is in effect a 'generalized other' (not an individual or person) which enables the member to organize and control their own nature and by reflecting on their experience as a member of the group, develop a sense of personal identity. Such personal or self development takes place through the use of language. Experience can only be reflected on through conceptualizations in words and through discussion with others, also in words and meaningful gestures. Hence the individual becomes socialized into the group, they experience a sense of belonging because they have adopted the principles, practices and attitudes of the group. In taking these generalized social attitudes of the group (or community) the individual becomes a person and the expression of associated and, presumably, acceptable attitudes constitute, at least part of the person's character.

Weick,[17] following Mead, discusses the self as 'sense maker' but there is no single sense maker, for each individual has many selves as self definition occurs through a process of interaction. In presenting 'self' to others a person tries to decide which self is appropriate. In defining the self in words, these words matter first and foremost to a larger collectivity. These words may constitute, for example:

- an ideology or belief system
- an organized control system
- the language of a professional or occupational group
- a theory of action – how to behave in or cope with particular situations
- the language of our predecessors and our understanding of tradition
- stories that enable us to relate our own and others' experience.[18]

The practicalities of personal development have been conceptualized holistically.[19] The development of the self concerns the whole of a person's life. The process can be managed by planning, setting out career and personal objectives, levels of personal wealth which are desired and those aspects of personal development and learning which need to be attended to. Clearly anyone at any age can set down on paper their own personal development plan. But what might this mean for the person who does not want to embark on a management career, but who is seeking to be self-employed and managing their own business? Box 5.1 discusses such cases.

This exercise shows how two owner-managers construct their business and personal 'realities' very differently. It is about how people manage their own life course and how, by being more self conscious, they can manage the process more effectively to help themselves to achieve their life goals.

Organizational learning

Organizational learning can be understood from a number of 'disciplinary' perspectives and should be distinguished from the learning organization. Easterby-Smith suggests there are six identifiable perspectives which comprise organizational learning, as shown in Table 5.2.[20]

Psychology and OD concern human development within the organizational context. Work in this area suggests a number of themes. There is the notion of a **learning hierarchy** – learning from the simple to the more complex, from stimulus-response type learning to learning situations where choice and change are involved. A further theme is that of the **cognitive process of learning**. In this instance, people build up 'cognitive maps', which frame thinking. Collective understanding occurs when individuals share their thoughts, although in several senses this may be problematic.

Experiential learning suggests a different kind of learning, which develops in stages from the concrete experience through abstraction/conceptualization resulting in action. This suggests a relationship between thought and

Box 5.1: Personal development profiles of two owner-managers, Chris and Sam

Chris

Sam

Career objectives

Has set up a small business in the 'rag trade', employing 15 people. Chris wishes to make a 'decent living', provide for family comfort, good holidays and a private education for the kids.

Has set up several small businesses but is looking for the 'main chance'. Sam is seeking business opportunities to create wealth. He has never been content running just one business; the thrill is to grow them and then move on to set up more businesses.

Personal relationships

Family is the most important. The family must be nurtured and provided for.

Sam prefers a loose and extensive network of relationships on the grounds that you never know when contacts might prove useful

Material wealth

What is important to Chris is person comfort, wanting for nothing; such ambitions are realistic.

Sam wishes to create enormous wealth. This is in large part a measure of one's achievement.

Personal development goals

Chris has had some difficulty recognizing that there may be such distinctly personal goals. It is realized that a better balance might be struck between work and play. Setting up the business meant working very long hours. This means learning how to maintain current levels of business activity, while remaining competitive in one's chosen market niche.

Hitherto Sam has taken little time to stop and think about personal development issues. Sam now recognizes that by engaging in certain activities (e.g. forming a strategic alliance) it is possible to learn a great deal. Learning experientially from concrete events is his preferred style of learning. Sam has now realized that by reflecting on these experiences further learning and development can be achieved.

Priorities

The family.
A comfortable living.
Learning to achieve a balance between work and play.

The business.
Wealth creation.
Learning in order to achieve more through successfully realizing further business opportunities.

Personal development activity now requires both Chris and Sam to be more reflective about what they do. Instead of simply 'doing things', they will need to be more experimental, trying and testing their ideas and evaluating which strategies and tactics work and which don't. The hardest part is learning to change habits where work routines and ways of doing have become established. This is particularly difficult for Chris.

action and has been referred to by some as 'action learning'.[21] A further psychological approach has concentrated on the idea of 'learning styles'. Here it is suggested that people have preferred ways of learning and that different environments favour different learning styles. Learning style is thought to be a subset of cognitive style – the way people think and 'process information'.

Table **5.2** Disciplines of organizational learning

Discipline	Ontology	Contribution/ideas	Problematics
Psychology and OD	Human development	Hierarchical organization, importance of context, cognition, underlying values, learning stiles, dialogue.	Defensive routines, individual to collective transfer.
Management science	Information processing	Knowledge, memory, holism, error correction, informating, single and double-loop.	Non-rational behaviour, short vs long term, information overload, unlearning
Sociology and organization theory	Social structures	Effects of power structure and hierarchy, conflict is normal, ideology and rhetoric, interests of actors.	Conflict of interests organizational politics.
Strategy	Competitiveness	Organization-environment interface, levels of learning progressively more desirable, networks, importance of direct experience, population-level learning.	Environmental alignment, competitive pressures, general vs technical learning.
Production management	Efficiency	Importance of productivity, learning curves, endogenous and exogenous sources of learning, links to production design.	Limitations of unidimensional measurement, uncertainty about outcomes.
Cultural anthropology	Meaning systems	Culture as cause and effect of organizational learning, beliefs, potential cultural superiority.	Instability and relativity of culture as barrier to transfer of ideas, whose perspective dominates?

Source: M. Easterby-Smith 1997 (see note 20): p.1087

... [Cognitive] styles are consistent individual differences in the ways of *organizing* experience into meanings, values, skills and strategies, whereas learning styles are consistent individual differences in the ways of *changing* meanings, values, skills and strategies.[22]

Alternatively, learning style has been defined simply as the consistent differences in the way people absorb or retain information.[23] On such an assumption, learning style has been linked to 'split brain' or the analytic-holistic (intuitive) mode of thinking and processing information. Using Allinson and Hayes' Cognitive Style Index,[24] Allinson, Chell and Hayes conducted a study of the cognitive style of growth entrepreneurs.[25] The proposition was that entrepreneurs would have a more holistic style than the general population. This was shown to be the case, although there is scope for further research.

However, there is still a problem about why individuals and organizations find it so hard to learn from experience. This is explained by Argyris and Schön.[26] Essentially they argue that people have a set of espoused beliefs which they may contradict by the way they behave. If confronted with such inconsistency, they are likely to become defensive and show every unwillingness to acknowledge this as a problem. Hence the confrontational approach, even by an external consultant, is unlikely to solve the problem because it begs the question of whose version of reality is correct. The solution appears to be through dialogue that enables the parties concerned to reach a consensus, greater awareness of the issues and build up a more solid relationship of trust.

The **management science perspective** concerns the gathering and processing of information about the organization and relates to managerial decision making (which is the subject of the next chapter). The key aspect of this approach is that of systems thinking. As such, learning is said to occur through the processing of information, which results in a change in behaviour. The system includes knowledge acquisition (including knowledge gained through the selection and recruitment of individuals), information distribution and interpretation; and organizational knowledge, which comprises a combination of explicit knowledge and tacit understanding. Further, the systems view includes the idea that through feedback mechanisms, what may have been a localized problem or reaction can affect the whole system.

The introduction of information technology can hinder rather than facilitate organizational learning. Any system requires a judgement to be made of what is 'normal' and what constitute 'deviations'. Clearly employees prefer to be publicly associated with working the system normally. However, at more senior levels where, for example scenario planning techniques are used, there may be more than one interpretation of what is 'normal'. This lessens the idea of sanctions and facilitates implementation.

Organizational learning may be hindered by political and nonrational behaviour. Employees may distort or suppress information. Such problems can be reduced through involvement and participation, ensuring that issues are openly discussed. A further potential problem concerns the time frames for organizational learning. The introduction of new/information technology may meet a short term need and its exploitation may result in anticipated efficiencies. However, learning in this case tends to be operational whereas the exploration of information technologies with a larger time frame can result in deeper, strategic learning. Finally related to this is the need for **unlearning** – discarding old ways of working in order to embrace the new.

Sociological and organizational theoretical approaches to organizational learning seek to address fundamental questions. Four perspectives have been identified.

The **functional approach** suggests that organizations do not learn as well as they might because there are structural impediments such as hierarchy, power differences, conflict and boundaries to be contended with. In this view these are inevitable aspects of organizational life.

The **contingency approach** suggests that what organizational learning means depends on the nature of organization. Thus in a bureaucracy or highly structured organizational arrangement there will be greater formality, planning and control (the adoption of an ISO9000 system of quality control is one such example). Learning will take place within these formal structures whereas in a more organically designed organization there will be greater informality. The latter will mean more opportunities for informal exchanges between employees and that learning can take place anywhere and at any time. Moreover there is wider 'ownership' of information and knowledge.

Social constructionists suggest that learning is more likely to take place through informal processes and that it will also occur as an outcome of critical events, for example where any discontinuity (i.e. the introduction of a new product or process, etc) results in the 'reconstruction' of knowledge.

Finally, the **critical theoretical perspective** seeks to address the issue of governance; who decides what shall be learnt and what knowledge shall be privileged. There are clearly problems, whether the answer is hierarchical (i.e. are the owner-manager, chief executive, top management learning the right things?) or decentralized (increased uncertainty of what is right and the political activity that ensues).

The **strategic perspective** considers how firms may achieve a competitive advantage through learning. There is no single view as to whether firms may increase their chances of survival through learning – these views vary from the relatively pessimistic to the more optimistic. Several types of learning may take place through, for example direct transfer of experience from one company to another and/or a general 'collective' learning across the organization. Moreover it is argued that strategy determines selection and interpretation of information, whilst learning style can determine what strategic options are countenanced. There are also different levels of learning from the lower level 'routine' to the higher level strategic, which takes place against a backdrop of uncertainty and ambiguity. Furthermore, if a competitive edge is to be secured, learning needs to occur quickly as well as efficiently. This is particularly true in the cases of technology transfer and scientific innovation where rapid change prevails and the need to get the nose ahead is imperative to success.

However, competitive pressures resulting in the need for rapid learning may have certain disadvantages, such as reducing thinking time. This lack of reflection and poor communication has implications for the effectiveness of organizational learning.

A major source of learning exemplified, in particular, through joint ventures between companies across country and cultural 'boundaries' is that which derives from direct experience and comprises tacit knowledge. It has been shown to be a problem getting senior managers who are more distanced from the 'action' to accept this source of knowledge. Another important lesson to be taken on board is that of how learning can best take place between countries. Detailed transference of ideas appears not to work because of cultural differences. It has therefore been suggested that the process works best if the principles of know-how and understanding are abstracted at a higher level of generality and then translated back to fit local needs and circumstances.

The **production management perspective** focuses on learning and organizational productivity and efficiency. The idea of a 'learning curve' and a linear, quantitative or accumulative approach to learning is found wanting. In particular it does not account for learning decay or the fact that production costs may over time increase rather than decrease relative to those of more recent competitors. Other non-quantifiable factors such as the approach taken by management and organizational design factors also need to be taken into account.

The **cultural approach** to learning invokes both organizational and national senses of 'culture'.[27] However, many of the studies which have invoked the concept of culture have dealt with the transference of ideas and knowledge between nations. This work begs a number of questions. For example are there identifiable learning abilities particular to a nation such as Japan? Can such learning abilities be transferred to other countries? What learning differences are there between nations that make it difficult for transference to occur?

There have been some major studies[28] which show distinct differences between Japanese and North American companies on a number of dimensions. For example internal communications in Japanese companies tended to be based on tacit understandings, whereas in US companies there was an explicit articulation of information through documentation. In contrast, information flows into these companies also differed. For the Japanese, the information was explicit and technical whereas in the US it was tacit and relied on specialists. Such work has raised questions about whether some cultures are superior to others in facilitating learning. Other studies, assuming a social constructivist perspective, argue that learning is very much context specific and cannot be transferred from one setting to another. This suggests the need for learning to be localized.

Organizational learning and transformation

The practitioner perspective on organizational learning tends to suggest that learning is for a purpose. Moreover, learning occurs with the advent of change. When a firm undergoes some degree of renewal or transformation the owner-manager or chief executive understands that this brings with it the need to learn, to acquire new knowledge and skills. The idea of 'organizational learning' *per se* carries little currency. Organizations are collections of individuals and as such organizations learn through the experience and actions of individuals.[29] But learning, as argued above, does not necessarily occur at the point of implementation. Take, for example a company's mission statement or its policy document on equal opportunities practice. Such statements or policies represent the 'espoused theories' of a company. Espoused theories of action are those normative theories to which individuals *and* organizations subscribe. The organization mission statement makes various assumptions about organizational goals, standards, achievement and so on to which each member of the organization (usually) publicly subscribes or at least pays lip service. The policy document is also formally and publicly acknowledged. But the knowledge and the implicit prescriptions to particular courses of action which such documents contain are not necessarily made manifest in the behaviour and actions of managers and other employees. The knowledge which governs their actual day to day behaviour is their 'theory-in-use'. This may or may not be consistent with the espoused theory enshrined in company policy.

Theories of action draw on the employees' experience and knowledge and the shared consensus of values which gives organizational life an 'objective reality' to its members. **Espoused theories** are the official theories of action and company values and beliefs to which the organization subscribes. Where there is a difference between espoused theory and theory of action there will be a tension and the potential for organizational learning to occur. Organizational learning is therefore about the testing and possible restructuring of organizational theories of action.

Box 5.2: Types of knowledge shared by organizational members

Dictionary knowledge – descriptive knowledge, 'the what?'
Directory knowledge – procedural knowledge, 'the how?'
Recipe knowledge – prescriptive knowledge, 'the should'.
Axiomatic knowledge – knowledge about reasons and causes, 'the why?'.[30]

The types of knowledge listed in Box 5.2 form the basis of employees' theories of action; shared beliefs and understandings of what is acceptable within the organization's culture, tested against the expectations of likely future activity. This consensual behaviour creates shared meanings and a rationale for past, current and future action. Clearly, if learning is to take place then there must be changes in organizational knowledge. This will expand the range of possible future actions and lead to a change in shared understandings of organizational ways of doing and being. This may be clarified by means of an example (see Box 5.3).

In the case of Maise Clothing, all forms of knowledge are being drawn upon by the members of the firm. The answers which the management have produced show that the potential for learning to occur happens when there is an impetus resulting from a fundamental change in the knowledge of the organization. However, the process of learning about new ways of doing and tackling the company's present crisis may take different forms. These include adaptive (**single loop**) learning, reconstructive (**double loop**) learning and process (**deutero-**) learning.

Single loop learning occurs when there is a need for system maintenance. Single loop learning is, in effect, the system adapting to, or correcting for, an error. Whether it be manufacturing or service industries, systems can refer to any number of established procedures such as quality control, ticketing,

Box 5.3: Maise Clothing Co. Ltd

Types of knowledge may be formulated in a series of questions. A dialogue, as a precursor to learning and organizational change, was being experienced at Maise Clothing Co. where the senior management team metaphorically scratched its head and pondered the question of what the present situation was *vis à vis* its competitors? The answer was evident; 'they're undercutting our price structure'. Clearly here was an impetus for change. But more thinking was required; how could the company proceed to steal a march on its competitors? Bob Maise's daughter. who had not been out of university long and was not particularly popular for her 'bright ideas', responded. She suggested that the company could either bring more work in-house or source more abroad and reduce costs. There was further discussion about this and other ideas concerning what strategy the company really should adopt. Pauline pushed her line of argument further: 'either we can adopt an aggressive cost cutting strategy which will increase efficiency of operations and enable us to compete on price or we could consider going upmarket', she said. After a pregnant pause, the harassed sales manager asked, 'why has this happened to us in the first place?' There was no articulated reply but a number of people gave each other knowing looks which said: 'because you took your eye off the ball!' but Bob Maise realized that it was he – the managing director – who was primarily responsible for the situation they were in. Now what they needed was accurate information about what the competitive situation was, what options were realistically open to them so that they could make an informed decision. Pauline was probably right, perhaps he'd give her the opportunity to prove herself!

billing customers, labelling, financial control and so on. When a defect, error or problem occurs in one such system, the first step to be taken is detection, the second step, correction. Once the problem has been rectified the system continues as normal. The learning which takes place concerns the types of thing which can go wrong with the particular system. Much of employee/management activity concerns the maintenance of systems; learning where faults are likely to occur and developing procedures for taking corrective action to create as little disruption as possible (see Figure 5.2).

To increase efficiency at Maise Clothing, the company has decided that there is a need to increase productivity – more garments must be produced by each machinist by continuing to do the same routines – and to reduce wastage by less reworking. Essentially no fundamental new learning has taken place. The system, whilst faster and more efficient, is still the same system.

Figure **5.2** Adaptive or single-loop learning

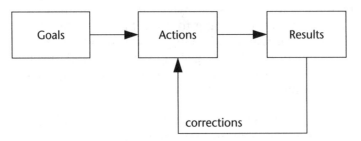

Source: Argyris and Schön 1978 (see note 26)

106

'Members of the organization respond to changes in the internal and external environments of the organization by detecting errors which they then correct so as to maintain the central features of organizational theory-in-use.'[31] Single loop learning is thus about the maintenance of organizational performance within specified *norms*. **Double loop learning** occurs where these fundamental norms and values are changed. This involves restructuring the organization's underlying values, often in the form of its priorities, that is what is now deemed to be the more important course of action. Learning can only be said to have occurred if these changes are accepted. This process leads to a questioning of old norms and values and the development of a new frame of reference. Often a weight of evidence is required before an organization will take heed and radical change occur.

To illustrate this further, Maise Clothing has now decided to source its manufacturing production abroad. This has meant a number of fundamental changes, including the reduction of its manufacturing plant. Instead of making the garment up, the plant now finishes, packages and despatches. The workforce has been reduced. New skills have been acquired, in particular the firm has entered into a strategic alliance with a Hong Kong based clothing manufacturer. This relationship has been further complicated by the subcontracting of work to new manufacturing units in the Republic of China. Senior management have been flying out frequently to oversee this process and it has been an 'eye opener' how much they could learn from their Chinese counterparts. Maise Clothing (UK) Ltd has thus learnt a new system of values and has begun to operate the firm along these lines (see Figure 5.3).

Accepting fundamental change in organizational patterns of behaviour is difficult for people who may have spent many years in a job which has required

Figure **5.3** Reconstructive or double-loop learning

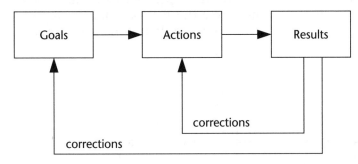

Source: Argyris and Schön 1978 (see note 26)

largely routine responses. Employees' behaviour patterns can become ossified around particular procedures and routines and, when faced with change, they may develop 'defensive behaviours' in order to resist it. Hence, if successful adaptive and, in particular, reconstructive learning is to take place employees must be given the opportunity to learn how to learn at this level. This involves developing the ability to reflect on the need for adaptive and reconstructive changes and to develop a new system of meaning or rationale for the requisite changes. Once each employee can understand this learning process and can see themselves operating within it, learning will take place (see Figure 5.4).

Senior management at Maise had been managing in a routine fashion for so long that they had lost sight of their direction and the encroaching competition. Machinery was antiquated, there had been no revision of their product-market strategy that anyone could recall and they were competitive on neither price nor quality. The crisis meant that, whilst there was union opposition and indeed opposition from various layers of management, the need to salvage the company or go under brought with it a new imperative. Defensive behaviour eventually gave way to a more constructive approach. New systems *had* to be introduced and there was a new feel about the place signified by a buzz of activity. But Bob shrewdly recognized that there was an opportunity to make some changes in the management team. His daughter had been impressive and so he promoted her to managing director, whilst putting himself in the role of chairman. With a shift in strategy and organizational structure, there was a need to strengthen the marketing, procurement and quality control departments. He discussed the shape of the new management team with Pauline; the need to bring in new talent and skills and the need to develop the remaining staff. This determined Pauline's next task: to carry out a systematic staff audit, prepare job specifications for a new marketing director, operations manager (as opposed to production manager) and quality controller.

People were also learning how to work with Pauline. She was good at translating her father's vision into practical reality. She delivered. She was seen to be hardworking and employees learnt that she could in fact be trusted to do what she had said she would do. It was becoming clear that the company was being rejuvenated and turned round. There was a feeling of confidence, vitality and strength from this and it was dawning on people that it might eventually be possible to expand the business from this new base and create some new jobs. This gave a lift and an impetus to the work of those who were left.

Figure **5.4** Process learning

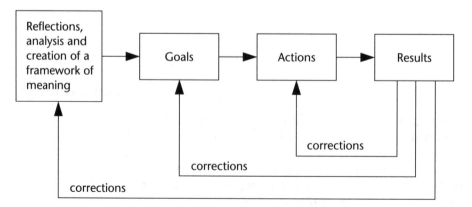

Source: Argyris and Schön 1978 (see note 26)

Triggers for organizational learning may be any or all of those organizational crises discussed earlier.[32] The means by which learning takes place, however, is primarily through communication and dialogue. People communicate their understanding of situations and what they believe a situation to mean and represent; different views of that reality are contested until a new reality or understanding of the situation becomes the dominant or shared one.

Within any organization there tends to be an elite or power group which dominates, indeed controls the process of learning and the definition of the 'new reality'. In an owner-managed firm, or a family business, the 'dominant coalition' will be the business owner and his or her management team or family. Any change in the leadership or ownership is likely to signal the need for new learning as the 'new broom sweeps clean', sweeping aside old values and practices, revising the organizational missions, arguing for new systems and ways of working and the requisite need for reconstructive learning to take place. There was evidence of such behaviours in the above case study of Maise Clothing. Clearly in a context of global competitiveness, the need to learn becomes imperative amongst teams, departments, functional areas and all levels of management. The major barrier to this process is the difficulty of *un*learning and the defensive postures which may be taken up where vested interests are being protected.

Applications of organizational learning

There are many applications of organizational learning, for example a company's commitment to **total quality management**,[33] or **Investors in People** require continuous learning. Companies with strong research and development departments engaging in product and/or process innovation are likely to require organizational relearning and restructuring. A Schumpeterian innovation[34] is one which will change an industry and create a need for change not only by the innovative firm but also by industry followers. However, any commitment on the part of an organization to the continuous training and development of its workforce, for example by adopting NVQ training at all levels, will trigger the need for extensive adaptive and reconstructive change.

Where the application of learning is concerned the literature has tended to focus upon models of learning organization. The key features include the idea of implementing organizational learning, the commitment to a desired end state and an action research agenda.[35] The main approaches to learning organization combine a management science/systems perspective with that of an organization development (OD) perspective. A management science perspective emphasizes the systems view and a concern with measurement, whereas OD is primarily concerned with issues of human development and emancipation at individual, group and organization levels. Senge, for example combines both but places a strong emphasis on OD.[36] There are five elements to his learning organization: **mental models** – assumptions which inform action, **shared vision** – personal perspectives of leaders which are articulated into a form which can be shared by all, **personal mastery** – commitment to lifelong learning, **team learning** – highlighting individuals' insights and managing those group dynamics which can undermine learning and **systems thinking** – the framing of the parts to construct an integrated pattern or whole.

A second tradition concerns itself almost exclusively with OD and takes on two forms – the cyclical and the evolutionary models. **Cyclical models** such as that of Kolb[37] do not have an end point whereas **evolutionary models** suggest progress through different stages of development.[38] In essence models of learning organization tend to assume a functionist paradigm; they are pragmatic, normative and aspirational.[39] A not untypical example is the model of a learning company developed by Burgoyne, Pedler and Boydell.[40]

The learning company

In reflecting on progress in training and development, Burgoyne *et al.*[41] note that training, personal development and organizational learning have gone through several 'movements', but as each finds a solution to a particular problem, yet another problem emerges. Still, however the question arises: training and development for what? Is it to satisfy people's deep need for meaning and understanding, for a sense of purpose? Work which has addressed these issues has focused on what these authors term the **spiritualization of organizations**. This indeed captures one sense of the term 'aspirational'. Has anything changed at the turn of the millennium? Learning appears to have more of a collective, social sense of purpose; to meet not only the goals of an organization but also national concerns and priorities. The concept of the learning company' attempts to address, at least in part, this broader, philosophical question.

There are 11 characteristics of a learning company which are associated with the practice of organizational learning. In addition there is an organizational learning process. Table 5.3 itemizes the characteristics.

The process underpinning the concept of the learning company relates thought and action of individuals and the collective to policy and practice at operations levels. In a learning company each of these aspects is energized and is in balance and there is a coherence in view and in practice. This has yielded four propositions.

1. Individual thought and action = individual learning.
2. Alignment of collective operations and individual action = managing.
3. Aligning policy and operations = directing.
4. Relating individual ideas to collective plans = participation.

In addition, Burgoyne *et al.* appear to have a fifth and sixth proposition.

5. Where operations and policy inform each other = collective learning.
6. Collective learning and emergent strategic thinking = strategic management.

Table 5.3 **Characteristics of a learning company**[42]

1. A learning approach to strategy.
2. A high level of participation of employees and stakeholders.
3. The use of information technology for sharing knowledge.
4. Feedback to develop the understanding of the effects of action, to learning and decision taking.
5. Internal relationships which facilitate mutual adjustment and adaptation.
6. Reward systems which give people incentives to learn.
7. Flexible organization structures allowing for change as a result of learning.
8. Employees working at the organizational boundary collecting external information for the improvement of internal processes.
9. Willingness and ability to learn from other organizations and companies.
10. A culture which encourages responsible experimentation and shared learning from both successes and failures.
11. Mechanisms and relationships which encourage and support self-development.

Finally, there are some important policy questions that need to be addressed in respect of the effectiveness of the learning company model.

- Are organizations which adopt the learning company precepts more effective in respect of their business performance?
- Is job satisfaction higher in learning companies than in companies which have not adopted the Learning Company principles and practices?

There are companies which have labelled themselves learning companies (such as Rover cars); it is important to give credence to the learning company/organization theory that there is real evidence of continuous learning processes and opportunities which, to coin a phrase, 'make a difference'.

Conclusions

'Learning', 'organizational learning' and 'learning organization' are concepts which have been shown in this chapter to have a rich provenance in theory. The importance for entrepreneurship is the link between learning and change. In business and the world of work the only constant is change. People need to learn new techniques, new skills, new meanings and they need to learn how to unlearn, adapt and modify their surroundings. Organizations need to rejuvenate, realign, reconfigure, readjust and reconsider in order to compete and deliver an effective and competent performance. This means, amongst other things, that they need to develop, through effective learning processes, tactics, strategies, operational plans, ideas, collaborative arrangements, new ventures, product portfolios, etc – and fundamental to such behaviour is learning.

The company which makes a step change in size suddenly will find itself with a new set of problems to be managed. A strategic alliance with a larger company is likely to mean the need to put new systems such as quality control and financial management systems in place, to relate to new ways of working and a different organizational culture and to learn how to manage the power relations and the new politics of organizational management. Hence the concomitant of organizational learning is the processing and, ultimately, the management of information and knowledge.

Additional reading

Probst, G.J.B. and Buchel, B.S.T. (1997) *Organizational Learning*, London: Prentice Hall.

Kolb, D.A. (1984) *Experiential Learning*, Englewood Cliffs, New Jersey: Prentice Hall.

Pedler, M., Burgoyne, J. and Boydell, T. (1978) *A Manager's Guide to Self-Development*, Maidenhead: McGraw-Hill.

CHAPTER 6

Decision making

Introduction

Being decisive can often win looks of admiration from other people; vacillation and dithering – quite the opposite! In a business the need to make clear decisions occurs constantly, but the information base for those decisions may simply not be there. What should be done? Should the person delay? (perhaps the situation will change and the need to make a decision disappear) Should they hazard a guess (and trust to luck)? Should they attempt to inform themselves and then take the decision? Clearly most people would select the latter option but reality may be more complex. There are issues of where to turn for the information; does it in fact exist? What kind of time pressures is the decision maker under?

In this chapter, some behavioural aspects of decision making theory are considered and illustrated from actual cases. In particular the chapter examines 'intention' and its relation to action, the decision to found a business and behave entrepreneurially. Beyond the founding stage, problems change and so do demands on the founder. To illuminate this issue there follows a discussion of cognitive style – the way in which different people approach decisions. This it is suggested could result in a 'schizophrenic enterprise', the tensions which can arise between the need to be systematic and managerial and the desire (on the part of the founder) to pursue business venturing in an instinctive, intuitive way. Such tensions can become embodied in different personalities, particularly as the business grows beyond the managerial scope of the founder.

As the chapter develops it is also clear that problem-solving is a particular case of decision making. Problems can take on crisis proportions. However, the astute entrepreneur can often turn crises into opportunities. An instance of this kind of behaviour is described through the case of ABC Engineering Ltd. It contains some salutary lessons which are picked up in the ensuing discussion.

The chapter moves on to a consideration of how decisions may be 'framed'. To illustrate this the Miles and Snow theory of 'adaptive strategic choice behaviour' is outlined. This leads naturally into some preliminary thoughts about the issue of risk and uncertainty. Given that business environments are characterized by uncertainty how might risk be viewed and handled? One way of managing and reducing risk is to develop and apply systems of rules consistently. This has the added advantage of increasing the predictability of situations. Finally there is a brief discussion of decision making as an attempt to make sense and impute meaning to particular situations. This is followed by an outline of the curious phenomenon – escalation of decision making – where people seem to become increasingly committed to a course of action despite the fact that it appears to be going wrong. This final section is illustrated by reference to the London Stock Exchange Taurus project, but is likely to strike many chords in the minds of executives who have been involved in decisions to introduce new technologically based systems of operating. First let us turn our thoughts to considering some basic propositions about the nature of decision making.

What is decision making?

According to March[1] decision making is intentional, consequential and optimizing. It is assumed that decisions are based on preferences (wants, needs interests, etc) and expectations of outcomes associated with alternative actions. Decision making is thus about choice amongst alternatives. It is also about thinking; identifying alternatives and selecting that option which, within the limitations of the information at the time, is deemed to be the most appropriate. Decision making in the practical everyday context is thus about judgement based on a consideration of the information that the incumbent is able to glean at a cost, in terms of time and effort, that they are prepared to pay. The theory upon which this common sense appraisal is based has a long and distinguished history.[2]

Of course such a theory of choice assumes that alternatives and the probability distribution of their consequences can be calculated. Moreover, it assumes that the resources and the information channels are available to the decision maker, who wants to make the process explicit. There are practical reasons why such openness would not be attractive in certain cases, for example in an aggressive competitive context. However, organization theorists have challenged the dogma of choice theory on a number of counts. Some of these objections include the difficulty and the costs of paying attention to all one's business goals simultaneously and, whilst it is possible to work out a number of options open to the firm, there are limitations to knowing all associated action possibilities and their consequences. A key issue therefore is what the decision maker chooses to pay attention to. It is likely to comprise:

- the political and organizational context of decision making, especially where there are multiple decision makers with potentially conflicting preferences and interests
- the need to distinguish between routine decision making over which there are rules and standard operating procedures, norms of custom and practice and the difficulties of the non-routine and the innovative[3]
- problems associated with ambiguity in respect of preferences, relevance, history and organizational learning and interpretation.

This set of issues only begins to scratch the surface of the problems of choice within the organization or business context. For example, how does experience and history affect the decision maker's capability? Are decisions likely to be more effective (because the person has learnt from past mistakes) and/or more efficiently arrived at (because a person has learnt how to shortcut the process) or can history and experience obscure rational decision making capability and cloud the judgement (due to the holding of prejudiced beliefs)? What of the size of the undertaking? How can the 'ecology' of decision makers in simple contexts be transposed to suit the ecologically complex contexts of organizations where there are multiple decision makers, multiple strategic goals and variability in organizational learning and competence or *vice versa*? Furthermore, if decisions are ultimately driven by subjective preferences and personal desires, how can an understanding of the processes of decision making be developed without a detailed knowledge and conceptualization of intentional action? Moreover, how can the theory which suggests that organizations *need* to integrate actions and provide coherent solutions to problems be reconciled with the reality of organizational life which indicates that organizations *at best* are working towards achieving overall coherence and integration rather than having accomplished it? Finally, decision theory which suggests that choices and preferences are a given (to be identified) avoids the complications of a behavioural approach, which problematizes those options by arguing that they are open to interpretation and that the meaning attributed to them is mediated and contested through language. To summarize such objections is to point out that decision making can no longer be seen as a wholly rational process but is one in which the dynamics of human behaviour need to be considered.

Intention

Intention appears to be a critical aspect of decision making in the entrepreneurial context. Entrepreneurs intend to found or set up businesses with the objective of capital accumulation and growth. However, the predictive power of intention in respect of expected business performance or other anticipated outcomes raises yet another objection to the assumption of a process based on rational, mechanistic assumptions.[4] It has been argued that 'intentions' work very much like beliefs, that is, there is a subjective probability associated with the strength with which the belief or intention is held.[5] Further, the strength of the intended action will depend on the individual's beliefs about the consequences of that action and his or her evaluation of those consequences. For example, an entrepreneur may intend to make a major investment in upgrading the technological base of the business. If the basis of the belief is that the investment will make the firm highly competitive and the most effective way of developing the business at the time, this assessment will strengthen the entrepreneur's intention to make the investment. However, this only increases the probability or likelihood that the entrepreneur will do it; the situation is still not certain, there may be other events which intervene. Such aspects have been referred to as **normative pressures.**

In order to understand 'normative pressures' one needs to distinguish between social norms (what an individual believes a given collective such as one's peers, customers or industrial association, would choose to do) and personal preferences,[6] which may be at variance with the assumed social norm and are governed by what an individual believes they should do given what they perceive to be other immediate, more greatly valued pressures. So, for example in times of high unemployment there may be a sense created that the socially and politically correct course of action would be to support an investment which would result in increased employment. For a high profile company this might be an important influencing factor. However, the entrepreneur's personal preference suggests that they should take a longer term, strategic view of the business and its viability. The upshot in this hypothetical case is likely to be that the entrepreneur has indeed made the investment in new plant, but it is to be located abroad. This decision is in large part based on the judgement that higher returns on such an investment will be realized.

The example gives the impression that the decision is a solo one – taken by the entrepreneur alone. Even in the microbusiness this is thought to be unlikely. For, even in this context, there will be alternatives, but also various social pressures on decisions. This is clear where there are business partners or family involved. As such there is considerable scope for conflict as illustrated in the vignette of a small alco-pops business (Box 6.1).

Box 6.1: Family decision taking in the alco-pops business

Timothy managed his own small firm in the alco-pops business. Due to a family disagreement over the 'right' strategic direction to take the business, Timothy had pulled out and set up in competition. He was clearly capable of making ruthless decisions and his business was thriving. Perhaps there would come a day when he would buy the original business back, presumably at a very attractive price.

Entrepreneurs are believed to make clear, quick judgements. However, even those individuals not known for a tendency to procrastinate may find themselves faced with some decisions which are less than clear cut. The higher profile given to ethical decision making, social responsibilities and 'green' issues suggests the need for entrepreneurs to consider the wider social context (consider the story recounted in Box 6.2 below).

It is clear that there is considerable scope for conflict over intended decisions which are not the prerogative of a single individual. There is a social context to many business decisions and there is likely to be a host of different influences which shape the normative pressures on the decision takers. These go beyond the rational, clinical, strategic options to a wider consideration of ethical and social responsibilities, as the examples amply illustrate.

Box 6.2: How fans can get in the way of an entrepreneurially owned and managed football club

Football is a dominant world sport. This story is about Newcastle United – a premier division football club – based in the North East of England. It has courted controversy for some years, in part due to its success and it has considerable influence on the culture of the city from where it derives its name.

The heart of the city of Newcastle has a green area known as the Town Moor – a protected area of land where cattle can graze and people can walk. A proposal was put forward some years ago to relocate the club's stadium – St James's Park – on the Town Moor. At one point it appeared that the Town Council was minded to support the proposal but pressure groups were formed. Local action groups and individual protestors demonstrated in prominent places, capturing much media attention and news coverage. The decision, if indeed it had reached a decision, was rescinded. An option to relocate the stadium several miles away just outside the city's boundaries was also rejected. Eventually it was decided to develop the original site. Even then the club courted controversy when it attempted to build corporate entertainment boxes and facilities in an area traditionally occupied by season ticket holders. This became acrimonious as the season ticket holders took the club to court, claiming that their season ticket for the seat included a ten year guarantee. The judge ruled in favour of the club, pointing out that the 'small print' did allow the club to move the season ticket holders to alternative seating with a view to extending the corporate entertainment boxes. This ruling did not satisfy the supporters, who were set to appeal against the judgement. The club, a privately owned and managed business, subsequently made some changes in its directorial board.

It is also clear that the beliefs and the informational basis of those beliefs is fundamental to the subsequent course of action. New information may make a difference as to how the proposed course of action is viewed and whether there are any grounds to the belief that the same course of action should be continued. Furthermore, as the example of Newcastle United Football Club shows, business decisions are embedded in a social context from which the entrepreneur and associates cannot be extracted. The social context and the consequent social interaction affect the attitude to the course of action being considered. Indeed various psychological states can also play a part in the degree of attachment or commitment to the idea. In the example, there was considerable publicly displayed, normative social pressure to prevent the Club's proposals being actioned. This may have had the desired or intended effect of weakening the Club's resolve. As it happened, it did not but, as they might see it, some concessions were made.

Lower profile businesses may not experience the same weight of countervailing force on the decisions which an entrepreneur and/or executive team may wish to push through. The absence of a testing decision context to deflect the entrepreneurial decision away from the intended course may not be to the advantage of the business over the longer term. A sub-optimal decision may be made and it may prove too late to reverse an investment decision (consider the example of Michael's cookie business in Box 6.3).

Box 6.3: Michael's' cookie business

It is said that many entrepreneurs learn from their mistakes. Michael attempted three different business ideas before founding his New Zealand based cookie business. After some initial teething problems and having made a critical decision to involve his brother in the business, the enterprise appeared to go from strength to strength. The brothers decided to purchase a marshmallow factory only to discover that the technology did not work. Eventually the problem was rectified and the opportunity to develop new business exploited. Next the brothers decided to set up a sales manager in Australia with a view to capturing a slice of the market. Was the decision premature or had they simply not thought through the management and control issues associated with this new enterprise? Either way it proved to be a costly mistake. Eventually they cut their losses and parted company with the germinal new venture.

The decision to found

Clearly one of the more important decisions an entrepreneur makes is the decision to found. Greenberger and Sexton[7] suggested that there are factors which moderate an individual's decision to set up a new venture. Such triggers may include sudden redundancy. In addition, situational factors such as support by family, financial support and a supportive environment will influence the decision to found. Learned[8] argued that there are three key influences on the decision to found: propensity to found (principally psychological traits and background factors which make a person more likely to attempt to found a business); intention to found; and sense making, that is the individual must be able to make sense of the information they receive in order to be able to make an appropriate decision to found or not. Hence, it was concluded that not all individuals have the potential to form a new venture. Of those which have, not all will attempt it and of those who attempt it, not all will succeed.

Bird[9] also confined herself largely to discussing the intention to set up a business. She argues that entrepreneurial intentions are underpinned by a combination of rational/analytic and intuitive thinking. Intentions are rational in so far as they are goal-directed and guided by an explicit strategic planning process. They are intuitive to the extent that action is a response to a 'hunch' or a vision and guided by an implicit strategy.[10] However, Boyd and Vozikis[11] have modified Bird's model by pointing out that a person's beliefs also have an influence on a person's subsequent behaviour. Beliefs are 'stored information', which shape attitudes and intentions to the behaviour – in the case in question – to found a business. However, that is not all, they argue further that a person must believe in their own ability or effectiveness if they are to carry out their intentions. Positive experiences, modelling oneself on successful others, positive feedback and encouragement and a person's physiological state (such as being highly anxious) will affect their feelings of self-efficacy. In other words, intention is not enough, the would-be founder must believe they can do it.

The decision to behave entrepreneurially

Naffziger and others[12] have taken into consideration the pre- and post-start up influences on the decision process. The pre-start up factors include (a) the entrepreneur's personal characteristics such as personality traits, (b) the entrepreneur's personal environment, for example family or employment situation, (c) the relevant business environment such as societal attitudes, the economic climate and access to funds, (d) the business idea and its evaluation and (e) the entrepreneur's goals, for instance what do they seek to accomplish – rapid growth, life style, cash out, retirement? Beyond this they argue that there must be a strong perceived link between the founder's managerial strategies and firm performance outcomes. Thus, if a founder did not believe that what they were doing would lead to successful outcomes, they would be unlikely to proceed. Furthermore, in considering the expected outcomes, the entrepreneur must believe that they will at least meet their expectations. Hence the likelihood of achieving certain outcomes will affect go/no-go decisions and future entrepreneurial activity.

The schizophrenic enterprise

Moving through the transition from founding a venture to managing the fledgling firm is a particularly difficult process, demanding adjustment to a different set of decisions and problems. Some firms and the individuals managing them may find this a tough experience. One problem is that of resolving the different ways that decisions may be approached. Should the owner-manager continue with their intuitive style and how might they integrate the thinking of others?

Research has suggested that the two hemispheres of the brain specialize: the left hemisphere emphasizes analytical, logical thinking whereas the right hemisphere is specialized for synthesis, integrating many inputs simultaneously and holistically.[13] People have preferred thinking styles though they can draw on a mixture of approaches.[14] Recent studies have suggested that successful entrepreneurs of high growth companies tend to have a preferred cognitive style, which is intuitive.[15] However, it is unlikely that all co-workers will operate in this way. Indeed a balanced 'partnership' may include contrasting styles of thought and behaviour.

In Figure 6.1 the left hand side of the diagram represents the rational analytic, linear process of thinking. It is likely to result in more formal approaches consistent with a managerial, planning style of decision making whereas the right hand side represents an intuitive, entrepreneurial style. It is governed by the ability to envision future possibilities and to create that future by taking decisions that amount to an implicit strategy focused and goal directed towards opportunity realization. Further, the entrepreneur's intentions to act are mediated by their personal values and beliefs and their attitude towards the intended action. This is consistent with the idea that it is rather more difficult to separate the entrepreneur from the company so that there tends to be a rather personalized idiosyncratic character to the firm and its culture.

The new venture, however, needs to be managed. Some entrepreneurs purposively attempt to develop such skills (for example Henri Strzelecki[16]) whereas others may delegate such tasks, for example by putting someone in charge of office management and administration. The formula of identifying a 'right hand person' can work well though they are usually handpicked or even poached! The requirement is for someone who is organized, systematic and logical in their approach – in other words a 'left-brain' person.

As the firm develops and becomes more professionally managed, the entrepreneur and founder has a choice of whether to adapt their style and grow with the company or disengage in order to found a new venture. Until such a time there may be a degree of discomfort between founder and senior management. For example, the board or senior team may create 'normative pressure' for actions to be taken in accordance with their agenda and/or business plans, which they may have had carefully documented. It would not be the first occasion in which a lone entrepreneur has had to battle it out amongst his or her boardroom colleagues who have arrived at different action alternatives through very different modes of thought (for example the now defunct firm Coloroll).

It should not be surprising that an entrepreneur will want to maintain tight control over business decision making for as long as possible. In this imagined (but very probable) context the entrepreneur needs to develop tactics and skills for handling his or her management team. This will be enabled if the entrepreneur has personal charisma – the ability through charm and presence to inspire people, the ability to construct persuasive arguments to influence colleagues and win them over, and the ability to galvanize support and respect. This highly personalized approach may be sufficient to counter the pressures from others resulting in actions which will have consequences for the firm.

Problem solving

A further aspect of decision making is problem solving. A problem may be considered to be the *perceived* context in which an individual chooses a course of action. It is perceived because problem identification is about how an individual chooses to construe a situation. The owner-manager who is intent on growing their business may perceive the situation in positive terms such as, for example presenting an opportunity. On the other hand, a stronger currency, the advent of another supplier or the development of a new competitive product by a rival firm are likely to be perceived as threats to the business.

Thus, a problem may be defined as the difference between an actual and a desired situation, whereas problem *solving* is the process of identifying a discrepancy between an actual and a desired state of affairs and taking action to resolve it.

An opportunity is an occasion offering a possibility. It may be argued therefore that it is the context which presents difficulties. Once such difficulties are

Figure **6.1** A schema of the decision process in the new venture

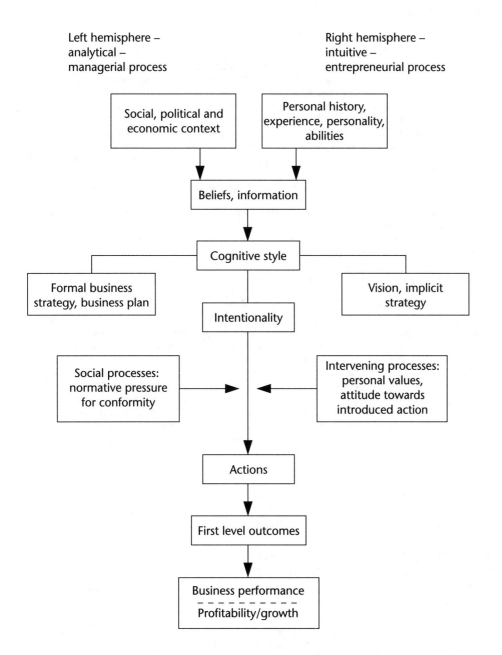

worked through the situation may be perceived as one which presents new possibilities to be exploited to advantage. The entrepreneur attempts to change the problem he or she is facing into an opportunity (see Box 6.4).

Box 6.4: Creating an opportunity out of a crisis

ABC Ltd: A tale of an engineering jobbing shop

ABC Ltd was a partnership up to the Spring of 1999. The two senior partners and founders had built the firm from nothing over the past 40 years to an employment level of 25 when crisis struck. A major customer (responsible for 45 per cent of their business) tried to renegotiate the terms on which they did business. The new relationship would have been more intrusive on the part of the customer, giving them in effect 'inside' knowledge of ABC's accounts, gross margins on jobs, etc. The upshot would have meant greater dependency, with the customer dictating the terms of future jobs, including how they would be priced. This was unacceptable to the senior partners, Bob and Jim. They decided that the solution was to part company with this particular customer. Thus over the next three months as the extraction process took effect ABC lost 45 per cent of its custom.

This crisis meant that the business could no longer support 18 shop floor workers and it needed new customers – and fast!

The management – Bob and Jim – and their two sons took the decision to incorporate the business. The management team plus the senior partners' wives became ABC Ltd's directors. They kept on the foreman who had been with them for 13 years and trimmed the shop floor to just five employees.

As 'hands-on' managers, the self-appointed directors got on the 'phone, having identified likely sources of custom and rebuilt the customer base. Now, 18 months on, the company may take on one or two new shop floor hands as the existing employees have been consistently working overtime for some months.

Management have discovered that the 'crisis' has had some beneficial effects. First they observed a 15 per cent rise in productivity. Second, they found that the business was being revitalized. Furthermore, they could now start to plan ahead. They moved into better premises with a view to future expansion. They were anticipating registering with ISO9000 because (a) they already had complete traceability of jobs and (b) they expected that this move would improve their ability to secure and develop their customer base. Further, Jim had effectively retired – certainly from the day to day management of the company. His partner Bob was also looking forward to his own retirement and was actively planning for the succession of the two sons. This gave a positive vitality to the business and a 'buzz' of activity as the team forged ahead with their vision of a new tomorrow.

Owner-managers, as discussed in an earlier part of this chapter, can vary considerably in their cognitive and affective style towards the way they approach and view decision contexts. They can:

- **Avoid** problems by ignoring information ... (the 'ostrich' syndrome)
- **React** to problems after they have occurred ... ('crisis management')
- **Seek** problems that is be proactive, anticipate problems before they occur ... ('anticipatory management').

They can also (as discussed in relation to Figure 6.1) approach problems **systematically** (that is, analytically) or **intuitively**.

To be **systematic** is to unpack the problem into its logical components and deal with it in a step by step fashion. This is purportedly typical of the large corporation though senior management increasingly has to respond quickly to new uncertainties. Under such circumstances they may respond intuitively.[17]

Intuitive thinking however is much more flexible and spontaneous than rational-analytic thinking. It enables owner-managers to respond holistically and imaginatively to problems. Hence they deal with many aspects of the problem at once and may respond to 'hunches' (having a feeling of what is the right thing to do) This method works well in situations of uncertainty and ambiguity. For instance, Bob saw the crisis ABC faced with its major customer holistically and dealt with it as such. Once the decision to part company had been made then the solution was obvious but not easy. It was however achievable and ABC succeeded in the end though at an initial cost.

It is clear that owner-managers have to deal with a range of situations. Problems vary in their enormity, type and content. As is now apparent, not all business problems are by any means financial. Setting aside the crisis faced by ABC, owner-managers may have difficulties from time to time managing their business partner(s), the workforce, key customers and various aspects of business development such as those associated with rapid expansion and over-trading or decline due to the inability to attract sufficient orders.

Owner-managers, also, are not only managers of their own business, they also have a personal life which may impact on business activity. Whatever the problem context the owner-manager needs to have a deep understanding of each aspect of the process. This includes, first and foremost, a true understanding of what the problem is and its possible causes. This presents the owner-manager and the firm with a learning opportunity. For example, Bob knew (especially with hindsight) that to have 45 per cent of the business with one customer was a mistake. For some firms it could have meant the loss of a customer in a different sense but in the case of ABC Ltd it increased the possibility of interdependence, with an imbalance of power and the smaller player having to dance to whatever tune the dominant firm wished to play. Thus, having identified why the problem arose, Bob needed to move quickly on to the identification of possible solutions. This required the generation of further information – by using Yellow Pages, new potential sources of customer were identified.

In any problem solving situation, an important consideration is to decide how much time to devote to each step. Bob crossed the Rubicon. It is difficult to see once he had made the decision to part with their major customer what other options were ahead. However not all problems take this form. Often there are options and the owner-manager may take a 'best bet' approach and test out a solution to the point where it clearly represents the correct way forward or not. Owner-managers often use valued customers, their accountant or family (where the business involves family) as a source of feedback and advice. Once a decision is reached it must be communicated and implemented. At this juncture the management of the problem and its solution may be wholly or partially delegated. How it is handled will depend on a number of factors including the seriousness of the situation and the presence of a competent other to whom delegation is a realistic possibility. Where it is considered to be critical then the owner-manager is likely to take an active interest in the resolution of the difficulty, monitoring results until the desired outcome is achieved.

An attribute of the entrepreneur is their information seeking behaviour; scanning the environment to identify opportunities and in some cases to create opportunities. Managers also need to develop this skill; to create and not merely respond to opportunities.[18] This is likely to mean that as owner-managed companies increase in size they need to develop entrepreneurial skills in their lower management team. Unstructured situations, ambiguity and uncertainty facilitate the creation of opportunity. Managers, on the whole, tend to deal with structured situations. The problems which arise are likely to be structured, that is familiar and straightforward, where it is clear what information is needed for their resolution. This facilitates planning ahead. Where conditions are stable, the ability to deal with familiar problems in a routine way creates efficiency. Problems can be dealt with by means of standard solutions. However, there are drawbacks; such 'routinization' tends to create complacency and the misguided belief in one way of approaching and managing problems. Hence it was clear in the case of ABC Ltd, prior to the 'crisis' it had dealt routinely with its major customer. The company had become complacent and this showed itself in a lack of concern by management of the prevalence of low productivity.

The unusual and unfamiliar raise problems which require new solutions. This creates a sense of urgency and alertness and the need to develop contingency plans to deal with such scenarios. It also means that close attention needs to be given to the specifics of the situation. Occasionally a problem, as illustrated, may take on the proportions of a crisis. A crisis is not only an unanticipated problem, it is one which may lead to disaster if not dealt with speedily and correctly. The situation may present a real test of an individual's judgement, decisiveness, diagnostic and leadership skills. Bob and ABC Ltd came through on all counts. Clearly any problem can be worsened if the diagnosis is incorrect or the focus is on solving the symptoms, not the cause. Sound diagnosis means dealing with the correct problem and to do this efficiently and effectively means setting priorities in order to deal with the most important problems first. ABC Ltd had to deal virtually simultaneously with the need to rationalize the workforce, rebuild the customer base and protect the remaining partners, employees and jobs.

The problem for a partnership but also for any self-employed individual is that they often bear both the responsibility and total cost of any decision made. But in the limited liability company, the responsibility for business situations arising in the first place and the consequences of any decision taken, are likely to be shared. Nonetheless, where other people are involved, possibly as employees and in particular where it has consequences for them, they will want to know why a particular decision was taken. In small enterprises like ABC Ltd it is likely that everyone knows. But such transparency may not always be evident. TSL Ltd, a small software house, was entrepreneurially led. The owner-manager dealt with a Scandinavian based client and he failed to articulate his vision for the company's future development. The workforce felt insecure, there was a high turnover of staff and consequently performance was lower than it need have been. Hence a problem with the intuitively based decision is that the decision maker may fail to communicate their decisions, they cannot always articulate the thought process and judgmental steps taken to reach their solution – the way forward they have envisioned. Not only do others feel excluded, they have no basis for feeling confidence in the proffered solution. An act of faith appears to be required!

Whilst formality renders the treatment of problems to systematic scrutiny, it may also mean that problems are shared at least by some in the company. The formal analysis of problems, for example using cost-benefit analysis, has the advantage of openness. It involves comparing the costs and benefits of each course of action. However, even where sophisticated quantitative techniques are used to evaluate alternatives, human judgement is involved to ensure that the right criteria are applied. Apart from asking what are the benefits and what are the costs of pursuing a particular course, other criteria include:

- **timeliness**, for example in respect of a new product launch
- **acceptability**, to other stakeholders who are involved
- **ethical soundness**, to what extent is mine or my company's reputation at stake?

As companies grow, their problems tend to change and so too do the types of approaches that become more or less attractive to their managers. Often there is much more at stake and the intuitive 'gut reaction' is generally still perceived to be the more risky and least preferred approach.

Framing the decision

It is rare that business decisions are discrete and have no wider implications. Owner-managers, indeed 'firms', are said to develop a particular orientation to a problem/opportunity which arises from past experience and their strategic perspective.[19] Miles and Snow[20] developed a theory of adaptive strategic choice behaviour in relation to the resolution of three problems: the entrepreneurial, the engineering and the administrative problems. An organization, that is, its top management, could adopt a particular strategic orientation to those problems. They suggested that there were evident three strategic types which they labelled **defenders**, **analysers** and **prospectors**. Table 6.1 shows some of the key differences between these types.

Defenders and prospectors tend to fall at the extremes of a continuum. The prospector could be said to be operating in the entrepreneurial domain, in a dynamic and uncertain environment, whereas the opposite is true for the defender. The analyser falls half way along and shares characteristics of each. The stark differences in problem orientation between the prospector and defender also result in different strategies for exploiting opportunities, different solutions to problems and a different cost-benefit basis for the decision taken.

Prospectors tend to run higher risks. They are primarily innovators who wish to maintain a reputation for product-market development. They scan a

Table **6.1** Problem orientation of the strategic types – prospectors, analysers and defenders

	Strategic type		
PROBLEM ORIENTATION	**PROSPECTOR**	**ANALYSER**	**DEFENDER**
Entrepreneurial problem	How to locate and exploit new product and market opportunities.	How to locate and exploit new product and market opportunities while simultaneously maintaining a firm base of traditional products and customers.	How to 'seal off' a portion of the total market to create a stable set of products and customers.
Engineering problem	How to avoid long-term commitments to a single technological process.	How to be efficient in stable portions of the domain and flexible in changing portions.	How to produce and distribute goods or services as efficiently as possible.
Administrative problem	How to facilitate and coordinate numerous and diverse operations.	How to differentiate the organization's structure and processes to accommodate both stable and dynamic areas of operations.	How to maintain strict control of the organization in order to ensure efficiency.

Source: Miles and Snow 1978 (see note 20)

broad area in order to locate new areas of opportunity and they are creators of change. The risks are that they may over extend their resources and the outcome may be low profitability. The defender, on the other hand, tends to operate primarily in stable markets, exploiting markets through increased penetration and new product development incrementally. The strategy is one of achieving efficiency of operations and may include vertical integration. They tend to adopt a mechanistic approach to structure and process in contrast to the flexibility and adaptability of the prospector.

In Miles and Snow's terminology senior managers adopt a particular orientation towards strategic choice which determines the kinds of decisions they are likely to make and solutions they will probably adopt. The nature of the risks associated with these contrasting orientations vary accordingly. Such an analysis is redolent of Stevenson's distinction between the 'promoter' whose strategic orientation is 'opportunity driven' and the 'trustee' with a 'resource driven' strategy.[21]

A further approach to the framing of decisions has been developed by Mintzberg.[22] He distinguishes between three different concepts of the term 'strategy'.

- Strategy as a **plan** – a consciously intended course of action.
- Strategy as a **pattern** – a stream of actions which are consistent.
- Strategy as a **position** – a means of locating the organization in its environment, e.g. its product-market domain, its 'niche'.

The owner-manager may (although it is unlikely) be operating with a formal strategic plan in which all the decisions taken are outlined and to which all members of the firm are committed. Much more likely however is the situation where the owner-manager makes decisions which are implicitly strategic in that they are internally consistent. This strategy may not be intended, it may simply emerge.

The decision environment: risk

The limits to an individual's or group's knowledge and the complexity of the environment in which decisions are taken suggest that all decisions are taken in situations of some degree of uncertainty and risk. 'Uncertainty arises from incomplete information, randomness, or unpredictability of events.'[23] Business planning helps manage uncertainty. However, the idea that the environment is a source of information to which probabilities can be attached seems far too simplistic. Other considerations are the stability and turbulence of the environment. Even so, this raises some interesting questions about the degree of foresight owner-managers and executives of firms may be expected to demonstrate. Crisis can occur suddenly. Moreover firms may be faced with a choice. For example ABC Ltd could have opted for a stable, routine, predictable situation by sticking with its major customer (and this would have continued as long as its major customer's competitive position in their market was assured), or the less stable option which they in fact chose, to 'go it alone' and experience the risk and uncertainty.

What has become evident is that the greater the instability and turbulence of the environment, the more flexible, adaptable and responsive the organizational action must be.[24] What is clear is that organizations must cope with uncertainty if they are to be effective and ensure their long term viability.

But how do people view risk?

March and Shapira[25] argue that the way chief executives view risk is very different from the way risk is presented in decision theory. These senior executives do not consider the probability distributions of all possible outcomes of their choice. Rather, there are three key differences.

- A risky choice is one that contains a threat of a very poor outcome, in other words it focuses on the negative and ignores the positives.
- Risk is not primarily a probability concept, it is about the amount that might be lost, that is it is not risk aversion but loss aversion or regret aversion.
- Executives show little desire to reduce risk to a single quantifiable construct, that is they show little desire to quantify the risk.

Risk taking propensity varies across individuals and situations due to differences in incentives and experience. People are encouraged to take risks as they take on more senior positions. However, organizational life inhibits risk taking and executives are willing only to take calculated risks, recognizing that there is an emotional investment in taking risks. They believe that fewer risks should be taken when things are going well and that survival of the business should not be risked. This is consistent with the attitude of young start up owner-managers whose view is that they have little to lose, compared with the owner-manager in the established business who can identify very clearly what he or she now has to lose.

On the whole risks are avoided by viewing them as being manageable, having the confidence to believe that they can be controlled. Interestingly executives distinguish sharply between gambling and risk taking. Gambling is simply unacceptable. In starting up a high risk venture, the entrepreneur does not present his or her decision as having gambled on his or her judgement, rather it is presented with the supreme confidence that the venture is going to succeed. It is not unknown for the marital partner to be the one who lies awake at night worrying about the risks involved! Having embarked on a course of action, one ploy is to reject the estimates of failure, to make efforts to revise these estimates by seeking new information and to continue to believe that they can 'beat the odds'. Risk is thus accepted because it is not believed that it will have to be borne.

Clearly, in practice executives display a considerable degree of insensitivity to probability estimates. They either do not understand, trust or use such estimates, though it is acknowledged that estimating the probabilities of outcomes is fraught with difficulties. What is apparent is the way in which executives focus their attention. The problem/opportunity may be simplified by focusing upon only a few key aspects at a time. Thus understanding action in the face of incomplete information may be about where the individual chooses to focus their attention rather than about the decision *per se*. Here one can see the tendency of the entrepreneur to refocus on opportunities, whereas the executive in a context of risk aversion will focus upon the dangers inherent in a particular course of action. Aspiration levels to succeed rather than fail will affect the focus of attention and risk preference.

Deciding how to decide

As is now apparent there is more than one model of decision making. Indeed it would broadly appear that there are three: the classical, the so-called administrative and the heuristic. The **classical** or rational decision making model assumes certainty and the ability to select the optimal solution whereas the **administrative** model recognizes the limits to human cognitive ability. Here rationality is bounded by the information available. Decisions made tend to be satisficing decisions because they involve choosing the most satisfactory alternative that comes to the decider's attention. In contrast, **judgemental heuristics** are simplifying strategies for decision making. People may use information which is readily available and thus introduce biases into the decision making process.

March[26] summarizes a set of contested issues which affect how a person understands and theorizes about decision making behaviour in organizations.

- Whether decisions are to be viewed as **choice-based** or **rule-based**. Is decision making about the logic of making choices amongst alternatives or is it about the logic of appropriateness, fulfilling roles and following rules?
- Whether decision making is typified by **clarity** and **consistency** or by **ambiguity** and **inconsistency**.
- Whether decision making is an **instrumental activity** or an **interpretative** activity.
- Whether outcomes of decision processes are seen as attributable primarily to **autonomous actors** or to the systemic properties of an **interacting ecology**.

Rational decision making is bounded by individual and organizational constraints. The classical version of theories of rational choice assumes that guesses are improbably precise. Furthermore, attempting to predict future preferences is problematic in practice. This is because it is possible for individuals to hold inconsistent and conflicting preferences. Moreover, preferences are often stated imprecisely and they can change over time. Preferences may thus be constructed or developed within this ambiguous context and hence are difficult to predict.

Risk taking is affected by human bias in making estimates of the risk involved, individual propensity to take risk in conditions of success or failure and the reliability of organizational actions. Within an organizational culture which is low on trust and where actions are perceived to be unreliable decisions will be seen to be risky. Risk taking is also influenced by an individual's target or aspiration level. Being above target results in greater risk taking because failure is unlikely due to the larger 'cushion', moreover the individual may be less attentive and less focused. On the other hand, as actions fall further and further below target, decisions will become more conservative and fewer risks will be taken.[27] Nevertheless where an individual chooses to pitch is of interest.

Most business environments are considered to be uncertain in the sense that uncertainty is largely judged to be a consequence of operating in an unpredictable world, incomplete knowledge of any specific aspect relevant business and economic affairs and, interestingly, the inability to negotiate contracts with key individuals. In the latter case the constraint is often a lack of strategic information, for example knowing and understanding what the competition is likely to do. It suggests a 'do nothing' decision outcome.

There is an alternative decision logic which is associated with rule-following – the logic of appropriateness, duty and obligation. This does not suggest an entrepreneurial mind-set. However, organizational behaviour is typified with actions of conformity, routine and acquiescence. Even in the small non-bureaucratic firm the employee usually wishes to please the boss, one too many challenges to their authority is likely to result in the two parties parting company. Hence working out what actions are appropriate to the situation and to their position (and hence their personal identity within that context) can be important.

Rules develop over time. They are chosen or adopted consciously and are accepted rationally. Management develops systems for the flow of work which are rule-governed, occasionally idiosyncratically so. Sometimes they recognize the need for an externally validated system of rules such as the introduction of ISO9000. Rules also receive modifications based on feedback and in this sense organizational learning takes place.[28]

Other types of rule become a basis for the particular culture of an organization, its way of doing and going about its business. 'This is how we do things around here' is also prescriptive. It tells people how they should behave. Moreover, classes of decision may be copied and imitated by decision makers in other organizations; decisions – the basis for action – are contagious, particularly where they are seen to be 'winning decisions'. 'They have one therefore we'll have one' or ' ...we'll *have to* have one ...' (rider – if the company is to stay competitive and in business).

Rules can become invariant though they may evolve over time. The professional manager's actions, for example are guided by reference to principles which are rules that concern the proper basis for action. However in some situations – crises for example – normal rules may no longer apply. This is certainly the case *in extremis* such as when the receiver has been called in to a company. Furthermore, no system of the application of rules is perfect; there may be inconsistencies and there is usually scope for interpretation and self-interested calculation.

Sense-making

Faced with uncertainty, it seems obvious that owner-managers will need to make sense of the external cues and information they are receiving.[29] Hence, a current view of decision making is that it is about sense-making[30] and the construction of meaning. So how do individuals process information to provide meaning? They decompose problems, focus on certain aspects and ignore others and work backwards from desired outcomes. How do they give meaning to their aspirations? Particular preferences are evoked and others ignored and targets are set. Achieving those targets is intimately tied up with the individual's identity and their aspirations.

The rational theory of decision making has assumed that decision makers are concerned with outcomes upon which actions are predicated. However, the sense-making theory of decision making suggests a re-emphasis away from action to the process, the generation of meaning. Decision making becomes a 'meaning factory' rather than an 'action factory'.[31] Hence negotiating one's way through life may be more concerned with interpretation than with making choices.

A further problem with the rational decision making model is that it concerns the individual decision maker and ignores the context of conflict, confusion and complexity in which that decision is made. This highlights the importance of social interaction and the 'ecology' of decision making. It means that it is important to consider the inconsistent preferences amongst a group, team or other collectivity and perhaps even more salient it means that decision making is organized by time rather than by causality.

In this particular vision of organizational life how are decisions made and conflicting preferences resolved? Collectivities are interconnected in multifarious ways. Within the firm conflicting demands are resolved through the price mechanism for labour, capital or goods. Hence there is a process of exchange in which the entrepreneur or chief executive negotiates deals so that business goals are met, wages are paid and there is a return on investment. The outcome is one of ordered priorities, rules governing hierarchy and subordination and the creation of identities. Hence identity, position and action are all negotiated through reaching understandings about ways of behaving which are consistent with a set of rules and translating those understandings into actions.

Escalation in decision making

From the foregoing, the idea that decision making is a totally rational process devoid of bias is clearly untenable. But what on the face of it is puzzling is that people can become increasingly committed to a course of action even after it has gone wrong. This 'escalation of commitment' in which further 'corrective' actions can only worsen the situation presents a particular dilemma: how does one explain why people throw good money after bad?

One of the key conditions is that people make decisions in conditions of uncertainty; they do not know the consequences of their decision, nor are they able to calculate the likelihood of particular outcomes. Staw[32] in seeking explanations of the escalation phenomenon drew the following conclusions.

He suggested that there are multiple causes of escalation. They include the economics of the investment decision associated with the particular project, psychological aspects such as optimism and the illusion of control, self-justification, the effects of risk preference and the psychological impact of sunk-costs on calculations of future action, social aspects such as having to account to others for one's actions and persistence which in other contexts would be highly valued, organizational determinants such as institutional inertia and finally, contextual factors to be found within the organization's environment, for example government policies or key firms who are large employers in a locality.

Escalation phenomena occur over time, they are not about snap decisions and escalation may arise out of action or inaction. Phase 1 tends to be dominated by the economics of the project. Estimates are made of the likely costs. However, such estimates may be biased by over optimism and enthusiasm which create an illusion of control over situations which are likely to be influenced by outside forces. Phase 2 commences when questionable or negative results are received (such as the unlikelihood of finishing on time and a revision of the estimate indicating the magnitude of likely losses to be incurred). At this juncture persistence and self justification commences. The costs assume importance and key individuals wish to save face. The losses mount. Phase 3 occurs as outside parties begin to notice. Contextual and organizational forces take hold. Opinion is mobilized against dropping the project as the consequences are rehearsed.

The time period over which escalation occurs allows a slow souring and for social and behavioural factors to take hold of decision making. If the economics of the project were known and understood at the outset then it is unlikely that the project would have received the go-ahead. But it is likely that behavioural factors play a part at an early stage, colouring views and calculations upon which the decision to mount the project are based. There is also a logical sequencing of effects according to Staw,[33] who argues that, while projects usually start with the vision and backing of an individual (e.g. product champion or entrepreneur), as the project develops social factors take over as others become involved and committed to the project. Finally, as the project matures organizational and possibly macro forces may come into play.

Drummond[34] published a case study of 'Taurus', the now notorious IT venture commissioned by the London Stock Exchange. Taurus was intended to replace London's antiquated share settlement procedures with a state-of-the-art electronic system. After three years the project collapsed at a cost to the Stock Exchange and the City of London of about £500 million. Drummond's monograph documents the events which led to the abandonment of Taurus and the resignation of Peter Rawlins, the then chief executive of the Stock Exchange. It is, as Drummond puts it, 'a salutary tale' but one from which lessons can be learnt.

Drummond emphasizes the need to take a 'multi-paradigm approach' in order to understand the multiple layers of complexity which characterize the Taurus project. At the macro level she argues for the importance of understanding the influence of the 'deep structure of power' of the Establishment which, in this case, comprised the conflicting agendas of the securities industry and the Stock Exchange. At a 'meso-level' Drummond describes the problem as 'the tragedy of the commons', that is, 'Taurus is destroyed by everyone pursuing their respective and sometimes conflicting interests.'[35] Thirdly, at the micro level, 'persistence emerges as the product of organizational and project forces which restrict decision makers' options.[36] Furthermore, 'face saving behaviour' she argues, is a *symptom* of loss of control, not a cause. Also contrary to theory it was evident that there was a high degree of commitment to the project at the very early stages and at that juncture the chief executive was unable to stop the project. But withdrawal from the project was not simply about information, it was about how power was used to explode one myth and replace it with another: ' ... information is potentially putty in the hands of decision makers ... Information serves as the basis for a competing rationale. However, it is not the information *per se* which is decisive but how it is interpreted and used.'[37]

Conclusions

It is clear that decision making is critically important to business practice. But making decisions is not easy if the decision maker wishes to make the 'right decision', given the information that it was possible to glean at the time. Certainly there are a great many problems of choice to be considered. However, this should not paralyse the organization into inaction, rather increased awareness of possible pitfalls will hone the senses to what are the realistic options.

This chapter has considered some of the influences which play a part in the effectiveness of decision taking. It is not sufficient to have strong intentions, there are social, behavioural and other pressures which should lead the decision taker to consider how they might introduce the decision or if indeed there is not another set of options that they may have overlooked. Secondly, it is clear that mistakes will be made. The conclusion is to learn the lesson and do what is necessary to avoid the same mistake being repeated. Third, the decision maker must believe in their ability to make a good decision – one which will 'stick' and have the desired effects. Self-confidence and self-efficacy[38] would appear to be important personal attributes which can be acquired. They can be developed and there is nothing like success to boost a person's confidence.

Fourth, and related to the last point, self-knowledge and self-awareness appear to be important if the executive is to continue to be effective, for example knowing one's 'cognitive style', that is whether one prefers to take decisions intuitively or in a systematic analytical way. Further, there may be consequences of clashes between senior staff who have strong but very different preferred ways of thinking about and arriving at decisions. This, it was suggested, may result in a 'schizophrenic enterprise'!

The fifth lesson that this chapter illustrates is not to allow a problem to result in defeat. It is possible to turn problems round and, as was the case with ABC Ltd, create an opportunity out of a crisis. This has implications for the leadership qualities of the executive such as their ability to be decisive, their judgement and the soundness of their diagnostic skills – drawing on tacit knowledge and demonstrating a thorough understanding of the situation being faced.

A sixth lesson which emerges is that of the need to share problems and decisions with the workforce. In a time of crisis it is particularly important for people to know and there is a heightened sense of insecurity which needs to be dealt with.

It is also clear that decisions are rarely discrete – the seventh lesson – they are framed by past experience and strategic choices. Once again it is evident that different types of executive will approach choice of strategy differently and that this will have implications for the kind of operational decisions taken.

An eighth issue tackled in this chapter is the need for executives and others to be aware of the nature of risk and its behavioural consequences. The lesson here emerged from the knowledge that individuals choose to focus their attention differently, for example on potential opportunities or inherent dangers. Certainly if a person is to take a positive view of the degree of risk it is crucial that they know how their actions will 'pull it off' otherwise pursuing such a course will appear to be mere foolhardiness.

There are ways of reducing the riskiness of situations and so the ninth lesson is the importance of developing a system of rules that enable the routine to be dealt with systematically so that attention can be focused upon the problematic, non-routine occurrences. Furthermore it is always worth remembering, as this chapter also brings out, that there is always more than one perspective on a problem. In attempting to make sense of it, people place their own construction on it. Hence, particularly in larger organizations, decisions can become politicized. The tenth lesson therefore is the need to develop an understanding of how to manage the politics of decision making.

Finally it is concluded that decision making is a much less rational process than many people would like to think. Whilst this point is illustrated throughout the chapter, it is also evident in the phenomenon of 'escalation in decision making'. Clearly there are many lessons to be learnt by executives who find themselves entering into a decision to commit resources to an uncertain project where costs may escalate and the ability of the contractor to deliver become highly problematic.

Exercise

Write your own case study which illustrates at least one decision making situation discussed in this chapter. Describe the context of the decision, the sequence of actions taken and by whom and identify the outcome(s) Now discuss what decision should have been taken and why.

CHAPTER 7

Motivation and control

Why should a person seek self-employment rather than to be employed? And once self-employed what is there to motivate them to remain in business for themselves? These are two of the crucial questions that are asked of owner-managers. Another is how, once the business is up and running, do owner-managers motivate other people?

There have been a great many general theories of motivation which have been variously divided into need, reinforcement, social learning, equity, expectancy and goal theories.[1] Such theories have been derived from and applied to individuals in large company organizational contexts that are established rather than emergent.[2] However, applying motivation theories to emergent organizations raises some interesting additional questions. For example if it is harder work, more stressful and initially, at least, unlikely to be financially rewarding what is it that motivates someone to start their own business? If that level of effort has to be maintained over a number of years, what are the incentives to sustain an individual and motivate them to remain in business? How can such behaviour which, on the face of it, appears to be contrary to expectations, be explained? In this chapter these questions will be approached through a combination of critical examination of theory, research and illustrative case material. First of all, the question why anyone would want to be self-employed is considered by studying a real case and then by reviewing the theory. This addresses the reasons why someone might take a particular course of action. Next the process of motivation and control are examined in a complex model that links actions and outcomes – both personal and business. The evidence in support of role motivation theories is then critically evaluated. Particularly problematic for such theories is the extent to which they may be 'culture-bound'. A provocative case is included to raise questions about cultural differences. The chapter then considers how owner-managers and entrepreneurs might motivate and control the people they employ. This can be achieved by the right style of management and clear goal-setting behaviour. Finally, the importance of context is reinforced through a detailed examination of the behavioural and motivational effects of operating a small firm which is interdependently linked within a Small-Firm-Network structure. But first the very interesting case of Ann David is presented.

Ann David's case is a reminder of the importance of context – both environmental and cultural. Kenya's economy is developing. What this means for the new business start up like Ann's is that basic infrastructure such as a supply of electricity or provision of a workspace cannot be taken for granted. Establishing a business under such conditions – literally from scratch – is

Box 7.1: Ann David's carpentry workshop, Kenya[3]

When this case study was prepared in the mid 1980s Ann David was 27 years of age. She had had educational and career aspirations to study at university and to secure a job in the media, neither of which had been realized. Instead she became an untrained teacher until she married in 1986 and started a family. With four children to care for she was eventually unable to continue her teaching position.

In 1988 she and her husband set up a small trading business buying maize from rural areas and selling it to the Cereals Board. Unfortunately the business failed after just 12 months, leaving the couple in debt. Ann's husband had to continue in employment in order to pay off the debt. Their next move was renting a plot of land just big enough for Ann to use as a site for a carpentry workshop. Initially the workshop had posts but no roof and no electricity and Ann and the two carpenters she hired had to work under the scorching sun.

She received two orders, but no payment for the work. The resultant bad debt put Ann out of business again. This time though she had learnt a lesson: never give credit! She started up again making stools and chairs, and the business slowly recovered. Four months later she approached the government economic development agency KIE for a loan. In order to secure the loan she had to produce a business plan. She had some business training and learnt how to prepare such a plan. The loan was granted. It enabled her to cut her own wood, install a lathe in a friend's workshop where there was electricity and expand the number of people she employed to five. However, it was hard work servicing two loans and there were a number of difficulties on the way. The deal with her friend did not work out and it took Ann a further 18 months to find a way to install electricity in her own workshop.

Still short of capital, Ann applied for a third loan from a financier. This was to fund another machine and working capital. By the time the loan came through after several reapplications she had assembled another home made machine – a circular saw – and fully roofed her shed.

By this time she had three machines in operation and she was employing seven people full time. She also used casual workers to help smooth out the fluctuations caused by big orders. She was now in a position to repay the KIE loan and her business was at last established. She continued with her own business training, developing her knowledge of bookkeeping and banking. She had also developed plans to buy another plot of land and erect a small factory to house her joinery business. She saw this as an opportunity to absorb some of the Kenyan youth and to develop their sense of self reliance. But apart from this pro-social motive, she felt proud to be the woman owner of a business in an industry that was normally dominated by men.

hard. Yet Ann persisted. So what motivated her? The livelihood that she made was a matter of survival if she was to provide for her family. She also had debts. Her earlier ambitions had been thwarted yet there was still the basic drive to make something of her life, to achieve something for herself and others. Further, what is the evidence that Ann is truly an entrepreneur rather than a business owner-manager? One very tangible piece of evidence is that of Ann's business plans, which were geared towards capital accumulation and business growth – growth that she succeeded in achieving year on year after the initial teething problems had been overcome. Hence Ann's was not a lifestyle nor was it a family business. Finally, one other set of motives is apparent. On a personal level, Ann could become a pillar of her local community, earning respect by providing employment and training for young people. This showed a sense of social responsibility and the desire to put something back into the community – a 'collectivist' motive consonant with local values and culture.

In the next section the discussion of the choice of self-employment as a career option is broadened and the underlying theory discussed.

Reasons for self-employment as a career choice

People are said to take action because the content of what they do fulfils a need. Need theories it has been suggested hold the key as to why an individual becomes self-employed. For example a person dislikes her present job and so quits because:

- she does not like her boss
- she feels she could do better elsewhere
- she would prefer to work for herself
- she prefers giving orders rather than taking them.

The content of the dependent clause(s) provide the reason why she has taken a particular course of action. The reason identifies the need. So, for example, 'she does not like her boss' suggests she may prefer greater autonomy – in 'need theory' terms, that she has a need for independence. If in addition she says that 'she would prefer to work for herself' this statement corroborates the suggested explanation for her action. On the other hand, if she says that 'she feels she could do better elsewhere' such a statement indicates aspirations and a desire to get on in life, to achieve. In pursuing a course of action for this reason then the need she is attempting to fulfil is a need to achieve. Finally, she may say 'she prefers giving orders rather than taking them'. This suggests that she prefers to be the boss, to be in charge and to organize others rather than be organized by someone whom she may not even rate very highly. A person who gives such reasons for their choice of action likes to be in control. Some may suggest that they have a need for power!

Noteworthy is the fact that this example does not identify money as a possible motive. In the developed economies of the west, wealth creation is often *one* motive but it is not necessarily the *primary* source of motivation. Rather, a person's discomfort with their present situation is likely to be an 'antecedent influence'. Moreover, in collectivist societies, amassing personal wealth may be considered an unworthy motive. In general, the theory suggests that there are three critical needs: the need to achieve,[4] the need for independence[5] and the need for power or control.[6]

- **Need for achievement** is a drive to excel and achieve a particular goal. The goal is set in relation to a standard and so the individual who is motivated in this way will strive to accomplish their goal. Such people David McClelland described as 'high achievers'. Characteristically they like to take personal responsibility for finding solutions to problems, they like rapid feedback and they aim to achieve moderately difficult tasks, that is tasks which are a challenge but not beyond their capabilities. This ensures worthwhile effort and results in feelings of accomplishment. Although this is a very attractive theory, when tested it did not demonstrate a direct connection between need for achievement with the decision to own and manage a business.[7]

- **Need for independence** has been suggested as a fundamental characteristic of small business owners.[8] Small business owners prefer to be their 'own boss', have often escaped from what they perceived to be hierarchical regimes of the large corporation and to have realized a sense of purpose through owning and managing their own business. Manfred Kets de Vries[9] suggested that entrepreneurs are deviant or marginal characters. Childhood experiences and family background were said largely to have contributed to the entrepreneur's inability to accept another's authority to fit comfortably into an organization. More recently James Curran has also supported the view that small business owners value autonomy and independence.[10] He has argued that desire for independence tends to create a 'fortress enterprise' mentality, shutting out external advice and linkages with the wider environment, with the consequence of constraining business activities.[11] It would seem that a large proportion of small business owner-managers may have reasons for limiting the growth of their enterprises. These people – the *petite bourgeoisie*[12] – form the fabric of local economic communities. For example, they are the people who are plying a trade (plumbers, electricians, running a local garage or a corner shop, etc) and who are ostensibly pursuing a livelihood through self-employment. They are likely to have very different motives to entrepreneurs who pursue profit opportunities for business development and growth.[13] In Eastern Europe, Scase argues[14] that the majority of small business owners running bars, restaurants and retail outlets are *proprietors* (as opposed to entrepreneurs). They consume the profits from their trade rather than reinvesting in the business. The niche they have carved out for themselves enables them to 'construct spheres of personal autonomy'.[15] Hence the motivation includes autonomy from bureaucratic, state controls and the ability to create a personal lifestyle through the ability to generate cash that can be consumed (as opposed to accumulated and invested in the business) in order to raise their personal standard of living.

- **The need for power or control** has also been suggested as a source of motivation. Power has been variously defined either as an attribute of an individual or as a structural phenomenon. The person with charisma has the power to exert influence over others, whereas situations may bestow 'position power' on the role occupant. People with a desire for power not only enjoy being in charge but also accumulate all the symbols and emoluments of power. They prefer to be placed into competitive and status oriented situations and tend to be more concerned with gaining influence over others and with their prestige than with effective performance. The stages of development of a power base are interesting but largely untested on the owner-manager. Table 7.1 outlines the four stages for the manager – theorized by McClelland[16] – and compares these with hypothesized stages attributable to the owner-manager. This theory suggests that people can structure situations in ways that enable the ability and need for control to manifest itself. For example, referring back to the case of Ann David, it is clear that Ann had no role model or mentor to guide her initially. This is probably the case for pioneering entrepreneurs. However, by strengthening the business, Ann was also able to strengthen herself, becoming increasingly more self-reliant as she discharged her debts and built up a client base. She also developed a useful network of contacts, ridding herself of a business partner and clients who had let her down. This enabled her to fulfil her business goals steadily. When the business was well established she was able to contemplate more socially oriented goals that were community-spirited.

Table **7.1** Stage of development of power base: the manager compared with the owner-manager

Stage of development of one's power base	Manager	Owner-manager
1. Drawing strength from others.	The loyal follower serving powerful others.	Identifies a role model, emulates another successful business owner/'copies' their business idea.
2. Strengthening oneself	Collects status symbols, plans one upmanship begins to dominate situations.	Sets about establishing a reputation for self and the business; develops the business profile; seeks to establish business in a dominant market position.
3. Has an impact on others.	Becomes self-assertive, attempts to manipulate situations and control other people's behaviour. Uses others in pursuit of own goals.	Develops a network of 'useful' contacts. Uses these contacts judicious in pursuit of their business goals. The more devious owner-manager may attempt to manipulate situations.
4. Acting as an instrument of higher authority.	Having reached a high status position, they now seek to subordinate their personal goals to those of the organization.	Having established themselves and the business, they may seek to pursue other goals – industry or community minded. This establishes them as a respected (and powerful) figure in the community.

Source: McClelland 1975 (see note 16)

The need for control has been construed to be a personality dimension called **locus of control**.[17] People with an *internal* locus of control were said to believe themselves to be in control of their destiny whereas individuals with an *external* locus of control believed that fate, chance or powerful others had a dominating influence over their lives. It was expected that business owners would have a higher internal locus of control than the population at large. However the problem with this argument is that managers also need to feel in control of those factors that influence business operations. It is perhaps not surprising therefore that no evidence had been found to distinguish business founders and non-founders (i.e. managers) on locus of control.[18]

Current thinking suggests that the business owner's reasons and motives are associated with their goals for the future development of the business.[19] From a sample of 405 new British businesses, Birley and Westhead were able to identify the following taxonomy of reasons for start up.

- **Need for approval** – this they reasoned is associated with personal development; venture initiation is a means by which the founder can progress his/her ideas.
- **Need for independence** – here they stress the owner-manager's individualistic desire to have personal control and freedom of choice.
- **Need for personal development** – this appeared to correspond to a need for continuous learning.
- **Welfare considerations** – this refers to a socially driven motive to contribute to the wider welfare of the group or community; it is ideological and philanthropic.
- **Perceived instrumentality of wealth** – wealth is viewed as a means to an end; the need is materialistic.
- **Tax reduction and indirect benefits** – this reflects the fact that some owners wish to increase their personal wealth by retaining previously earned money.

Owner-managers rarely give only one reason for founding a business, therefore understanding the underlying complexity of their motives requires careful analysis.

Kolvereid[20] surveyed a cohort of Norwegian masters students in order to discover the reasons for their career choice: self-employment or employment. The classification of reasons for their choice of employment is given in Table 7.2.

It seems that the reasons for having a preference for the different types of employment are distinct. Those preferring organizational employment gave as their reasons security, social environment, workload and to avoid responsibility and career, while those preferring self-employment gave economic opportunity, authority, autonomy, challenge, self realization and participation in the whole process as their reasons. Of these Kolvereid suggests that the most important reasons for career choice appear to be security, workload and autonomy.

The search for universal principles

Content theories of motivation have a long pedigree,[21] yet when cultural specifics are considered some content theories may not hold up. This is true, for example of Maslow's need hierarchy theory and may also apply to McClelland's theory of achievement motivation.[22] In the latter case, according to Hofstede the concept of 'achievement' is hardly translatable into a language other than English! Anglo-American countries were found to have a high need for achievement but Latin American countries did not.

Table **7.2** Classes of reasons for employment status preferences

	Reason given for preferring	
	Self-employment	Organizational employment
1. **Security** (risk, security, safety, stability, fixed income)	2 (27.3)	67 (41.7)
2. **Economic opportunity** (increased wages, economic opportunity, development potential, wages dependent effort, direct measurement of results)	6 (2.8)	1 4.2)
3. **Authority** (authority, control, steering, responsibility)	14 (5.9)	1 (9.1)
4. **Autonomy** (freedom, independence, be your own boss, choose own work tasks)	37 (15.8)	3 (24.2)
5. **Social environment** (larger social environment, social membership. colleagues, mutuality)	0 (4.7)	12 (7.3)
6. **Workload** (requires too much effort, family/leisure, fixed working hours, laziness, simpler, less stressful, low complexity)	1 (15.5)	38 (23.6)
7. **Challenge** (challenging, motivating, inspiring, interesting, exciting)	17 (7.5)	2 (11.5)
8. **Self-realization** (self-realization, realize one's dreams, creative need, create something)	11 (4.4)	0 (6.6)
9. **Participate in the whole process** (participate in the whole process, follow work tasks from a to z)	2 (0.8)	0 (1.2)
10. **Avoid responsibility** (avoid responsibility, not committing)	0 (4.0)	10 (6.0)
11. **Career** (career opportunity, promotion)	1 (2.4)	5 (3.6)
N	91	139

Source: Kolvereid 1996 (see note 20): p.28

When attempting to apply content theories of motivation to a business situation several difficulties are revealed. Firstly, people do not seem to have a single reason for behaving in the way that they do and even a reason that took predominance at one point in time may change. For example unemployment or forced redundancy may be the reason why someone considers self-employment. In fact it is a circumstance; a trigger that enables them to contemplate a new possibility – indeed one of which they may have harboured thoughts for a long time. Whatever is the case the new situation of unemployment has presented them with the need to consider future career options – one of which is likely to include that of self-employment. With no clear idea of what self-employment might entail, some people may still decide to 'give it a go'. Some will do well; they will discover that they enjoy working for themselves and they are able to create quite a good living. However, this will not invariably be the case, as the statistics on business failures arguably demonstrate.

Hence, a person's motives to select self-employment, given the tenuous assumption that they will be successful, will include:

- working for themselves (independence and autonomy)
- life style (desiring to fulfil a personal dream, to achieve meaning in life)
- security (providing for the family)
- wealth creation (as a measure of one's achievement, as a means of bestowing status, as a means to other ends)
- production/craft (pride in achievement)
- organization builder (desire to create a structure, an outer embodiment of one's vision)
- philanthropy/social entrepreneurship (the desire to produce something through which the community or group will benefit)
- tax avoidance (the desire to keep for oneself all that one feels one has produced).

The cross cutting effects of culture mean that no one reason is likely to apply; within a society different groups are likely to have different reasons for preferring self-employment. These groupings will be based on gender (for example men are more likely than women to give security as a reason), marginalization (for example minority ethnic owner-managers may prefer the independence and status achieved from self-employment); class-based on manual or white collar occupations (for example a tradesperson – plumber, electrician etc – may work for themselves because that is 'normal' in the particular industry culture of their espoused business, similar reasoning may also apply to a veterinary surgeon). Reasons like tax avoidance and philanthropy are perhaps less understood. For example tax avoidance and an illicit black economy prevails in many countries; it is a means whereby an individual or group can generate more cash for their personal consumption. Clearly this possible source of motivation requires further investigation in specific contexts. Philanthropy was a feature of business life in Victorian England and there now seems to be something of a revival of interest in social entrepreneurship. This is an area where culture and local mores can play an important part.

The process of motivation and control

Whilst need theories may help explain why a person initiates a venture, they do not explain how that person sustains it, expands it by setting up additional businesses or abandons entrepreneurship as a career choice. In order to do this a theory about the process of motivation is needed.

One such theory is Porter and Lawler's VIE (Valence-Instrumentality-Expectancy) theory.[23] This theory is important because it integrates several others, including need and equity theories. However, in organizational behaviour it has generally been used to explain how a manager can motivate their subordinates. Certainly it would be useful to consider its application to the owner-manager as a leader and motivator of their employees but in the following instance it is applied to the owner-manager's self motivation and seeks to explain how they are motivated to sustain their own entrepreneurial performance.

Figure **7.1** The process of entrepreneurial motivation

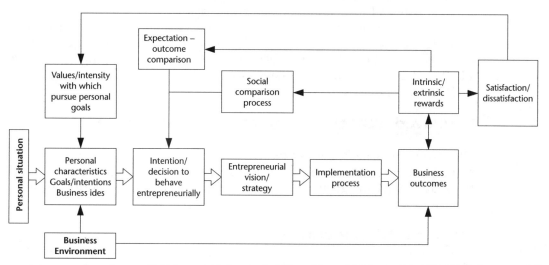

Source: Naffziger *et al.* (see note 25): p.33 and Porter and Lawler 1968 (see note 23)

The key features of this model are:

● the linkage between the implementation decision with business performance outcomes
● the impact of both intrinsic and extrinsic rewards in sustaining entrepreneurial behaviour
● the value of rewards and their sustaining effect
● integration of start up, strategy formulation and implementation and sustained entrepreneurial behaviour.

The model commences with the initial decision to start up and suggests that there are five key influences at this stage: personal characteristics of the founder, their personal situation, the relevant business environment, the business idea and the founder's goals/intentions.

- **personal characteristics** are largely based on needs but may also include personality traits
- **personal situation** includes family, gender, societal position (e.g. marginality)
- local and social environment make up the **business environment** – a local culture that views business start up positively will be supportive
- the existence and evaluation of **ideas** is critically important – not all ideas become viable businesses
- the personal **goals and intentions** vary with each business founder according to life circumstance, age and vision for the business.

Perceived implementation-outcome relationship

The founder must believe that the strategies, business decisions and tactics adopted will lead to desired outcomes such as increased sales, profit or market share. The stronger this basic belief, the stronger the motivation to continue to behave entrepreneurially. The results (i.e. whether the founder achieves what they want) will feed back, confirming or failing to support whether the desired outcomes have been achieved and, consequently, what their knock-on effects might be.

Perceived expectation-outcome relationship

The owner-manager's perception will be that business outcomes (performance) will meet or exceed expectations. The extent to which these expectations are met, the greater the motivation to engage in entrepreneurial behaviour.

Strategic management

The strategic management of the venture will vary in content according to the stage of development of the business and the owner-manager's overall intentions and business acumen. Business strategies adopted will also be appropriate for dealing with the competitive environment.

Outcomes

Outcomes are viewed as rewards for one's efforts and these rewards may be **intrinsic** (intangible/psychological) or **extrinsic** (tangible/physical). Intrinsic rewards include feelings of satisfaction, control of one's destiny and a sense of responsibility for the successes achieved. Extrinsic rewards are likely to include financial performance of the business. These outcomes are valued by the owner-manager; they are also compared with expected outcomes and provided they meet or exceed expectations they will be motivating.

Sustained entrepreneurial behaviour

Equity theory of motivation suggests that individuals compare actual outcomes of their performance with expected outcomes with actual and expected outcomes for a comparator – ANO. This gives a standard by which one's own performance can be evaluated.[24] The individual may be doing better than they had expected but relative to the performance of another owner-manager in the same industry they may be doing relatively poorly.[25] The actual goals that the owner-manager has set will vary over the various stages of development of the business. Initially therefore actual survival or breaking even may be the outcome they wish to achieve, whereas once the business is established, making a profit that enables further investment and business development is likely to be a more desirable outcome. Other important outcomes used as comparators are market share. Here the owner-manager may be quite keen not only to protect their market niche, but also to compare the position of the business relative to a close rival. Benchmarking is an example of this kind of behaviour.

Whilst the business is young and small the goals of the founder tend to be synonymous with the goals of the firm. However, when the business reaches the stage of being professionally managed and/or is incorporated as a limited company it is very likely that there are other stakeholders involved whose goals for the business may be different from those of the founder. The motivational process will then become more complicated as other players' interests will also need to be considered and the payback to the original founder may thereby be reduced. However, the theory predicts that should the outcomes for the owner-manager cease to meet expectations then options other than continuing with that particular business are open. She or he may sell out, disengage and/or develop new business ideas.

Role motivation theories

During their working lives people have a role to play at their place of work. Roles vary enormously. They vary in respect of hierarchical position, whether managerial or not and as a consequence of functional requirements. Mintzberg[26] has suggested that there are ten organizational roles that managers may assume, while Miner[27] points out the relationship between roles and organizational types. These organizational types are:

- the **hierarchic organization** or bureaucracy
- the **professional organization** e.g. law firm, university
- the **task organization** especially the entrepreneurially-led enterprise
- the **group organization** where people empowerment and teamwork are crucial.

Complex organizations may operate with more than one system. For example a university operates as a professional organization but it also has overlaying that a managerial or hierarchic organization. However, it is the task organization and the model of the entrepreneurially-led business that Miner develops and which is of interest here. The prototype includes an owner-manager who is involved in all aspects of the business and an enterprise which is managed with a large amount of informality where there is a focus on task achievement and financial reward. The defining characteristics of such a system are itemized by Miner[28] as follows.

- Work rules and regulations are established by oneself to ensure goal accomplishment.
- Rewards accrue as a consequence of effective task accomplishment.
- Responsibility for daily work loads belongs to the individual.
- Job results are evaluated by the individual.
- Competence is judged by the individual.
- Long hours are accepted to gain personal rewards and achievement.
- Day-to-day work decisions are determined by personal job goals.
- Job changes are made by the individual without permission from anyone.
- Personal drive is the most valued characteristic of workers.
- Risk taking is considered necessary for personal achievement.
- Pay is based on successful task completion.
- Daily work judgements are determined largely by personal goals.
- Personal drive is directed to the achievement of personal goals.
- Punishments are directly related to failure to achieve personal goals.
- Advancement is based on personal goal accomplishment.

The role links the organization and the individual. The pattern of motivations is typical of the role. Where there is a good fit between individual motive pattern and organizational role requirements, the theory suggests that the individual will perform well and be successful. Conversely, where there is a poor fit then the individual is likely to perform badly and be unsuccessful. However, this is not about one person operating in role or otherwise, it is about the whole organizational system of roles. Where staff motivational structure is inappropriate the whole system is likely to operate inefficiently if not ineffectively. The above set of role-related characteristics is compatible with the operation of a small prototypical entrepreneurial firm[29] that lacks formal structure and has low role definition, where task accomplishment is valued highly and rewards are performance based.

The theory builds on the work of McClelland[30] – a theory that suggested a close link between entrepreneurship and the achievement motive. Miner however, identifies five task-role motivation patterns.

- **Desire to avoid risk** represents one point of contrast between McClelland's theory, which predicted that the high achiever takes calculated risks and the lay perspective, which believes that entrepreneurs are risk takers.
- **Desire for feedback on performance** is critical to understanding whether one has performed well. True entrepreneurs are concerned with their performance (which is intimately linked with the performance of the busi-

Figure **7.2** The relationship among the set of five entrepreneurial role requirements

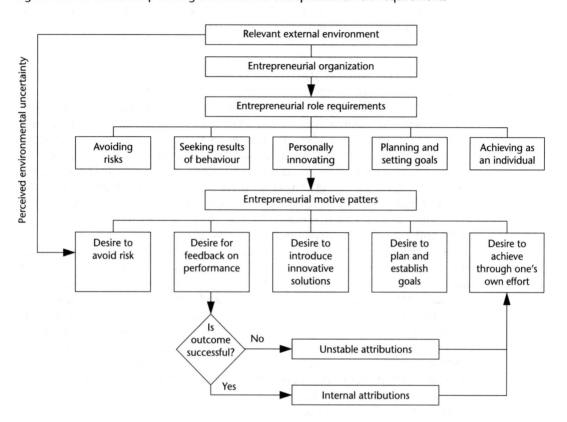

Source: Miner 1993 (see note 27)

ness) and prefer to have clear feedback so that they know the extent to which what they are doing is having the desired effect.

- **Desire to introduce innovative solutions** is central to the concept of individual achievement. Through innovation (doing something different if not unique) the entrepreneur can attribute their success to their own efforts and take personal credit for this achievement.
- **Desire to plan and establish goals** concerns thinking about and anticipating future possibilities which hold the prospect of future rewards.
- **Desire to achieve through one's own effort** such that one can take sole responsibility for success or failure. It is also driven by pride and desire to enhance one's self esteem.

Task motivation is said to result in task success and, ultimately, to affect organization performance. Task motivation theory has been tested against a sample of 'opportunist entrepreneurs',[31] high technology entrepreneurs,[32] and female entrepreneurs.[33] Whilst the study involving 'opportunist entrepreneurs' did not show any encouraging results, the study of high technology entrepreneurs did. A comparison was made between the task motivation scores of founders and manager-scientists of high technology companies. The researchers found that high growth founders of high technology businesses had a significantly higher task role motivation score (on all five dimensions) than manager-scientists or low growth founders of high technology businesses.

In the study of female owner-managers, a sample of 47 female business founders was compared with that of 66 female managers in respect of their task motivation. Overall there was a significant difference shown in task role motivation and self achievement. Women managers tended to attribute the causes of failure to themselves (rather than some external cause) significantly more than did female founders. Both women founders and women managers tended to attribute success to their own actions. This lack of a difference between the two groups on this dimension was not expected. It was suggested by way of explanation that these women faced greater adverse conditions than their male counterparts. Whether women are founders or managers they have many obstacles to overcome. Where they succeed that success is hard fought and they rightly attribute the success to their own efforts.

Role motivation theory has, like most theories, both strengths and weaknesses. Its strength is that it relates the driving forces that motivate the individual to behave in particular ways to the role they play at work. That organizational role shapes both their goals and their needs. The nature of the needs and motives are contingent upon the type of organization if there is to be a 'good fit' and effective performance. However, there are two major weaknesses to this theory. One is that it is likely to be culture-bound: that is, achievement oriented, individualistic behaviour may well typify the American 'entrepreneur' but may not be typical globally.[34, 35] This is evident when considering specific elements of the model. For example in Singaporean society there is a low tolerance of failure (see the case of Mr Tan, Box 7.2). In general therefore this will colour a Singaporean's attitude towards risk taking. This contrasts with the North American culture where individuals are encouraged to pursue their dreams, be courageous risk-takers, dare to be rich and become modern day heroes.[36] Secondly, the method of 'measuring' motivation – the Miner Sentence Completion Scale (MSCS),[37] like the Thematic Apperception Test (TAT) used by McClelland[38] – has been criticized for low intercoder reliability. Not withstanding such criticisms, role motivation theory both develops McClelland's theory of achievement motivation further and places motivation within an organization/environmental context.

Exercise
Suggest ways in which the case of Mr Tan demonstrates Miner's task-role motivation theory.

Controlling and motivating others

Once the business is established and employs others the owner-manager has the management task of motivating and controlling their employees. This means (amongst other things) understanding what motivates them to per-

Box 7.2: Mr Tan: A stationery entrepreneur based in Singapore[39]

Mr Tan is a qualified professional accountant who attained a high status position as a financial controller in a large company. He went against all expectations and Singaporean sentiments when he gave up this secure, well paid job to set up his own business. His prior job was in the stationery business so this gave him a tacit understanding of the trade. As a national chess champion with an analytical caste of mind, he rapidly developed a strategy which enabled him to take some of his existing contacts with him and so quickly establish the business. Nevertheless there were some difficulties to overcome, from customers through to bank managers who could not countenance his reasons for becoming self-employed. The home market was very constrained and so Mr Tan looked overseas, taking an international approach to business development. This meant carefully developing business plans and negotiating deals with other interested parties, including those based overseas. He enjoyed playing this business stratagem game. The results speak for themselves: he has successfully established businesses in Malaysia, Australia and Indonesia and sold them on to other multinational companies. He has had joint ventures, for example with a major German stationery manufacturer and now he manages two companies – based in Singapore and Indonesia.

form effectively and how to motivate and control them. A recognition that motivation and control is an interactive, interpersonal process that can be developed indicates the fulfilment of an important personal learning objective.

The theory is closely related to that of management style. McGregor[40] for example, discussed two contrasting styles, which he labelled Theory X and Theory Y. They were based on assumptions about human nature. The manager who adopts a 'Theory X-style' assumes that their employees are basically lazy, motivated by self interest and greed. The most effective management techniques indicated by this theory are the 'stick' (primarily) or the 'carrot' (secondarily)! The owner-manager who adopts a Theory Y approach, however, assumes that employees want to work, enjoy their work and have a sense of responsibility and commitment to their employer and to others they work with. They are more likely to be motivated by recognition, praise and job challenge than monetary rewards.

McGregor's Theory X and Y relates well to Herzberg's two factor theory of motivation.[41] Herzberg distinguishes between 'hygiene factors' and 'motivators'. **Hygiene factors** are those aspects of the job environment which need to be maintained to an acceptable level if feelings of dissatisfaction are to be avoided. These factors are *extrinsic* to the person and include working conditions – canteen facilities, cleanliness, ambient temperature, safety, etc. **Motivators** on the other hand, include interpersonal relations, recognition, advancement, responsibility and job challenge – just enough to stretch the individual. One of the practical implications of Herzberg's theory was to suggest that instead of *enlarging* the job, jobs could be *enriched* to include the motivators. This raises some interesting practical questions. For example would the owner-manager be sufficiently interested to restructure and redesign jobs in order to motivate their workforce? Clearly, owner-managers

Box 7.3: Two contrasting management styles

	Modern		Traditional	
Theory Y	Style		Style	Theory X
	Participative		Autocratic	
	Cooperative		Controlling/	
			directive	
Work is	Communicative		Orders	Work is
natural	Creativity		Security	a necessity
and				and
enjoyable				disliked
	Motivation		*Motivation*	
	Intrinsic		*Extrinsic*	
	Challenge		Carrot and	
	Commitment		stick	

Box 7.4: Jodhpurs Ltd provides crèche facilities for its employees

Jodhpurs Ltd is an SME based in a small town in Northern England. It produces equestrian riding wear, anoraks and associated clothing for the 'outdoor-type'. Jodhpurs Ltd is an old established family business that has succeeded in capturing a market niche in specialist riding wear. As such it needs expert sewing machinists to produce the riding wear to a quality standard. The company aims to produce quality riding gear at affordable prices. Being well placed in the market for its goods it can command a good price and pay competitive rates of pay. In this location there are several clothing firms competing for skilled labour. Providing a good, clean, pleasant working environment helps keep the workforce happy. But where the company has really scored is through the purchase and conversion of a neighbouring house into a crèche. The crèche is within yards of the women's place of work, which is an added advantage given that many of the women do not run their own car. This provided for an added sense of security knowing that the child was close at hand and well looked after.

vary in their experience, capability and insight in this respect. However, there is no inherent reason why this particular skill cannot be developed particularly if a 'pay off' can be shown.

Goal setting theory of motivation

Owner-managers , as demonstrated above, are primarily task and performance oriented. As owners of their business they want to see a relationship between their own effort (and that of others) and bottom line performance. Locke's goal setting theory[42] suggests that more effective performance derives from clearly set goals at an appropriate level of difficulty, that is the goals should present a challenge but they should also be doable. The following are the chief findings from this empirically tested theory.

- Difficult goals lead to higher performance than moderate or easy goals.
- Specific, difficult goals lead to higher performance than vague, broad goals or 'do your best' goals.
- Feedback about goal-directed behaviour is necessary for goal setting work.
- People need to be committed to achieving goals.

Furthermore, there are various characteristics that affect goal-directed performance.

- People's skills, abilities and knowledge. Rather obviously, the more able will be capable of tackling the more complex tasks.
- Self confidence affects the choice of tasks.
- Task complexity can be self defeating. Specifying challenging goals on simple tasks leads to clearer improvements in performance than on complex tasks where there are likely to many demands to be attended to.
- Goal-choice is influenced by what the individual (or group) would ideally like to achieve, what they expect to achieve and what they believe is the minimum they should achieve.
- Goal-commitment is critical. The individual must see the goal as important and be committed to achieving it even in the face of setbacks. It is in large part up to the boss to ensure that employees see the importance of the goals and that they are achievable.
- Informed feedback helps clarify what has worked in the past and what might work again. It is also stimulating, producing greater effort next time.

There are some clear implications for the owner-manager of this approach. These include leadership style (see chapter 9), communications effectiveness, recruitment and training (see chapter 14). There are also implications for self-development that concern notions of empowerment and self-efficacy, self-regulation and self-management training.

Stakeholders and networking behaviour

Owner-managers are often in a very different position to directors of large corporations: (a) they may be the sole or principal owner and (b) there is more likely to be family involvement – family to whom the owner-manager has both business and personal responsibilities. These personal and social responsibilities provide for deeply held values that govern the owner-manager's levels of motivation and demotivation. These close personal relationships form what Granovetter[43] has termed 'strong ties'. Over and above this the owner-managed firm is embedded in a set of external relationships which control the business process. Such relationships may involve subcontractors, suppliers, customers, bankers/venture capitalists or business angels – all of whom have an interest in the firm's performance. For the owner-manager the issue is one of control; whether networked relationships are based on a formal or informal footing, it is crucially important that the owner-manager manages the relationships well and through this process establishes a good reputation.[44]

Perrow[45] has described a 'small-firm-network' (SFN) structure as an alternative organizational structure. He argues that it presents a different system of organization of business processes, wealth creation and distribution and role relationships. The SFN provides a basis for cooperation, flexibility, innovation and problem solving. This stimulates the sharing of information and experience, the development of long term relationships and a sense of collective fate. In addition it shapes motivational and leadership style. Figure 7.3 depicts a formal SFN according to Perrow. It shows the linkages between the producers and other parties to the network, both upstream and downstream. According to this model, the SFN is within an infrastructure that further support business activity.

Perrow also argues for a structural basis for cooperation and motivation (see Figure 2.2 and related discussion in chapter 2). First of all he has compared and contrasted the organizational structure that typifies the old capitalist model with the SFN. Within capitalism there is scope for the producer to play off one customer or supplier against another. The SFN structure creates a situation where customers and suppliers have choices. This provides a *structural basis* for cooperation, flexibility and the raising of quality standards. Placing the owner-manager back into this situation creates the motivational structure to compete positively in order to maintain effective networked rela-

Figure **7.3** Small firm networks

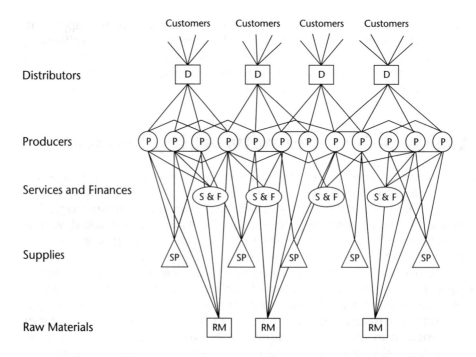

Source: Perrow 1992 (see note 45): p.455

tionships and levels and quality of output. This model of the SFN is not universally or globally prevalent. It exists, for example, in the Emilia-Romagna district of Italy, but hardly at all in the US or the UK. However, other types of networking behaviour occur in these countries.

Amongst European and North American scholars there are two schools of thought. Advocates of entrepreneurship suggest that networking is a fundamental part of entrepreneurial behaviour.[46] The argument is that in seeking business growth, entrepreneurs pursue opportunity development through networking activity. However, empirical studies do not consistently support this proposition.[47] James Curran argues that small firms (in the UK) do not actively engage in networking activities either formally or through kinship and friendship networks. Figure 7.4 shows these models of entrepreneurial behaviour and small business trading behaviour and their motivational linkages. This apparent contradiction can be reconciled because an economy comprises of a variety of firms, whose owner-directors have different aspirations and goals for themselves and the business. The entrepreneurially-led businesses are the growth businesses of tomorrow, whereas the non-entrepreneurially-led businesses tend to form the stable core of owner-managed businesses whose owner-managers pursue personal goals associated with life style and family welfare.[48] Indeed it is these firms that have been variously referred to in this chapter as being run by proprietors or the *petite bourgeoisie* (see earlier section).

The idea of being part of a network of relationships also adds to our understanding of motives for independence and power. The small firm viewed as a link in a network of economic relationships suggests that, while at start up the owner-manager may wish to be their own boss, that degree of autonomy

Figure **7.4** Skilled networking behaviour – the key to enhanced business performance

(a) Entrepreneurial-led business

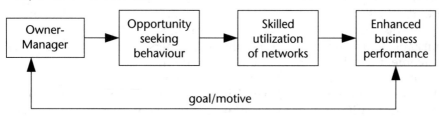

(b) Non-entrepreneurially-led business

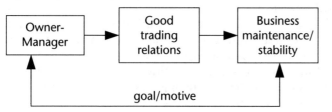

is tempered by multiple interdependencies. These include: internally, the motives and wishes of a business partner, family and/or other stakeholders in the business, the adoption of quality systems, Investors in People (IiP) etc and externally, subcontracting, franchizing and buyer-supplier relationships and interaction with economic institutions and support agencies. It is thus difficult to sustain an argument for the independence of the **small business owner-manager.** At best, the desire to be one's own boss and to have overall control of the choices made for the future direction of the business may give an illusion of independence because there is a plethora of relations that delimit choice and autonomy.

The idea of the socio-economy is one of interdependence of relations. The position of the owner-manager within this structure affects their power to mobilize resources. Position is not neutral, it has associated with it prestige and the ability to influence. A person who positions themselves well can achieve greater access over social and other resources. This position power, Granovetter[49] argues, is enhanced by the strength of weak ties. Weak ties contrast with close personal relations. They enable the individual to reach out beyond their close social circle to more distant parts of the socio-economic structure and draw upon more and better resources.[50] Thus, position and ties indirectly affect business performance.

Conclusions

Why anyone makes a particular decision, chooses a course of action and acts in a particular way cannot be completely known. However, sufficient research has been conducted to build knowledge of motivating and demotivating circumstances, reasons, processes and outcomes. Moreover, there are no definitive answers because circumstances – contexts – vary, though they can be documented systematically in order to add to the stock of knowledge. The case studies that have been included in this chapter by way of illustration testify to this variability. They reveal only a glimpse of people's different circumstances – the obstacles (some physical, others cultural) they may have to overcome, their determination and ingenuity in so doing.

Contexts change. The development of the internet and the apparent ability to become a 'global company' in a very short time has created a new highly motivating set of circumstances for many aspiring entrepreneurs. Certainly one of the key motivators appears to be summed up in the question 'who wants to be a millionaire?' The rapid hike in valuations of internet companies fanned the enthusiasm of the aspirants and their backers until, almost as quickly, the bubble burst. It seems that establishing a global internet company requires rather more than youthful enthusiasm and a bottomless purse for advertising purposes. It requires, as do all successful businesses, strong effective management and business acumen. Now there is a period of rapid adjustment as people refocus on the serious business of entrepreneuring and understanding the processes that create success.

CHAPTER 8

Gender, self-employment and business performance

Women's economic role has changed profoundly. In the 17th century, for example, a woman's role and her work centred around the home. In the typical rural family, a woman's domestic responsibilities extended to farm work, the production of dairy produce, beer, meat and cloth. The family home was an economic unit and it was the wife who went to market to sell domestic products and to buy goods for the house.[1] This situation pre-dated the Industrial Revolution and so the home was, by and large, also the economic base for the husband. Post Industrial Revolution, the idea that 'a woman's place was in the home' firmly took root despite the fact that in 1851, of the 8 million females of working age (i.e. aged ten or over) a quarter went out to work![2]

In the 20th century, post the Second World War, a woman's place was once again 'in the home'. However, this view was challenged in the mid-1970s by a seminal study on the nature of housework.[3] Housework, which is unpaid labour, creates dependency and a tendency towards social isolation. In a society where economic independence is valued, it has presented the structural conditions for women's subordination. Furthermore, owing to employment segregation and the gendering of work, women who did work found that their choice of jobs was limited to the lowest paid sectors of the economy.

One solution to the woman's dilemma of dependency and limited employment opportunities has been that of taking in homework.[4] A favourite type of homework in the late 19th century was sewing and embroidery, often taken in by women in the 'lower middle classes'. It had the advantage of enabling women who needed to work to do so clandestinely. This 'requirement' of invisibility continued in the inter-war Depression and post the Second World War there was again an increase in the numbers of homeworkers. The exploitation of women and ethnic minorities as homeworkers continues to date. 'Homework cannot be relegated to history and indeed shows every indication of remaining a good economic proposition for employers for many years to come' (see note 2 of this chapter).

Homeworking was just one example of the social problem of gender inequality. As discourse about such problems developed questions about the nature of gender were raised – what is a woman? how is masculinity to be defined? The use to which language is put is the socio-cultural manifestation of deeply held values and beliefs a people share about such issues. For example, in the UK the word 'tough' when applied to a woman is something of a slight on her character, whereas when the same adjective is applied to a man it is by way of a compliment to him. This is not a trivial point. Because the argument then goes, if women were to operate in the business world – a 'man's world' – they would need to be tough. If they acted 'tough' they could be said to be aping men, or they were being unnatural and hence undesirable. Furthermore, the only way to succeed in the business world is to be tough, therefore if the woman was not tough she would not survive. Hence either way the woman could not win, she was to be excluded from the economic sphere.

But attitudes were changing, there were growing numbers of women and men across the globe who knew this argument to be both unfair and a nonsense. Nevertheless it was going to be difficult for those women who were to be the first to break through those socio-cultural 'barricades' to enter the business world as effective forces and as women.

Perhaps only a minority of people are prepared in their lives to pursue a difficult course because they believe it to be fundamentally right. So the question remained hanging in the air for some time: why should women bother to enter the economic sphere in a way and in numbers that had not been seen before? Why not stay at home and be 'kept'?

Retreating to a post-Second World War position where women were encouraged to stay at home and let the men take the jobs was no longer a recognizable or viable social scenario. From the 1960s and beyond, families had become accustomed to two wages or dual salaries and a commensurate life style. Women therefore were in a position to compare themselves with their male counterparts, to witness inequalities in pay, for example, and resistance was building. This raised further issues about the structure of the labour market.

The labour market

It is argued that it is impossible to understand women's economic role unless one understands how the labour market is structured. The history of the development of the socio-economic structures in society has set the scene for this. Thus in contemporary society the concept of skill is socially constructed because it depends on which gender performs the task![5] To avoid equal pay for the same work, work is gendered both horizontally (there is work which is predominantly seen as 'women's' and that which is 'men's') and vertically (ensuring male domination of the top jobs). Theories as to why this situation should have arisen vary and there is no one universally accepted explanation, most are controversial.[6]

Attempts to break down the barriers of gender segregation of the labour force (which of course affect both men and women) are being made in the UK through such schemes as Opportunity 2000 launched in 1991 through the auspices of Business in the Community and the Equal Opportunities Commission. Opportunity 2000 continues to make progress. There is visible evidence of men taking on 'women's jobs' such as cleaning and operating supermarket checkouts whilst women make inroads into non-traditional areas of work and levels of management from which they were largely excluded.

The enterprise culture

In the 1980s it was a major plank of the then UK government policy to develop an 'enterprise culture', the rationale for which appeared to be an attempt to reduce the levels of unemployment – levels which had risen sharply at the beginning of that decade. Criticisms of this as a policy are well documented;[7] they range from the criticism of the vagueness of the term 'enterprise' to specific criticisms of particular schemes. For example, attempts were made to develop a 'spirit of enterprise' in school children (defined, it would appear, as becoming 'innovative' and 'risk taking' in attitude and behaviour). Such schemes achieved mixed success.[8] Perhaps one of the problems was that they were too ambitious: just as not every child enjoys the opportunity to participate in sport and 'games' so too not every child should be expected to enjoy participating in setting up and managing a small business. Business owners are heterogeneous and only a proportion are entrepreneurial in the sense of intending to create wealth and accumulate capital. Business games run from schools that reflect the fact that children can play different roles in the business and show that all roles which contribute to eventual achievement are the results of the team effort, are likely to be more effective.

It was also thought to be a problem that too high a proportion of the business start ups during this period were of the self-employed. Many were said to be pseudo-self-employed, that is homeworking or carrying out subcontracted work. This was apparently particularly true of women.[9] Moreover it was suggested that economic development agencies during this decade set up training and development support that was primarily targeted at men with family support behind them. The lack of provision of child care facilities and a culture in which male partners did not take an equal share in domestic responsibilities meant that women started off at a disadvantage. This issue began to be addressed through 'Fair Play' schemes and European Union funded programmes aimed at addressing the training needs of women, in particular certain categories such as 'women returners', to give them the skills and the confidence to play a full and successful role in the economy.

At this time, two types of women tended to pursue self-employment: extremely poor women, who saw it as a way out of the poverty trap and professional women, who saw their future promotion prospects blocked. It remains to be seen to what extent such programmes have helped these very different groups of women. Some work has been carried out that suggests a partial answer and some very positive outcomes for women. It claims to have an answer to the question of what characteristics typify a woman, indeed a woman who is likely to be successful in the business sphere (see Box 8.1). Now a new generation of women is emerging. One category, which might be categorized as characteristically young, middle class and professional, is demonstrating that a combination of IT capability realized through the internet, an imaginative business idea which fulfils a market need and flair may be providing an answer.[10].

Box 8.1: Women entrepreneurs

Sarah Gracie sounds a more up-beat note for women owner-managers in the UK.[11] She reports on a rapid increase in businesses founded by women: in 1997 almost a third of new businesses were started by women. Women appear to have overcome initial disadvantages acknowledged by both men and women by developing:

- a more cautious approach (due in part to the fact that they have unequal access to capital)
- greater survival skills (honed by experience of household financial management and multiple tasking)
- superior interpersonal skills (including communications, team management, emotional support, cooperation and openness).

Finally, the success and speed of development of an enterprise culture in a country is arguably affected by its education policies and practice. In the UK, the idea of receiving a business education and, in particular, one that includes the pursuit of enterprise, has been impeded by deeply ingrained attitudes that business knowledge and understanding cannot be taught but only imparted through experience. The question why teaching business knowledge should be thought to be any different from teaching medical, engineering or architectural knowledge, for example, gives the lie to this particular issue. However, a recent Government White Paper[12] marks a fundamental change at least at the political level. This plus the earlier recommendations of the Dearing Report into Higher Education, if acted on, will present more opportunities for both men and women to study entrepreneurship at degree level. This will help both, but in particular it will enable women who have been caught in the predicament of lacking experience, having insufficient business training and where there has been an absence of female role models to facilitate and encourage their pursuit of business ownership as a career option.

Ownership

The question of who owns business in the widest sense of the question – for example whether it is in public or private hands – is largely beyond the scope of this chapter. On the whole we are concerned with private ownership and within that category questions have already been raised about the gender of ownership. Other questions concern whether the ownership is in the hands of a family. A further question is whether it actually matters. Do any of these factors affect business performance?

Gender and business performance

The absolute numbers of female owned businesses is still fewer than that for male owners. Also women have been owning and managing businesses for a relatively short time. The accumulated wisdom, business experience and business know-who that might be expected would be less for women than for men. How might this manifest itself? First of all it affects the woman's level of confidence, whether she wishes to set up in the first place and to have similar aspirations to those of men. Secondly, it is likely to manifest itself in terms of cultural expectations. Hence because men have that head start, society quite reasonably expects more of them in terms of their ability to manage better and show higher 'bottom line results' than women. But are women owner-managers that far behind?

The first thing to say is that both male and female business owners show a great variety of intention, aspiration and capability within their gender category. This has been known for some time. For example, male owner-managers have been variously described as craftsmen versus opportunists, *petite bourgeoisie*, small business owners versus entrepreneurs – all having implications for aspirations, desire to grow the business, and values and commitment to business ideals.[13] Female owner-managers have been described in other terms. Goffee and Scase[14] suggested a fourfold typology.

- **Conventional women** owner-managers are highly committed to succeeding as wives and mothers as well as being successful in business.
- **Innovative women** owner-managers are more interested in developing a successful business than in fulfilling traditional sex roles.
- **Domestic women** owner-managers give high priority to their families, while giving the business less attention.
- **Radical women** owner-managers generally start their businesses to champion women's issues but do not adhere to traditional business values.

In this typology there is an explicit recognition of cultural expectations of women that in general if they work they have a dual role to fulfil. The question being addressed is how they have variously dealt with that issue.

Carter and Cannon[15] suggest a fivefold categorization.

- **Drifters** – where young women are 'pushed' into self-employment, and there are low interest levels but may develop into:
- **Young achievers** – business ownership is a career option; training and development is undertaken. Some become high achievers.
- **Achievement oriented** – comprises older, career experienced women with high aspirations from the start. They tended to put the business first.
- **Returners** – these women returned after having career breaks to have families. The business was seen as a long term career option and their intentions became those of the 'achievement oriented' woman.
- **Traditionalists** – mostly older women, few had to choose between family and business commitments and they often had a network of family members who could take over the business temporarily.

Both of the above studies of women owner-managers show a preoccupation with the woman's career and life cycle, that is the intermingling with and coping strategies for, domestic and business commitments throughout their active life. It is perhaps understandable why such issues should have been considered in respect of women business owners, what is more difficult to explain is why questions in respect of men's personal lives and their careers as owner-managers have not been directed at men. In fact this problem of researchers asking different questions of male and female respondents in separate studies and thereby not being able to shed light on gender issues is now being addressed. Dyer and Handler[16] report on the kinds of conflicts between work and family that may arise for owner-managers. They point out that mar-

---

Box 8.2: Gender, a man's perspective
– PR Publicity Ltd

PR Publicity Ltd was founded in 1985 by two men who had been employed by a major television company. It was the idea of the younger man, Paul, who described himself at that time as 'the classic yuppie who crashed his BMW'. He was aggressively ambitious and motivated by money. The business was set up in London where Paul and his partner were located, although Paul had started his career in the North East of England as a journalist. He still had contacts there and it was an opportunity in 1990 of a lucrative PR contract that initiated major changes for the business and consequent family tensions. Paul was married, his wife had a salaried occupation and their home – a modest terrace house – her family and their friends were all located in the South East.

In 1990, Paul's partner, Steve, looked after the London office but he still needed Paul's contribution to the management of that aspect of the business. Moreover, the recession was biting in the South East, quite severely. The work got less and less, the relationship between the two business partners deteriorated and eventually they parted company. To Steve's embarrassment, the business in the South East 'dried up', whilst in the North East, the business 'took off'. But that left Paul with a major problem:

'Well my wife refuses to move here, which has caused me a lot of fatigue and some anger and annoyance and bitterness, because I would like to structure the company ... I want to live in Northumberland. The idea is I live in Northumberland with an office on site.'

From a business perspective this would make sense: he could build up the business in the North East and still maintain a presence in London, he could 'commute to London because the office I have in London is actually a flat. I could ... live in London when I have to, in the office, and then come back here to the North East.' Paul could see the benefits for his family. As things were, he was 'living off adrenaline'. He often gets up at 5 am, has a punishing schedule of travelling, meetings, missing meals, working weekends and rising and going to bed when the family are asleep. 'My big regret is seeing my son grow up down the telephone line'. 'It's our tenth anniversary tomorrow (I've got to get a card) and you just don't have time to spend together ... and all the grievances and all the – things, you know – they've bottled up, so when you do spend time together you're bound to have a row.' On the other hand, if he could move the family up to the North East, he could 'save money, buy a lovely house – much better than the one in the South East. ... It would cut costs – I could actually save a lot of money, and live in a style to which my wife would love to be accustomed.' Moreover, Paul believes that his son would love it. 'But I don't think it's going to happen ... I think the other alternative would be to get divorced. I might have to do that anyway.'

ital conflict, neglect of children and divorce can all be outcomes if work-family issues are not managed well. The next section discusses such issues in the context of the family business.

In the above case, Paul is paying the price for entrepreneurial ambitions that were born at a time when the economy was growing rapidly. He rode that crest like so many others until the wave broke. But the wealth of opportunities and the relative ease of establishing the business appeared to have blinded him into thinking through what he and his family might gain from the business to enrich their personal lives. Whilst he can see a solution, it is only a solution for *him*. He seemingly can only handle the schism that his decisions have created by deepening it. He deeply regrets going into partnership. This lost him the London business and had repercussions for his personal life. There is no question that Paul – head in hands – also regrets the impact that his decisions are having on his wife and family, but it appears inevitable in this case that Paul will put the business first and that will mean having to come to terms with the consequences for his wife, his son and their personal lives.

Hence, gender is not simply an issue for women, it is also an issue for men. In Paul's case, there are deeply embedded gender issues which have had both social and economic consequences. Furthermore, this case does appear to suggest that gender *is* a factor affecting business performance.

A recent study[17] has thrown further light on the issue of gender and business performance. In this study the variety of business owners in respect of both their gender and their business aspirations and entrepreneurial intentions was reflected. An important issue was raised. This was whether women's performance in business should be assessed in the same way as men's. This is not an unreasonable question to pose because if men's and women's experience of founding, managing and sustaining a business are very different then perhaps they should be assessed by different criteria. However, the idea implicit in the above question, that women's businesses underperform relative to their male counterparts, is controversial and has not been demonstrated conclusively.[18]

Table **8.1** Form of business ownership by business turnover[19]

	Form of ownership				
Turnover	Sole Male	Sole Female	Two or more	Spouse	Totals
£100k or less	31 (78%)	13 (65%)	3 (18%)	9 (43%)	56
£101k or more	9 (22%)	7 (35%)	14 (82%)	12 (57%)	42
Totals	40	20	17	21	98

Chi squared test of significance = 19.85135 at $p = 0.00018$ with 3 df.

Source: Chell and Baines 1998 (see note 19): p.125

The data in Table 8.1 show no significant difference between the performance of sole male and sole female owner-managers of microbusinesses in the business services sector. The results that were critical were the larger, growth-oriented businesses managed by 'two or more' male owners and the moderately higher performing spouse owned businesses. Whilst there were a few very successful, women-joint-owned business owners these were too few to include in the analysis.

This study raised two further important questions in respect of the possible influence of gender: do women tend to integrate their business into their personal lives, whilst men keep their business and personal lives separate? Is there any evidence that culture affects men's and women's roles and the performance of their businesses?

These researchers suggested a fourfold distinction:

1. **Voluntary integration**: the ideal of harmonious integration of family and business lives, which are closely and intentionally interwoven.
2. **Forced integration**: a business owner uses the family to shore up the business – an action spurred on by adverse circumstances.
3. **Voluntary separation**: occurs where there is a deliberate attempt to compartmentalize business and family matters.
4. **Forced separation**: a business owner desires family involvement that the domestic partner resists.

The results of the study showed no clear pattern: an equal number of female owners fell into the separation and integration categories. Of the male owners 13 fell into the 'separation' category (and for four of these it was 'forced', that is, against their wishes), while the remaining four fell into the 'integration' category. Of the mixed gender couples, seven fell into the 'integration' category and one into the 'separation' category. 'This appears to demonstrate that men also value their family lives and are not only prepared to, but positively, pursue a strategy of integration of the two.' Nor do women invariably attempt to integrate business and their personal lives. When they have small dependent children it may be convenient to integrate, both whereas in other circumstances such as no children and a thriving business they may prefer to keep them separate.[20]

An important issue when considering the possible effects of gender is that of cultural presuppositions, that is being able to identify accurately what assumptions are being made about the respective roles of men and women in society and their implications for work and economic roles. Different countries hold different beliefs and values on a number of dimensions,[21] including gender roles, and so it is important to consider carefully national differences and not to generalize beyond them.

In the UK-based study being reported, cultural presuppositions were assessed in the following ways.

- The performance of spouse-owned and other co-owned businesses (where the business partners were not married or cohabiting). The other co-owners outperformed the spouse-owned businesses significantly.

Box 8.3: The Peach Recruitment Agency Ltd

Sally was made redundant at the age of 42 and she used her redundancy money to set up an employment consultancy. Initially she worked from home. Her husband, then aged 60, was very supportive. He acted as a 'sounding board' for her ideas, gave her financial advice plus some practical assistance, for example answering the telephone, doing some driving and providing some useful contacts.

Sally took the business very seriously. It was not a hobby. Rather it was important to her self-image and her self-esteem. After 18 months and with advice from a personal friend and her accountant, she made two important decisions: to become a limited company and to move the business out of the home into an office.

At home she had employed two women on a full time basis and her step-daughter part time. They had all worked out of a small back bedroom. Also, she said, 'when I was working here at home ... I had no motivation. It was very easy for the dog to give me a nudge and say "the sun's shining, let's go for a walk, put the answerphone on and go out." And I have very little will power. I have the will power to get up in the morning and walk in here because I know I have to open the office. I didn't have that [before] ... now it is a proper place of work and [I can] give the family back the house.'

- The hours worked reflected the fact that, generally, small business owner-managers work long hours (at least 48 hours per week). However, in the spouse-owned businesses, the wife put in on average 27 hours, this reflected the fact that she was managing dual responsibilities for the business and the family.
- Who assumes responsibility for domestic tasks and childcare is a good indicator of culture. The more traditional response is that the women take them on, the less traditional response is for a sharing of responsibilities between male and female cohabiting partners. The research showed that spouse-owned businesses reflected the more traditional values, followed by sole male owners, sole female owners and the joint male business owners tending to share more of the domestic responsibilities. Interestingly the latter were the best performing businesses!
- Of the tasks performed in the businesses, these were professional/managerial or clerical/secretarial. In the spouse-owned businesses the man tended to assume the 'professional role' with his spouse in a subordinate, supportive position carrying out clerical or secretarial duties. Whilst men tended to employ their wives in the business, no married woman (not already jointly in business with her husband as a spouse partnership) employed her husband.
- Women in business with their husbands often undertook tasks for which they had little experience, taste or prior training. This contrasted with the higher achieving businesses (male or female owned) that did not call on their family and maintained a wide network of support for generating information, ideas and skills.

It must be remembered that this account is of one study of women and men owner-managers of microbusinesses in the business service sector. It would clearly be wrong to generalize the findings to other size bands of small to medium sized businesses in other industrial sectors. Nonetheless the study raises some fundamental issues and in particular the need to examine data very carefully before drawing any conclusions in respect of the effects of gender on business performance.

The family and business

The above discussion suggests that the family business may not be the most effective form of business ownership. However, further research is needed to demonstrate this conclusively. The family business does create certain problems (over and above those highlighted in the above section), which other non-family businesses simply do not have. These may be summarized as:

- managing obligations to work and family
- employing family members
- managing different forms of inter-role conflict
- managing career progression within the family business
- managing business succession.

The case of the Matchovitch Winery is probably everyone's idea of an ideal family business. The family took both pleasure from and pride in the business. They formed a well-integrated team and this helped create a climate of social harmony. The obligations to the family and to the business were well balanced, for example whilst father worked hard in developing the business he also played a part in bringing up his offspring. When employed in the business, there was little role conflict, indeed, there was overlap between the brothers' roles, which was found to be beneficial. Employees' views were respected and so any potential problems of suspected nepotism were allayed. The business and family both ran on 'traditional' lines; succession was managed through seniority and the male line in both domains. Provided everyone accepted the assumptions of patriarchy then all worked smoothly. However, there was no role for the daughter to play in the business. In order to achieve the responsibilities and status of a managerial position, she had to work outside the family business. So, even the idealized patriarchal family business is not perfect for all.

In general, however, the problems associated with managing obligations to work and family is not peculiar to, but may certainly be heightened in, the context of the family business. Research suggests that for women owner-managers, where a family has been started or there are dependent children, the needs of the family tend to take precedence.[22] How male owner-managers manage this situation is less clear. Any divergence in the case of male owner-managers is likely to rest on their goals for the business. Where there are entrepreneurial intentions then commitment to the business and its ideals are likely to be high, whereas where the balance of commitment is personal then commitment to family rather than business is the more probable outcome. This ties in with the earlier discussion of women entrepreneurs by Goffee and Scase.[23]

Employing family members ensures that the dynamics of business and family are brought together. This may be neither good for the business nor

Box 8.4: A close-knit family business, Matchovitch Winery, New Zealand

Michael Matchovitch was a third generation New Zealander and owner-manager, along with his mother and two brothers, of a well known, up-market viniculture business. The business was inherited from his father. Both sets of grandparents had emigrated from Croatia. On Michael's father's side the grandparents settled in New Zealand in 1938. For three years they lived and worked on the 'gum fields'. They started a dairy farm and were able to put sufficient aside until, in 1944 they were able to buy a small vineyard. Grandfather Matchovitch planted more vines and grew more grapes until he had developed two vineyards. At this time, as the market demanded, he produced fortified wines – port and sherry – and only a little dry red wine.

It was Michael's father, Bill, who developed the wine side of the business. In those early years Bill's wife, Mary, and grandma Matchovitch helped out with the bottling – there was no bottling machinery at that time. Throughout the next two decades Bill and Mary built up the business and Bill became a well-known figure in the New Zealand wine industry. They had four children. They sent the eldest, Bob, to college in Australia to take a three year degree programme in the art of wine making. Their second son took a degree in chemical engineering. He too eventually came into the business. Their youngest son was also educated to degree level usefully in marketing, before joining his brothers in the business. The other child – a daughter – entered the hospitality industry where she was a successful sales manager until she left and started a family.

In 1992, Bill died and Bob took over as managing director. He had been in the business since 1982 and worked alongside his father developing the land so that they could plant more vines. Bob was able to put into practice techniques that he had learnt at college. 'Dad always said, "I haven't sent you to college for nothing, I've got to give you a chance"; and, although he always kept the reins on, it was really good that I could do exactly as I wanted.' He acknowledged however, that a major factor in the company's development was his father's foresight. It was 'growing the right varieties, and varieties that sell, varieties that can achieve a high price per unit. Because we are quite a small company we have to do that sort of thing; you can't work on volume, low price commodity type marketing; it's got to be new product and something that people really like ... and that's exactly what we've done.'

The Croatian culture of not being in debt was an influence, to some extent grandma had held Bill back. But at one stage they bought 100 acres, when interest rates were running at 19 per cent and they had to spend a further 30 000 dollars; they finally sold it 'but it was really hard work'. They had witnessed a lot of family businesses in New Zealand that had grown too big too quickly, whereas by exercising prudence they had maintained a family business for 50 years. A key motivation was being one's own boss, but whilst it was not clearly articulated, Bob said that despite the hard work, 'being in a family business is really quite special'. They saw their family as being blessed with good fortune; they had a role model in their father 'who really enjoyed the life'.

The roles of the brothers overlapped, as in many small businesses. The future wasn't clearly mapped out, but they knew that if the business was to support a further generation it would have to grow. The management style was one of involvement: 'there's one guy we have to take a lot of notice of; he runs the cellar'. But there are other matters which they feel they should ask other staff about; the thinking tends to be very inclusive: 'You think, I'd better get everyone's feelings on this and make sure everyone's in agreement with it'. Occasionally the brothers would argue, but that was felt to be 'only natural'. This was outweighed, it would seem, by the degree of commitment, the unstinting hard work, satisfaction and independence that they all enjoyed.

good for the family.[24] Certainly evidence is accumulating of the difficulties that couples and their families may face in trying to develop a successful business and harmonious family relations. The problem is that the values that underpin the family and those that underpin a business are fundamentally different. They give rise to potential areas of conflict. This is vividly illustrated in the following case study.

Box 8.5: Typesetting 'R Us (TRU)

TRU is a small business owned and managed by a married couple. It produces artwork and, in particular, computer graphics either for printers or graphic designers. It is based in a new town in the South East of England. TRU's owners Graham and Maggie had four children, none of whom were yet old enough to make a contribution in the business. They did, however, employ Graham's brother, Rob.

The company ran into major difficulties, after making a major financial investment in new technological equipment, it lost a major customer account. Graham was fearful of going bankrupt and not being able to support the family. A friend helped out. But what about the brother, did he help at all?

Graham: 'He just wanted to be paid – he was not involved in the long term impact on the business'.

Maggie: 'He's a very selfish person – he thinks the world owes him a living.'

There were harsh words for Rob. For Graham it now meant rising at 4 am and working until bedtime.

Maggie: 'The effect on the children was Graham not being around because of the hours he has to put in. ... I have to be mother, father and handyman. I think it's worse than being a single parent. If you're a single parent at least you know what you have to do. But we keep hoping and expecting that he's going to come home. We [Maggie and the children] have formed our own structure and it's hard to fit him in when he *is* at home. I know it's for the business but logic and emotion don't go together. I feel a lot of resentment ...'

The interviewer asked whether it would have been harder for Maggie if she had not been involved in the business.

Maggie replied that, on the contrary, she would have found it easier because she would have known what her role was:

'I think it's the opposite of what you're suggesting. At first – when things were going well – I was a partner in name only – for tax reasons. But I take it seriously. When Graham says he can't cope I help him with the office work. I hate office work. I'd rather walk the streets in the driving rain. But if he needs me I help. I have the pull of the family and the pull of the business – a dual role. If I was not involved in the business at least I would know what my role was.'

The situation with Rob was both acrimonious and bitter. Maggie was particularly condemnatory and unforgiving. They made Rob redundant although Maggie 'wished they'd sacked him [as] he did things that were sackable offences.'

Graham defended his decision to offer his brother a job on the grounds that he needed to replace a good employee who had left. He thought it was fortuitous that Rob was available. It would save him the trouble of advertising and recruitment (which he hated doing) and his brother was 'technically brilliant'.

'When he worked for my father' (who had once owned his own small printing firm), 'there were lots of arguments. I got on with my father but was shocked by how many arguments they had.' But Rob had since married and they both felt that he was mellowing.

Graham continued: 'I thought it was safe to offer him a job. But it was hard for him. He's seven years older than me and he had his own business (which failed). It was demeaning for him to work for me.'

The upshot was tears and arguments, which involved the wives and not simply the brothers.

Maggie concluded: 'We don't speak now. The rift is still not healed. The children are affected because I will not let them go round.'

Managing family members is much more problematic than managing non-family employees, as the case of Typesetting 'R Us has illustrated. It is quite impossible to envisage how Graham might have used any standard managerial procedures in order to control his brother effectively. How might Graham, for example, have administered performance appraisal in such a context? Performance appraisal implies an hierarchical relationship, which Rob would not have accepted. Conflict would most certainly have been in evidence.

But even where there is a well integrated family business such as that of the Matchovitch family, performance appraisal might still have raised potential conflict issues, though of a different sort. For example is it possible to apply dispassionately performance appraisal to employees – some of whom are family whilst others are not? At the nub of this is the issue of which comes first, the family or the business? To put the family first constantly can raise problems with non-family employees, who see nepotism, favouritism and perhaps inequitable treatment. The family therefore needs to be seen to be fair, even-handed and balanced in its resolution of (in particular) interpersonal difficulties. Part of this stems from managing expectation of both family and non-family members. The development of explicit policies to which all employees must adhere from the outset will help lay down guidelines for the management of future, as yet not experienced, issues.

It is difficult to maintain a business at a particular level for long. Furthermore, as the family grows there is a clear need for the business to grow if it is to provide the same level of support for all. Growing a business raises a new set of problems. Most small business owners prefer to be fully in control of decisions, have difficulty with delegation and may attempt to resolve this problem by 'keeping it in the family'. Ultimately, however, this can stifle growth.

Once established, a business needs to deal with the problems of growth transitions. An established small business may still carry out much of its management informally. Role and job descriptions may be unclear and overlap, meetings may be held casually as the need arises, be unminuted, and crucial decisions may be taken outside meetings. Whilst the firm is small, employees can work out what is going on and resolve interpersonal issues informally. As the business grows this becomes more difficult. The next stage of development is characterized by **increased professionalization**. This means greater role clarity, the development of a top management team and the increased systematization of management practice. For the family business this is likely to mean bringing in new blood from outside the family at very senior levels. In some firms, however, anticipating this problem offspring will have worked outside the family business for some years to gain other experience and/or may have taken higher level management programmes (e.g. MBAs) in order to assume the roles of professional management of the business.

Table 8.2 summarizes the differences between the family and business as systems. As the business changes over the course of its development so too do its systems; essentially they become more formalized, rule-governed and impersonal. Such values, which govern the growth-oriented or professionally managed business, contrast starkly with those of the family.

Table **8.2** A comparison of family and business systems (according to stage of development)

	Family system	Business system		
		Start up	Establishment	Growth
Goals	Support and nurture the family.	Survival; secure sufficient business to continue in business.	Maintenance. Keep present customers happy, secure sufficient other business to maintain present levels of activity and performance.	Growth. Focus on opportunities for increased profitability, increased revenue, efficiency and growth.
Relationships	Deeply personal.	Ape the family.	Close and paternalistic.	Become impersonal.
Rules	Unwritten, part of the family culture and 'way of being;' shapes expectations.	Informal: 'way of doing' is developed.	'Rules' tacitly understood. Expectations developed.	Increased formality. Written rules and formality derived expectations.
Evaluation	Rewards based on who you are within the family not necessarily on 'merit'. Love and support is unconditional.	Rewards are based on effort. Support is conditional.	Rewards are based on effort and results. Support is conditional.	Rewards are based on results. Performance formally appraised. Employees can be promoted or fired.
Succession	Caused by death or divorce.	Leaving, break up of a business partnership.	Promotion or leaving, retirement.	Retirement, promotion or leaving.

Source: Chell *et al.* 1991 (see note 29, chapter 7) and Dyer 1992: *The Entrepreneurial Experience* (San Francisco: Jossey-Bass).

Inter-role conflict

When a married couple set up a business together the work/family conflict of such business/marriage partnerships is potentially more intense than work/family conflict in a dual career family (where the pressure at work and in the family come from different sources). This was illustrated by Maggie in the case of Typesetting 'R Us. Thus the spouse-run business presents a particular form of inter-role conflict defined as **when participation in one role is made more difficult by participation in another.**[25]

In this case the work and family domains are not separate, the primary source of pressure (role sender) for work and family is one and the same person and there are expectations of the other partner associated with role performance in each domain. Work-family conflict is experienced for marriage/business partners when **the individuals who make up a partnership disagree over the allocation of time that each gives to work and family roles.**[26]

Each partner brings personal characteristics, including attitudes regarding traditional sex roles, skills and abilities, business roles in the founding process, and preferences for work-family roles. The key issues in respect of their individual inputs are:

- the extent to which each partner agrees on the allocation of time to work and family roles
- the perception of his/her own inputs and those of the partner
- the gap in perceptions of equity in respect of the couple's decision making processes, parental responsibilities, mutuality of support and role overload.

Outputs from this process are experienced by each individual in terms of (a) satisfaction with the relationship, (b) satisfaction with the support of the other partner and, generally, (c) satisfaction with life. These individual experiences of satisfaction result in an output for the couple in respect of the quality of their relationship and the effect of this on business performance. The critical point made by this research is that a couple should agree on their respective roles, whether or not they decide to follow traditional gender lines. Where there is greater agreement, satisfaction with both family and work will be the result and this will have a positive (or negative where there is conflict) impact on the marital relationship, feelings of personal well-being and business success.[27]

The succession problem

Who is to take over when the founder dies or wishes to transfer ownership? To what extent is succession planned? In some businesses a son or daughter enters the business and is groomed for succession, as was evident in the Matchovitch family business. In others, either there is no son/daughter and heir, or the offspring have decided upon an independent career path. There are a number of key issues which need to be addressed in order to facilitate successful succession.

- Handling the retirement of the founder, particularly where that individual continues to have a need for control, power and meaning in life through the business.
- Recognition of the difficulties of the family who are loyal to, and unwilling to upset, the founder.
- The role of the next generation, their interest in the business, the extent to which their psychosocial and lifestyle needs can also be met through the business.
- The extent of sibling rivalry or accommodation.
- Changing power relationships and the extent to which they can be accommodated.
- Taking care of the founder's retirement, tax and financial planning.
- Handling other family members not selected for business leadership.
- Training and development of the successor.

- Managing non-family employees in respect of the next generation of leadership.[28]

Conclusions

There are more women choosing self-employment and business owner-managership than ever before. However, women's opportunities are still hampered by cultural expectations. They have greater difficulty financing their business than do their male counterparts, for example.[29] Overcoming such barriers demands a cultural shift in expectations and a redefinition of work and family roles, which indicates a willingness by both parties to share equally power, tasks and responsibilities for work and family, with the allocation of such roles and responsibilities not on gender lines but on the basis of capability.

There are practical implications for the training and development of both men and women for entrepreneurial careers and for support agencies, including the banks, for supporting women-owned businesses to the same extent that they support those of men.

Part 3
The Business Team

CHAPTER 9

Leadership and the management of enterprise

Owning a business is one way in which the founder can exert control and experience a sense of autonomy. This puts them in a key position to develop the business' character and culture and attempt to determine its performance. However, many businesses are founded with an active business partner, a sleeping partner and/or a family member. Businesses may also be bought (outright), bought into (as in a management buy in) or bought out (as in a management buyout). Further, businesses may be inherited. How the business is acquired is likely to have some impact on how it is managed and led.

The person's antecedents, in particular their educational and family background, their work and management experience, are all likely to have a bearing on their leadership and management style once they have acquired their own business. Furthermore, entrepreneurial intentions – to grow a business or not – help shape the vision, strategy and operational tactics for goal achievement.

The concepts of 'owner-management' and 'entrepreneurship' have not been clearly aligned with the concepts of leadership and management. Of course, common sense suggests that the business founder when sole owner will play a major role both in leading and managing the business. But what does this really mean? Many businesses are run in partnership so who owns and leads may be a moot point: many business partnerships have dissolved acrimoniously because the issue of direction could not be agreed. This highlights two key ingredients of leadership: the need to have a clearly articulated and agreed vision and the need to manage others effectively.

In this chapter the nature of management and leadership will be examined by comparing and contrasting the two roles – leader and manager. In developing an understanding of leadership the focus will be on a new leadership style. This has its roots in the notion of 'charisma' – a magical if not mystical way to exercise influence – and its essence in the concept of change. The transformational leadership style that emerges will be discussed in relation to organizational strategic processes, in particular turnround and renewal, the exercise of entrepreneurial intentions for growth and competitive positioning and the skills and capability requirements for personal and organizational effectiveness. Finally, the question 'how can it be known whether more effective, better trained leaders yields improvements in firm performance?' will be addressed.

Management

Management is the cornerstone of organizational effectiveness and is concerned with arrangements for carrying out organizational processes and the execution of work. Because of the nature of organization(s), management – and thereby managers – are embedded in a system of authority relations. This tends to give a difference of perspective (the frame of reference tends to be unitary or corporatist). Authority relations imply the need to delegate, to control, to engender trust, to be able to deal with status differences. Authority relations also imply their counterpart – obedience. People, on the whole, have a predilection to obey. Employees are 'agents within a hierarchical system' and compliance tends to be the easier option, ultimately giving a sense of satisfaction. Compliance is rewarded within the system. Authority relations also bring with them responsibilities; however, freedom from responsibilities can make many employees happy, they are neither responsible for the decision nor can they be blamed if it goes wrong!

Within the formal system of hierarchical relationships, that is the line management system, managers are expected to assume leadership. However, the organization is not complete unless one considers the way it operates informally. Leaders can emerge through the informal route. Hence there are likely to be subtle differences between leadership and management. Leaders may emerge in non-structured situations. A person who has not been appointed as leader may nevertheless be a very effective leader. Thus, not all leaders are managers. Not all managers are leaders. Leaders are often able to bring about long term changes in people's attitudes and are also often inspirational.

Therefore to answer our initial question – is management and leadership different? – we need to give deeper consideration to each function.

The role and function of management

Historical overview

Management theory, in its 100 or so years history, has developed, indeed metamorphosed, from one era or definition of itself to another. It is worth noting these changes because for one thing no ideas ever completely die and, for another, it helps inform our current understanding of management.

Some may consider that management can be taken even further back in time, but in terms of sheer influence many would consider that Frederick W. Taylor (1856–1915) was one of the first theoreticians to develop a system of management. This system became known as **Taylorism** or **scientific management**.[1] The objective of the system was to increase worker productivity and efficiency. Taylor developed a set of principles by which work should be performed. He did so on the basis of analysis of each job. He studied the best way that the job could be carried out. This would establish a standard of workmanship to be emulated by the rest of the workforce. Employees were then trained to that standard. The job was also timed and pay was based on the achievement of the standard. This system had its desired effect and brought with it a differential payment system.

Box 9.1: The McDonaldization 'Paradigm'

The McDonaldization Paradigm is **the process by which the principles of the fast food restaurant are coming to dominate more and more sectors of American society as well as the rest of the world.**[2]

McDonald's fast food restaurants and many other areas of contemporary society exhibit the rational features of Weber's bureaucracy – efficiency, predictability, calculability and the adoption of non-human technologies for the control of people. The mechanized and 'scripted' employee customer relationship, for example, makes the restaurants a dehumanizing place to work. McDonald's also adopts the principles of scientific management when it assumes that there is 'one best way' to do a job.

The basic approach – high speed, large volume and low price with assembly-line procedures for cooking and serving the food – was developed by the McDonald brothers and extended by Ray Kroc who bought them out in 1961 and created the McDonald 'empire' through innovative franchising techniques.

Now McDonald's fast food restaurants are worldwide but, not only that, the principles upon which these and other fast food restaurants have been built have been extended into other areas, including health care, education, hospitality (such as motels), shopping centres and malls, pre-prepared microwaveable meals, publishing, etc. McDonald's may be a phenomenon but Ritzer argues it has implications for health, for the environment and for society at large.

Administrative management was distinguished by the contributions from three writers at the turn of the 19th century – Henri Fayol (1841–1925), Max Weber (1864–1920) and Mary Parker Follett (1868–1933). All three have continued to influence modern day management thought and practice. Fayol attempted to identify the principles and skills of management.[3] The skills could be developed in people and the principles taught. The five functions of management he suggested are:

- planning
- organizing
- commanding
- coordinating
- controlling.

His principles closely matched these functions, for example he identified the principle of unity of command, span of control and the need for a clear unbroken line of communication from top to bottom of an organization. However, his main focus was on the operation of management and the crucial functions to be performed for management practice to be effective.

Max Weber is famously known for his ideas on bureaucracy.[4] Weber's concept of the bureaucratic form could not be further from the entrepreneurially-led organization – an organization which is flexible and responsive to change. Weber's objective was to depersonalize management, to create uniformity, standardization and hierarchisation. This organizational form was to operate according to a strict code of rules, a clear chain of command and measures such as discipline to achieve tight control. It operated best in conditions of stability and certainty. The contemporary problems of externally driven change and global competitiveness have not augured well for this organizational form. Indeed, Burns and Stalker brought this problem to light when they contrasted the mechanistic and organic organizational forms in structure, behaviour and effective performance.[5] Much of contemporary management thought has gone into a consideration of how to loosen up the 'iron cage' of the bureaucratically organized corporation to enable it to become more innovative, competitive and enterprising.

Mary Parker Follett's writings are in the process of being rediscovered. Many of her ideas have contemporary relevance.[6] For example, her approach to leadership stressed the importance of people; how to lead in a way that encourages employees to give their best. Groups were important vehicles through which employees could resolve differences, overcome conflict and integrate people's interests. She has much to say on the issue of empowerment and facilitation as a leadership style rather than tight control.

Follett's writings prepared the way for a new approach to management, which became known as the Human Relations School. A key figure in shaping this movement was Elton Mayo (1880–1949) who was programme director of the research conducted between 1927 and 1932 that became known as the Hawthorne Studies.[7] This research underscored the importance of people: 'the organization is people' might have been the motto! Mayo's main discoveries with his co-workers (Roethlisberger and Dickson) was the importance of *social* (as opposed to economic) motivation and the need for a commensurate management style. The research programme did not set out to 'discover' or 'demonstrate' the importance of employees' social needs, on the contrary, the study was designed as a series of field experiments to monitor the effects of changes in working conditions (heating and lighting, for example) on employee performance. The research team discovered that the special attention given to the workgroup in itself resulted in improved performance. This became known as the **Hawthorne Effect**. The team went on to study the effect of the social environment on performance and discovered that workgroup pressure (normative behaviour) had considerable influence on performance, indeed more so than management controls. This brought to the fore the importance of people management skills for effective management practice.

The Human Relations School or behavioural approach continued predominantly into the 1970s and was overlain by emergent approaches such as systems theory. In general, systems theory enabled management to develop an overview of the operations of the organization as a system of interdependent subsystems.[8] The characteristics of an open system are its openness to its environment, the permeability of its boundaries, the flows of resources – information, materials and energy – through the system, the inputs to, the transformation process within and output from, the system to produce goods and services, a feedback mechanism that facilitates self-regulation and control and synergy which emphasizes the need for interrelationships between all parts of the system.[9] Any size of organization could function as a system. The mechanistic model of organizational functioning that typified the bureaucratic form was vanquished for a more appropriate metaphor – that of a biological organism which has the crucial attribute of adaptability. This biological analogy has persisted into current thinking, for instance organizational ecology and the view of the organization as an occupant of a 'niche'. As the theory states that there can be only one occupant of a niche, the theory can be extended to competitive behaviour between rival firms.

A major reason why the above management schools of thought persist lies in the development of contingency theory. Contingency theory emphasizes the 'no one best way' philosophy. Pragmatically it suggests that a solution may be found which works in one situation but not in others. The task of management therefore is to identify the most appropriate solution to the particular situation and problem. Organizational effectiveness is not now seen as solely a function of the appropriateness of structure but also of changes in the environment – internal and external (see chapter 1 of this volume). Environments can be stable and predictable or turbulent, requiring a flexibility of approach as they constantly change. The relationship between the external and internal environments also needs managing. The deployment of technology and the organization of tasks and of people are constraints which have to be carefully considered and appropriately managed if the organization is to function effectively.

Child distinguished between task and political contingency theory.[10] The primary purpose of the **task contingency approach** is the effective and efficient performance of tasks in order to meet organizational goals. In contract, the **political contingency perspective** suggests that the choice of organizational design is not simply a function of efficiencies that may accrue, but rather of what is acceptable to various power groups within the organization. It has been suggested that the small entrepreneurial organization may be characterized as a task organization (see chapter 7 of this volume). Moreover, small organizations tend to be organized around a central hub – the owner-manager – where power tends to be concentrated. Within larger, organizationally complex businesses with line management arrangements and separate functional departments managers have scope to manoeuvre themselves into positions to influence or resist policies.

The art of management has become that of being able to analyse each situation, draw on different schools and decide on the most appropriate action. Thus in the 1980s contingency theory was taken to its logical conclusion. Management must be aware of the complexity of each situation and take an active role in trying to work out what is the best course of action in every case. This requires considerable diagnostic skill, the assumption of a great deal of responsibility and the need to be personally very flexible in style and approach.[11] In this school of thought managers are encouraged to push the decision down to the point of action, thus requiring of them a further skill, that of effective delegation. This philosophy results in greater employee empowerment as it assumes that those people who have to implement a decision should make it. This further development indicated the need for an integrative approach to management, drawing on the different schools (especially systems and contingency theories) and allowing for the existence of self management teams.[12] This provided for a complex organizational system within which there might be found considerable variety amongst its sub systems. So, for example, R&D departments could be run on a team management basis whilst production is much closer to the scientific management model. Marketing could exhibit considerable employee empowerment, flat hierarchy and autonomy. All these different attributes show differences between organizational subcultures.

Organizational culture

Recent theorizing about the nature of management has attempted to address the issue of organizational culture.[13] The managerial role is seen as one that must manage the organizational culture effectively, addressing and accepting the dominant beliefs and values held within the particular organization and instigating actions which are consonant with that culture. Decisions are based on experience and accumulated understanding of the culture. This presents an 'organizational view of the world'. In this model of the corporate world, change on the whole occurs incrementally and decisions build on each other such that past decisions mould future strategy. This particular model of corporate culture does not necessarily fit the real world of the small business owner or the entrepreneur. Handy, for example, has used the metaphor of a wheel or a web to describe the nature of organizational structure and culture in small organizations. [14] What is being suggested is a centrality of power and decision making around the owner-manager, whose personality, style, way of doing and being shapes the dominant culture of the business. In the small business context there is 'less room to hide' for the subordinate who does not share the assumptions and values of his or her boss. Furthermore the culture of growth versus the culture of stability will be a major determinant of organizational culture. Certainly in the small firm managing the culture is also a major part of the managerial role, but in the enterprising growth-oriented firm, managing change and the discontinuities that this may bring is likely to be a major challenge for management.

What do managers do?

One body of research in small business has coined the label 'owner-manager' for the founder/owner of a small business, without defining precisely what is meant by the term 'manager'. Rather it is assumed that an owner-manager functions at an operational level, implementing decisions and taking a view on the level of activity and performance required to meet orders. Owner-managers of small businesses tend to assume more than one role – they are, for example, both the production manager and the marketing director rolled into one. They may be involved in procurement and logistics. In effect they may have to turn their hand to any job that needs doing at the time in order to meet the exigencies of a particular situation.

This analysis of 'what do owner-managers do?' begs a number of questions. Firstly, if there is such variety in their work, what range of skills and competencies are required of them in order that they may successfully accomplish their many and varied tasks? Secondly, the question is raised as to whether the job of owner-management in the small firm differs significantly from the job of management as it pertains to the medium to large organization.

The textbook definition of a manager is: 'a person in an organization who is responsible for the work performance of one or more other persons.'

Indeed managers are people to whom others report: 'Managers get things done through other people.'

Box 9.2: The regular duties of a manager

- Ensures that the organization fulfils its basic purpose.
- Designs and maintains the stability of the organization's operations.
- Takes charge of the organization's strategy; helps adapt organizational behaviour in a controlled way to its changing environment.
- Interprets the organization's values and culture and directs subordinates towards organizational preferences.
- Is the key informational link between organization and environment.
- Maintains the organization's formal system of authority.

Exercise

Replace the word 'organization' in Box 9.2 with 'small firm' and the word 'strategy' with 'vision' and consider whether the essentials of the owner-manager's managerial role are covered in this list.

Of course, at a more detailed level of day to day activity it is possible to unpack the manager's job. Rosemary Stewart[15] was one of the first people to ask: 'how can managers' jobs be compared and evaluated?' and 'how do managers spend their time?' For example how much time do they spend thinking, in the office, travelling etc? What are the particular activities performed? What do they depend on?

Not surprisingly she concluded that there is considerable variability depending upon the nature of the job. The job varies due to different functional areas and responsibilities, different companies and industrial sectors so, for example some managers may be more desk based than others, some may spend more time pushing paper, others firefighting and managing people in face to face situations, some may spend a large proportion of their time out of the firm.

Henry Mintzberg in a similarly conceived piece of work[16] suggested that managers:

- work long hours

- work at an intense pace
- work at fragmented and varied tasks
- work through many communications media
- work through other people (interpersonal relations/networking)
- work at exercising control over situations.

The above checklist could be applied to the role of the small firm's owner-manager. Mintzberg however took his analysis one stage further and suggested that there are ten managerial roles, which fall into three categories: the **interpersonal**, which involves interaction with other people; **informational**, which involves all aspects of handling information; and the **decisional**, which applies to problem solving, addressing opportunities and the use of information in decision making. Figure 9.1 shows the ten roles identified by Mintzberg.

Figure **9.1** Mintzberg's ten managerial roles

Interpersonal – involves interaction with other people
- figurehead
- leader
- liaison

Informational – involves exchanging and processing information
- monitor
- disseminator
- spokesperson

Decisional – Involves the use of information in decision making
- entrepreneur
- disturbance handler
- resource allocator
- negotiator

Source: Mintzberg 1973 (see note 16)

A senior manager or owner-manager is the one who on the whole 'calls the shots'. It is this person who sets the priorities and the agenda of what work, aims and objectives shall be pursued. They will also have something to say about the timeframe over which the work is to be completed. The manager/owner-manager will use a variety of settings (both formal and informal) in which to develop and pursue their agenda. Agendas are met by working with and through other people both inside and outside the business. Networking is the process of building and maintaining positive relationships with people whose help may be needed to develop and implement the ideas and vision which lie behind the owner-manager's agenda. The successful manager (and indeed the successful entrepreneur) devotes a great deal of time to developing such a network.

The interpersonal role of the manager/owner-manager is not only important in respect of the networking capability but also internally in managing effective working relationships. Often the manager/owner-manager is seen as

Figure **9.2** The management of effective working relationships in a small firm and their impact on business performance

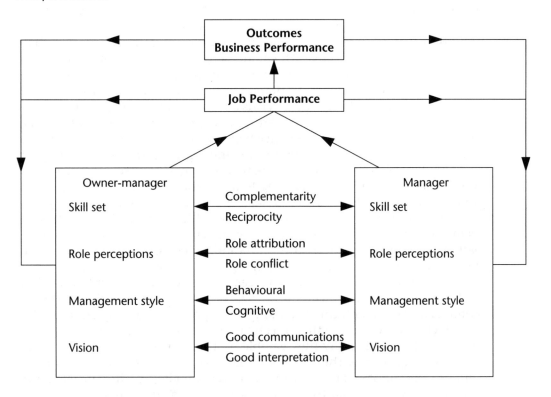

Source: Chell and Rhodes 1998 (see note 17)

an isolated individual ploughing their furrow whereas the reality of managing through other people is the crucial importance of the relationships built up with others. The tag 'superior-subordinate' or 'leader-follower' does not capture the critical elements that make for a successful working relationship. Figure 9.2 models such a relationship.[17]

The management of effective working relationships encapsulated in Figure 9.2 suggests the importance of:

- skills
- role perception
- management style
- vision.

The skills set includes the technical skills of the job, including tacit knowledge of the industry and business, and the interpersonal skills which affect the working relationship. The skills sets may be complementary (where for example, the owner-manager is highly entrepreneurial and the manager very practical and capable of implementing entrepreneurial intentions). Role perceptions include role attribution, role ambiguity and intra-role conflict. The clearer the role perceptions, the greater their complementarity and the lower the conflict. On the whole, whilst creative tension may occur between the two roles, an effective working relationship will only be sustained where role expectations are met on both sides. Ultimately these are bound up with the realization of the owner-manager's strategic goals or intentions. There are three dimensions by which management style may be characterized: behavioural, cognitive and affective. The model suggests that the management style may be characterized by way the other party is engaged in interaction (that is, a participative versus authoritarian style), the nature of the thinking process (suggested to be intuitive versus analytic) and the emotional affective relationship (for example, formal-informal, relaxed-tense, playful-serious). The issue is the degree of consonance between the parties in the relationship.

In the large corporation, long term planning, formalizing the strategy in documentary terms, was the textbook way of managing at senior levels. Now, in fast changing environments, long term planning, even in a large corporation, is becoming a thing of the past. The vision that is developed as a steer for the small firm is likewise becoming the vehicle for creating the strategic reality of the large enterprise. Managing the envisioning process is a critical part of aligning relationships at the appropriate levels. The process of socially constructing reality is one in which thoughts and ideas are expressed in order to facilitate a social process of engagement which requires interpretation, understanding and conveying meaning.[18] The use of imagination and envisioning is a particular form of thinking. Entrepreneurs not only tend to think intuitively,[19] they also use their imagination to perceive the potential of situations.[20] Characteristically they gamble on their imaginations. In this working relationship, it is the owner-manager who envisages the potential of various opportunities and it is the manager (middle/first line or whatever) who must interpret what that vision means. The greater the opportunity for discussion and articulation of the vision, the closer will be the manager's interpretation of the owner-manager's intentions and the more effective the implementation. This is the **vision realization process**.

The outcomes of this process are: good or poor vision communications and interpretation, good or poor implementation i.e. job performance and successful or unsuccessful business performance.

The management of effective working relationships is thus critical to firm performance. In so far as the owner-manager is producing the ideas and the manager is interpreting and implementing those ideas there would appear to be a very effective leader-follower relationship. In the next section we will examine leadership theory with a view to comparing the nature of leadership and management.

Leadership

Historical overview

Leadership is one of the most researched and poorest understood of all the organizational behaviour concepts. Adair[21] suggests that our understanding of leaderships stems from the Greeks, where knowledge (that is, technical and professional competence) was held to be the key to leadership responsibility. This was knowing what to do and how to do it to lead by example and encourage others to follow. To take the lead particularly in times of crisis was to earn the respect of the followership.

However, the idea that there might be traits (or characteristics) which typify a leader has largely been discredited. This idea took hold at the turn of the 20th century but no solid evidence was amassed to identify what traits these might be. It is also problematic because it suggests that leaders are born, that is the leadership traits are genetically endowed. The issue is then one of identifying people with such traits and placing them in leadership positions.

If leaders are not born, what is it that leaders do and how well or effectively do (or should) they do it?

The identification of leadership behaviour had its roots in research on behaviour in groups. Within this context, emergent leaders were observed to adopt two distinct role related behavioural characteristics, termed **task orientation** and **socio-emotional leader behaviour**.[22] These observations were confirmed by Bales' contemporaries. In particular, another influential programme of work – the Ohio State University Studies of leader behaviour – took further the identification and measurement of such leader behaviours.[23] These studies revealed four leader behaviours of which 'consideration' and 'initiating structure' were the most significant. **Consideration** was the extent to which the leader showed consideration for subordinates. **Initiating structure** was the extent to which the leader defined and structured their role and that of their subordinates. There was an extensive programme of research associated with the measurement of these two dimensions, however, a number of problems were revealed.

- The difficulty of demonstrating that these two dimensions were independent.
- That either or both dimensions affect outcomes such as feelings of job satisfaction, labour turnover, grievances, etc.
- The research design – the contexts in which leaders and their subordinates acted out decisions was ignored.
- The direction of causality was not established. Was leadership behaviour a cause or an outcome?[24]
- The data was not based on the observation of actual leader behaviour but relied on the perceptions and recollections of subordinates.

Despite these problems, the research was influential. For example, the work of Blake and Mouton appears to have been influenced by these studies. They distinguished between 'concerns for people' and 'concerns for production'. These two opposing forces became the dimensions of leader behaviour which they used to construct their **managerial grid**.[25] The managerial grid shown in Figure 9.3 below identifies five leadership orientations:

- **Impoverished management** (1,1) assumed that the leader does the minimum required both in respect of production and the staff working under them.

- **Organization management** (5,5) depicts an 'adequate performance'. The leader balances the necessity of getting work out with staff morale and as such tends to work at a 'steady pace'.
- **Country club management** (1,9) describes leader behaviour which focuses on satisfying employee needs with a low concern for production. A comfortable working atmosphere is engendered.
- **Authority-obedience style** (9,1) shows extreme concern for production with little regard for employees. Here the leader concentrates on maximizing production by exercising power, authority and control.
- **Team management** (9,9) where the leader integrates high production and people concerns by a goal-centred team approach which maximizes commitment and involvement through participation.

Blake and Mouton used the managerial grid as a training device. Managers were encouraged to identify their leadership style and were given guidance as to how to develop it. The idea was to develop a leadership style akin to those of the 9,9 leader.

The inadequacies of personality traits and behaviours to predict leader effectiveness became apparent. This led to the idea of the need to consider the context or situation and its impact on leader and followers. Behaviour was thus thought to be contingent upon the situation and as such affected group performance. The **Contingency Model of Leadership Effectiveness** was developed by Fiedler[26]. The elements of the situation which Fiedler measured

Figure **9.3** The managerial grid

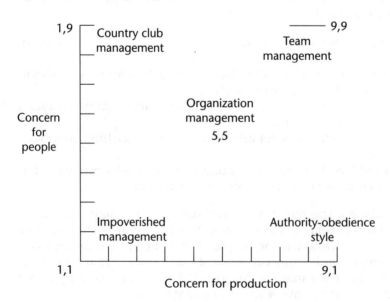

Source: Blake and Mouton 1964 (see note 25)

were: leader-member relations (good or poor), task structure (structured or unstructured) and power position (strong or weak). The leadership style he distinguished as being either predominantly **task oriented** (concerned with task accomplishment) or **relationship orientated** (aims to maintain smooth interpersonal relations within the group). He discovered that a particular leadership style was more effective in some situations and not in others. So, where the situation was either very favourable or very unfavourable, task oriented leaders were the more effective. Relationship oriented leaders were more effective in the moderately favourable situations. Fiedler's initial position was that leader-orientation was very difficult to change and so one could achieve leader effectiveness by manipulating the situation. Much of the research carried out in the early 1970s in order to test the contingency model was unable to validate it and it remains a controversial but interesting idea.[27]

The next major development in leadership theory was the path-goal theory of leadership effectiveness proposed by House.[28] This theory built on the Ohio Studies of leadership style, the expectancy theory of motivation and path-goal theory. The idea was that a leader should be able to identify subordinates' needs and reward them accordingly so motivating them to do their jobs well. By clear guidance an effective leader will 'clarify the path' and enable the employee to achieve better performance for which they will be rewarded. House developed this into a contingency theory by introducing situational variables: the nature of the task, the organization's formal authority system and the work-group. The theory suggested that a different leadership style is required according to whether tasks are routine or non-routine. A relationship oriented style is more effective where the leader has more upward influence in a hierarchical authority system; where workers are interdependent there is a greater need for path-goal clarification and where employees are essentially working on their own and know what to do, a relationship oriented leadership style is more effective.

Tannenbaum and Schmidt suggested that leadership style could be characterized in terms of a continuum from autocratic to democratic to *laissez faire* behaviours.[29] They suggested four influences that affect the manager's choice of style.

- Personal characteristics including experience.
- Characteristics of subordinates especially their willingness to accept responsibility for decisions.
- Situations, such as the nature of the tasks to be performed and time pressures.
- Types of problem which can be handled on their own or those which should be resolved jointly.

They suggest that the manager considers a full range of options before deciding how to act. However, it illustrates a very important practical issue when evaluating management style research, that is, the self-fulfilling prophecy. People decide how to act often dependent on management style. This may convince management that they were justified in their choice of behaviour, for example an autocratic style may be demotivating and lead to low performance, low performance then 'justifies' telling people what to do and keeping a tight reign over work behaviour.

As discussed in chapter 6, much of management behaviour is about taking decisions. The problem was how to make effective decisions and what does effectiveness mean in this context? Earlier work by Maier suggested two criteria: quality of the solution and acceptance by subordinates.[30] A **quality solution** is one which solves the technical aspects of the problem. However, there are often circumstances where subordinates have a legitimate view as to whether what is being proposed is acceptable. **Leadership style**, suggested Vroom and Yetton, must be sufficiently flexible to meet the exigencies of particular problem solving situations.[31] Leadership style is therefore best characterized by the degree of participation with subordinates.

- The leader makes the decision on their own.
- The leader consults subordinates individually but makes the decision on their own.
- The leader shares the problem with subordinates individually, obtains their ideas, but then makes the decision on their own (which may or may not reflect subordinates' ideas).
- The leader shares the problem with subordinates *collectively*, obtains their ideas and suggestions, but makes the decision on their own (which may or may not reflect subordinates' ideas).
- The leader shares the problem with the group, discusses possible solutions until a consensus is reached and a solution arrived at which is then implemented.

The decision style adopted depends very much on whether quality of solution is important and whether the leader has the information needed to take the decision. Furthermore, the decision style adopted is also dependent on whether acceptance of the solution by subordinates is critical to implementation. Where more than one option is open to the manager, then two other criteria are suggested.

- When decisions need to be made quickly, then the more authoritarian style is appropriate (they are time efficient).
- When it is important to develop subordinates' knowledge and understanding of the issues, then the more participative styles should be selected (time investment).

The model offers guidance to the busy manager as to when it is appropriate to engage in different levels of participation in decision making. Vroom[32] has extended the model in an attempt to reflect more closely the reality of decision situations. It has been argued that the model is too complex but the principles that underpin the model are very few and they are ones which will present little difficulty to most managers in assimilating. Moreover, the model appears to reflect the reality of most management situations in that all managers will want to consult over some issues and will believe it not unreasonable to take a decision on their own in some circumstances.

The rational decision making model indicates a range of leadership styles combined with the need to show flexibility and responsiveness to particular situational contingencies. By the same token this model is about how these situations should best be handled. The practical implications for a leader/manager if they are to be really effective are the need to develop the following.

- Diagnostic skills
- Person management skills in face to face, consultative and participative situations
- The ability to implement decisions once taken.

The above theories of leadership effectiveness have tended to place an onus on the leader to act in particular appropriate ways on the group or team of subordinates. The group would respond accordingly. More recent theories also recognize that team members have choices and do not necessarily respond as followers, that is, sheep-like! Hersey and Blanchard's situational leadership theory assumed that leadership depended on the maturity of sub-ordinates.[33] 'Maturity' was defined as desire for achievement and willingness to accept responsibility. They suggest further that the relationship moves through phases starting from the new employee who is prepared to accept instructions and close supervision until they know the ropes. As the employee becomes more familiar with the job and procedures, the manager may be expected to provide more by way of explanation and 'sell' an idea. With even greater familiarity a participative approach may become appropriate and with it the recognition that employees themselves have something to contribute to job development and associated decision making. This may lead eventually to delegation and the assumption of greater levels of responsibility for task management by subordinates. This raises a particularly interesting issue, if not challenge, to the small business owner-manager who reputedly finds delegation a difficult skill to master.

The mid-1980s saw a change in direction in leadership research; there was a resumption of interest in the personal quality – **charisma**. Many great leaders are said to have had this special quality but not all were effective. The leader with charisma is someone with a personal quality or gift that enables them to impress and influence. For Weber charisma was just one basis for leader authority.[34] Once leadership is recognized it is a powerful force commanding personal devotion and complete obedience. Burns referred to it as 'heroic leadership'[35]. It is in this sense that we tend to think of charismatic leadership, for it conjures up ideas of past heroes or great leaders. Adair identifies some notable cases in Alexander the Great, Napoleon and Lawrence of Arabia. However, whilst charisma may arouse popular loyalty and enthusiasm it does not necessarily imply leadership effectiveness for which, he suggests, there are other notable qualities – steadiness, patience, concentration, consideration and technical capability.[36]

Bass, however, following Burns, distinguished between two types of leader-follower relationship: transactional and transformational.[37] A transactional relationship is based on reciprocity and exchange. It is the striking of a bargain. Follower behaviour is controlled by reward and punishment. The goal is

Box 9.3: Charismatic leaders

Charismatic leaders are role models who are admired, respected and trusted. They have extraordinary capabilities, persistence and determination. They are willing to take risks, they are reliable, consistent and 'do the right thing'. They motivate and inspire by providing meaning and challenge. They involve others in envisioning attractive future states. They also provide intellectual stimulation. By providing challenges, they stimulate others to be innovative and creative. By questioning assumptions they also reframe problems. They also provide special attention to each individual follower's need for achievement and growth by acting as a coach and mentor.

task completion but there is no other purpose holding the parties together. The transformational leader, on the other hand, is inspirational and transcends individual self-interest. The transformational leader motivates others to achieve beyond their expectations.

One problem with Bass's theory is whether he is not talking about the truly exceptional individual. Some examples he gives are Mahatma Gandhi, Martin Luther King and Theodore D. Roosevelt. This is one reason why some reject this as a general theory of leadership. Critics have pointed out that there are many cases of inspirational leaders whose aims and objectives have been immoral and corrupt. To take care of this criticism Bass has distinguished between socialized and personalized charismatic leadership. The former is egalitarian, serves the collective interests and develops and empowers others, whereas personalized charismatic leadership is based on personal dominance, authoritarian, self-aggrandizing, self-interested and exploitative behaviour. He concludes that transformational leadership is socialized and must be 'morally uplifting'. Personalized transformational leadership, on the other hand, is pseudotransformational.

Leadership and management: are they different?

The development of thinking about the differences between leadership and management has been aimed at creating understanding.[38] To do so it has been necessary to create a new language with which to describe effective leadership behaviour in order to develop opinion and create a new vision of future possibilities. Handy sets the scene by presenting a new set of concepts – federalism, subsidiarity, trust, forgiveness, limited tenure, inverted doughnuts and networks – whilst other authors have dealt more specifically with special issues such as gender and management, addressing the questions of style, culture and opportunity.

Kotter, in contrasting management and leadership, made the point that they concern two entirely different systems of action.[39] It is therefore possible for an organization to be overmanaged and underled or *vice versa*. What, he suggests, organizations need is both strong leadership and strong manage-

Box 9.4: The new language of organizational behaviour according to Handy

This language of politics is particularly appropriate for the large corporation that wishes to transform itself into an organization of enterprising and achieving people.

Federalism
- coordinates, facilitates, enables
- possesses a small essential core
- energy and initiative stems from the periphery not the central core.

Subsidiarity
- embodies the principle that a higher order body should not do anything that can be done by a lower order body
- as such it is delegation underpinned by a moral imperative
- means the need to trust people to make mistakes and forgive the genuine mistake; reverses the notion of a 'blame culture' and empowers people to act.

Limited tenure
- real responsibility should be given to a person for only a limited time to avoid abuse and possible corruption
- unlimited tenure is a recipe for dictatorship.

Inverted doughnut
- a metaphor for empowerment – there should be a solid core of essentials to a job with an empty 'ring' capable of being filled by discretion and initiative, but bounded.

Networks
- the importance of making connections, especially to the outside world.

ment. Management concerns dealing with complexity, which is particularly evident in the large organization. Without good management organizational behaviour disintegrates into chaos. Leadership, he suggests, is about the ability to cope with change. The skills and competencies associated with each system are complementary.

Arguably, in the smaller, newly founded organization, the leadership skills are likely to predominate though with an increasing need to get things organized and under control in order to implement the vision, that is, business idea. Hence good leadership is essential while effective management quickly becomes increasingly important.

Creating a culture of effective leadership depends on the ability to support 'multiple leadership initiatives' through the development of extensive informal networks. Clearly, in small businesses there is not the same complexity that size bestows. However, once any group reaches eight or more people its tendency is to fragment. Organizational structure that emphasizes departmentalization also tends towards fragmentation, rivalries and conflict. It is being able to develop a culture that overcomes the structural difficulties of the overmanaged organization which is the essence of effective leadership. Such a culture can be developed by giving employees challenging opportunities at an early stage in their career. The experience gained, the freedom given to take some risks and make some mistakes, develops leadership capability.

Table **9.1** How companies manage complexity – two contrasting styles

Management	Leadership
Planning Setting targets: identifying steps to goal achievement and allocating resources to achieve them.	**Envisioning** Setting direction: creating a vision for the future along with strategies for its achievement.
Organizing Creating a structure: identifying jobs and staffing requirements, communicating the plan and delegating responsibility to those job holders for carrying them out.	**Aligning people** Communicating the vision and marshalling support; getting people to believe the message and empowering them with a clear sense of direction and strength in unity.
Controlling and problem solving The installation of control systems to detect deviations from the plan. The purpose is to complete routine jobs successfully.	**Motivating/inspiring** Energizing people through need fulfilment and involvement in the process. It includes supporting employee's efforts and recognizing and rewarding their successes. Coordination occurs through strong networks of informal relationships.

Source: Kotter 1990 (see note 39)

Employees given such opportunities in large companies may be well equipped to move into and lead the small to medium-sized enterprise.

The differences between leaders and managers has also been demonstrated by contrasting the traditional functional responsibilities of the manager with the less tangible aspects of leader behaviour. The idea of a 'manager' suggests routine, efficiency, planning, paperwork, procedures, regulations, control and consistency. This implies a particular style of management. Traditional managers tend to:

● adopt impersonal or passive attitudes to goals
● compromise in order to resolve conflicting values and reach a solution
● maintain a low level of emotional involvement with others
● conserve the status quo.

In contrast, the term 'leader' suggests vision, energy, dynamism, creativity, change and risk taking. Hence, leaders tend to:

● adopt a more personal and active attitude
● create excitement
● empathize with others
● work in, but not belong to, the organization
● search for opportunities for change.

Whilst management is concerned with planning, organizing, directing and controlling, leadership is concerned with motivating. Watson brought out the significance of this contrast in the **7-S organizational framework.**[40] Strategy, Structure and Systems are the province of management. Style, Staff, Skills and Shared goals are those of the leader. Clearly to be an effective manager it is necessary to exercise the role of leadership. In this sense leadership is a sub-set of management. New management shows a movement away from reliance on position power and operates within a flattened hierarchy, empowering others and using symbols of power and control. Employees are given credit for achievement and the motivation is more personal, charismatic. This is in the context of the need to transform and change the organization.

Transformational leadership

There has been considerable interest in transformational leadership because of its perceived utility in organizational development and change. Transformational leadership is based on the idea of 'charisma' but is not the same as 'charismatic leadership'. It picks up the leader-manager distinction, emphasizing that leaders are interested in instituting change.[41]

The transformational leadership style has been developed strategically as a framework for primarily organizational transformation but also individual transformation. The main thrust of this work has been to examine the processes by which strategic leaders can transform and revitalize organizations (for example, Tichy and Devanna[42]). The basic framework is:

- a **trigger event** – a crisis or realization of a need to change the organization
- a **felt need for change** – must be experienced by key personnel
- **creation of a vision** – the transformational leader must communicate the vision of a desired future for the business
- **mobilization of commitmen**t – a critical mass of people must make the vision happen
- a **new organization culture** must be developed.

Several large corporations have attempted image and organizational culture

Box 9.5: Transformational versus transactional leadership characteristics

Change	v	Stability
Restructuring	v	Consolidation
Negotiation	v	Exchange
Vision	v	Planning
Fluidity	v	Routine
Inspired	v	Controlled performance

transformations but not all have been successful. For example, British Airways as one aspect of an attempt at image transformation removed the British flag – the Union Jack – from the tail fins of its planes to be replaced by a range of abstract images to signify its aspiring international identity as an airline. Whilst symbols are important to signify culture and meaning, this symbolic gesture towards internationalism signified nothing to other nations and to some rather more conservative Britons it signified a betrayal of national identity. Leaders and chief executives who take such bold steps must succeed otherwise the duration of their tenure is likely to be curtailed.

Tichy and Devanna emphasize the need for the leader to have a thorough understanding of the technical, political and cultural aspects of organizational change so that they can articulate new norms, values and ways of doing to lever a smooth passage for change and reduce resistance. The transformational leader as per the prototypical entrepreneur must see themselves as change agents, want the changes to come about and not experience change as hassle.[43]

Conger takes the idea of the transformational leader further by emphasizing a staged process requiring different skills[44] (see Figure 9.4). Conger's model of the charismatic leader has parallels in the high profile ('opportunistic') entrepreneur.[45] It would, however, be difficult to demonstrate Conger's stages. Such charismatic figures have seemingly boundless energy, present 'larger than life' figures and are concerned with image. Nigel, an entrepreneur and business owner of a small firm in men's designer clothing exhibited such characteristics. The value of the product was in the brand and so company image and Nigel's image were intricately interwoven. It was important that the quality and exclusivity of this brand was known to potential clients and that Nigel could express this verbally and non-verbally. This signified the need for a degree of arrogance and eccentricity, of self-importance, boosting personal and product images simultaneously. Moreover, it was apparent that employees also believed in the image and in Nigel's embodiment of it; in this sense they were followers not employees.

Nigel also carried out consultancy work for major clients (principally in Australia, the UK and the USA). He would personally assess what was needed then bring in his deputy, Bob, to put his vision into operation. This gave Bob considerable power which he never abused. Having tried to run his own business many years ago without success he had the utmost respect for Nigel. Bob was also valuable in that he could work effectively with others – external clients as well as the internal team. Nigel, on the other hand, tended to be brusque and outspoken; he had been known to 'ruffle a few feathers' when jobs were being implemented. He now knew that it was better to withdraw and leave it to Bob, whom he could trust. The trust extended to the shared values, commitment and agreement about what was needed. However, the idea that there was 'low internal conflict' requires some qualification. Nigel's team (inclusive of Nigel) argued about every last detail – colour matching, fabric, finished look, etc – and some temperament would be displayed. But this was professional discussion; there was no angry or acrimonious displays and once agreement was reached, everyone pulled together to deliver to the specification, design and delivery date.

Figure **9.4** A stage model of charismatic leadership

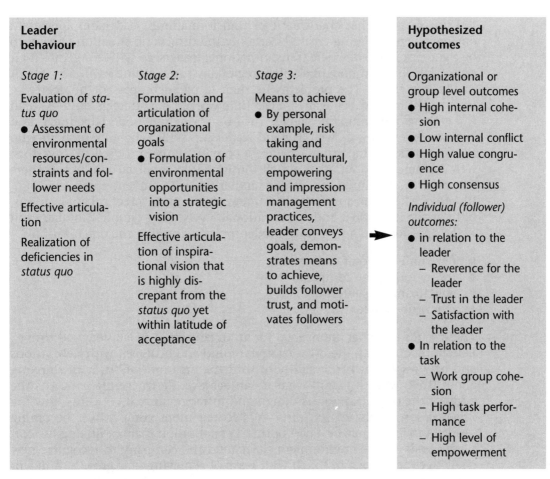

Leader behaviour			Hypothesized outcomes
Stage 1:	*Stage 2:*	*Stage 3:*	Organizational or group level outcomes
Evaluation of *status quo*	Formulation and articulation of organizational goals	Means to achieve	● High internal cohesion
● Assessment of environmental resources/constraints and follower needs	● Formulation of environmental opportunities into a strategic vision	● By personal example, risk taking and countercultural, empowering and impression management practices, leader conveys goals, demonstrates means to achieve, builds follower trust, and motivates followers	● Low internal conflict ● High value congruence ● High consensus
Effective articulation	Effective articulation of inspirational vision that is highly discrepant from the *status quo* yet within latitude of acceptance		*Individual (follower) outcomes:* ● in relation to the leader – Reverence for the leader – Trust in the leader – Satisfaction with the leader ● In relation to the task – Work group cohesion – High task performance – High level of empowerment
Realization of deficiencies in *status quo*			

Source: Conger 1989 (see note 44)

In sum, the key skills that this model and the work of Tichy and Devanna and of Chell, suggest are:

● **envisioning, articulating/communicating the vision**
● **environmental sensitivity:** information scanning, assimilation, decision making and judgement
● **unconventional behaviour:** challenging the status quo, being different
● **personal risk:** to deliver the vision, enhance reputation of self and the business
● **sensitivity to stakeholder needs:** a sense of collective responsibility
● **interpersonal skills:** such as persuasion, developing trust, empowering others, self efficacy.

This set of characteristics is paralleled in the work of Sashkin.[46] Kotter also uses the term 'agenda setting' rather than envisioning and 'network building'.[47] Such alternative terminology serves to reinforce rather than contradict the profile.[48]

Hunt suggests that charismatic or transformational leadership appears to emerge where there is a crisis.[49] Certainly the turnround situation appears to be a good example of where transformational leadership skills come into their own. Malcolm Hart bought a failing regionally based airline – Gill Air – for £1 in the late 1980s. The problems he then faced encompassed the degree of investment needed, set against a carefully worked out strategic business plan for making the company viable. Turnrounds require sound technical and business know-how as well as good leadership skills. The entrepreneur who turns rounds a company must have a convincing plan to 'sell to' investors, new customers and suppliers and disillusioned/demoralized employees. There are, as already pointed out, strong similarities with the entrepreneurial profile. Hence, the transformational framework has many practical applications, both at the individual and organizational levels. For example, Gouillart and Kelly[50] put forward a four stage model for 'transforming the organization':

- reframing corporate direction
- restructuring the company
- revitalizing the enterprise
- renewing people.

These **4 'R's** are what are needed for an organization to 'survive and thrive'. Reframing opens up the organizational mind and infuses it with new visions and new resolve. It is the ability to shift the organization's way of thinking about itself, what it is and what it can achieve. Restructuring concerns the body of the organization; its design and infrastructure. It concerns how the organization 'girds up its loins' to become more competitive; becoming 'leaner and fitter' may be a part of this. Revitalization is about linking the corporate body to the environment. It enables the company to recognize new challenges and to get in touch with ways of achieving new growth. A downsized business can easily stagnate hence revitalization is essential to begin to achieve new growth and take on new challenges. Renewal deals with the spirit of the organization. It concerns investing individuals with new skills, new purpose and a new metabolism thus enabling the organization to regenerate itself.

The need to rejuvenate a business is not a function of age or size of that business. Hence the 'new leadership profile' (see Table 9.3 below) is likely to be broadly relevant to organizations where change, increased competitiveness and a transformational orientation is deemed to be critical. The practical implications of this analysis are summarized in Table 9.2, which identifies some entrepreneurial capabilities associated with a transformational leadership style.

Table **9.2** The transformational style and the implications for entrepreneurial capability

Transformational style	Entrepreneurial capabilities
• Places less reliance on structure and authority system.	Informality energizes, encourages flexibility and cross-organizational linkages.
• Greater emphasis placed on social skills development.	Lack of formality or hierarchy but strong task orientation suggests the need for good social and and interpersonal skills and good HRM policies.
• More depth understanding of 'culture' – both internal and external.	Need to build networks and develop both internal and external linkages.
• Sensitivity to situational differences and cultural norms and expectations.	Exercise of sound judgement.
• Greater need to handle organizational politics and decision processes.	The need to have a strong vision, implementation process and plan for effective resource allocation.
• Balance required between charismatic style and implementation of effective developmental processes.	Reputation for delivery must be maintained, otherwise 'charisma' becomes tarnished and hollow.
• Increased importance of the competitive environment and the demands for organizational change.	Environmental scanning is critical; ability to rise to demands of challenges and desire to achieve.
• Selection and appropriate placing of employees in jobs.	Recruitment strategy crucial especially in the smaller organization.
• Need for continuous organizational learning and adaptation.	Repetition of mistakes is costly, it could mean the difference between survival and demise.

Table **9.3** A comparison of old and new leadership styles

Old leadership	New leadership
• Planning	Vision/mission
• Allocating responsibility	Infusing vision
• Controlling and problem-solving	Motivating and inspiring
• Creating routine equilibrium	Creating change and innovating
• Power retention	Empowering others
• Creating compliance	Creating commitment
• Emphasizing contractual obligations	Simulating extra effort
• Detachment and rationality of the leader	Interest in others and intuition of the leaders
• Reactive approach to the environment	Proactive approach to the environment

Leadership development and effectiveness

The relevance of leadership theory and research has been identified in the skills and competencies exhibited by an effective leader. Effectiveness operationally defined means being able to get things done through other people. The specific skills include the ability to translate knowledge into action that results in desired performance. At one level of abstraction, technical (knowledge/know-how), social (interpersonal/human relations) and conceptual (thinking/reasoning) skills can be distinguished. Whilst at a 'lower' level, types of skills are associated with particular behaviours, for example planning, and are likely to be contextually related (the week's work, production flow, etc). The exercise of planning competency is concerned with setting goals, assessing risks and developing a sequence of goal related actions.[51] Competencies are functionally related managerially and task related in respect of entrepreneurial behaviour.

However, whilst much is known about the types of competencies that may be identified, there would be little point from the practitioner's perspective in giving it further consideration if it were not believed that skilled leader behaviour will (ultimately) make a difference in terms of firm performance. This suggests the need to take training and skills development to a level of proficiency to enable the firm to achieve increases in efficiency, effectiveness, productivity, market penetration, sales, etc, leading to higher growth and/or profitability of the firm. For the entrepreneur 'buying in' the best people (often through word of mouth recommendation) is a substitution for skills training. Indeed this also suggests that the growth-oriented leader knows that they are only as effective as their weakest employee. But little of the training is at leadership/owner-manager level. It is variable across sectors and it is more prevalent in innovative, growth-oriented firms.[52] Unfortunately whilst common sense suggests that better skilled individuals will perform more effectively, no link has been demonstrated between training and firm performance.[53] Amos also confirms the weakness of this link.[54]

Not all studies have been of a quantitative nature – some have been case study based. Thus, in a different way the 'excellence models' have attempted to identify exemplars of managerial excellence and company performance,[55] but the formula has lacked reliability and replicability. Achievement can be sought and its fruits gained but the underlying complexity has proved difficult to model.

The EFQM[56] Excellence Model is another such approach aimed at enabling firms to improve their performance and achieve longer term success. The advantages of this model are that it provides a framework for the total organization spearheaded by leadership and purposeful behaviour. It is multi-level in respect of 'inputs' from people, external partnerships, other internal resources and strategy. There are also multiple levels of outcome or results. The role of the leadership is to develop a vision and values which imbue organizational culture, manage internal systems to ensure successful achievement of goals and involve, motivate and support others. This combines both a visionary (inspirational) role with the more conventional integrating roles of management. Whilst there are many large corporate subscribers (in name) to this model it has to be said that there is still too little that is known about *how* such processes are managed by the leadership, *what* the critical difficulties are, *how* they are overcome, *what* (if any) learning takes place and *how* these behaviours manifest themselves in respect of managerial/entrepreneurial skills or competencies.

Conclusions

Leadership and management research appears to have come a long way. However, the concepts discussed in this chapter are constructions. This is apparent in the notion of the 'transformational leader' for whom there is clearly an implied if not articulated mission; it is to rise to the challenge of global competitiveness, to change the business organization so that it can, not only, meet such challenges, but 'exceed above expectations', in other words, aim to become a world class business run by a world class leader.

The military imperative – to defend one's country – no longer holds sway in shaping models of leadership effectiveness. Whilst there do appear to be strong overtones of 'agency', these are counterbalanced by the need to be sensitive to the team, the culture and the socio-economic environment and to recognize interdependency and the importance of developing networks and linkages. The 'new leadership style' therefore suggests the need for a blend of characteristics – those of agency and communion[57] – if the leader is to manage both the internal dynamics of organizational change and competitive positioning on a world stage. The appropriate skills complement is also recognized as that to be developed in young prospective leaders of the future.

Finally this chapter has demonstrated that (a) there is no shortage of research on the nature of leadership and management, (b) there has been a convergence of thinking in respect of the mix and overlap between leadership and management skills and (c) there is a dearth of research that demonstrates the effectiveness of such a skills profile in terms of business performance. To demonstrate such linkages requires the expertise of a multidisciplinary research team investigating the issues longitudinally and over an extended time frame. Too little investment has gone into research of this nature.

CHAPTER 10

Team management and development

Two heads are always better than one.

Private ownership and entrepreneurship have been portrayed in the media as the 'economics of individualism'. A potent image has been developed of a charismatic entrepreneur – the man or woman owner-manager – who has masterminded the business, is 'multifunctional' that is, is capable of discharging a variety of duties, is fully in control and carries sole responsibility for the businesses' success or failure. There may be some truth in this image in some businesses although the image has been criticized. It has been criticized for the language that is used to characterize this type of entrepreneur, in particular that of hero(ine). Second, it has been suggested that a very high proportion of business start ups are made by two or more partners.[1] These partners could be said to form an 'inner team', it is they who influence the behaviour, decisions and strategic direction of the business.

However, whether a business is founded by an individual or a team, there is a secondary process of team development which is much needed if the venture is to be a success. This process creates an outer team.[2]

This chapter builds on the previous one where models of leadership which stressed interdependency were discussed and considers the need for the leader – in this case owner-manager – to develop a range of social and interpersonal skills in order to persuade and impress others to follow their lead. Leadership was thus about having a vision or idea which others could be persuaded to 'buy into' whilst management was the process of aligning people around the implementation of that idea. Hence, if management is the ability to work through other people, then a key to business growth and development is the ability to create and manage effective teams.

In this chapter, a model is assumed where, within a specifiable context, there is an input (team composition), process (team/group dynamics) and outcomes (performance of the team/success of the venture). The chapter opens by depicting a suitable life cycle model of an organization and considers the management and entrepreneurial leadership behaviours necessary for team and organization development in the embryonic business.

Context to group management

Baliga and Hunt[3] suggested a model of work group effectiveness that has its starting point in a life cycle model of organization development (see Figure 10.1).

Figure **10.1** Phases and stages of the organizational life cycle

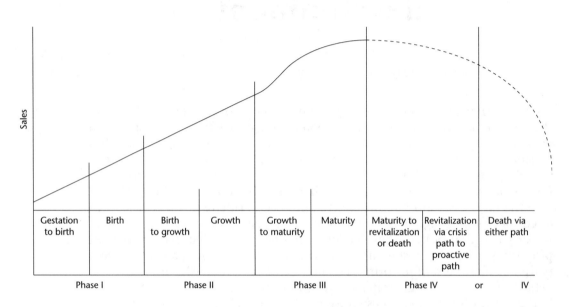

Source: Baliga and Hunt 1988 (see note 3)

Their analysis of the manager's role in this context is based on Stewart's analysis of the components of the job of management:

- **Demands** (what must be done)
- **Choices** (the discretionary element of the job)
- **Constraints** (those elements such as finance, human resources etc, that limit what a manager can do).[4]

These demands, choices and constraints, they suggest, vary over the life cycle. Hence, if 'managers do the right thing' and 'leaders do things right' it is possible to develop a framework for the identification of effective management and leadership based on the above three criteria. This implies the following propositions.

- An ineffective manager is unable to fulfil demands of the job consistently.
- An effective manager/marginal leader is able to fulfil demands but is not able to reduce the constraints or capitalize beneficially on the choices available to them.

- An effective manager/effective leader is able to fulfil demands, reduce/ modify favourably the constraints and choices and create some organizational slack (an excess of resources over and above those required to meet demands).
- An effective manager/very effective leader fulfils demands with a minimum level of resource, minimizes constraints, maximizes choices and creates favourable future demands in order to generate considerable slack.

In Figure 10.1, within the 'gestation to birth' transition, there are some key demands made on the owner-manager. They are to:

- develop a viable strategy
- acquire the necessary financial, material and human resources to translate the vision into organizational reality.

This process may be carried out more successfully by an entrepreneurial team that has a wider range of capabilities to draw upon. The following case study (Box 10.1), based on an actual business, depicts one approach to an entrepreneurial team start. The founder had previous experience of setting up a business venture but not in the hospitality industry. However, having reached middle age and after a personal life crisis, the launch of a successful business venture was a conscious and very deliberate decision on the part of this particular entrepreneur.

Box 10.1: The launch of a new restaurant:
a sushi bar

Some of the key steps which the founder took are as follows.

1. He developed a high profile vision of the sushi bar, its design and operations.
2. He presented the idea to a number of financiers and acquired the necessary equipment, including the purchase (or lease) of a building to locate the business.
3. He identified key people to make up a team, particularly important was the chef. Further plans were developed *together* – the chef played a critical role in the development of the operational plans.
4. A day was planned for the opening and launch of the restaurant. Such an event is likely to involve internal and external stakeholder scrutiny; also immediate customer evaluation. In the event, the press were invited to give the restaurant a high profile opening.
5. There was further socialization of employees, management systems were put in place for day to day running of the restaurant and a management/leadership style developed which was inclusive, participative and supportive.
6. Unusually perhaps, roles were quite clearly distinguished from the outset. The owner-manager would be responsible for opportunity identification and development, the expansion of the resource base and the beneficial (to the business) exploitation of these developments.
7. There would be increased demands on resources due to expansion – the pace of which needed to be managed. Vision development was necessary in order to maintain the commitment and morale of the staff and to deliver outcomes.

At a very early stage of business development, crucial issues highlighted in the above case study were those of the founder's effective leadership, management and marshalling of resources. These resources include the staff. In a kitchen or production unit the roles, the responsibilities for task delivery, the division of labour and so on, are the staffing element of detailed operational planning. Arguably, this skill was fundamental to the sushi bar's rapid success.

In this chapter, the discussion will focus on putting together effective teams, whereas in chapter 14 the human resource management aspects of team management and development will be considered. In the next section how effective teams are created from groups of individuals is examined.

What is a group?

Teams are very special forms of group.[5] Therefore some basic knowledge of the nature of groups is essential if the owner-manager is to put together an effective team or teams. A group is more than a collection of individuals; it is not a crowd at a football match or the eight individuals who happen to be squashed in the lift. A group has a purpose, perceive themselves to be a group and are in some sense interdependent. Groups may be defined by their purpose; the nature of their task – the job of work formally defined – or the social needs they fulfil. A group of people may come together for social reasons on a regular or *ad hoc* basis, at a particular venue or different venues according to the wishes of group members. However, a group of people may come together for the sole purpose of completing a job of work, they may fulfil some social psychological needs in each other during task completion, but that is not the objective. The degree of interdependence of members of the group is critical to task completion. For example, based on the above case study, in a well organized kitchen completed dishes from the menu cannot be prepared unless there is coordination of effort, good timing and a shared set of values, beliefs and common purpose. These values might be around quality, presentation and beliefs about what the customer (and perhaps more importantly!) what the boss wants. The greater the mutual agreement and sharing of these beliefs, values and purposes, the more cohesive the group.

At work the formal function of a group is to fulfil goals that help realize the organization's mission. The mission may have started out as the owner-manager's vision which has been articulated and communicated both directly and via the chef, through whom it has been formalized into detailed operational plans, down to task level. The pace of work in the kitchen, for example, will largely be dictated by the busy-ness of the restaurant, the quality and type of food. The chef also controls the pace and instructions are given on the hoof. The owner-manager (where they are not the chef) may be at 'front of house', seating customers, overseeing the table service and so on. In such a fast moving environment, where service matters, realization of expectations, role clarity-enactment and the delivery of unambiguous instructions at all times contributes to an effective, smooth operating environment. In this example, the group is functioning as an effective team.

As a coacting, interdependent operational unit as in the above example, the group must be well coordinated. Groups, however, can and do operate at all organizational levels (for example, the top management team, sales teams, *ad hoc* committees, research and development units) and as such they have clear advantages over individuals. They have:

- the ability to work on complex interdependent tasks
- the means of generating new ideas and creative solutions to complex problems
- superiority for purposes of liaison and coordination
- the capability to implement complex decisions
- greater suitability as vehicles for change
- the capacity for socialization and training of new members.

Such task functions may be achieved more effectively and efficiently by means of a group but the group fulfils other needs of the individual. A cohesive, well managed group can also:

- give friendship and support
- develop the individual's sense of identity and self esteem
- provide a basis for the construction of social reality through discussion, questioning and talking about events and sharing perspectives about how events should be defined.
- help reduce feelings of insecurity, anxiety and powerlessness
- facilitate problem solving
- be entertaining, helping boost morale and reduce boredom
- provide a means by which members can counter managerial power.

Hence, managed effectively the group is an asset to the business. The power of a group is generated by the group's **norms**. Group norms prescribe how a group will behave. Norms are rules of conduct, usually tacitly understood, developed during interaction and established to maintain the consistency with which the group goes about its business. Some norms may be counterproductive from the organization's perspective, for example restrictive practices, whereas other norms such as the desire to do a job well may help the firm maintain quality. Some important characteristics of norms are that:

- they cannot be imposed from outside the group
- they are formed with respect to matters of significance to the group
- they usually apply to all members of the group
- they are more powerful the greater the acceptance by all members
- there will be differences in tolerance for deviations from normative behaviour, for example high status members have more latitude to deviate from group norms.
- they simplify the influence process
- they apply to group behaviour
- they develop and change slowly.

Groups go through a process of development which has been characterized as

forming, **norming**, **storming** and **performing**. In the newly established business, as the owner-manager puts together a team, norms will begin to develop. Clearly the owner-manager can influence this process by setting standards, communicating the vision and their expectations and clarifying what needs to be done. There will be much to discuss, some things to grumble about and others which cause excitement if not a little anxiety. The group 'storming' stage does not necessarily mean violent disagreement, but it does mean open discussion, questioning and reaching agreement on the way forward. The more open the management style at this crucial juncture the more likely it will be that anxieties will surface, and the greater commitment to the agreed plan and course of action will be. Openness enables the owner-manager to establish trust and in return give support. This will only be effective if they can deliver on the promises, the resources and the vision realization. Initially the group will commit to the plan if there is evidence that the owner-manager is able to deliver their side of the bargain. This may appear to be transactional leadership in operation – exchanges, reciprocity, a bargain being struck. However, with vision realization and the development of slack the excess of resources over demands will put the owner-manager in a strong position *vis à vis* the group; demonstrating their effectiveness and providing the motivational rationale for commitment to requisite performance.

Discussion is also important because norms can help establish standards of achievement and quality of task performance. Only through discussion will the group understand the importance of the standard and develop an acceptance of the reasons for it. Hence a participative management style in such circumstances is more likely to deliver the results.

Conformity to group norms is a powerful dynamic and one which suggests the need for skilful handling. The owner-manager who is a powerful visionary leader will be able to exert influence on group norms, and help shape and develop the standards and ways of doing that they can approve. In contrast, where the management style is transactional or Tayloristic, work standards will be 'externally' imposed (that is, from outside the group) or at least they will be experienced as such. The firm will then need some compensating feature which will enable the work group to 'buy into' the concept and adopt the standards (for example 'McDonaldization'). However, not all companies have compensating features. Here management *influence* will be weak (although there may be plenty of evidence of control systems in place) and the group will develop a set of norms independent of management (for example, the Bank Wiring Room of the Hawthorne Works – Mayo[6]).

It must also be remembered that in most work situations an employee may not have very much choice of group membership. Their commitment needs to be won. The battle is partially won through the selection and recruitment process, but not always, especially if the group is a low trust, low support group.[7] Here the management task is likely to involve an attempt to dilute the negative influences of extant normative behaviour by introducing (minimally) two new recruits – one of whom is in a senior position. In this way management will facilitate the introduction of new ideas, new ways of working and new people to champion subtle changes in group culture, which will garner trust, engender support and result in higher performance. However, managing the pressures to conform to extant group norms is a difficult but not impossible process.[8]

Group think

Irving Janis identified a powerful dynamic of highly cohesive in-groups.[9] In-groups are those groups that are evaluated positively through in-group-out-group comparisons. They are deemed to be superior in some sense. They may, for example, be the more powerful. Social comparison processes may exaggerate the strength of the in-group. Nevertheless when this group develops a strong dynamic towards conformity and internal consensus the conditions for group think are extant. Such a group requires that members concur above all else and overrides any realistic appraisal of alternative courses of action (Janis, 1971). A real danger is that independent critical thinking is replaced by group think which, according to Janis, is likely to result in irrational and dehumanizing actions directed against the out-group. Key symptoms of group think are the following.

- Team members share an illusion of **invulnerability**; this leads to over-optimism and a willingness to take extraordinary risks.
- Team members collectively construct **rationalizations** in order to discount warnings and negative feedback which, if taken seriously might lead to the questioning of the assumptions underlying past decisions.
- Team members believe unquestioningly in the inherent **morality** of their own group; it inclines them to stop short of considering the ethical or moral consequences of their decisions.
- Team members hold **stereotyped** views of the leaders of enemy or opposing groups.
- Team members apply **direct pressure** to any member who expresses doubts about any of the group's shared illusions or who questions the validity of the arguments supporting a course of action favoured by the group.
- Team members keep silent about their misgivings and are **self censoring**.
- Team members share an **illusion of unanimity**; silence is interpreted as concordance.
- Some team members appoint themselves as **mindguards** to protect the leaders and fellow members from adverse information.

The consequences of group think are poor decision making and inadequate problem solving. This is because there is limited discussion and too few proposed solutions. There is also little reevaluation and reconsideration of proposals. No attempt is made to obtain expert views from outside the group. There is a tendency to plough on with the course of action first thought of. Attention is highly selective; facts and opinions that do not support the policy are ignored. There is little or no contingency planning. It is difficult to believe that such groups could survive or exist for very long; what organizations could house and protect groups whose thinking may be critical to organization direction but so woefully inadequate?

However there are ways in which such cosiness can be broken up and decision making made more effective.

- Encourage critical thinking.
- Commence with an impartial stance to encourage open debate.
- Set up alternative groups to address the same or similar questions.
- Encourage employees to discuss and provide feedback on the team's deliberations.
- Open the group to external membership by experts.
- Study the opposition's strategy.
- Form subgroups to consider alternative courses of action and strategies.
- Hold sufficient meetings to allow people to express any lingering doubts.

Although Janis studies top policy decision making groups, 'group think' is a dynamic which can affect any cohesive group. An owner-manager, for example, is in a prime position – at the very heart of the business – to develop and perhaps want around them uncritical management teams. The message is: beware! because group think ultimately leads to sub-optimal decision making.

Team working

Practitioners, consultants and leading management 'gurus' from the mid 1980s to the mid 1990s strongly advocated the importance of working with and through teams. This prescription was primarily motivated by the perceived need to restructure large corporations in order to create the conditions for increased competitiveness on a global scale by using the group or team as a vehicle for bringing about change. Peters[10] commended the use of groups at all times through the downsizing and restructuring of large corporations into smaller business units. Whilst there were other strong voices (Kanter[11]) on the effectiveness of teams, others pointed out that teams were not always universally effective.[12] What therefore might be meant by an effective or an ineffective team? Under what circumstances is it appropriate to use a team? Are there different types of team and how might they be characterized?

Early research on the effectiveness of groups led to the conclusion that there is a level of interpersonal operations within a group which is essential for it to function properly. Such interpersonal and intragroup processes McGregor termed 'group atmosphere'. The following table (10.1) compares the workings of effective and ineffective groups.

The table shows the fundamental importance of intragroup relationships, the skilled handling of communications, information exchange and decision making, and the relative absence of hierarchy. The 'atmosphere' is relaxed and friendly, that is, people feel confident that they can contribute openly to the issue being deliberated. Participation through a group mechanism serves a number of purposes.

Table **10.1** Contrasting behaviours in effective and ineffective teams

Effective groups	Ineffective groups
1. Group atmosphere is informal, comfortable, relaxed; no obvious tensions; no boredom; a working atmosphere of people who are both involved and interested.	1. The atmosphere reflects indifference, boredom or tension. The group is not challenged by its task nor genuinely involved in it.
2. Lot of discussion which is task relevant and in which everyone participates.	2. A few people dominate the discussion and contributions are frequently off the point with no attempts made to keep the group on track.
3. The task or objective of the group is well understood; it has been arrived at through discussion and all members are committed to it.	3. From what is said, it is difficult to understand what the group task or objective is; people have different, private objectives which they are attempting to achieve in the group; there is no common objective.
4. People listen to each other and ideas are freely expressed.	4. People do not really listen to each other and ideas are ignored or overridden; people leave such meetings having failed to express their ideas and feelings, being afraid of ridicule or undue criticism.
5. Disagreement is expressed, not suppressed or overridden by premature group action; those who disagree do so genuinely and expect to be heard.	5. Disagreements are generally not dealt with effectively; they may be suppressed for fear of open conflict; where they are not suppressed, there may be 'open warfare' of one faction attempting to dominate another, there may be 'tyranny of the minority' in which an individual or subgroup is so aggressive that the majority accedes to their wishes in order to preserve the peace or get on with the task.
6. Decisions are reached by consensus, but the group does not allow apparent consensus to mask real disagreement; formal voting is minimized, as it tends to be divisive; the group does not accept a single majority as a proper basis for action.	6. Decisions/actions are often taken prematurely, before the real issues are examined or resolved; a simple majority is considered to be sufficient, without the majority expected to go along with the decision; this creates resentment and a lack of commitment to the decision by the minority.
7. Constructive criticism occurs and is not of a personal kind.	7. Criticism creates embarrassment and tension; it is often personal and destructive.
8. People are free to express their personal feelings as well as their ideas.	8. People hide their feelings; they are not considered an appropriate area for discussion.
9. When action is taken, clear assignments are made and accepted.	9. Responsibility for action when it is taken is unclear, and there is a lack of confidence that individuals who have been so designated will carry out their responsibilities.
10. The chairperson does not dominate discussion, rather leadership shifts depending upon the issue under discussion.	10. The leadership is fixed and resides in the chairperson who sits at the 'head of the table'.
11. The group is self-conscious about its own operations: whether the problem is procedural or interpersonal, the group will try to resolve the problem before proceeding.	11. There is no discussion in the group about its own operations or maintenance functions.
12. Power struggles as such do not occur in the group; the issue is not *who* controls but *how* the job gets done.	

Source: McGregor 1960 (note 12)

- It helps people recognize what it is they do not yet know but should.
- It is an occasion for members of the group to get answers to questions.
- It provides an opportunity to seek and obtain advice on matters over which there are anxieties.
- It enables the sharing of ideas such that a common wisdom or consensus may be reached.
- It is a way for people to learn about each other.

This type of group does not necessarily meet in order to take decisions – it may have no executive authority – but through the consultation process it serves both educational and advisory purposes. As a work group it may have the added advantage of diffusing problems – 'nipping them in the bud'. Thus, even in an effective group regular consultations with the supervisor/leader can have beneficial effects. Where the group is not very effective the supervisor may have a particular role to play in order to break down barriers where people are reluctant to take part in discussions, lack ideas and/or fail to give and take.

Tsosvold argues that if a group or team is to be effective it must be motivated towards achieving actions which contribute towards the organizational mission.[13] A 'dynamic' team has these features. It also has the group capability to deal with issues concerned with intragroup processes and effective self management and improvement. This ensures the continuance of the group – a feature which is not an inevitability.

Table **10.2** Two contrasting group cultures: stagnate and dynamic

Stagnate	Dynamic
Lack of coherent vision	Good vision articulation
Individualistic, competitive atmosphere	Collective, collaborative and cohesive group behaviour
Hierarchical organization, power associated with position and status	Flattened organization, power devolved, group members empowered
New ideas either stifled or lacking	Idea-seeking and exploration
Automatic, routinization of behaviour	Opportunity for reflection, discovery and development of ideas

Chaudry-Lawton *et al.* take a broader, pragmatic view of team effectiveness. They point out that 'successful teams bring together a rich mix of competencies, personalities, experiences and values',[14] but such teams also have a good understanding of their environment. Their profile of the successful team anticipates much of the current literature. See Table 10.3.

Table **10.3** The secrets of effective teams

- PURPOSE AND GOALS
  They are persistent and obsessive in the pursuit of their goals, but creatively flexible in how they get there. They constantly ask themselves the question, 'What are we trying to achieve?'
- REMOVE BARRIERS
  They try to remove barriers and obstacles and are willing and able to confront people or situations that are not helpful.
- PERFORMANCE EXPECTATIONS
  They are committed to quality in their own performance and their expectations of each other are very high.
- UNDERSTAND THEIR ENVIRONMENT
  They appear to have a good understanding of the philosophy, strategy and value of their organization.
- CLEAR VISION
  They have a clear vision of what they are trying to achieve. They use this vision to provide them with direction. They also have very clear strategies for moving beyond their vision into the action stage.
- BUILD NETWORKS
  They are good at building networks both inside and outside the organization by identifying individuals who can help them achieve their goal or support them in other ways.
- OPEN AND AVAILABLE
  They are visible and available to others. Although they have strong values and communicate to others what they stand for, they are also willing to receive feedback and advice from other people.
- DRIVEN BY SUCCESS
  They are driven by success and thrive on energy, excitement and commitment, which come with feelings of success. They enjoy the recognition and rewards that success brings.
- TAKE INITIATIVE
  They are action-orientated. They do not wait for things to happen to them. They initiate a lot of activities and make things happen. They respond quickly and positively to any problems or opportunities that they can see.

- ASSUME RESPONSIBILITY
  They appear to be in touch with their parent organization's goals and are committed to their organization's success. They thrive in a supportive and open culture where they can assume responsibility and produce results.
- INFLUENCE EFFECTIVELY
  They influence their organization and other teams within it. They tend to use their credibility rather than their authority to get things done.
- REMAIN FLEXIBLE
  They work best with broad guidelines and principles rather than with rigid rule. In this way, they are able to remain flexible.
- URGENT AND CRITICAL
  They are able to distinguish between the important activities and the urgent. They welcome change and are able to integrate it in their plans smoothly.
- SHARED LEADERSHIP
  They like leaders who can provide them with direction and help to maintain the team's energy and commitment. They expect the leader to negotiate with others in the organization for support and resources. Leadership shifts from time to time depending on the circumstances, the needs of the group and the skills of team members. Team members are prepared to assume leadership when necessary.
- COMMUNICATION
  They maintain a high level of communication even when they are working apart. Team members feel free to express their feelings about the task and the team's operations.
- INNOVATE
  They tend to be innovative and are creative and prepared to take risks in order to enhance the team's performance.
- CONTINUOUS IMPROVEMENT
  They are interested in continuously improving their own performance. They look for ways to do things differently and to do things better.
- CO-OPERATION VERSUS COMPETITION
  They are able to work with others easily and focus on co-operation rather than working against others.

Source: Chaudry-Lawton *et al.* 1992 (note 14)

Quality control circles[15]

The idea of a quality control circle (QCC) is that it allows the workgroup to identify and tackle problems within their immediate work environment.[16] This enables them to develop a degree of self-control which should enhance commitment. The QCC draws on their expertise, increases their sense of responsibility and facilitates cost savings. The benefits are:

- increased employee involvement
- enhanced business effectiveness
- an opportunity to change company culture.

The central tenet is the achievement of quality and the reason is to increase the company's competitiveness. This means enabling the firm to produce the best product/service efficiently while increasing customer satisfaction.

Each QCC may involve between three and ten members and meet regularly. They are trained to identify, analyse and solve some of the problems that occur in their line of work, present these solutions to management and, if approved, implement the solution. When the QCC works at its best it is responsible for the whole cycle of planning, doing, checking and taking action. It is thus responsible for setting and achieving its own targets within the overall framework of company goals.

The QCC does not attain self control immediately but goes through four distinct stages.

1. Training and development
2. Monitoring and problem solving
3. Innovation
4. Self control.

Initially the work group learns how to identify, analyse and solve some of the more pressing problems in its work area. This can be achieved by brainstorming and eliminating problems outside the group's sphere of control. The analysis involves an attempt to identify the causes of the problem. This is done systematically and the possible causes are categorized as: people problems, equipment, method, for example the job specification or inadequate instructions and materials. These possible causes are then further evaluated by the group until eventually it is satisfied that it has identified the major causes. These are prioritized or ranked and the findings presented to management. Management then decides whether to accept the circle's recommendation. If QCCs are to function effectively then any hindrances to their operation must be removed and they must be properly supported and encouraged. The QCC lends itself to a 'path-goal' participative style of leadership. However, it is essential that management creates a climate conducive to the successful operation of QCCs so that they can become part of the culture of the organization. It has to be said however that QCCs have not been particularly successful in the West.[17]

The collective mind

The behaviour of groups and teams has been considered primarily in terms of what those **behaviours** might be which contribute to effective group performance. This has been examined in particular in the context of a pressured environment, where change and business development are common place and where performance matters. Reference has also been made to the **affective** side of group behaviour, that is how group members feel about their experiences as a group. Weick and Roberts[18] suggest that there is a third, much neglected dimension of group behaviour – the **cognitive**. However, whilst individuals have minds and think, is it sensible to discuss group thinking or rather the sense of a 'collective mind'?

Weick and Roberts developed their theory of **collective mind** by analysing the behaviour of men during air operations on the flight deck of an aircraft carrier. One of the specifics of this kind of operation is the need for high reliability; any errors can be fatal. The team included air traffic controllers, landing signal officers, the control tower, navigators, deck hands and the helmsman: up to 30 people may be engaged in the 'recovery' of an aircraft at any one time.

Hitherto, the language of group behaviour has indicated the need for coordinated responses and a sense of the integration of operations. Weick and Roberts add to this by adding a cognitive dimension; that of **heedful interrelating**. Their analogy is that of a neural network. A network has structure and content, but it is also the pattern of interconnections which give meaning. Similarly with mind, it is not simply the action, but the process – being mindful (or not) of what one is doing – which is a critically important dimension and incidentally suggests intelligent (or stupid) behaviour. They use the term 'collective' rather than 'group' or 'organization' because collective refers to people who act as if they are a group.

> People who act as if they are a group interrelate their actions with more or less care, and focusing on the way this interrelating is done reveals collective mental processes that differ in their degree of development ... [A] collective mind is distinct from an individual mind because *it inheres in the pattern of interrelated activities among many people*, (see note 18: p.360, my emphasis).

Heedful interrelating signifies such qualities of mind as noticing, taking care, attending, applying one's mind, concentrating, putting one's heart into something, thinking about what one is doing, alertness, interest, intentness, studying and trying. People act heedfully when they 'act more or less carefully, critically, consistently, purposefully, attentively, studiously, vigilantly, conscientiously and pertinaciously'. Hence when heed declines, performance may be described as careless, thoughtless, mindless and indifferent. This, however, describes the mind of an individual not that of a group. To extend the concept to group behaviour Weick and Roberts suggested the following.

● People in groups behave as if there were social forces organizing them – for example, the pilot receives integrated information from several sources (the tower, landing signal officers, air operations) that in reality are operating relatively independently.

- When acting as if there are social forces at work, people construct their actions whilst envisaging a system of joint actions and interrelate that constructed action within the envisaged system (subordination) – for example, the pilot taxies on to the catapult for launching purposes. As he envisages what is going on, he is also vigilant to see if the various operations are being correctly interrelated. 'Does it feel right?' relates not to the aircraft but the joint situation to which he has subordinated himself.
- This combination of actions (contributing), envisaging (representing) and interrelating (subordinating) create a system – for example, when the whole team works together in an interrelated way to recover an aircraft.
- The effects produced by a pattern of interrelated activities vary according to style (for example, heedful/heedless) and strength (for example, loose/tight) – for example, individuals in a group can work with, for, or against each other. It is these varying forms of interrelating that embody the collective mind.

Collective mind exists as a kind of capacity and emerges in the style with which activities are interrelated. The collective mind is more developed and more capable of intelligent action, and so the interrelating is done more heedfully. Heedful interrelating raises the level of comprehension and ability to deal with unexpected events, by:

- the increased ability to draw on more know-how from the past and apply it into new, prospective contingencies
- making the connections between activities across a wider span of the task sequence
- the ability to link levels of experience e.g. the newcomer and the 'old-timer'.

Heedful interrelating has implications for the socialization of employees and organizational learning, the development of competence and the ability to raise the organization's capability to deal with increasing complexity. The authors cite actual examples of heedful interrelating such as landing and taxiing on a carrier deck at night, and the job of bosun – the person responsible for deck operations. In the latter case the bosun gets up an hour earlier in order to think through the kind of environment he will create on deck that day. He bears in mind the collective operations and how individuals will carry out their duties. Thus he plans with a representation of the collectivity in his mind.

Weick and Roberts also give an example of heedless interrelating showing how a particular incident can result in events becoming more incomprehensible as people fail to understand what is going on and a deterioration in interrelating. They point out that it is important to disentangle the development of a collective mind from the dynamics of group development (i.e. forming, storming, norming and performing). Figure 10.2 shows a two by two

Figure **10.2** Different types of group

	Group think cults	Superteam
Mature/ developed		
Immature/ underdeveloped	Divided, blame-oriented disaffected group	*Ad hoc* project teams

Group (vertical axis label)

Underdeveloped   Developed

Mind

Source: Weick and Roberts (see note 18)

matrix indicating group development and mind development along either axis.

The 'developed group-undeveloped mind' is found in the phenomenon group think.[19] The combination of 'undeveloped group-developed mind' can be found in *ad hoc* project teams. Across the other diagonal is the 'developed group-developed mind' – termed the 'superteam'. In this team there is both a coordination of actions combined with the interrelation and aligning of thought processes. There is a sharing of information, heedful contributing, mutual respect and heedful subordinating characterized by trust. The upshot is sharpened apprehension and comprehension of an envisioned complex task that can only be collectively known, understood and mastered. Its opposite – the fragmented, uncoordinated group – is likely to be careful in the way members behave toward each other, irresponsible in so far as its commitment to group goals are limited and show little understanding and divisive, in that the lack of coordination results in mistakes which are not 'owned' and reveal low levels of trust and a 'blame culture'.

McGrath, MacMillan and Ventakaraman[20] operationalized the Weick and Roberts construct of 'collective mind' in an attempt to investigate the management processes by which activities are translated by teams into competitive advantage and enhanced business performance. They argue that where new initiatives are being developed the problems facing the team are incomplete information and the difficulty of interpretation. Hence if the team is to operate effectively it must develop competence in what it is doing. They define competence as **the purposive combination of resources which enable the team to accomplish a given task.**

But to develop new competencies means being able to combine resources in new ways in order to gain competitive advantage. To be seen to be competent the team must be able to meet or exceed its objectives, in other words there must be a convergence between its intended and its realized objectives. The crucial questions are:

● How does the team come to know what are the critical combination of resources that will achieve competitive advantage? (comprehension)
● How might it develop working relationships which allow the effective execution of its objectives? (collective mind)

They argue that a team which has developed such a 'collective mind' operates **deftly**. Operating deftly (or smartly) reduces the costs of interaction. Opportunity costs are reduced because there is a high level of trust in the team, therefore interaction is highly efficient. Transaction costs are also thereby reduced, as are agency costs. The team is controlled through its own social processes, there is no need to invest in forms of control. After empirical testing, the conceptual model appeared to be as shown in Figure 10.3.

Figure **10.3** A model of the antecendents which lead to enhanced business performance

Source: McGrath *et al.* 1995 (see note 20)

The conditions in which heedful interrelations or deftness in operations within teams are appropriate are the following.

● **Reliability** – where accuracy, precision and/or timeliness in operations are critical to task accomplishment; team members depend upon each other to achieve such high levels of performance and there is a need for high levels of dependability and trust.
● **Efficiency** – where the viability and/or competitiveness of a company requires the control of the costs of resourcing an operation. This may mean effecting cost savings, controlling waste, streamlining operations, or identifying innovative ways of task accomplishment. Such measures cannot be implemented by individuals acting independently.
● **Effectiveness** – when goals, targets and output are achieved and there are high levels of satisfaction amongst the team performing the work. Effectiveness is only achieved when people are so minded. Where each team acts interdependently, recognizing the complexities of the work to be accomplished, then the organization is positioned for high levels of performance.

There is clearly a need for further research and more case study material to exemplify best practice in this area. McGrath *et al.* cite the case of the 3Ms as a high performing organization which works deftly. More examples are needed so that the implications for organizational learning may be explored. Other comparative research might be undertaken to enable the development of our understanding of how self-managed teams and quality circles work.

Indeed, whether armed with the concepts of 'collective mind', 'deftness' etc. there is a need to ensure that such teams learn to manage themselves more effectively.

Multicultural teams

Cultural diversity amongst team members has an impact on team process and productivity. The team process is likely to be more complex, therefore creating difficulties of integration and interrelating of team members. However, where the team is able to manage its multicultural perspectives then the resultant diversity is likely to facilitate more innovative solutions to problems and to increase both the quality and quantity of outputs.[21] Table 10.4 summarizes the advantages and disadvantages of diversity in multicultural teams.

In addition to these advantages and disadvantages the multicultural team reduces the likelihood of 'group think' because the members are less likely to so limit their perspectives. The multicultural team's productivity also depends

Table **10.4** Advantages and disadvantages of diversity in multicultural teams

Advantages	Disadvantages
Diversity permits increased creativity	*Diversity causes a lack of cohesion*
Wider range of perspective	Mistrust
More and better ideas	Lower interpersonal attractiveness
Less group think	Stereotyping
	More within-culture conversations
Diversity forces enhanced concentration to understand others'	
Ideas	Miscommunication
Meanings	Slower speech: non-native speakers and translation problems
Arguments	Less accuracy
Increased creativity can lead to	Stress
● Better problem definition	More counterproductive behaviour
● More alternatives	Less disagreement on content
● Better solutions	Tension
● Better decisions	
	Lack of cohesion causes an inability to
Teams can become	● Validate ideas and people
● More effective	● Agree when agreement is needed
● More productive	● Gain consensus on decisions
	● Take concerted action
	Teams can become
	● Less efficient
	● Less effective
	● Less productive
	Source: Adler 1997 (see note 21)

on the task and stage of development of the group. Furthermore, diversity becomes most valuable when the needs for cohesion remain low relative to the needs for creativity.[22]

The more senior the team the less likely it is to be engaged in routine tasks. Hence multicultural diversity facilitates the innovation process if the team is managed effectively. This ability to reveal divergence of views is more prevalent in the early stages of group formation, hence younger teams are more innovative. However, there are preconditions to ensure such outcomes. They are that:

- each member recognizes and accepts member differences
- team members are selected for their ability, not their ethnicity
- there is no dominant ethnic group, so there is an equitable balance of power
- members share the same goals
- the team is given positive feedback on its performance as a team
- members must respect each other if they are to work together effectively.

Maznevski and Peterson suggest that team processes are about event management.[23] Differences in cultural perspective may mean that the objectives of the social processes are quite different, for example building up confidence in the decision, or building up relationships and developing trust. However, *all* teams are about making sense of events. An event must be noticed and interpreted and a meaning attributed to it. In a team such processes occur interactively. Culture systematically influences the process of noticing, interpreting and responding to events. In multicultural teams, having an understanding of cultural difference enables each team member to develop realistic expectations of fellow members. Furthermore the team also responds to the environment. Cultural values affect such responses, hence in a multicultural team culturally held beliefs and values will have a strong influence on the types of event which the team must address. Table 10.5 summarizes the likely effect of cultural orientation on the event management process.

Maznevski and Peterson ask 'when is culture most likely to influence behaviour?' And, what characteristics of events must lend themselves to be noticed, interpreted and responded to using culture-related scripts rather than person or situation related ones? Strong situations (i.e. where the environmental and social cues to behaviour are clear) present people with a 'script to follow' (e.g. the storm breaks and people run for cover). Weak situations, in contrast, are highly ambiguous. Hence personality will influence an individual's response more strongly in such situations. By the same token, in strong situations culture is not as relevant as it is in influencing interpretation and action in weak situations. Situations facing multicultural teams tend to be complex and ambiguous i.e. 'weak' and thus lend themselves to the effects of cultural difference. Whilst it might be tempting to develop strong situations and hence reduce ambiguity this does not necessarily lead to the most effective teams. In a competitive situation effective management of diversity and the capturing of different perspectives and ideas is likely to result in greatly enhanced team performance.[24]

Table **10.5** Cultural orientations and their effects on the event management process an potential contributions of members in multicultural teams

Orientation	Variation	Assumption	Event management process			
			What is noticed	Sources for interpretation	Preferred response	Potential contributions
Relation to nature	Mastery	Control nature and environment	Events implying loss of control	Control procedures, problem-solving experts	Active interventions designed to increase control	Identify and implement potential interventions to improve
	Subjugation	Controlled by nature or supernatural	Unavoidable constraints	Cultural norms, supernatural	No attempt to change the unchangeable, 'do one's best' to address the rest	Prevent wasted effort at attempting to change relatively fixed constraints
	Harmony	Balance relations among elements of environment, including self	Imbalances in organizational systems	Sources with holistic approaches	Restore and maintain harmony and balance	Identify and implement whole system, synergistic approaches
Time	Past	Respect for past and tradition	Discrepancies with past and tradition	Traditions, stories, records	Consistent with past practice	Identify similarities between past and current situations; learn from past
	Present	Today's needs most important, also short term future	Failure to address immediate concerns	Current data, short term projections	Address immediate criteria, little concern for past or future	Promote sense of urgency, address immediate threats and opportunities
	Future	Focus on long term future	Potential long term implications	Forecasts of trends into future	Sacrifice today for long term future benefits	Draw attention to events with long term implications, incorporate into current planning and action

Table **10.5** Continued

Orientation	Variation	Assumption	Event management process			
			What is noticed	Sources for interpretation	Preferred response	Potential contributions
Nature of humans[a]	Evil	Humans' basic nature is evil, harmful acts are normal and expected	Harmful and untrustworthy behaviour, situations with potential for such behaviour	Those harmed by an action, sources designed to prevent harm (e.g. legal and corporate control systems)	Little or no trust until relationship well established; continual monitoring	Monitor people and behaviour, prevent team/company from being taken advantage of
	Good	Humans' basic nature is good, harmful acts are anomalies	Helpful and trustworthy behaviour	For harmful events-external situational explanations	Trust, little monitoring	Encourage trusting environment group, encourage information, or sharing, nonpersonal explanations
Relationships among people	Individualistic	Responsibility to and for self and immediate family	Will not notice those who do not make themselves noticed explicitly	Topic experts regardless of group membership or status	Preserve own self-interests first	Expect self and others to contribute fully, uniquely, and in important ways
	Collective	Responsible to and for larger group, for example, extended family, peer group	Whether others respect lateral group relations	Sources that would not cause loss of face for anyone	Preserve interests of group, if necessary at expense of own self-interests	Maintain group relations, promote active listening
	Hierarchical	Unequal distribution of power and responsibility, those higher have power over and responsibility for those lower	Whether deference is offered to senior people, offered by junior people	Supervisors, senior team members, those with high status	Senior members to control group; junior members to obey others in group	Make good use of senior members', supervisors' and outside experts' knowledge and experience

Table **10.5** Continued

Orientation	Variation	Assumption	What is noticed	Event management process		
				Sources for interpretation	Preferred response	Potential contributions
Mode of activity	Doing-achieving	Constantly strive to achieve goals and continually engage in productive work; live to work	Discrepancies between plan and actual	Anything that provides satisfactory, immediate meaning; may skip explicit interpretation	Immediate action to achieve goal as quickly as possible	Set goals; ensure goals are achieved
	Being-feeling	Do what you want when you want; work to live	Feelings, intuitions at least as much as external events	Own and others' intuitions, feelings; trusted sources	Response that feels right, when time is right	Maintain group relations, draw attention to affective information
	Thinking-reflecting	Rational, developmental approach; think through everything carefully	Evidence that plans have or have not been thought through carefully	Wide variety of sources rationally justified; extensive interpretation	Rational response, may be delayed due to interpretation	Ensure multiple analyses and explanations are considered

Source: Maznevski and Peterson 1997 (see note 23): p.68-71

a. A third variation is 'mixed', which assumes humans' nature is a mixture of good and evil. A fourth variation is 'neutral', which assumes that humans' nature is neither good nor evil and behavioural tendencies are determined by the environment. Their implications can be seen as a combination of those outlined for 'good' and 'evil' here.

Team building and development

Team building and team development would appear to be critical to effective business functioning whatever the size of firm, though where the firm is small there are some important differences in how teams are developed and managed. For example in the very small firm people can rarely avoid each other, whereas this tactic is entirely possible in the larger enterprise. Additionally, truncated hierarchies, pressures to empower at lower levels and enable employees to realize their full potential suggest the need to take teams seriously. It is evident that within organizational contexts effective working teams do not just happen, they need to be managed. How might this be done?

In an earlier volume the issue of team building was discussed at some length.[25] In the limited space remaining in this chapter one particular approach to team development will be discussed: that of Meredith Belbin and his work at Cambridge on team roles. Team members are human resources. The crucial question they sought to answer is: what combination of personnel is required to make a balanced and effective team? The answer is the balance between the team roles identified by Belbin and their mix. In the original study[26] Belbin identified eight team roles and discussed them in terms of their 'positive qualities' and 'allowable weaknesses'. Subsequent work has resulted in some changes: an additional team role, the 'specialist' and a change in the labelling of two of the extant roles – 'chairman' becoming 'coordinator' and 'company worker' becoming 'implementer'. The revised list of team roles with their definitions is presented below (see Table 10.6).

Whilst a person's functional role may be well understood, it is not obvious what team role or roles they may be best suited to. The problem of identification was solved by the administration of psychometric tests and the observations made on team members performing a management game. The expression of team role behaviour is, however, subject to a number of influences (see Figure 10.4).

Functional roles require a person to be technically equipped to carry out a task or job but the qualifications a person has may be neither necessary nor sufficient to assure effective job performance. For the small firm, or any firm where its competitive performance is crucial for survival and growth, getting the right person in particular positions is clearly fundamental. A person who is eligible in terms of their qualifications may not prove to be suitable (for example, they may not 'fit in'). Occasionally the ineligible may prove to be surprisingly suitable.

Behaviours that Belbin has termed 'allowable weaknesses' may develop into behaviours which are unacceptable (see Table 10.7). The 'allowable weakness' is part of the team role; it facilitates stronger recognition of the specific role, giving role clarity and an enhanced team role image.

Just as senior executive jobs are less highly specified so too is that of the owner-manager. The person makes the job, its ultimate success may also depend on the extent to which they can relate to other senior members of the firm. Relationships are thus determined in part by the team roles being played

Table **10.6** The nine team roles

Roles and descriptions – team-role contribution	Allowable weaknesses
Plant: Creative, imaginative, unorthodox: Solves difficult problems.	Ignores details. Too preoccupied to communicate effectively.
Resource investigator: Extrovert, enthusiastic, communicative. Explores opportunities. Develops contacts.	Overoptimistic. Loses interest once initial enthusiasm has passed.
Co-ordinator: Mature, confident, a good chairperson. Clarifies goals, promotes decision making, delegates well.	Can be seen as manipulative. Delegates personal work.
Shaper: Challenging, dynamic, thrives on pressure. Has the drive and courage to overcome obstacles.	Can provoke others. Hurts people's feelings.
Monitor/evaluator: Sober, strategic and discerning. Sees all options. Judges accurately.	Lacks drive and ability to inspire others. Overly critical.
Teamworker: Co-operative, mild perceptive and diplomatic. Listens, builds, averts friction, calms the waters.	Indecisive in crunch situations. Can be easily influenced.
Implementer: Disciplined, reliable, conservative and efficient. Turns ideas into practical actions.	Somewhat inflexible: Slow to respond to new possibilities.
Completer: Painstaking, conscientious anxious. Searches out errors and omissions. Delivers on time.	Inclined to worry unduly. Reluctant to delegate. Can be a nit-picker.
Specialist: Single-minded, self-starting, dedicated. Provides knowledge and skills in rare supply.	Contributes only on a narrow front. Dwells on technicalities. Overlooks the 'big picture'.

NB Strength of contribution in any one of the roles is commonly associated with particular weaknesses. These are called 'allowable weaknesses'. Executives are seldom strong in all nine team roles.

Source: Belbin 1993 (see note 27): p.22

out by either party. As strangers people will tend to act out a single role, for example, the 'shaper' may be overbearing but the other – a 'teamworker' – responds predictably in a conciliatory and diplomatic fashion. The upshot: this particular dyad works well together. However, people at work may hold multiple role relationships. For example, a shaper/plant boss may have a teamworker/monitor/evaluator subordinate. The primary relationship is of a

Figure **10.4** Influences on team-role behaviour

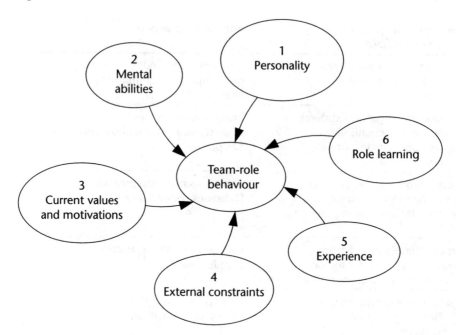

Key to Figure 10.4

1. Personality was measured using the Cattell 16PF personality inventory.
2. Ability was measured using the Watson Glaser Critical Thinking Appraisal (CTA) inventory; high level reasoning ability can override personality according to Belbin. It was a particularly important predictor of the behaviour of the plant and the monitor evaluator.
3. Cherished values that are often developed through cultural influences shape particular behaviours.
4. Environmental factors such as context or situation, whether the boss is present or absent, influence behaviour.
5. Personal experience and cultural influences affect behaviour to take account of conventions.
6. Awareness of role differences and learning to play a role improves personal versatility.

directive nature with a shaper controlling a teamworker. But then the boss thinks of an idea that could have important consequences if everything proceeds as planned … 'Let me try this idea out on you', says the boss to the subordinate. The relationship has ceased to be directive. The plant is talking to the monitor evaluator and is ready to receive advice.[27]

This switching of roles without loss of face is possible within a relationship of some standing either where people have worked together for a long time or, for example, are close kin involved in a family business. However, the latter tie is no guarantee of success.

Relations at work can be strained. In small companies ways of dealing with such situations are important as few firms can afford the luxury of underperforming personnel. Some tactics are to identify the individual's strengths,

Table **10.7** A thin line can separate some allowable weaknesses from unacceptable behaviour

	Weaknesses	
Team role	Allowable	Not allowable
Plant	Preoccupied with ideas and neglect of practical matters.	Strong 'ownership' of idea when co-operating with others would yield better results.
Resource Investigator	Loss of enthusiasm once initial excitement has passed.	Letting clients down by neglecting to follow up arrangements.
Co-ordinator	An inclination to be lazy if someone else can be found to do the work.	Taking credit for the effort of of a team.
Shaper	A proneness to frustration and irritation.	Inability to recover situation with good humour or apology.
Monitor/ evaluator	Scepticism with logic.	Cynicism without logic.
Teamworker	Indecision on crucial issues.	Avoiding situations that may entail pressure.
Implementer	Adherence to the orthodox and proven.	Obstructing change.
Completer	Perfectionism.	Obsessional behaviour.
Specialist	Acquiring knowledge for its own sake.	Ignoring factors outside own area of competence.

Source: Belbin 1993 (see note 27): p.5l

modify one's own role behaviour and develop ways of handling 'paradoxical relationships'.

The **paradoxical relationship** also illustrates another principle, which is that sometimes a relationship will work through the auspices of a third party. However, this is not invariably the case. In a study of microbusinesses in business services, it was found that in a small proportion of spouse owned and managed businesses, taking on an employee did not always work. It was as if this additional person intruded upon an established, interpersonal working relationship between husband and wife. It was an interesting and somewhat unexpected deterrent to business growth!

How might the 'budding entrepreneur' put together an effective team? Let us assume that the incumbent is a 'prototypical entrepreneur'[28] and as such may have some of the characteristics of a plant (creative, ideas person), a shaper (dynamism, full of drive and energy) and a resource investigator (enthusiastically explores opportunities). To have a business partner or other team member at the early stages of the business who also may be characterized in one or other of the above three team roles is probably asking for trouble: at some stage there is likely to be a clash of personalities. The break up of

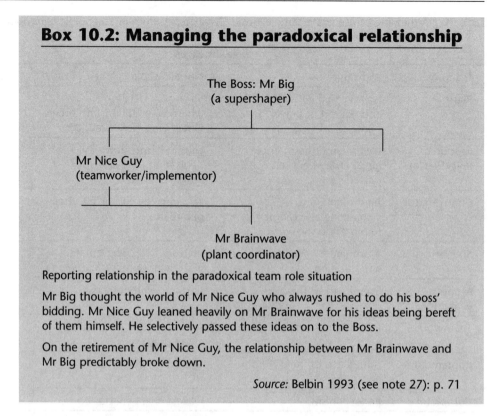

Box 10.2: Managing the paradoxical relationship

The Boss: Mr Big
(a supershaper)

Mr Nice Guy
(teamworker/implementor)

Mr Brainwave
(plant coordinator)

Reporting relationship in the paradoxical team role situation

Mr Big thought the world of Mr Nice Guy who always rushed to do his boss' bidding. Mr Nice Guy leaned heavily on Mr Brainwave for his ideas being bereft of them himself. He selectively passed these ideas on to the Boss.

On the retirement of Mr Nice Guy, the relationship between Mr Brainwave and Mr Big predictably broke down.

Source: Belbin 1993 (see note 27): p. 71

a business partnership puts the business in jeopardy. Ideally, the appropriate business partner or 'right hand man' is an implementer (or in old terminology company worker). Such a person is reliable, efficient and able to turn ideas into practical action. The implementer may want a completer (who is conscientious and delivers on time), a teamworker (who is cooperative and unchallenging) and possibly a specialist (who has particular knowledge and skills) working under them. What is critical is setting up the business with the right mix of people so that they can work effectively together.

Conclusions

The image of the lone but heroic entrepreneur has been criticized as being a part of legend and myth. Successful businesses may be started by individuals but very often they are founded by business partners. However, whatever the size of the business founding unit, there is a need to galvanize human (and other) resources in order to develop a broader (in scope) but well integrated entrepreneurial team which can take the business forward. This suggests the need to develop a deep understanding of group processes and what this may mean for the quality of social interaction in entrepreneurial teams. This work must encompass an understanding of the functioning of entrepreneurial teams both horizontally and vertically within the small but growing enterprise.

CHAPTER 11

The management of innovation

The idea of innovation as a central strand of entrepreneurship would seem to be obvious to the layperson. It is, after all, the innovator who captures new markets and stands to make considerable wealth. But what does it mean 'to innovate' and what part does creativity play in this process? In this chapter the notion of creativity is first explored, focusing in particular on the part played by creative individuals in the innovation process. Next, innovation in the Schumpeterian sense is introduced and its alleged effects – such as heightening firm performances as a consequence of competitive behaviour – discussed.

There are different degrees and types of innovation, from the radical to the routine, all of which have to be managed effectively. Ultimately innovation is down to the performance of people, individuals and teams in the firm, thus leadership and management skills are needed to manage high levels of innovative performance. This is an important issue and much of the space of this chapter is devoted to its consideration.

However, while people management may be necessary, the strategy of the entrepreneur and the firm is critical if the opportunity created is to be harvested. Thus the chapter goes on to discuss value innovations as a major new innovation strategy in the knowledge economy. Not all firms will pursue such a strategy and there certainly is a need to consider the particular problems of the technology based enterprise. The final part of the chapter therefore takes another look at the conditions needed to facilitate 'business spin offs' and the continued importance of science-based enterprise to an economy. But first, the chapter opens with a consideration of the nature of creativity.

Creativity

People tend to operate with a 19th century notion of 'creativity' as the romantic hero, working solo, perhaps in a garret or backroom, pushing out their works of genius. Contrary to this notion, however, current thinking on the nature of 'creativity' suggests that it is a social rather than an individually driven phenomenon and that creative ideas are context specific. Hence creativity has been defined as: 'a context specific, subjective judgement of the novelty and value of an individual's or a collective's behavior.'[1]

Creativity is a context-specific judgement because the evaluation of creative ideas can vary from one group, organization or culture to the next. Creativity is not an inherent quality of an object, it is an assessment that people make and whether an action is regarded as creative depends on the level of agreement among people making the judgement. Creativity also refers to an outcome that someone has produced. Thus, those sitting in judgement can usually see, touch or hear the object in order to assess its novelty and value. Hence people are only considered creative if they produce creative products on a regular basis. Furthermore, contexts can bias judgements as to what is considered to be the more creative.

Much of past research has suggested that to understand creativity one must identify those personal attributes of individuals which have led them to be creative. This approach has ignored the contexts, in particular when and where those acts of creativity were executed. Past research (which has tended to focus on individuals) has tended to addressed three questions: (1) *why* are people creative? (2) *what* key influences are there to encourage or discourage creative activity, (3) *what* feelings facilitate creativity?

Why are people creative?

People are creative because they are interested in doing creative or novel things out of curiosity, playfulness, adventurousness or an appreciation of aesthetics. Moreover, creativity enables them to maintain a variety of interests and new experiences. It fulfils a need for independence, self-determination and solitude. It enables the individual to achieve and, more particularly, to achieve a position of power through dominance in their field or profession. If this set of motives is true the creative individual is unlikely to feel comfortable in the conventional bureaucratic organizational form. It is not difficult to see how they might aspire to self-employment or employment in a company that facilitates creative behaviour. But what are the characteristics of such companies?

Key influences

Key influences that affect personal motivation include the individual's expectations of their own performance. If a person harbours doubts then this will affect their self confidence and they will be unlikely to put themselves in a position which will expose themselves to adverse criticism. The person who is confident that they have creative talent will also be comfortable in ill-defined and ambiguous situations.

Feelings influencing creativity

Interest and curiosity drive energy levels. Thus the creative individual tends to be open to new experiences and is emotionally expressive; discovery includes the ups and downs and the joys of finding out something new.

However, a major problem with such approaches is that they are devoid of theory, at best they tend to state the obvious – that creative people tend to be creative! This is clearly not the whole story! For example, we need to know what skills are needed for the creative person to be creative and what impact opportunity has. Skills or abilities that have been identified include the possession of divergent thinking skills (for example how many uses can you think of for a brick?) and skills of association (for example lateral thinking and the ability to make connections) Creative performance increases with intelligence up to an IQ level of 120. Education helps but too much may impede creativity! Intuitive capability and social competence are also associated with creativity. However, this approach tends to suggest that people are born with creative talent, though some research has shown that creativity can be enhanced through training.[2] The nature argument is problematic because it: suggests that there is a limit to creative talent and the proportion of people in a given population who possess it; presents a problem of identification and selection of the talented person; and is difficult to establish where the 'cut off point' lies.

Interactionist approaches to personality have shown the importance of contextualizing behaviour. It is perhaps not surprising therefore that opportunity provides an important context facilitating creativity. The broad context includes the leadership style. Essentially the leadership style conducive to creative behaviour was found to be supportive, participative and outcome-oriented. Participative leadership includes structure, support and trust. As a precursor for creativity it depends on the quality of the relationship developed between the leader/manager and the employee(s). The leader/manager must be confident in the employees' competence or capability and trust their motives, whilst the employee must trust management's competence and motives. These are not only essential preconditions for good working relations but also critically important for the development of *mutual respect.*

A further aspect of context, according to Ford's review, is the development of effective communication networks by the creative individual. These are professional rather than social networks and show that creative individuals seek to enhance their work by developing effective working relationships. Other situational factors are said to include: a change-oriented mindset on the part of management which promises a receptivity to new ideas, a nurturing organizational culture, a reward system geared to motivating talented employees, adequate resources to support creative efforts and a climate in which management encourages people to think creatively and produce creative solutions to problems. The message is that creative ability is more widespread in the population than the elitist, boffin or 'romantic hero' notions have hitherto led us to believe.

Capturing knowledge about creativity is not an academic exercise which should encompass only an academic perspective. If creativity is to mean something in the business context understanding it must include the practitioner perspective. Gioia[3] summarized some of the contrasts between these two perspectives (See Table 11.1)

In essence there is still the novelty, the eccentric, intuitive and nonrational perceptions of creativity by the academic. However, the importance of context, prior knowledge, experience and skill are also identified and importantly that creativity is a social process. Practitioners are less romantic about the

Table **11.1** Contrasts in academic and practitioner creativity themes

Academic	Practitioner
Academics dwell on the novelty dimension of creativity.	Practitioners dwell on the value dimension.
Academics seek novel solutions and look for value.	Practitioners seek value and look for novel solutions.
Academics emphasise the divergent thinking and acting involved in creativity.	Practitioners emphasise the convergent thinking and acting involved.
Academics think of creativity as thinking differently.	Practitioners think of creativity as doing differently.
Academics seek the impetus for creativity within the organization.	Practitioners seek the impetus for creativity outside the organization.
Academics focus on producing diverse ideas.	Practitioners focus on satisfying diverse interests.
Academics make more general, global statements about creativity.	Practitioners make specific, local statements about creativity.
Academics treat creativity as an unbounded enterprise.	Practitioners treat creativity as a pragmatically bounded enterprise.
Academics talk about creativity as an aesthetic accomplishment.	Practitioners talk about creativity as a practical prelude to innovation.
Academics are more dispassionate and removed in their discussions of creativity.	Practitioners are more passionate and personally involved in their discussions of creativity.

Source: Gioia 1995 (see note 3)

notion of creativity. Their interest lies in the production of something of value which is market driven. Usefulness is the standard through which all inventiveness must pass: 'Ideas must display technology-market connections which means that R&D labs cannot be anarchies. Solutions must be capable of implementation, and they must have quality, however defined by the end user' (Gioia, 1995, see note 3).

Moreover, strategic relevance and the need to stay focused on the problem are essential. With a clear recognition of the risks involved practitioners suggest the need for strong management support in order to foster the creative process. Also emphasized is an appropriate organizational culture; that is, one that allows sufficient freedom, venturesomeness and flexibility to enable the generation of creative solutions. Practitioners also emphasize the importance of the team, of collaboration and the ability to draw upon complementary skills in order to enhance creativity. Hence some of the contrasts between academics and practitioners are those of emphasis rather than of kind. Taken together they provide a strong knowledge base for building a deeper understanding of creative processes within organizations. Table 11.2 provides a summary of this transdisciplinary knowledge.

If creativity concerns organizational processes and not simply individual

Table **11.2** Capturing knowledge about creativity – a summary of knowledge gleaned from academic and practitioner perspectives.

1. Creativity in organizations is typically a team enterprise, not an individual phenomenon.
2. Creativity is a risky business.
3. New ideas alone do not contribute to creativity; they must pass the test of practical relevance and deployment in the market place.
4. Hence creativity in organizations comprises novelty, value and effectiveness.
5. Creative processes in organizations include the rational and non-rational.
6. Creativity is goal-directed, deliberate and considered, but it is also enabled by luck, insight and opportunity.
7. Managerial leadership and support are critical. A guiding vision, support in the form of resources, rewards and recognition and a blame free culture facilitate creativity.
8. Traditional bureaucratic hierarchies are impediments to creativity.
9. Creative ability is widely spread and therefore should be seen as a normal part of organizational life.
10. Employees should be encouraged to produce creative solutions to problems.

Source: Gioia 1995 (see note 3)

action, what might this process look like? Ford[4] has put forward a model which assumes multiple stakeholders representing multiple domains who act as gatekeepers to new ideas and creative solutions to problems. Domains that are external to the organization and comprise the organization's environment form the backcloth to changing situations, opportunities, threats, etc which are picked up internally as cues. 'Cues' must be interpreted and generally made sense of. Organization members can do this in one of two ways: they can draw on their existing experience and invoke standard behavioural repertoires (in other words habits/tried and tested responses, etc) to deal with the situation or they may recognize or acknowledge that the situation is unusual and demands a different, nonroutine response. It is the ambiguity inherent in the latter situation and the willingness to respond to it which results in the development of creative solutions. Moreover, those creative solutions are likely to confer competitive advantage on the firm. The creative individual will enjoy the freedom to pursue novel solutions, in contrast to the firm where personal goals and organizational goals yield few opportunities for the exercise of varied and independent action. Creative action, however, will not be pursued unless the individual feels capable of responding effectively and is confident that they can produce a solution that will be received positively by one or more stakeholders. Where these conditions do not hold the individual will not feel motivated to expose themselves to criticism or censure, instead they will sink back to the familiar and the comfortable, sticking with the knitting and reproducing the routine and very familiar solutions. In the latter context there will be a low level of skills development in the organization and organizational learning will characteristically be single loop learning.

The creative employee (or team) will not only feel confident of their capability but they will invest considerable energy in producing a solution. Hence they will have an emotional investment in its success. This strong basis for the creative team's motivation will also draw on their individual and collective talents to perform. Such talent will include a variety of knowledge, thinking and behavioural skills. Moreover, as learning occurs the definition of the situation will also change and learning becomes double loop or generative learning.

The upshot is creative action, which is judged by multiple stakeholders from their various domains. Here a relationship of trust is important – ability to trust opinions – as the gatekeepers have the power to influence the emergence of those creative ideas and actions. Finally, it is these creative actions which are necessary to create meaning in ambiguous situations. Creative actions are more likely to be competitive and to provide the business with a competitive advantage. Figure 11.1 describes this process.

The map identifies two paths: an outer path, which follows the routine and familiar action possibilities and an inner path, which pursues the unfamiliar and makes sense of it sufficiently to develop novel and innovative solutions. Each path carries with it other behavioural and affective elements, the outcomes of which, being either routine or creative action, are judged by external stakeholders and players in the market place.

Figure **11.1** A multiple domain model of organizational action, showing routine and creative action-taking

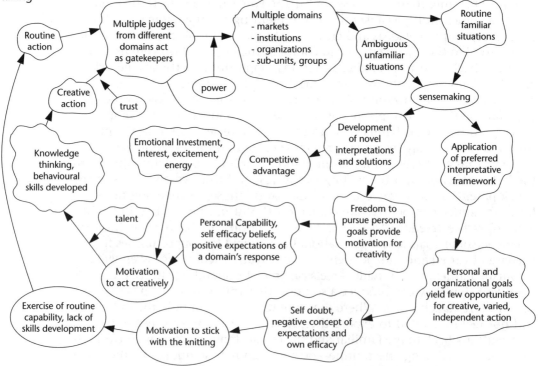

Source: based on Ford 1995 (see note 4)

Summary: action imperatives

The key features of organizational circumstances and contexts which may be managed in such a way as to lead to enhanced creative action are summarized in Table 11.3 below.

Table **11.3** Summary: action imperatives

1. People create certainty by imposing familiar interpretasions on ambiguous or unfamiliar situations.
   Action guideline: Doubt what you think you know.
2. Creative actions occur mainly as a response to ambiguity.
   Action guideline: Treat ambiguity as an opportunity.
3. Creative actions in organizations are usually judged to the standards of multiple social domains (e.g. sponsors, other departments, external organizations – suppliers, banks, investors, etc).
   Action guideline: By means of a 'stakeholder analysis', tailor creative acts and products to key evaluative domains.
4. Goals for creativity are surely articulated and thereby are implicitly discouraged in many organizations.
   Action guideline: Establish explicit creativity goals for tasks, projects, and programmes.
5. People often lack confidence in their own creative capability because of inexperience due to work environments that reinforce routine, habit and sameness.
   Action guideline: Enhance creative capability by providing people with the opportunity to develop new skills that are acknowledged and built on.
6. Confidently held beliefs that an organization is receptive to creative actions are key. Negative beliefs strongly favour familiar over creative actions.
   Action guideline: People may undertake creative actions to the extent that they expect them to confer advantages relative to other options.
7. Negative emotions favour habitual action; positive emotions, such as enthusiasm, favour creative action.
   Action guideline: Ambiguity leads to anxiety as well as creativity. Creativity is served by dispelling fears and engendering positive emotions.
8. Talent matters, but knowledge and skills that facilitate creative action can be developed.
   Action guideline: Hire creatively talented people, but also develop thinking and communications skills. Knowledge and experience pertaining to the specific domain of application are important. Training programmes should be designed which are domain relevant.
9. Creative actions produce meaning out of ambiguity. People socially construct order out of ambiguity often without recognising the degree of the doubt and uncertainty. In highly ambiguous situations analysis can be ineffectual.
   Action guideline: Creative action should replace analysis on the key method for making sense of the environment.

Innovation

The above section has developed an argument that creativity in organizations is about creating something novel which is also of value. But how does this differ from the notion of 'innovation'? Innovation as a concept is more closely tied to entrepreneurship, indeed many writers have suggested that it is a key defining characteristic of the entrepreneur. Joseph Schumpeter,[5] for example, suggested that the entrepreneur's economic role was disturbance of the economic equilibrium – that is the balance of supply and demand for a particular good which assured stability of prices. This disturbance arose from innovation – the creation of something new in the marketplace which altered the supply-demand equation. By recombining the factors of production to create something new (an **innovation**) the entrepreneur creates a demand for the innovation, thereby supplanting the old. However, innovation for Schumpeter could take a number of different forms.

- The creation of a new product or alteration in some of its attributes.
- The development of a new method of production.
- The opening of a new market.
- The capture of a new source of supply.
- A new organization of industry.

'Everyone is an entrepreneur only when he actually carries out new combinations, and loses that character as soon as he has built up his business, when he settles down to running it as other people run their businesses'[6]

This kind of innovation assumes a depth of understanding of an industry, including technological and product market knowledge and leadership ability.[7]

Kanter[8] largely follows the Schumpeterian line of reasoning. She points out that, although most people would think of innovations as being scientific in character, there are many other kinds of changes that count as innovations, for example new tax laws, the creation of enterprise zones, quality circles and problem solving task forces. The fact that people tend not to think of social and organizational changes as innovation she regards as unfortunate:

> Indeed, it is a virtual truism that if technical innovation runs far ahead of complementary social and organizational innovation, its use in practice can be either dysfunctional or negligible. Innovation refers to the process of bringing any new, *problem solving* idea into use. Ideas for reorganizing, cutting costs, putting in new budgetary systems, improving communication or assembling products in teams are also innovations. *Innovation is the generation, acceptance and implementation of new ideas, processes, products or services* .... Application and implementation are central to this definition; it involves the capacity to change and adapt. pp.20–21 (My emphasis)

West[9] also defines innovation simply as the introduction of new and improved ways of doing things at work. A more complex, psychological definition he suggests is that innovation is:

> The intentional introduction and application within a job, work team or organization of ideas, processes, products or procedures which are new to that job, work team or organization and which are designed to benefit the job, the work team or organization.'
> (note 9)

This psychological definition introduces the idea of **intention** and the linkage with personal and/or organizational goals. This suggests that there is a human dimension of organizing if an innovation is to be implemented successfully. An innovation can be a change that is introduced in a particular context but may have been tried elsewhere and as such it is not strictly new. Hence, whilst creativity is the generation of novel or original ideas at work, innovation is their implementation.

Implicit in the works of Schumpeter and Kanter is the idea that innovation leads to better performance, it gives a business a competitive edge thus enabling it to outperform its competitors and the innovation is better than its predecessors, which it has or aims to supplant. It suggests that technical or technological innovations do lead to better economic performance of companies, however there may be social and organizational costs arising from resistance to the implementation of a requisite change. A critical management problem therefore is how to deal with the human and organizational aspects of innovation.

Abernathy and Clark discuss the nature of competitive advantage arising from innovative activity.[10] On the technology/production side they suggest it is the resources, skills and knowledge that affect design and production which ultimately create competitive advantage. Skills and knowledge are embodied in individuals but over and above this there is a collective understanding that is incorporated into teamwork routines, procedures and practices. This emphasizes the importance of the organization of factors of production and of information for the development of product innovation. They stress further that market and customer knowledge are also critical aspects of innovation activity. This includes the relationship with the customer, the composition of the customer base, channels of distribution, customer knowledge and nature of communication with the customer.

The impact of an innovation on production and/or markets can be conservative or radical. Not all innovations need be radical and disruptive (in the Schumpeterian sense), they emphasize. Where the innovation is largely 'conservative' the knowledge and competence within the firm is enhanced. In contrast, radical innovations tend to reduce the value of existing competence, displacing it with a requirement for reskilling. Hence new industries can be created and old ones destroyed. They refer to this as the **transilience of an innovation**, that is how, in competitive terms, the innovation impacts the value and applicability of established competence. Figure 11.2 depicts the Abernathy-Clark 'transilience map'.

Figure **11.2** The Abernathy-Clark transilience map

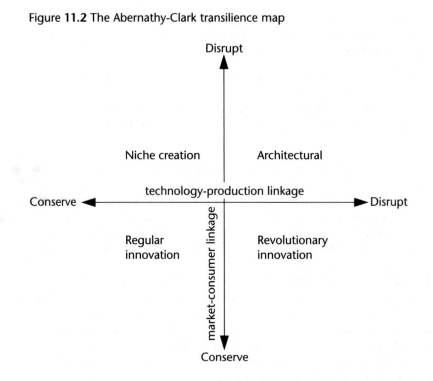

Source: Abernathy and Clark 1988 (see note 10): p.61

Architectural innovations include both the development of an innovation and its application in an entirely new market. In other words there is a departure from established ways of doing and new markets are opened up. Examples include the invention of the radio, phototypesetting in the printing industry, development of breathable fabrics and foulweather clothing. Henri-Lloyd originally designed high specification foulweather gear for yachtsman, the functional purpose of which was protective. However, the clothing was also very attractively designed, so much so that it became a 'fashion item' and exported as such to young consumer markets in Italy.[11] The Body Shop developed new innovative product ranges in cosmetics, body lotions and treatments, targeted at a lower income consumer group, thus undermining the exclusivity of the traditional cosmetics industry.[12]

Niche creation comprises the opening of new market opportunities through the use of existing technology. Examples include the clothing/apparel industry. Some of these innovations in design/product concept may be relatively short lived, as in the case of waxed cotton jackets as a fashion item (mid 1980s); other examples include electronic consumer products such as food processors. The advantage created is likely to be temporary and depends very much on a sequence of new product/innovative designs in order to compete with rivals. Timing and quick reactions appear to be crucially important.

Regular innovation involves change that builds on established technical and production competence applied to existing markets and customers. The effect is to entrench existing skills and resources. Examples include synthetic fibre production and computer technology. Typically, regular innovation takes place over a lengthy period, changes can be small and incremental but cumulatively significant in terms of product improvement. Further incremental change in process technology tends to raise productivity and increase capacity and results in further economies of scale.

Revolutionary innovation disrupts and renders existing technology obsolete yet is applied to existing markets. Examples include television valves, mechanical calculators and gas mantles. The typewriter is also a piece of office equipment of the past. Now software such as Microsoft has revolutionized wordprocessing. In the food industry the ability to produce chilled fresh foods and bread with a longer shelf life has impacted on the nature of the products that fill supermarket shelves.

The transilience map provides a framework in which the relationship between innovation, competition and the evolution of industries can be examined, as well as gaining insight into the strategies and tactics of competitors. Further, each quadrant requires a different set of managerial competencies in order for the innovation to be successful. In the architectural phase, management must synthesize creatively the information gleaned with respect to new user needs and technological possibilities. This is not only the management of creativity but also business risk. Niche creation concerns the ability to size up new market opportunities, develop a product which exploits them and being able to respond quickly – to get in there first. The regular innovation environment requires the skills of methodical planning, consistency and stability of production design and sourcing of materials. The aim is steadily to improve product quality and cost efficiencies. This is a job for the administrator and functionally oriented engineer. The revolutionary innovation requires investment in new technology development and so crucially must include the ability to marshal the requisite financial resources combined with the ability to focus on market possibilities. It requires good technical insight but also good team management across functional areas – product and process designers and market planners.

Van de Ven[13] also follows the Schumpeterian approach. In a seminal article he highlights some of the key problems associated with the management of innovation. In sum, they are:

- managing attention so that people focus on new ideas
- implementing ideas – managing the social and political dynamics of innovation
- managing the multidisciplinary innovative process in a way that enables individuals to see not only their own part but also how it relates to the whole
- managing the strategic problem of creating an infrastructure that is conducive to innovation – this is predicated on the necessity of leadership predisposed to foster innovation.

A fundamental issue is the source of the innovative idea: is it technology driven or market led? Whilst need that governs the market is the preferred option, a model which suggests a linear process in the stages of innovation is favoured less than one in which all the necessary parts respond simultaneously.[14] This implies the need to group together key resources and interdependent functions. The unit must have the scope to self-organize and flexibility to solve its own problems. Information technology and other structural aspects of the unit enable individuals to see their own activity in relation to the 'bigger picture'. Further, innovation does not result from the enterprise of a single entrepreneur but from a network of effort focused upon, and committed to, the implementation of a set of ideas. This network is both internal and external to the business. It requires the kind of leadership which fosters innovation.

Box 11.1: VSW Scientific Instruments

Don, the founder of VSW, had the desire to build the best manufacturing company of advanced scientific instruments in the world. This, he recognized, was a major challenge but one to which he aspired. He wished to have a successful business with an international reputation. Don was not a scientist, yet he had the ability to spot opportunities and exploit them. The special capabilities that Don brought to the company when he was its MD were those of a catalyst, a networker, a resource investigator and team leader. 'He sees his role as a catalyst, bringing the right ingredients together and makes things happen. He ... developed an extensive network of contacts in this highly specialist field. The network extends from the USA to Japan. He never pretends to be a scientist but will take scientists abroad with him.'[15] How did Don achieve this? 'He gambles on his experience, backed by that of experts. He ... first establishes the scientific validity of a new idea and then will assess the likely demand by sounding out potential customers.'[16] Don's approach has been collaborative, working with the universities, giving and receiving help and advice. He recognized the risks he was taking especially in the early days and as the company grew cushioned it from the effects of risk with a large order book. Finally, developing innovation was not solely about business ideas, it also had human resource management consequences. For example the need to recruit good quality staff and develop teamwork was recognized. Communications, information exchange and the development of ideas through internal seminars, and staff training were all areas of well established practice.

Managing creative and innovative teams

So far in this chapter it has been established that innovation tends not to be a solo activity but ultimately depends on the efforts of others. This may be achieved by the exercise of a combination of higher order skills that result in coordinated effort and heedful interrelating to achieve and sustain high levels of performance. These fundamental team skills were discussed in chapter 10. In this chapter it is suggested that there are additional management and leadership skills that foster innovation and that managing innovation is a quite conscious and deliberate activity. It requires an awareness of the innovation process combined with an appropriate set of tactics or strategy. In this sense managers can be trained to handle innovation and innovative teams more effectively.

West[17] has suggested a four phase innovation cycle: **recognition** of a performance gap, an external innovation or a potentially useful innovation, **initiation** which comprises proposing the idea or innovation to others, **implementation**, which occurs when the innovation is first developed and used, and **stabilization** when the innovation becomes adopted and a routinized part of the system (see Figure 11.3)

Figure **11.3** Factors associated with group innovation theory and their impact on the innovation cycle

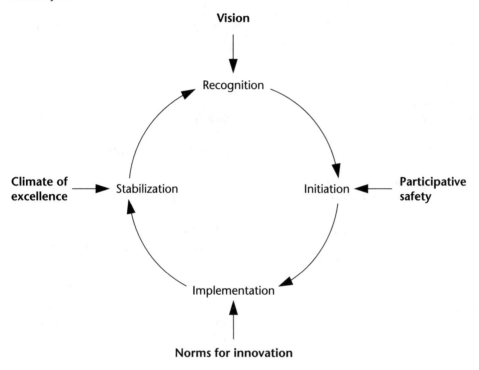

Source: West 1990 (see note 17)

Further four critical aspects of group process will affect this cycle – vision, participative safety, norms for innovation and climate for excellence. **Vision** influences the recognition process. Vision is defined as 'an idea of a valued outcome which represents a higher order goal and motivating force at work'. [18] Vision influences a group or team if it has the following characteristics. **Clarity** indicates a negotiated and shared set of objectives or mission which are evolving and attainable and as such clarity of purposes is valued within the group. **Participative safety** suggests 'involvement in decision making is motivated and reinforced while occurring in an environment which is perceived as interpersonally non-threatening.'[19] This is the opposite of the blame culture, it is a non-judgemental supportive environment where people feel free to put forward ideas without fear of being ridiculed, censored or penalized. The third group process is the creation of **norms for innovation** or 'the expectation, approval and practical support of attempts to introduce (innovations).'[20] West distinguishes between articulated and enacted support. In other words, managers may pay lip service to innovation but fall short of giving any practical support. Both articulated and enacted support are essential. **Climate for excellence** is 'a shared concern with excellence of quality of task performance in relation to shared vision or outcomes, characterized by evaluations, modifications, control systems and critical appraisals'.[21] Commitment to achieving excellence creates a demanding team environment and culture in which new ideas are appraised and challenged in a constructive way, high standards of performance are encouraged and a diversity of approaches to achieving excellence are tolerated.

In a later study, West also examines the effect of team composition on innovation.[22] He suggests the following six characteristics affect team creativity.[23]

- **Size**: larger teams tend to be less creative, with a maximum size of 10–12 people.
- **Diversity**: differences in personality, training, background and gender are important for high quality team decision making.
- **Tenure**: long serving teams can become complacent and less innovative. Project newcomers tend to stimulate creativity.
- **The proportion of innovators**: the greater the proportion of innovators (i.e. people with an innovative tendency) the more likely innovation will take place.
- **Knowledge, skills and abilities (KSAs)**: KSAs also influence outcomes. They include domain relevant KSAs as well as team-functioning KSAs.
- **Team task**: task complexity leads to higher levels of team creativity.

Not all SMEs are small, some are of sufficient size to be managed by a professional management team. When considering the management of innovation, Kuhn[24] identifies an important distinction between 'creative managers' and 'managers of creativity'. The skills sets for each are very different. An entrepreneur may be the one who generates the ideas or they may be a cata-

---

Box 11.2: Stimulating creativity

Brainstorming

With your group or team generate as many ideas as possible for a new business start up (product or service). The aim is to generate a large number of ideas, suspend judgement and accept all ideas offered at face value. Use other people's ideas to stimulate further ideas.

Negative brainstorming

Take each of the ideas generated and critically evaluate them in turn.

The aim is to generate a list of all possible negative aspects. Consider the most salient criticisms in greater detail. Agree which ideas are the most workable in practice.

What is your new business concept? _____

lyst, stimulating and managing others in their production of new ideas. In the business environment there are steps to the management of creative and innovative problem solving (see Table 11.4)

Kuhn points out that a problem solving procedure can only be transformed into a creative one by breaking constraints such as 'conventional wisdom', 'not invented here-pressures' etc. Contrary to rational decision making processes, Kuhn advises the development of ideas initially without external information (step 2) and then a further gestation period (step 4) after the information search process. This is to facilitate in-depth understanding of the problem. Dealing with problems is at several levels, the **cognitive** though rational analytical is only part of the apprehension of the problem, the **affective** deals with uncertainty, ambiguity and all the doubts and risk associated with the problem solution – what is the right thing to do? – the **behavioural** concerns deciding between various action alternatives, choosing and taking a particular course of action. Brood. Cogitate. Meditate. Agonize. Uncertainty, ambiguity, and doubt are all friends of the creative process. Experience tension, frustration, stress. Creativity breeds suffering, but such suffering engenders deep fulfilment.[25]

The behavioural aspect also includes management style. Participative decision making (PDM) enables a degree of problem and information sharing, enabling the resolution of a problem with both high quality solution and general acceptance.[26] The team leadership style is thus critical. Kuhn[27] identifies four different 'executive stereotypes' (see Figure 11.4 below) Executives, owner-managers or team leaders vary in the extent to which they use infor-

Table **11.4** Steps in creative problem-solving

1. **Problem recognition.** (finding or sensing an unstable situation disturbance).
2. **'Naive' incubation/gestation** (personal immersion time of reflection and quiet contemplation, allowing subconscious manipulation, restructuring and new pattern making).
3. **Information/knowledge search and detailed preparation** (learning everything about the problem – factual information and expert opinion, each from diverse veiwpoints).
4. **'Knowledgeable' incubation/gestation** (personal consideration of unusual approaches and ideas, now melding naive notions of step 2 with factual information and expert opinion of step 3).
5. **Alternative solution formulation** (group intuitive phase generating numerous possibilities, using creativity-enhancing techniques such as brainstorming, analogies and the like).
6. **Alternative solution evaluation** (group analytical phase involving rigorous testing of possibilities by tough-minded methodologies).
7. **Chosen solution implementation** (putting ideas into action).
8. **Feedback and reassessment** (judging by results, improving the original idea).
Source: Kuhn 1989 (see note 27): pp. 224–5

mation (in order to aid the decision making process) and the way they think. Hence, a manager who has little use for information and thinks in only one dimension – decisive and independent – is termed a **dictator**. The person who uses a great deal of information but again thinks in only one dimension – tending to be analytical and rigorous – is referred to as a **computer program**. If the individual uses little information but thinks in many dimensions – is flexible and fleeting – this type Kuhn labels a **scatterbrain**. If, on the other hand, the executive who uses a great deal of information and thinks in many dimensions – transformational and synthetic – is referred to as an **alchemist**. However, being focused and single minded in some situations can be the more effective way of handling the decision situation, but the alchemist would appear to characterize the prototypical entrepreneur!

Figure **11.4** Executive stereotypes

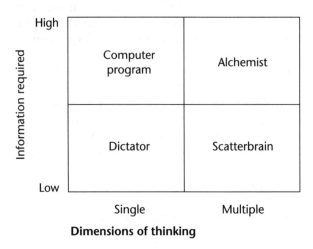

Source: Kuhn 1989 (see note 27): p.251

Managing the creative and innovative process at organizational level

Managing the creative process at team and organizational level means developing an appropriate culture. The following five characteristics need to be in place:

1. **Encourage risk by increasing reward or 'have the guts to fail!'** In medium to large size companies pursuing new venture strategies must be seen as a 'good thing', and a failed attempt not a career damning exercise.
2. **Facilitate creative types.** Some people are more naturally creative than others. They should be encouraged, whilst creative and innovative potential should be developed in others.

3. **Focus the firm's investment policy on innovation** or 'put your money where your mouth is!' Do not just *talk* innovation, take steps to promote and invest in it.

4. **Understand the creative process.** Educate the whole workforce to understand creative and innovative behaviour. Enable everyone to show their innovative capability, for example, through the use of quality circles.

5. **Promote interaction among departments.** Once a business employs 15 or more people, an organizational structure develops around jobs. Separation and departmentalization begin and there is a greater need for communication across these groupings. An active innovative environment can be maintained by the use of task forces or multidisciplinary groups. Hence it is necessary to promote intergroup cooperation, and reduce the socio-dynamics of territoriality and dominance.

Kanter 1983 researched hundreds of corporate 'entrepreneurs' whom she termed 'change masters'.[28] The change masters typically:

- formulate and sell a vision
- find the power to promote an idea
- maintain the necessary momentum to accomplish their mission.

They also have some key skills.

- **Kaleidoscopic thinking.** This is the ability to take an existing situation and examine it from a multitude of different angles, as if it has been shaken and turned upside down. This creates a new pattern and consequent set of action possibilities. It challenges accepted wisdom, as indicated above.
- **Communicating visions.** Innovations are generally positive concepts after they have been successfully implemented. To reach that point the person with the vision needs to sell it hard and be prepared to jump over a number of high hurdles.
- **Persistence.** This means keeping working at one's ideas and not letting go.
- **Coalition building.** The innovator or change master must enlist support for their ideas. This means getting other people to 'buy into' the innovative idea, the project or product. This gives the necessary power to energize further activity in developing the innovation.
- **Working through teams.** Participative management again is stressed, so is the need for people's commitment.
- **Sharing the credit.** The best change masters are said to make heroes out of their subordinates!

Environments that foster innovation in the medium-sized company are redolent of the small firm environment. Kanter[29] identifies four such conditions.

1. **Broadly defined jobs.** Jobs are described widely and a range of employee skills are in use. Skills are vertical and enable the employee to get a feel for the company as a whole. Tasks tend to focus on achievement and there is scope for individual initiative. In the small company there tends to be low

job definition and typically employees have to 'wear more than one hat'. Multi-tasking and multi-skilling are the norm for the competitive small firm. As such task achievement is crucial as it often defines the difference between survival and failure.

2. **Small but complete structures.** Appropriate team size is recognized so that many innovative companies set strict limits to the size of their business units or divisions. This apes the small business environment.

3. **Culture of 'people pride'.** Employees are valued in the highly innovative firm. Motivation and reward systems are geared towards enabling people to achieve their maximum potential. Whether the firm is an SME or a large corporation, if it is attempting to gain a competitive edge through innovation, motivating employees to this end is crucial.

4. **Power tools.** Three kinds of 'power tools' are necessary if ideas are to be converted into action: availability of information and open lines of communication; support or collaboration through 'dense networks'; flexible resources and managerial discretion in the allocation of resources for investment purposes. This means a degree of organizational 'slack'.

Ambidextrous organizations

In established organizations innovation and product/process development take place through incremental improvements and/or discontinuous innovation. Tushman, Anderson and O'Reilly[30] argue that organizations must develop the ability to be 'ambidextrous', that is they must be able, within a given technology, to generate incremental improvements to a design in order to compete effectively in the marketplace for that product whilst at the same time they need to be able to work on the development of the next technological innovation which will supplant the existing dominant design. SSIH (the Swiss Watch Consortium) and Oticon (the Danish hearing aid firm) were prime examples of companies which had dominated their worldwide markets in the 1970s and 1980s respectively and lost their market positions within a matter of a few years because of organizational complacency and inertia. Both SSIH and Oticon were out-innovated by more nimble, foresightful competitors. The paradox of success – 'core competencies become core rigidities' – is not inevitable, companies through proactive management are able to develop new organizational/technological competencies and make the necessary shifts. For example, Seiko (the quartz watch manufacturer) and Starkey (the US hearing aid company) were both able to make a technological design shift which resulted in new industry standards.

In order to ensure sustained competitive advantage a company must be able to create both incremental and discontinuous innovations. This duality of purpose requires different, inconsistent organizational architectures which are in operation concurrently. Such dual or ambidextrous organizations build on the experimentation, improvisation and luck associated with small organizations, along with efficiency, consistency and reliability associated with larger organizations. The management team associated with such organizations needs to:

- have a strategic vision which makes sense to both technologically led streams
- shape technological developments in line with market requirements
- be able to manage system-wide organizational change and development.

Fundamental to this management process the company must be able to compete in respect of technological design. This technological development process is characterized by a period of ferment in which there is design competition and out of which emerges a dominant design. Such dominance arises out of competition between alternative technological trajectories initiated and promoted by a variety of stakeholders, including competitors, alliance groups and government regulators, all of whom have their different social, economic and political agendas.

After a dominant design has emerged, attention is shifted to process improvements within this design technology. Typically incremental innovation will be evident. This leads to the development of product families, enabling lead companies to dominate the market in a particular product-market technology, for example the Sony Walkman. Such periods of incremental innovation are broken subsequently by a technological discontinuity. There may also be evident architectural innovations which reconfigure the same core technology and take that reconfigured technology to fundamentally different markets.

Managing these innovation streams means building different organizational structures in order to deal with both incremental and discontinuous innovation. Table 11.5 shows these contrasting architectures.

This approach suggests that if large organizations are to maintain their globally competitive position they have to incorporate and manage both the organic and bureaucratic[31] management systems. Some of the implications of this for their managements are: the need to develop management teams with strategic vision which cover multiple time frames; the need to create a balance between efficiency in core product-markets, whilst allowing for inefficiencies in the development of radical innovations; and the ability to learn and develop the knowledge base and requisite core competencies and for organizational learning to enable shifts to occur in understanding its own processes, assumptions and ways of operating.

Value innovations

Kim and Mauborgne[32] suggest that there has been a dramatic shift away from technological to value innovation in global economies. Neoclassical economics is premised exogenous (to the firm) competitive conditions which drive innovations. However, where supply exceeds demand, competing for a share of a dwindling market is seen as a 'second best' strategy. Value innovators in contrast are amongst the world's most rapidly growing companies (examples

Table **11.5** Contrasting organizational architectures for incremental and discontinuous innovations

Organizational Architectures	
Structured/mechanistic	Unstructured/organic
Incremental innovation	Discontinuous innovation
• structured roles and responsibilities • centralized procedures • efficiency-oriented cultures • highly engineered work processes • strong manufacturing and sales capabilities • demographically more homogeneous • older and more experienced human resource This set of characteristics yields increased efficiency, well developed knowledge systems learned through continuous incremental improvement. It tends towards inertia despite any past glory in product innovation-market leadership	The structure tends to be loose, the organizational arrangement small – 'an entrepreneurial skunk works' characterized by strong entrepreneurial and technical competencies. Tends to have a relatively young, heterogeneous human resource profile. Its work is likely to be experimental, with failures and showing considerable variations in the ability to draw on new knowledge bases and develop new variants, one of which may become the future dominant design technology. The venture is risky as no one knows *ex ante* what the future dominant design will be. Apart from inefficiency, it is rarely profitable and there are unlikely to be any established histories.

Source: Tushman *et al.* 1997 (see note 30)

are SAP, Microsoft and Wal-Mart), they succeed through market expansion, not traditional low-cost or differentiation strategies. Such companies have high market valuations because of their stock of knowledge. Unlike land, labour and capital, knowledge is an infinite economic good. This suggests revisions in economic theorizing such that growth and innovations are created from knowledge and ideas within a system. That system, Kim and Mauborgne argue, may be the firm. Furthermore, by creating new demand innovation can be a sustainable strategy. Firms that have pursued a value innovation strategy, '[t]heir strategic focus was not on outcompeting within given industry conditions, but on creating fundamentally new and superior value, making their competitors irrelevant. They went beyond competing in existing markets to expanding the demand side of the economy.'[33]

Value innovation anchors innovation with buyer value by linking innovation to what the mass of customers value. To achieve this, companies must offer customers radically superior value at an accessible price point. In other words, they must offer customers a superior product at prices they can afford. Such a strategy focuses on the performance criteria that matter to buyers and create new market space.[34] Examples of companies that have successfully adopted such market strategies are IKEA and Starbucks coffee shops. Unlike technological innovations, however, value innovations are not inalienable goods, they may be copied or imitated. How, therefore, can a firm that adopts such a strategy deal with the problem of market *free-riding*?

The answer lies in the adoption of a non-traditional product-market strategy. Whereas the conventional strategy of a new technology innovator would be high price, superior product, market skim, reduce price to maintain dominant market position as new entrants begin to compete and undercut the monopolist on price, the strategy of the value innovator would be to enter the market with a highly differentiated (superior) product at a low price, thus gaining the advantages of economies of scale and the ability to sustain its competitive advantage. Strategic pricing both leads to high volume and enables the company to establish a powerful brand. Combined with target costing, the company can create an effective cost structure which yields attractive profit margins. Both the value innovator and the customer win, and the would-be competitors find it hard to compete – a noteworthy example of this being Microsoft. Thus on the three bases of strategy – competition, customers and corporate capabilities – the value innovation strategy differs from the conventional. It seeks a radically superior product to make the competition irrelevant (e.g. Microsoft), it targets mass buyers by following non-customers (e.g. SMH and Swatch), and it shows a willingness to combine with other companies' capabilities by using a network of partners (e.g. SAP).

It is clear that value innovation strategies are becoming dominant strategies that quickly enable a firm to become a global competitor and market leader in its field. The key resource of such firms are ideas and knowledge, not technology; as such they need not require high initial investment (for example, The Body Shop, Starbucks coffee shops) Moreover, such strategies can and have been shown to be successful across a range of industries from watches to low cost retailing and software. Competition based strategies will continue in many sectors of the economy but Kim and Mauborgne predict they will become less significant as the knowledge economy increases its global penetration.

Business spin offs

The generation of new technology businesses and the conditions under which they may survive and flourish has been a topic of considerable debate and concern. On the one hand, it is possible to identify geographical area, where there have been considerable innovative activity leading to a critical mass of new technology based firms (such as Cambridge, UK and Silicon Valley, California). By the same token it is also possible to identify regions where there are low levels of innovation (for example the North East of England) It would appear that there are differences in the conditions and climate which lead to high or low innovation.

A primary problem is that the development of scientific ideas for the market place can take five years or more. In the initial stages, where there is merely the germ of an idea, there is the dual problem of low investment and high risk. No one knows at this stage whether the idea can be developed successfully. This can be depicted graphically (see Figure 11.5)

Figure **11.5** Risk and level of investment by stage of development of the science-based enterprise

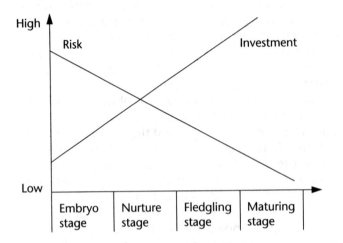

Source: Bolton, W. Enterprise Development Seminar, September 1998, Cambridge, UK

   Venture capitalists tend not to want to invest in such ventures until the 'fledgling stage'. Clearly there is a 'funding gap problem' of how to support an innovative idea at the 'embryo' and 'nurture' stages. Data from UK Science Parks with respect to start up funding suggests that by far the highest proportion of funds come from personal savings (57 per cent) and the second most important source of funding is the clearing banks (17 per cent). At this stage venture capitalists provide only 3 per cent of required funding. An existing business, public agency or grant/loan scheme are other sources of funding but of modest proportions only. Such a risk averse culture explains to some extent the UK's acknowledged problem of global competitiveness.[35]
   Bill Bolton's 'enterprise paradigm' (see Figure 11.6) shows the basic conditions that need to be in place to enable the business development process to conclude with the emergence of commercially viable businesses. The operational environment is as is, although government, through its fiscal policies, legislative programme and initiatives to stimulate entrepreneurship, affects the operational environment. The support infrastructure includes primary support through such institutional arrangements as the universities, private and governmental laboratories, business incubators and science parks. In addition direct financial support may be obtained through government agency programmes, seed corn and venture capital funds and banking support schemes. Secondary support includes local amenities, the telecommunications and transport infrastructure, housing, shops and schools. Business resources in the form of supplier and subcontractor firms, training and

Figure **11.6** The enterprise paradigm

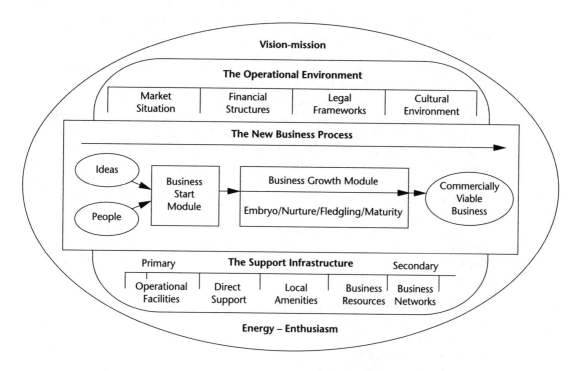

Source: Bolton 1997 (see note 21, chapter 12)

recruitment companies and marketing and management consultants are also important sources of support. Implied but not explicit in this model are the labour market characteristics: skills and competencies that may be drawn upon in the early development of the firm. Last but not least, business networks are increasingly thought to be associated with entrepreneurial development of companies. These may include the chamber of industry and commerce, professional associations and informal or personal networks developed by the 'budding entrepreneur'.

Where might this process start?

Business ideas need to be developed through commercial support, market testing and so on so that they become viable, whilst people who have the potential for managing the start up business entrepreneurially need to be developed. With scientific or technological potential business start ups, there is a protracted staged development process. The university laboratory may be the place where the embryo idea is 'hatched' and tested to see if it works 'in principle'. This 'proof' is essential to the decision as to whether there is a potential product in the making, and the decision to develop a working prototype can then be made. Evaluation of the prototype is done with the customer/market in mind and the further nurturing is likely to be carried out off campus in a business incubator unit. Working with a business plan, the technology entrepreneur will attempt to develop their first saleable product. As a 'fledgling business' with a small customer base the next stage of development work is likely to be in an innovation centre on a nearby science park. Working from a product-market perspective the entrepreneur will produce a product range, getting the product name established to the point of take off. Success will mean a further move for the company from the innovation centre to its own building as a mature business with an established market position. This process will take at least five years and each stage will require considerable work and involve some setbacks. These problems include winning sufficient support in the form of financial backing to survive over the period, being able to deliver a product specification which meets market demands – especially where a major customer is also a major investor or source of seedcorn funding – managing the development of a small business around the product, protecting the innovation through patents and finding a market niche whereby the product has the best chance of establishing its dominance, ensuring that one has an equitable shareholding in the mature business.

It is clear that creating and establishing science based businesses from scratch is a high risk business and one from which, with notable exceptions, the university sector has shied away. There are no guarantees but there are known critical success factors.

- A good business idea or concept.
- Good methodologies.
- Outstanding individuals.
- Practical management structures.
- Formal operational procedures.
- Sound financing.

This formidable list suggests the need on the part of support agencies and other interested parties to be able to screen ideas and people carefully and effectively, train and develop potential entrepreneurs in business management and development and be able to provide the support structures, systems and requisite levels of investment. Hence developing a successful technology-based business is certainly not for the faint-hearted, it is for those who enjoy challenge, who are able to persist through difficulties and solve problems and especially win the support of others. The rewards of 'fame and fortune' for the successful business will materialize, but other rewards – both intrinsic and personal – will be the ones which keep the entrepreneur committed to the success of the venture.

Conclusions

It is clear that developed economies are undergoing changes arising from progress in information technology. At present the dominant innovation strategy is one premised on competition. This is consistent with Schumpeterian economics, which suggests that innovations disturb the equilibrium and may be so profound as to revolutionize industries. In this chapter examples of such radical innovations have been cited. This approach also suggests that firms that can produce radical new ideas and protect those ideas from competitors will steal a march on them for long enough to establish a dominant position in the marketplace. Moreover, having commanded a high price for the novel good they have produced, they are able to recoup the costs of their investment and then reduce the price to expand their hold on the market. Along with this theory is the notion of the fundamental importance of the source of ideas. For Schumpeter and many theorists of entrepreneurship, it is the entrepreneur who is that source. Certainly, however, it would appear that there are industrial sectors dependent on the generation of good, commercial ideas – from culture-based to science and technology-based industries, through hospitality and the service sector. Ideas generation requires a particular mind set, the ability to think round corners, laterally and beyond the problem at hand. Creativity can be developed and so in this sense the particular capability is not as restrictive as it might first appear. However, the 'value innovations' strategy is based on a different set of premises. Importantly it suggests that *anyone* can have an idea; ideas are not the exclusive prerogative of the entrepreneur. Such ideas can easily be copied and by the same token are difficult to protect. To be successful the entrepreneur needs to adopt a different strategy and tactics. They must 'add value' to the concept (develop a superior product) and be able to enter the industry with low costs and at a price point that will appeal to a mass market. This enables the business to establish a dominant position and makes the competition irrelevant. Certainly there is much for the would-be entrepreneur to consider – the development of an idea alone is necessary but not sufficient, strategy and tactics are critical to ensuring the business gets established. This also suggests the importance of the team supporting the developing business. The new entrepreneur clearly must have a range of skills: *either* personal creativity *or* the ability to manage the ideas generated by others; an ability to think strategically and tactically; sound judgement; the ability to build a supportive team to take the establishment of the innovative business idea forward; people management and networking skills. It is concluded that awareness of these needs will help facilitate their development and ultimately the development of the business.

Exercise

Study the case of Microsoft.[36] Consider the following themes: the role of Bill Gates *qua entrepreneur*; Microsoft software as an innovative idea and its impact on the industry; the strategy adopted by the company – could it be considered to be an example of a value innovation strategy?

Part 4

The Professional
Management of Enterprise

CHAPTER 12

The development of enterprise

Introduction

There have been many changes in industry, employment and organization that make the notion of the development of enterprise an interesting one both from the perspective of the theoretician who wishes to make predictions concerning industrial and organizational futures,[1] and the practitioner who is concerned about their present and future ways of making a living. So many companies have downsized that there is a wealth of available expertise to be refocused on self-employment. There is also a higher profile being given to self-employment as a career option from graduate or even school leaving age. But what form that self-employment might take is just one crucial question for each individual who considers it.

This chapter addresses such issues obliquely. In the first section the nature and type of organization are discussed in terms of their shape and potential and the kinds of problems they can present managerially. These forms range from the traditional to the emergent virtual organization. In the ensuing section the issue of stages of development of enterprise is presented and a number of so called stage models are outlined and discussed. Such models have largely been applied to the more traditional organizational form – even then they are thought by some to be controversial – so might they be applied to the virtual organization? The next section discusses the problems of the growth of enterprises. A range of factors which purportedly affect growth is identified and an integrative model, which pulls together 12 factors, is outlined. It becomes clear that growth and development of enterprise is highly complex, shaped by a multiplicity of interacting factors, many but not all of which can be controlled. Ultimately, however, it is the wishes and intentions of the founder that constitute a critical driving force. The chapter attempts to identify what else is important and opens by discussing different organizational forms.

Organizational forms and enterprise

There is no single organizational form, but some forms have been found to be more conducive to enterprising behaviour than others. The reasons for this have been shown in classic studies which have contrasted the organizational and managerial behaviour associated with **mechanistic** and **organic** firms in, for example, the electronics industry.[2] Key features of the organic type include greater flexibility, innovation, fluidity and effectiveness of communications and the emergence of natural groups. Mechanistic organizations tend to suffer from rigidities of process, routinization, hierarchical command and communication structures and formality of team and departmental management. In general therefore it is pertinent to ask what design features might the enterprising organization have and how might management counteract the problems associated with design features? Also, what new organizational forms might be emerging, what are their essential features and in what ways do they facilitate entrepreneurial behaviour?

A useful starting point for approaching this problem is through Mintzberg's early work, which identified five classic organizational forms and the particular design features associated with each.[3] The number '5' appears throughout this book as Mintzberg proceeds to demonstrate the quintuple nature of the design elements of organizations. Further, there is no one view of how organizations function: indeed Mintzberg noted that there are five theoretical views of how organizations work.

1. There are assumptions about the nature of **formal authority** in organizations. This view suggests that authority, power and control reside in the hierarchical structure of organization and that the flow of authority follows this structure (see Figure 12.1a).
2. Another view suggests that organizations function through the flow of **regulated activity** – through the command structure (both up and down the organization), the support departments cutting across but helpful to line management at those nodes of interaction where interventions/support are required and the flow of production work at the very base of the organization (see Figure 12.1b).
3. A third theoretical approach has focused on the *informal* organization manifested through **informal communication** processes and internal organizational networks of relationships (see Figure 12.1c).
4. A fourth approach has been to consider the organization as being made up of **work constellations**. This theory suggests that people cluster together in peer groups to get work done in ways unrelated to the formal hierarchy (see Figure 12.1.d).
5. A further alternative theory is to suggest that organizations function through **ad hoc decision making processes** (see Figure 12.1e).

Furthermore, Mintzberg suggests that organizations function in all five ways and that it is this complexity of process with which management must contend. Hence the smaller the organization the fewer these complexities, the

Figure **12.1** Five views (or theories) of how the organization functions

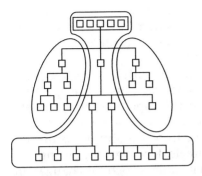

1 The flow of formal authority

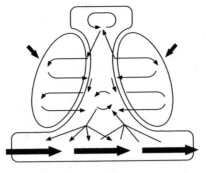

2 The flow of regulated activity

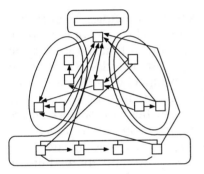

3 The flow of informal communication (adapted from Pfenner, J.M. and Sherwood, F. (1960) *Administrative organization*, Englewood Cliffs, New Jersey: Prentice-Hall, p.291

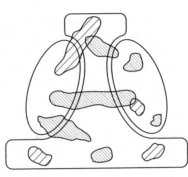

4 The set of work constellations

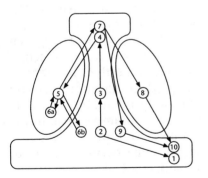

5 The flow of an ad hoc decision process

Source: Mintzberg 1983 (see note 3): p.20

less rigid the structure and the more responsive the organization can be to external contingencies, problems, threats or opportunities.

To learn that organizations become more complex with growth is perhaps not profound as an observation, but the difficulties that this has presented to the managements of large companies that need to be innovative and develop a competitive edge is not to be underestimated.[4]

Keeping with the number '5' Mintzberg continues with his explanation of what he terms, 'the 5 elements of structure': the strategic apex, the operating core, the middle line, the technostructure and the support staff. These elements are differentially balanced to produce five different types of organization. He also suggests that organizations evolve from the **simple form**; that their continuous development is based on strategic decisions (suggesting that strategy implies changes in structure) and that other structural changes are arrived at through the application of principles of organizational design. This issue of the growth and development of organizations is discussed later in the chapter.

Organizational theorists have identified five key principles of organizational design and their implications for management. The small or microbusiness is an example of the simple form. It is in this context that the application of organizational design principles can be viewed in practice. **Division of labour** is one such principle, which arises out of **job specialization**. It is often said that the owner-manager of the newly formed, small firm 'wears many hats', meaning that there is insufficient capital in the business or work on the order book to sustain a specialist workforce, employees are multi-tasked and the owner-manager may do a variety of jobs from packing, loading and delivering, to planning and selling. As the business grows and more staff are recruited, greater specialization occurs. A second principle is that of **span of control**, which suggests that there is an optimal number of people that a supervisor can control or manage dependent in part on the nature of the work to be supervised. The need for **supervision** thus has important implications for design through the building of hierarchical relationships. A small firm may have only one layer between the owner-manager and shop floor – that of the supervisor – whereas large organizations are multi-layered. The danger of this became evident over the past two decades as companies *delayered* in order to reduce the in-built inflexibility of hierarchy. However, even small firms must coordinate and exert management control over their activities, thus **coordination** is another principle of design. Further, in order to achieve certain quality standards, procedures, product specifications and operational processes need to be formalized. As firms grow and become more competitive this principle of **standardization** becomes an imperative. In the simple form there are fewer people and less of a need for formal procedures; job specifications may not be written down, meetings may occur on an *ad hoc* basis, apparently without an agenda and informally conducted, as everyone in the firm knows everyone else. However, as the business grows so does the need for more formal procedures, the development of the formal authority structures through the application of **the principles of administration**. Such organizational development through the application of design principles has wide reaching implications for the management of organizations, most of which are tied up with the performance of individuals, teams and the business, the assessment of those performances and the ability to achieve increased efficiency and effectiveness through the appropriate application of principles.

Mintzberg's five types of organization are termed:

1. the **simple structure**, which he associated with the entrepreneurial firm
2. the **machine bureaucracy**, which suggests the sector specific firm, for example in steel production, engineering or car manufacture
3. the **professional bureaucracy** – organizations which typically are in the public services domain, for example, the civil service, education, hospitals
4. the **divisionalised form**, which typically has a headquarters and a number of companies forming the 'divisions', examples are numerous and can occur in any industrial or business sector
5. the **adhocracy**, depicted as the innovative firm focused on R&D, design or project/consultancy work.

Mintzberg was concerned to identify the effects of poor design, deficiencies in structure and the absence of principles. Taking each of the above five forms what might be their limitations?

The **simple structure** has the major advantage of being adaptive. In the absence of formality, 'red tape', procedures and other impediments to rapid decision making, the simple structure facilitates responsiveness and the ability to be opportunistic. However, this structure tends to be centralized in decision making and control. There is considerable dependence on the 'strategic head' (owner-manager), too little formality and a lack of role definition. The small firm can outgrow its founder's capability, who quickly becomes the problem, the inhibiting factor in respect of growth and further development of the business. A small engineering consultancy firm was founded by three business partners. It remained the same size for two decades, when one partner died and another retired. The third took over the business and in the next five years tripled its size. Many business owners simply grow their business to a size that they feel they can easily control and that enables them to achieve a comfortable standard of living with not too much hassle. Employees who do not fit in or who are ambitious will feel frustrated in such a business and they tend to move on.

The **machine bureaucracy** is designed to handle mass production. However, whilst it has delivered many advantages to the consumer, not least of which is value for money, with products at prices the ordinary person can afford it also has, as a design, a number of deficiencies. The machine analogy is appropriate as it implies a mechanistic view of management. This has resulted in routinization (mechanical throughput) – such a process stifles innovation, an obsession with control and the destruction of the meaning of work. For the worker in this work environment, routinization, deskilling and standardization have meant boredom, low productivity and little job satisfaction. The mechanistic departmentalization of operations has also lent itself to greater conflict, particularly between departments. Importantly, it is an organizational form where resistance to change is rife. There are clear implications for management in respect of the techniques available to them to address those issues of change that make the firm uncompetitive and lacking in entrepreneurial drive.

It is important that **professional bureaucracies** meet the performance criteria of efficiency and effectiveness but not that it should be entrepreneurial. However in the 1980s in the UK there was a government initiative to create an 'internal market' within the health service and for various quasi-governmental bodies to be privatized so that they might learn to compete in a market economy. However, changing the professional bureaucracy has proved challenging. There are certain features of these organizations that have proved difficult to change. For example they are peopled with highly autonomous professionals who control their own work and who have individualized notions of 'strategy'. They tend not to respond to control outside their profession, which in itself brings a particular ethos. Although managed on a democratic, consultative basis they are also highly individualistic with a *prima donna* approach to headship. A great deal of discretion rests with individuals and there are usually cultural norms for dealing with incompetence. The management problems therefore are a lack of overall strategic direction, dependence on the quality of individuals and their teams, a lack of cohesiveness and an unwieldiness which results in inflexibility.

The **divisionalised form** is typical of large corporations. One of the most problematic aspects of its design is the tension which is created between headquarters (HQ) and a division. HQ tends to usurp the power of the division bosses by, for example, centralizing key decisions over resource allocation, product-market developments etc. The lack of autonomy of the division discourages entrepreneurial and innovative behaviours giving rise to a tendency to stagnate. More specifically it encourages counter-organizational practices such as hiding problems from senior management, 'massaging the figures', risk aversion, size maintenance and resistance to growth and change. Over all the sheer size of the corporation can create problems of competitiveness and power tends to be concentrated in the hands of only a few.

The **adhocracy**, according to Mintzberg, is a highly organic structure. It pays little attention to the classical principles of management, it is 'youthful', relies on the coordination of the work of specialists and tends to be organized around a 'matrix' structure. Project work tends to be 'one offs' and standardization is not a feature. Project teams consist of specialists, technicians and people with innovative capability. There is a narrow span of control with many managers relative to 'lower' level employees. The job of management is also distinctive; it comprises considerable liaison work, it is facilitative and involves negotiation and coordinating skills. Power is decentralized to project level and there is no true strategic apex; strategy is formulated implicitly through the decisions made. Due to high stress levels, pressures to meet deadlines, solve complex problems and achieve agreement in an unstructured environment, conflict arises. Senior management therefore tend to have an important part to play in defusing conflict, channelling aggression, monitoring projects and handling external liaison. The high degree of ambiguity and the politicized environment require tolerance and diplomatic skills. Several specific person-management problems arise over the difficulty of balancing workloads and the high cost of communication. This is an organizational form which is difficult to sustain; it has a tendency to grow towards a bureaucracy, which destroys its innovative capability.

Other organizational forms

The idea that there are just five organizational forms sets an unnecessary limitation, other important forms have emerged over the past 20 years. These include the matrix, network and virtual organizational structures.

The **matrix structure** is so arranged to facilitate the formation of cross-functional teams. It forms a lattice, with functions arranged vertically and projects (or products) horizontally. Projects may change and different teams of people can be put together to give maximum flexibility and optimization of human resources. A strength and a disadvantage is that the team member has both a functional boss and a team/project leader. Such a structure clearly needs expert management if it is to work effectively. When it does, it enables greater coordination and cooperation across functions, effective customer service and accountability for results. It has the potential to improve decision making because decisions are forced down to team level where there is the necessary information and it also releases functional managers from the routine to enable them to take a more strategic approach to their job. There are however some dangers, the project team can become too focused on itself so team management skills are crucial. There are also increased overhead costs generated by the introduction of project managers' salaries. Matrix organization can be applied to any size of organization including that of a global corporation. In that case the vertical lines may be geographic, with the country HQ coordinating all the affiliates in a particular country and reporting to the HQ of each product division (laterally organized). Even on this scale the problems of effective communication, good interpersonal and team skills are essentially the same. Despite these potential drawbacks the matrix structure should give the medium to large organization the entrepreneurial organizational attributes of flexibility and responsiveness and the conditions to promote innovation. It can also give scope to individuals to develop their potential and their general management and specific project-related skills. Matrix organization has been around rather longer than the newer approach to departmentalization – the network structure and is therefore tried and tested.

The **network organizational structure** is not 'networking' the behaviour. There is no one network structure. Broadly networks may be *intra*-organizational (formed by a collection of individuals and sub-units of the same organization) or *inter*-organizational (formed by a collection of independent individual companies). A network has a unified purpose which binds the network together and keeps it on track. It has independent members who can stand on their own but who recognize the benefits of collaboration. The network has a multitude of links which strengthen through increased interaction. There is no single leader of a network structure but many leaders who can make their own unique contribution, thus strengthening the network further. Networks are not flat but multi-level, formed by clusters of coalitions and different hierarchical levels. There are three different types of inter-organizational network.[5]

- **The internal network** firm owns most of the assets associated with a particular business. It operates with the market price and innovates to improve individual and overall performance. Examples are large multinational corporations organized around separate strategic business units (SBUs) or where separate organizational functions have become profit centres.
- **The stable network** is organized around a lead or parent firm which outsources different elements of its business. An advantage is that assets are owned by several firms, thus spreading risk, and there is some built-in flexibility. However, in hard times the dependent firms are likely to need protection from the 'parent'. The need for close cooperation in scheduling and quality standards may detract from flexibility.
- **The dynamic network** involves extensive outsourcing. There is usually a lead operator who acts as a network broker, deciding which partner is in or out of the network on any one deal or at any one time. This makes collaboration highly fluid and ensures that the network is always dynamic.

The **virtual organization** is yet another organizational form which emerged in the mid-1980s. 'Virtual' means not actual. One form of virtual organization is an intra-organizational creation. Where there is available information it makes the separation of location and time as well as distribution of fragmented processes possible. The key elements of the virtual organization are orientation to the market and use of information technology to achieve competitive advantage in the marketplace. Information technology in this context gives flexibility and as such confers competitive advantage. With the focus on core competencies and the design of an optimal value chain for the particular company, the elements of virtual organization are complete.

The **virtual corporation** is a temporary network of companies and may be termed an *inter*-organizational structure. The companies come together to exploit opportunities and are linked via information technology. The IT enables them to share skills, costs and markets. Once the opportunity is exploited the network organization is likely to disband. This virtual form enables independent companies the option of continuing their day-to-day business in addition to partnering companies in multiple virtual corporations. The virtual structure may be integrated horizontally or vertically. An example of a horizontal virtual service company is Coopers and Lybrand.[6] Coopers and Lybrand companies cooperate with one another to offer a 'one-stop service' internationally. This means that each independent company's markets are extended geographically and the sharing of resources improves the competitiveness of the whole organization. Virtual organizations have been made feasible owing to IT and the Internet, which facilitate information sharing across a dispersed area. This facilitates the coordination of activities and makes partnering effective.

The **virtual web** is the hub of virtual corporations. It is an open-ended pool of pre-qualified partners who agree to form the potential members of virtual corporations. It is a resource, capability and core competence warehouse from which the necessary items are picked off to meet customer expectations and market opportunities. According to Kluber[7] the virtual web is 'the organizational framework at a macro-organizational level' whereas 'virtual corporation is the actual (*sic*) performing unit on the micro-organizational level'. In sum the virtual web has the following six attributes.

1. A pool of companies with distinct resources and partners with complementary core competencies facilitating the design of a world-class value chain.
2. The ability to unite quickly to exploit an apparent market opportunity. This is enabled by the use of memoranda of understanding which build a trust culture.
3. The interrelation of member companies in the virtual web affects the output of the whole system. This is because the participating companies contribute essential complementary resources leading to an effective, highly cooperative unit with low internal competition. In order to achieve this desirable state, member companies must establish trust. This also means that the number of participating companies will effectively be circumscribed.
4. High motivation not to disappoint collaborators as this could mean not being considered in future projects.
5. Virtual webs may achieve a degree of stability and create their own culture.
6. The ability to form cooperative networks irrespective of geographical dispersion. The sharing of information facilitates joint planning, operation and control of all processes in virtual corporations.

Finally, the **net-broker** is the facilitator in the organizational network and acts as a catalyst.[8] The net-broker benefits from the smooth working of the interrelationships within the network and shares several characteristics with an entrepreneur, in particular the identification and creation of business opportunities and combining resources to form new ventures. A shared core competence is that of social contracting. However, the net-broker is an entrepreneur in a different organizational setting and social milieu.

Another form of virtual organization is the loose coupling of free agent individuals to a lean management centre.[9] This type of organization is dispersed around 'an interconnected world of information systems' and has the potential to be 'totally electronic, with no clear real world, physical identity'.[10] The bases of this organizational form are computer-mediated communications technologies such as e-mail, network conferencing facilities and PC video links and the software and hardware of teleworking – the PC and the modem or an integrated services digital network (ISDN) link. However, teleworking *per se* does not constitute a truly virtual organization. The virtual organization of individuals necessitates a different relationship between the organization and its human resource. This arises from the use of freelance and subcontractual personnel on a large scale. Individuals operating as free agents come together when necessity dictates and outsourcing occurs at the level of the individual not the organization (as in the net-broker virtual organization form). This takes the workforce outside the traditional employment relationship.

The case of Cavendish Management Resources (CMR) exemplifies the virtual organization of individuals within a management consultancy operation.[11] This organizational form was inspired by its founder Mike Downing to solve the problem that SMEs face of having difficulty in accessing financial and management expertise to realize future growth potential. By pooling the expertise of 150 experienced owner-managers acting on a sole trader basis, CMR can offer clients a much wider range of expertise. CMR members are carefully selected and in fact pay a fee for membership irrespective of whether CMR finds project work for them. This turns the 'employment relationship' on its head by placing responsibility on the member to ensure that the image of CMR works for them. As members, they are also given stationery, a marketing brochure and card which they can use when carrying out consultancy work not generated by CMR. This presents the image of being a member of a larger organization and increases client confidence in the quality of service the consultant can offer. From the sole trader perspective, belonging to a larger organization enables them to smooth out the peaks and troughs of work, prevents overtrading and offers excess capacity available elsewhere in the network. To facilitate networking, CMR organizes monthly meetings around dinners. This has several advantages; it reduces the sense of isolation that portfolio life can present, it enables members to get to know each other and, more particularly, the type of expertise they have to offer and it has the social binding effect of maintaining loyalty to the organization. From a management perspective such a virtual organization is highly cost effective. In the case of CMR it is run from a London office with two secretaries. Overheads are minimal. Members use hotel lobbies and airport and motorway lounges and facilities as meeting places with clients.

It is interesting that the two cases cited above are consultancy operations. However, other cases of virtual organizations are emerging, for example in the music industry.

The development of enterprise

As discussed above, not all business owner-managers desire growth, a high proportion are self-employed or are micro-businesses employing only as and when necessary. The proportion of high growth, entrepreneurial businesses has been set as low as 3–4 per cent by some commentators[12] although others have set in much higher – 20–30 per cent. It depends on how growth is measured and whether to include owner-managers who wish to grow but have not overcome certain barriers. Certainly the statistics suggest that there is a correlation between the size of firm and growth aspirations of the owner-manager.[13] More specifically, Hakim contrasts the low growth aspirations of the self-employed home based business with those of the owner-managers of limited companies. Furthermore, the proportion of small firms that aspire to achieve growth is greater than that which actually achieves growth. One reason for this, as already alluded to, is the problem of overcoming barriers to growth.

Stages of development

At its inception, the business start up is at a germinal stage. Its management and administrative processes are likely to be underdeveloped or under development. With growth, however, and the putting in place of management and administration, the business changes fundamentally in character. Theorists have suggested that the business moves through a number of stages of development. Stage theories, as they are known, are somewhat controversial if not problematic. Different theorists suggest a different number of stages that the business will pass through (from 1 to 11+)[14] and identification of the end of one stage and the beginning of another is not without its difficulties. Age is not an indicator of stage either, though size is likely to go hand in hand with the development of various formal procedures. However, given such caveats, stage models do have their uses. They highlight:

- the necessary changes in the behaviour and management practices of the owner which enable the progression of the business to another stage
- the awareness and ability to deal with the different problems encountered at each of the stages
- the changes in degree of informality of operations brought about by increases in size and the need to professionalize management.

Several authors[15] have put forward a general stage model of small firm growth. Churchill[16] suggests that once a business has been founded (or acquired) there are five stages to its development – **existence, survival, success, take off** and **resource mature**. Each stage has key problems which typically characterize the business. For example, at the outset the owner-manager is concerned to build up a customer base to ensure viability of the business and to secure sufficient funds to finance proposed growth. At the **survival** stage, the problem has shifted from viability to existing profitably. Once the business is profitable the problem changes in the **success** stage to a choice between further expansion or stabilization. If the latter course is selected, the owner-manager will disengage from day-to-day management and turn their energies to other things. If on the other hand, the owner chooses growth, then the nature of the problems at this stage will reflect that goal and include financing, motivating others and implementing systems for managing growth. The **take off** stage presents a number of challenges including the problem of delegation and decentralization. Once these problems have been resolved, the business will have reached the **resource mature** stage. Key problems now include the ability to consolidate and control success and not lose the entrepreneurial spirit.

Churchill[17] has updated the original model and created six stages by splitting and renaming stage 3 ('success') **profitability/stabilization** and **profitability/growth**. He points out that each stage is 'characterized by an index of increasing size, complexity and/or dispersion and described by five management factors: management style, organizational structure, the extent of formal systems, major strategic goals and the owner's involvement in the business'.[18] Manoeuvring the firm through these stages, he suggests, has major implications for managerial/leadership skills, team functioning and organizational culture. Furthermore, he maintains that the exercise of such skills *is* related to the financial performance of organizations.

Flamholtz[19] put forward a four stage model of organizational growth. The critical development areas in stage 1 (**new venture**) are identifying a market niche and developing the product or service. Stage 2 (**expansion**) is typified by stretched resources. At this stage ' ... the company needs an infrastructure of operational systems that lets it operate efficiently and effectively on a day-to-day basis. Unfortunately, many entrepreneurs are not interested in such "organizational plumbing".'

Stages 1 and 2 represent the entrepreneurial phase of the company's development. Beyond that, the company must make the transition to a professionally managed business. Stage 3 – **professionalization** – is thus the beginning of this stage of development. Typically there is a need for the implementation of formal systems of planning, organizing, development and control. The fourth stage Flamholtz terms **consolidation**. At this stage the key area to receive attention is organizational culture. As the company has grown, the informal systems for the socialization of waves of new employees becomes inadequate. To remedy this the company needs to develop a more conscious and formal method of transmitting the organizational culture.

Flamholtz makes a sharp distinction between the entrepreneurial business which is characterized by informality, a lack of systems and a 'free-spirited nature', and the professionally-managed business. The latter he describes as being more formal, with well developed management systems and a tendency to be disciplined and profit-oriented in its approach.

Kanzanjian[20] attempted to identify the strategic and operational problems associated with different stages in the development of new technology-based firms. His stage model reflects the nature of the business in that stage 1, termed 'pre-start up', includes invention and the building of prototypes. Major concerns are securing financial backing and strategic positioning. Stage 2 includes the development of the production technology, acquiring plant, refining the product design, etc. The development of the business in stage 3 is typified by growth and the attainment of profitability. Sales and marketing predominate. This includes developing market share and providing product support and customer service. Stage 4 is reached when the firm dominates its chosen market niche, is developing a second generation of products and is attempting to achieve a balance between bureaucratic and innovative tasks. The strategic positioning of the business assumes importance once more.

More recently Bolton[21] has presented a four stage model of business growth of science and technology-based enterprise. The underlying idea or metaphor is that of biological growth stages found in the natural world. Bolton's 'pre-start up stage', which in fact precedes the four growth stages, is the generation and testing of a business idea ('proof of principle') to demonstrate that it is in fact viable. His first stage he terms the 'embryo stage'. The team at this stage develops the idea to a working prototype and is likely to be carried out in the laboratory. He suggests that ideally this stage is supported by a business team who will enable the thinking about the potential product from 'technology push' to 'market pull'. The product passes to the 'nurture stage' whilst still being developed and tested. It is likely to have customers and be moved out of the laboratory into an incubator unit. At the next, the 'fledgling stage', the product will have been developed further, probably to present the customer with a product range. The small company will need to develop its resource base further and may need to move premises. At this stage Bolton argues the science enterprise park or innovation centre can offer shared premises, facilities and management services which enable the fledgling company to reach take off in a relatively secure environment. The fourth stage – the 'maturing stage' – is that of the established, though still vulnerable business. It requires business acumen and a mature management style to ensure that the business is developed beyond the 'hobby' or 'lifestyle' business to gain an established market position. The duration of this period of development Bolton estimates at eight to ten years (see Table 12.1)

Table **12.1** Bolton's four stage model of the development of science and technology-based businesses

	EMBRYO STAGE STAGE	NURTURE STAGE	FLEDGLING STAGE	MATURE
Location	University lab	Business incubator	Innovation centre	Science park
Duration	Six to nine months	One year	Three years	Five years
Product development	Working prototype	First saleable product	Range of products	Recognized position in market place
Support	Business team and full support package needed	Reduced support and watching brief	Support resources available	General resources available

Source: Bolton 1997 (see note 21)

Greiner[22] has taken a different approach. He identified key crises which occurred during each phase of growth, a view echoed by Scott and Bruce who also believe in the importance of crises affecting major change in the transition from one stage to the next. The latter authors point out that '[These] crises are extremely important to the entrepreneur in terms of both his business and personal life'.[23] This is an interesting observation, which appears to have some support from other more recent research.[24] The day-to-day management of businesses – small and large – may be characterized by the need to solve problems. So within a 'stage' it might be argued that the successful resolution of problems results in evolutionary growth, whereas the successful resolution of a crisis heralds revolutionary change and a step change in the

Table **12.2** Scott and Bruce's five stage model of small business growth

	Stage 1. Inception	Stage 2. Survival	Stage 3. Growth	Stage 4. Expansion	Stage 5. Maturity
Stage of industry	Emerging, fragmented	Emerging, fragmented	Growth, some larger competitors, new entries	Growth, shakeout	Growth/shakeout or mature/declining
Key issues	Obtaining customers, economic production	Revenues and expenses	Managed growth, ensuring resources	Financing growth, maintaining control	Expense control, productivity, niche marketing if industry declining
Top management role	Direct supervision	Supervised supervision	Delegation, co-ordination	Decentralization	Decentralization
Management style	Entrepreneurial, individualistic	Entrepreneurial, administrative	Entrepreneurial, co-ordinate	Professional, administrative	Watchdog
Organization structure	Unstructured	Simple	Functional, centralized	Functional, decentralized	Decentralized Functional/product
Product and market research	None	Little	Some new product development	New product innovation, market research	Product innovation
Systems and controls	Simple bookkeeping, eyeball control	Simple bookkeeping personal control	Accounting systems, simple control reports	Budgeting systems, monthly sales and production reports, delegated control	Formal control systems, management by objectives
Major source of finance	Owners, friends and relatives, suppliers leasing	Owners, suppliers, banks	Banks, new partners, retained earnings	Retained earnings, new partners, secured long term debts	Retained earnings, long term debt
Cash generation	Negative	Negative/breakeven	Positive but reinvested	Positive with small dividend	Cash generator, higher dividend
Major investments	Plant and equipment	Working capital	Working capital, extended plant	New operating units	Maintenance of plant market position
Product-market	Single line and limited channels and market	Single line and market increasing scale and channels	Broadened but limited line, single market, multiple channels	Extended range, increased markets and channels	Contained lines, markets and channels

Source: Scott and Bruce 1987 (see note 15): p.48

growth and management of the business. However, Storey remains sceptical, suggesting that the identification of crises which trigger movement from one stage to another may be an untestable proposition.[25] Table 12.2 shows Scott and Bruce's five stage of business development.

1. **Start up/inception**. The managerial emphasis at this stage is on the development of a viable product or service and to do this by establishing a customer base. But other problems may arise through the various constraints arising from liquidity, resources and customer base. Typical crises, which if successfully resolved tip the business into a second stage, are to generate a positive cash flow and make the business profitable, formalize systems and record keeping and delegate work. The management style of the new enterprise is typically 'entrepreneurial'. However, with increasing demands on the owner-manager's time, this signals a need to change the style from 'crisis management' to a more managerial one of delegation, monitoring and supervision.

2. **Survival**. Some growth has been achieved, which suggests the need to finance increased inventories and market expansion. Crises include overtrading and uncontrolled growth, the need to hold on to customers and expand the customer base and restructure to accommodate further and more distant delegation and coordination practices, the need to address the basis of competitive performance and its implications and information management. Expansion also has important implications for the selection and recruitment of new employees. As will be shown in chapter 14, this dimension of management is crucial to get right in the small firm.

3. **Growth**. In order to sustain growth, profits will need to be ploughed back into the business. Its development will mean the need for a more formal organization (moving beyond the simple structure). Liquidity is likely to continue to be a major problem. The firm must be able to capitalize on opportunities, which will take it to the next stage of development. Likely crises are from other larger competitors and the demands that arise due to expansion into new markets. A professional rather than an entrepreneurial approach to organization management is needed. This suggests the need for decentralization and heralds a major change for the entrepreneur.

4. **Expansion/take off**. Increased systematization and formalization of management control will require the professional management of the company. Issues of long term funding will need to be addressed and this may be resolved by taking on equity partners. There may also be a 'crisis of culture' given that the new professional management will not have the same commitment to the business as the founding team. The most likely crises are decentralization and the distancing of the entrepreneur/founder with the concomitant dilution of his/her power base. Greater external focus will be needed in order to meet customer needs (and as such compete effectively) and consolidate the product/market portfolio.

5. **Maturity**. The company is still likely to be growing but it will no longer be classed as a 'small business'. There will be a number of key managerial issues, such as expense control, productivity and finding new growth opportunities. Decisions will be taken to make major investments in mar-

keting the product, upgrading plant, etc. Consolidation may occur with possible shrinkage or growth through acquisition or flotation. The final crises will be ensuring the future of the company and managing the succession problem.

This model suggests that the firm moves through three stages of enterprise development before reaching the final two stages of professional management. It is the successful management of crises which typifies a particular stage and ensures that the business grows. However, by no means all businesses reach the later stages and their development may be arrested at any stage.

Chell[26] has suggested a three stage model (see Figure 12.2 below) Similar to the Bruce and Scott model, this stage model assumed critical nodes at the point of movement from one stage to another. Within this model other assumptions include those of choice and management style. For example the entrepreneur tends actively to seek expansion opportunities whereas the life style owner-manager sees growth as hassle, consequently the latter individual would be looking to arrest business development. This results in a flatter growth curve as the firm becomes established (usually) as a niche business. The alternative here could be rapid decline for both types of owner-managed firm. If the enterprise successfully negotiates the established stage then a further crisis may be reached – that of succession. Bringing in new blood can have a rejuvenating effect. However, this is not inevitable, the founder may disengage and be succeeded by a professional management team (buy-in, per-

Figure **12.2** Stages of growth of a small business

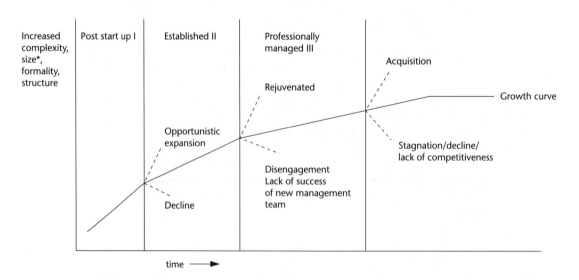

*numbers employed, change in turnover,
change in size of premises over three-year period

Source: Chell *et al.* 1991 (see note 26): p.72

haps), not all of which are successful. Finally, the mature business may grow through acquisition or stagnate and decline if it lacks competitiveness.

Figure 12.2 shows a sequential process model – the stages of growth – depicting small business development. Unlike some growth models it is based on 'nodes of choice' though like others, such as the Greiner and the Scott and Bruce models, these nodes focus on critical events. Unlike these models, the Chell Stages Model assumes a typology of business owner which is manifested in the differences in decisions taken at the nodes. So, for example in the case of Printco (see Box 12.1 below), Martin has grown the business to the 'established stage' and now wishes to disengage – not to found another business as might an habitual or portfolio entrepreneur, but to pursue life style motives. Like the **quasi-entrepreneur**,[27] he was willing to pursue opportunities to grow the business but not with the relentlessness of the **entrepreneur**.[28] There are opportunities to grow the business to a further stage of development, which Martin is now actively resisting.

Box 12.1: Printco

Martin was employed in an owner-managed printing company where he served an apprenticeship and acquired printing skills and knowledge of the industry. He watched his boss with envy: he could be like him, he could own his own print business, earn sufficient to fund a nice life style – car, travel, holidays – and not have to work hard until retirement. So he left and set up Printco, working from his garage. All he needed was basic printing equipment, a business concept and a customer. His concept was that of promotion and advertising material, and an early customer was the local newspaper. He expanded the business rapidly over the next seven years, moving into premises, purchasing equipment and employing 17 people at a high point in employment terms. However, he had reached a threshold. How was he to sustain that level of growth? Did he want to?

Martin made a number of critical decisions in the next couple of years. He moved the business to larger premises and bought additional equipment (for example a laminating machine) so that he could reduce the amount of work to be subcontracted. He also purchased and replaced existing print machinery with their faster equivalents; he bought the 'best' (the 'Rolls Royce' as he put it) on the market.

During this two to three year period he had built up the workforce, but that was not without person-management problems. However, with increased reliance on technological solutions, he was able to rationalize the workforce, retaining his most reliable, experienced and trusted employees. His next decision was also critical. He employed someone from outside the printing industry as a trainee general manager with special responsibility for sales.

Neil was young, enthusiastic and delighted to have been given a chance to prove himself capable of a senior management position in the company. He made several mistakes early on, primarily by being too trusting with clients. This resulted in some bad debts. Nevertheless Martin believed in learning from experience and Neil certainly had learnt from his mistakes.

Grooming Neil to take over as managing director was enabling Martin to disengage from the business. Now he could see his life style dream coming true. But at 40 would this be enough?

Factors affecting growth

The factors affecting the growth of firms have been identified by Storey as characteristics of the owner-manager and of the firm and business strategy. Furthermore, he suggests that all three components need to combine in order to ensure rapid growth.

Table 12.3 shows these dimensions and their characteristics.

Table **12.3** Factors influencing growth in small firms

The entrepreneur/resources	The firm	Strategy
1 Motivation	1 Age	1 Workforce training
2 Unemployment	2 Sector	2 Management training
3 Education	3 Legal form	3 External equity
4 Management experience	4 Location	4 Technological sophistication
5 Number of founders	5 Size	5 Market positioning
6 Prior self-employment	6 Ownership	6 Market adjustments
7 Family history		7 Planning
8 Social marginality		8 New products
9 Functional skills		9 Management recruitment
10 Training		10 State support
11 Age		11 Customer concentration
12 Prior business failure		12 Competition
13 Prior sector experience		13 Information and advice
14 Prior firm size experience		14 Exporting
15 Gender		

Source: Storey 1994 (see note 25): p.123

Characteristics of the owner-manager

Omitting any mention of personality characteristics, Storey reviews research findings in respect of 15 characteristics and concludes:

- there is no single study which has measured all 15 characteristics and so evidence for the strength of any single characteristic is weak; it would clearly be much stronger if all 15 were taken together
- motivation is important in that individuals 'pushed' into self-employment are less likely to found successful growth businesses
- the more highly educated are more likely to found high growth businesses

- more rapidly growing firms are more likely to be founded by groups
- middle aged owners are more likely to found rapidly growing firms.

Characteristics of the firm

Many of these characteristics reflect decisions made by the owner-manager, such as the time when the business started, business sector, legal form, ownership pattern, size and location. Storey concludes:

- younger firms grow more rapidly and there are sectoral differences
- limited companies grow more rapidly than sole traders or partnerships
- location is important: firms located in accessible rural areas grow more rapidly than those in urban or inaccessible rural areas
- firm size is complex, though the smallest firms are least likely to grow.

Strategy

Strategy concerns the decisions taken by the owner-manager within discrete operational or functional areas for example, training, finance and planning. Storey identifies 14 areas. He concludes:

- growing firms are more likely to have owners who share equity with outside individuals
- growing firms have made conscious decisions on market positioning and occupy particular niches or segments
- growing firms tend to introduce new products
- growth is associated with a willingness on the part of the owner-manager to devolve decision making to non-owning managers.

Barriers to growth

Barriers to growth include access to finance, the role of government and skills shortages. A survey of 1900 SMEs ranked 11 possible constraints for fast growth and stable/declining firms. The two most important factors were availability of finance and market demand. Of less importance, though still important, was availability of skilled labour, including management skills. The overall pattern of constraints for fast growth businesses relates to finance, employment and markets.

The approaches that Storey's analysis and review summarize reveal the limitations of the methodological approach which attempts to identify and measure lists of independent factors and combine them in a multivariate model in order to attempt to predict small firm growth. The problem is the absence of an underpinning conceptual framework or set of ideas which integrate the factors and enable an explanation to be constructed of what is happening to facilitate or inhibit growth. The Chell Stages Model (Figure 12.2 above) goes a long way towards achieving such a framework. An alternative approach

Figure **12.3** Perren's framework of independent and interim factors affecting growth

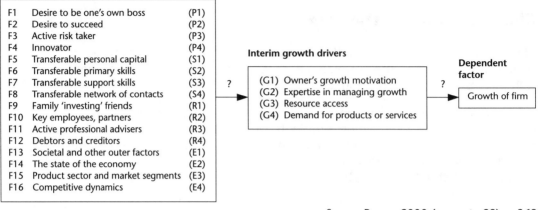

Independent factors

F1	Desire to be one's own boss	(P1)
F2	Desire to succeed	(P2)
F3	Active risk taker	(P3)
F4	Innovator	(P4)
F5	Transferable personal capital	(S1)
F6	Transferable primary skills	(S2)
F7	Transferable support skills	(S3)
F8	Transferable network of contacts	(S4)
F9	Family 'investing' friends	(R1)
F10	Key employees, partners	(R2)
F11	Active professional advisers	(R3)
F12	Debtors and creditors	(R4)
F13	Societal and other outer factors	(E1)
F14	The state of the economy	(E2)
F15	Product sector and market segments	(E3)
F16	Competitive dynamics	(E4)

Interim growth drivers

(G1) Owner's growth motivation
(G2) Expertise in managing growth
(G3) Resource access
(G4) Demand for products or services

Dependent factor

Growth of firm

Source: Perren 2000 (see note 29): p.369

within this genre (though one which dispenses with the idea of developmental stages) is that of Perren.[29] Figure 12.3 shows Perren's framework of independent and interim factors affecting firm growth.

From empirical research Perren was able to show the differential effects of the independent factors on the interim growth drivers (Figure 12.4).

Perren's framework is based on grounded empirical research though it is limited to 16 cases taken from a convenience sample. The model falls rather neatly into four sets of factors: personality attributes (P), transferable experiences (S), stakeholder patronage (R) and external influences (E). Here the interpretation of what the factors mean is critical. For example, what for Perren is a 'transferable experience' might for others be a skill, competence or resource. F8 – 'transferable network of contacts', a 'transferable experience' factor – was explained as 'the owner-manager having access to an adviser who has set up a similar type of firm can be a positive influence'.[30] This is based, it would appear, on one case. The wider literature, however, would suggest that the development by an owner-manager of a personal network of contacts is instrumental in affecting entrepreneurial growth.[31] Furthermore, a personal network then becomes a resource to be developed and used. F5 – 'transferable personal capital' – is described as 'the owner-manager possessing and being willing to use his/her personal capital to support the growth of the firm' (and its converse). Whilst it may be argued that experience may affect a person's willingness to use their own funds, personal capital and access to it is none the less a resource. A further issue is the fact that Perren appears to have attached little significance to the factor 'opportunism', this may be due to the limitations of the convenience sample. However, 'opportunism' is thought by many authors to be a key attribute of the entrepreneur.[32] Perren deals with 'opportunities' in relation to Factor 15 – product sector and market segments – which he construes in terms of 'low/good opportunities for targeting specific niches ...'. This is the view that 'opportunities' exist 'out there' to be picked like flowers and is contrary to the view that the entrepreneur creates

Figure **12.4a** Factors affecting an owner's growth motivation

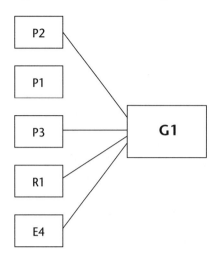

P2 – Desire to succeed – was found to be the dominant factor

Key
P factors –   Personality attributes
S factors –   Transferable experiences
R factors –   Stakeholder patronage
E factors –   External influences

Source: Perren 2000 (see note 29): p.373

Figure **12.4b** Factors affecting expertise in managing growth (G2)

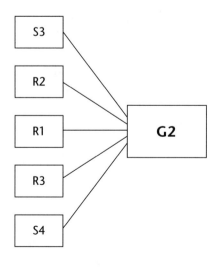

Source: Perren 2000 (see note 29): p.373

Figure **12.4c** Factors affecting resource access (G3)

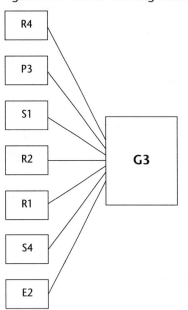

Source: Perren 2000 (see note 29): p.373

Figure **12.4d** Factors affecting demand (G4)

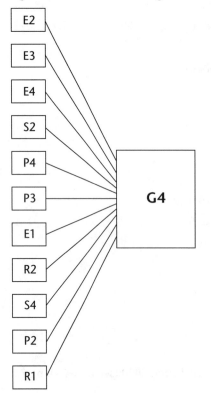

Source: Perren 2000 (see note 29): p.373

opportunities i.e. constructs situations in order to create opportunities. This can be by using one's network of contacts to advantage and usually involves the exercise of vision and imagination to identity gaps in the market for particular products or services.[33]

Finally, however, Perren points to an important but under researched dimension of models that purport to investigate growth of firms and that is '... the complex temporal process of factor interaction'. In other words influences are unlikely to be simultaneous and they can be timely or not. Perren concludes therefore that in policy terms what is needed is for 'tailored and timely support to be offered to micro-enterprises'.[34]

Conclusions

It is clear, that despite the rhetoric of various governments and academics, not all business owners concur with the idea that business growth is desirable. Ultimately the growth and direction a firm takes is down to the decisions and choices of one or a handful of individuals as to the growth and direction the firm takes. Because this is difficult to assess it is often ignored. As has been shown in this chapter some models of growth and development do not ignore the human factor, but there is still a great deal of work to be done by those who aspire to develop a predictive model and enable the economic development agent or the academic to 'pick winners'.

Exercises

1 Examine critically factors that may affect the growth and development of enterprise. How might you go about testing the validity of the factors?

2 Write a case study that exemplifies one structural form of organization. Discuss the case's entrepreneurial potential. How much of this potential can be attributed to structure as opposed to strategic, human resource or other named factors?

CHAPTER 13

Strategy formulation and application

In order that I exist, two gamblers, one Obsessive, the other Compulsive, must meet. A door must open at a certain time. Opposite the door, a red plush settee is necessary. The Obsessive, the one with sixteen bound volumes of eight hundred and eighty pages, ten columns per page, must sit on this red settee, the Book of Common Prayer open on his rumpled lap. The Compulsive gambler must feel herself propelled forward from the open doorway. She must travel towards the Obsessive and say an untruth (although she can have no prior knowledge of her own speech): 'I am in the habit of making my confession.'

Peter Carey, *Oscar and Lucinda*, London: Faber & Faber, 1988, p. 225.

When human behaviour is considered there is little difficulty in recognizing that there are many styles and ways of doing, being and thinking. This variety extends itself to managerial and entrepreneurial behaviour. There is not one way to gamble; one person can be quite systematic about it – obsessively so – whereas another person can lack any system, but simply feed off an insatiable desire. It is individuals who adopt these different styles and ways of living their lives.

In chapter 6 – on decision making – it was noted that gambling in a business context is frowned upon. However, the idea that the business person or entrepreneur can take a decision (say an investment decision) in conditions other than uncertainty was shown to be improbable. Therefore it might be thought that sanitized terms like 'investment' or 'business development opportunity' are often used euphemistically to disguise the risk which is being taken. Indeed, do managers and entrepreneurs understand the basis of risk and uncertainty? Entrepreneurs are said to 'gamble on their imagination'.[1] They assume personal risks, but what of the risks they may take affect that others? The compulsive or indeed the obsessive gambler may be said to lose sight of responsibility. It is not unreasonable therefore to ask what part a sense of responsibility plays in business and entrepreneurial venturing to oneself and to others.

Gambling is an individual act or acts. Each decision to place a bet is independent of every other decision, although in the mind of the gambler it may not be, as they blow the dice and fondly believe that this time they will recoup their losses. When on a winning 'roll' is it not sensible to 'play it out' or is it yet again just the thrill? But what of strategy? Is it not possible to develop a system – like Oscar – to increase one's chances of winning?

Strategy

Strategy is and was a military term for the development of tactics on the battlefield to outflank and outmanoeuvre the enemy. But it is now used in other contexts, for example a person can develop very subtle strategies in a bid to win at bridge or chess. But in business, it is a relatively new concept though one that has been developed by the management academic and adopted in the business school context. Hence, just as managers were found not to calculate probabilities of possible outcomes associated with a decision, executives and owner-managers, especially in the smaller enterprise, do not necessarily develop an explicit business strategy. So what is strategy?

> A **strategy** is the pattern or plan that integrates an organization's major goals, policies and action sequences into a cohesive whole. A well formulated strategy helps to marshal and allocate an organization's resources into a unique and viable posture based on its relative internal competencies and shortcomings, anticipated changes in the environment and contingent moves by intelligent opponents.[2]

Strategic decisions are those that determine the overall direction of an enterprise and its ultimate viability in the light of the predictable, the unpredictable and the unknowable changes that may occur in its most important surrounding environments. They intimately shape the true goals of the enterprise. They help delineate the broad limits within which the enterprise operates. They dictate both the resources the enterprise will have accessible for its tasks and the principal pattern in which these resources will be allocated. And they determine the effectiveness of the enterprise – whether its major thrusts are in the right directions given its resource potentials – rather than whether individual tasks are performed efficiently.[3]

Drawing up a business plan epitomizes one approach to strategic behaviour; the plan is an explicit statement of business goals, intentions, tactics, resources, aspirations and expected outcomes. The new business owner is exhorted to develop such a plan and use it as part of their armoury for thinking through the early stages of the development of their business and for persuading a bank or financier to back them. In this sense of the term 'strategy' the strategy is intended and deliberate.

Another sense of the term is in the pattern of consequent behaviours. Such a stream of actions (perhaps labelled *post hoc* as strategic decisions) may not be intended but may emerge. A further sense of the term is as a position, that is, being able to locate the business in its 'environment'. Strategic perspective on the other hand looks at the firm from the inside out. It concerns the 'collective mind' of the organization, it is its character. Strategy in this sense is shared and can thus be related to organization culture.

There are about eight different kinds of strategy – from the deliberate to the emergent – which can be identified,[4] each having different implications for management. The following table, based on work by Mintzberg and Waters, shows eight types of mutually exclusive strategy, which draw on different key skills and orientations to management.

Table **13.1** Various kinds of strategies, from the deliberate to the mostly emergent

Planned strategy

Precise intentions are formulated and articulated by a central leadership and backed up by formal controls to ensure their surprise-free implementation in an environment that is benign, controllable or predictable (to ensure no distortion of intentions); these strategies are highly deliberate.

Key behavioural element:	Intentional, planned behaviour.
Management implications:	The development of associated leadership skills.

Entrepreneurial strategy

Intentions exist as the personal, unarticulated vision of a single leader, and so are adaptable to new opportunities; the organization is under the personal control of the leader and located in a protected niche in its environment; these strategies are relatively deliberate but can also emerge.

Key behavioural element:	Ability to envision opportunities; strategy is entrepreneurial and personal.
Management implications:	Centralization of decision making, control.

Ideological strategy

Intentions exist as the collective vision of all the members of the organization, controlled through strong shared norms; the organization is often proactive *vis-a-vis* its environment; these strategies are rather deliberate.

Key behavioural elements:	Collective, organizational culture perspective.
Management implications:	Understanding and being able to manipulate organizational culture.

Umbrella strategy

A leadership in partial control of organizational actions defines strategic targets or boundaries within which others must act (for example, that all new products be high priced and at the technological cutting edge, although what these actual products are to be is left to emerge); as a result, strategies are partly deliberate (the boundaries) and partly emergent (the patterns within them); this strategy can also be called deliberately emergent, in that this leadership purposefully allows others the flexibility to manoeuvre and form patterns within the boundaries.

Key behavioural elements:	Goal setting, strategic targets.
Management implications:	Control, with flexibility and room to manoeuvre.

Table **13.1** Continued

Process strategy

The leadership controls the process aspects of strategy (who gets hired and so gets a chance to influence strategy, what structures they work within, etc), leaving the actual content of strategy to others; strategies are again partly deliberate (concerning process), partly emergent (concerning content), and deliberately emergent.

Key behavioural elements:	Divorce of operational and strategic elements.
Management implications:	Need for careful coordination to ensure that operational decisions do not constrain strategic options.

Disconnected strategy

Members or subunits loosely coupled to the rest of the organization produce patterns in the streams of their own actions in the absence of, or in direct contradiction to, the central or common intentions of the organization at large; the strategies can be deliberate for those who make them.

Key behavioural elements:	Strategic initiatives taken in different parts of the organization.
Management implications:	Lack of centralized control or overall strategic vision? possible 'loose cannons'.

Consensus strategy

Through mutual adjustment, various members converge on patterns that pervade the organization in the absence of central or common intentions; these strategies are rather emergent in nature.

Key behavioural elements:	Emergent, consensual behaviour.
Management implications:	Difficult to control and direct.

Imposed strategy

The external environment dictates patterns in actions, either through direct imposition (say, by an outside owner or by a strong customer) or through implicitly pre-empting or bounding organizational choice (as in a large airline that must fly jumbo jets to remain viable); these strategies are organizationally emergent, although they may be internalized and made deliberate.

Key behavioural elements:	External locus of control dictating strategy.
Management implications:	Requires a step change in thinking (such as a radical innovation) for the organization to regain the initiative and be in control of its own destiny.

Source: Mintzberg and Waters 1985 (see note 4): p.270

However deliberate the strategy, however precisely formulated, its goals may be unrealized. Similarly, emergent strategies may be realized or unrealized. Entrepreneurial strategies tend to be emergent as will be argued later, entrepreneurs have a different orientation to management.

Culture and strategy

Once a business grows beyond the employment of a single individual, arguably all its subsequent decisions, if not arrived at collectively, are implemented collectively (due to a combination of explicit and subtle influence processes). Such collective behaviour arises from the cultural mores of the firm. This suggests that strategic decision making does not sit comfortably with the rational objective view of organizational decision making. There is another sense in which such a view is rendered less tenable. As Schneider[5] argues, from the 1960s onwards the notion of strategy became popularized, and in the large company context managers bent their minds to strategic planning using the latest tool, whether it be SWOT analysis, BCG matrices or Porter's model for enabling business to identify its competitive advantage. These tools however were fads or fashions and in that sense cultural artefacts. Hence strategies are abstractions or social constructions.

Schneider identifies those cultural assumptions which are relevant to the alignment of strategy to the external environment. These assumptions pertain to the way uncertainty and control are viewed. At the level of national culture she observes that the Nordics and Anglos tend to adopt a controlling strategy, whereas the Latin Europeans and Asians adopt an adapting strategy. The controlling strategy is rational-analytic fuelled by a belief that it is possible to control the external environment through formalized planning approaches. The adapting strategy, in contrast, is based on a belief in greater uncertainty and less ability to control the environment. It tends to be arrived at through more informal means; it is more personal and subjective, involving a wider range of views and perspectives and it is informal and consensual. The Japanese have been shown to follow the adaptive emergent strategic decision making model. There is a notable absence of rigid planning systems and greater reliance on intuition, insight and feeling.[6]

This cultural variation can also be related to the strategic profile exhibited by the particular business organization. Schneider again argues that the controlling model tends to be related to a 'defender' strategic profile while the adapting model is consistent with a 'prospector' profile.[7] Another way of expressing this is that strategies must be internally coherent; the strategic process, profile and content should be consistent.

Formulation of strategy

Small to medium-sized firms are not renowned for their strategic thinking and business planning. At best the strategy is embedded in the actions and decisions taken but there tends not to be an explicit strategy, laid down and rigidly adhered to. Indeed, the very advantages of being small are the characteristics of flexibility and responsiveness which militate against the pursuit of long term, unbending goals and objectives. However if the SME is to achieve growth then the plan for doing so needs to be developed and *communicated*. Thus to manage its human resource effectively the owner-manager needs to develop explicit plans which are shared and discussed and for which there is support and built-in contingencies.

In order to develop a strategic plan the owner-manager and team need to ask a set of fundamental questions.

- What business are we in?
- What resources do we need?
- What are the key things we have to do?
- What are the indicators that we are on target?
- What external factors must we keep under review?

The next step is to commence analysis. A simple but effective tool is the SWOT – a two way matrix that enables the business team to consider (a) questions in relation to the environment – opportunities and threats, and (b) questions in respect of the company's characteristics – its strengths and weaknesses. A poor strategy is usually the result of inadequate awareness of the company's environment.[8] Companies need to be aware of their principal competition, to be able to name them and consider *their* characteristics! Thus in completing this matrix it is important to consider whether sufficient time is being afforded to all aspects – in particular the environment.[9] Entrepreneurially-led businesses appear to give considerable attention to the 'opportunities'.[10] It is perhaps a matter of speculation as to whether they generally devote sufficient time to considering the negative aspects of their environment and/or their business.

The strategic environment of the business comprises competitors, customers, suppliers and new products.[11] This strategic environment may be considered in relation to the wider socio-political environment. The SME is likely to occupy a market niche or segment.[12] Nevertheless the owner-manager needs to understand the wider market for that good or service and to know what the competition is doing, how much of a threat it presents and what strategies are being adopted. New competitors, new products, customers and suppliers are all factors in the competitive struggle, which Houlden sums up as 'pressure factors'.[13] So, for example, where barriers to entry are low, there is likely to be considerable new competition which will reduce the profitability of the particular enterprise for all. Clearly, an analysis of how each factor is operating in isolation is not sufficient to grasp the dynamics of competitor and strategic analysis. The business executive with the finger on the pulse will understand how these factors interact. A moot point is the owner-manager's preferred style of decision making. The owner-manager/executive with an intuitive style is more likely to have a tacit understanding of the marketplace;[14] he or she may have genuine difficulty in describing the steps of the analysis that led to the particular strategic decision taken. Understanding entrepreneurial strategies may well be a retrospective process of deduction from actions taken.[15]

It is very easy to look beyond the business and consider that the problem of the company's performance lies 'out there' in the environment. This may not be the case. Therefore a tough part of this analysis is to consider possible company weaknesses. These may arise in:

- operational systems and processes
- the accounts
- the management
- sales and marketing
- production and distribution
- innovation.

Good observation, followed up if necessary by an audit in the area suspected of weakness, is the preliminary step needed. Is there too much waste? Are stocks too high? Has volume of sales fallen? Has performance been disappointing – if so why and what action has been taken? Is the business a family business? Is the management strong and effective? Is the pattern of sales changing and what does this mean in respect of the customer base? Are costs under control and is productivity at an appropriate level? Is the customer 'cared for', is the company responding appropriately to their needs? Is the company generating new ideas for new products and services, and if so how? These are all typical but not exhaustive questions which the senior management needs to ask when analysing critically the strengths and weaknesses of the business.

Entrepreneurial strategies

Stevenson argues that entrepreneurship is an approach to management which is defined as 'the pursuit of opportunity without regard to resources currently controlled.'[16] He and his co-authors suggest that there are six dimensions of business practice that define critically the differences between the executive types, which they label 'promoters' and 'trustees'. The **promoter** is the person who feels confident of their ability to seize opportunities regardless of the resources under current control, whereas the **trustee** emphasizes the efficient use of existing resources. They identify six dimensions of business practice through which they are able to demonstrate the two contrasting styles of management: strategic orientation, commitment to opportunity, commitment of resources, control of resources, management structure and reward philosophy. As management style or business practice largely defines the corporate or business culture then the contrasting ways of doing by promoters and trustees yields well structured differences between an entrepreneurial and an administrative culture.

Creative strategies

Kuhn[17] addressed the problem of competitiveness of the medium-sized enterprise. This size of business, established but probably plateaued, was vulnerable; it had neither the advantages of being small such as flexibility and responsiveness nor those of large corporations with the considerably larger resource base. The research he carried out analysed the strategies of over 100

Figure **13.1** The entrepreneurial management style

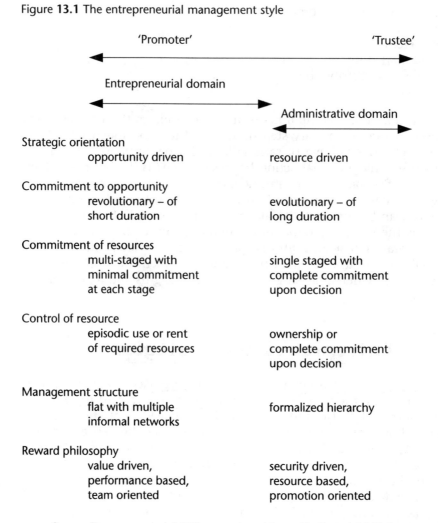

'Promoter'   'Trustee'

Entrepreneurial domain

Administrative domain

Strategic orientation
    opportunity driven   resource driven

Commitment to opportunity
    revolutionary – of   evolutionary – of
    short duration   long duration

Commitment of resources
    multi-staged with   single staged with
    minimal commitment   complete commitment
    at each stage   upon decision

Control of resource
    episodic use or rent   ownership or
    of required resources   complete commitment
                                    upon decision

Management structure
    flat with multiple   formalized hierarchy
    informal networks

Reward philosophy
    value driven,   security driven,
    performance based,   resource based,
    team oriented   promotion oriented

Source: Stevenson *et al.* 1989, reproduced from Chell *et al.* 1991 (see note 19): p.59

companies. The data were reduced to just ten creative strategies, (see Box 13.2)

The 'creative' strategies of Kuhn reflect much of the literature, for example, Porter's generic strategy – the need to focus. They are empirically grounded and thereby common sense prescriptions to help shape the entrepreneurial action plan. The case of Insulate Ltd demonstrates how even small companies can 'dominate their market niche' locally. Technologically and science-based enterprises are exhorted to be 'led by the market' and to be 'customer-oriented' even at the early 'embryo-stage' of product development (see chapter 12). Porter's 'generic strategies'[18] include 'differentiation'; business executives, including owner-managers, have a choice as to what they believe to be the appropriate generic strategy to adopt. According to Porter, pursuit of a 'differentiation strategy' excludes that of 'cost' (i.e. the pursuit of efficiencies and

Box 13.1: Insulate Ltd

Insulate Ltd operates within the petrochemical and construction industries with its main business directed at the off-shore industry, supplying insulation for underwater pipes. These days its business is mainly within the UK.

Bill, the sole owner-manager, gained his management experience with a large oil company in the early 1970s. When he left he went into partnership, running a jointly owned company for five years until he decided to sell out. He bought into an existing business – Insulate Ltd – when its two owners retired in 1979.

The company has a relatively flat, lean structure. Apart from Bill there is the works manager, a quality manager and the 'accounts department', run by Bill's wife on a part-time basis with a junior clerk bookkeeper. The remainder of the workforce is shopfloor. Being ISO9000 certificated is necessary if Insulate Ltd is to tender for jobs and have any dealings with other companies in the industry. This apart, documentation and formality is kept to a minimum. 'We're too small to minute meetings; we (the works manager, quality manager and Bill) meet daily and discuss the day's work. Everybody knows what's going on …'

Up until 1986, Insulate Ltd took on outside contract work, which meant travel and periods of time away from home and the company. Work of this nature could be lucrative but, on the other hand, 'there are plenty of sharks in this industry … sometimes you wouldn't get paid for a job and it often wasn't worth going to Court for …'. Bill decided he'd had enough and for the past 14 years he has concentrated the business on manufacture. It is in a niche market and the company is often in a position of having to develop tailored solutions to meet specific customer needs. To this extent the company is innovative but Bill does not believe there are many really new ideas. Still Bill needs to keep his ear to the ground, seeking opportunities which he can pursue.

In the last three years, the company's fluctuating fortunes have reflected the downturn in the off-shore industry. The size of the workforce has expanded and contracted varying from 25 to 8, where it currently stands. Its turnover is about £1.2 million per annum though this year it is making a loss.

'We retain a core of eight skilled workers; some of the people we had to let go hadn't been with the company very long so the redundancy payments weren't so great … it's regrettable that you have to make people redundant but you have to be realistic'.

Exercise
Discuss Bill's strategy with respect to Insulate Ltd. Is the company successful in your estimation? What do you project to be Bill's future strategic options?

---

possibly price competition). Furthermore, Porter would also endorse the idea that the effectively competitive firm must 'know the industrial market environment', that is, be aware of industrial trends, keep the finger on the pulse and not be surprised by upturns or downturns in the industry. Owner-managers like Bill (see Box 13.1) have a tacit understanding of the industry they have worked in all their working life (in Bill's case about 30 years), but this knowledge was reinforced daily through contacts with customers, contractors and other close associates. It need not take 30 years to build up such knowledge, on the contrary the new founder needs to make it their business to get to know their chosen industry quickly. To be so clearly focused, supported by knowledge and understanding will enable the executive to concentrate on another critically important dimension of strategy – the 'bottom-line'.

Box 13.2: Creative strategies

1.	**Dominance**	'Dominate your market niche'
2.	**Product emphasis**	'Be product oriented'
3.	**Distinctiveness**	'Be different'
4.	**Focus**	'Strive for strategic tightness'
5.	**High profile CEO**	'Radiate charisma and commitment'
6.	**Employee opportunity**	'Be people oriented'
7.	**Efficient innovation**	'Optimize new products, services, methods'
8.	**External perception**	'Know the industrial market environment'
9.	**Growth-profits trade off**	'Concentrate on the bottom-line'
10.	**Flexibility/opportunism**	'Change direction and move quickly'

Source: Kuhn 1989 (see note 17): p.11–13

Opportunities need to be carefully assessed for their ability to contribute to the firm's profit; growth in turnover alone is no guarantee of profitability. Low profitability jobs may occasionally be taken but there is an important principle of trade off to be considered. As a tactic – the 'sprat to catch the mackerel' – it might work in some situations and lever further work. But there is always the danger thereafter of having to underprice jobs. It might be considered whether adoption of this tactic might work in an industry like the construction industry!

The idea of a 'high profile CEO' does not usually feature in a conventional 'rational-analytic' list of strategic dimensions. However, research has shown that the 'high profile image-maker' in the form of the growth-oriented entrepreneur exists.[19] This 'orientation' appears to be more than a marketing ploy; the high profile image of the entrepreneur/executive goes hand in hand with the high profile being created for the business. British examples of this include the internationally known Richard Branson (the Virgin Empire), Roger McKechnie, co-founder in the North East of England, of Phileas Fogg Snack Foods (now owned by KP plc), and Henry Strzelecki,[20] founder and chairman of Henri-Lloyd Ltd – a Manchester-based company – whose original product, foul weather gear for yachtsmen and women was developed as a 'fashion item' through a product range of designer outerwear aimed at the youth, adventure market. Henri-Lloyd's success as an exporter to the Italian market testifies to the importance of quality in design as a further feature of this successful company's marketing strategy.

Innovation is clearly an entrepreneurial strategy, which was highlighted famously by the economist, Joseph Schumpeter.[21] Kuhn, in effect following Schumpeter's early lead, points out that innovation strategies need not be confined to products and adds 'services and methods'. However, this dimension also encompasses innovation strategies with respect to markets and the industry. For example, Bill Gates is a prime example of an innovator whose products revolutionized the computer industry. Anita Roddick, in the cosmetics and toiletries industry, has also made such a revolutionary impact. Her strategy included an ethical philosophy, pursuing 'green' issues and humane testing of products. She has attempted to source 'natural ingredients' for her products worldwide, but in particular from developing countries. There are few High Street retailers (certainly in the UK) who do not sell competing organic and herbal products.

Finally, Kuhn refers to 'flexibility' and 'opportunism' as further dimensions of his list of creative entrepreneurial strategies. In what ways are they creative?[22] Flexibility enables the entrepreneur to put together 'new combinations' (to use Schumpeter's phrase), and 'opportunism' may certainly be interpreted as a sign of a creative mind at work. In this sense, the entrepreneur uses information in an imaginative way, considering and testing possibilities before deciding on the 'right strategy or way forward'.

It is clear that, after each exhortation listed on the right hand side of Box 13.2, there is the unstated thought of the pragmatist: 'how?'. Strategic thinking invites operational and tactical thinking. Kuhn's creative strategies are really only the beginning.

Competitive strategy and the SME

One of the reasons for advocating the development of explicit strategies by the small to medium-sized company is that, when analysed, they are likely to experience many competitive forces operating simultaneously, and the most appropriate strategy may be the least obvious, highly innovative and even counterintuitive (for example, see shipbuilding in chapter 2). Thinking through their strategy can be helpful.

Slevin and Covin[23] have developed a model of 'total competitiveness' in which they identify 12 factors that affect a firm's competitive position and ultimately its performance (see Figure 13.2).

Twelve competitiveness factors

1. **Strategy/direction**. Concerns the long term goals being pursued by the owner-manager and the decisions being taken in order to achieve their goals.
2. **Human resource policies and practices**. Human resource management (HRM) is a much neglected area of small business management. It is arguable that HRM practice is probably underdeveloped in the small business environment. Certainly practice is variable.[24] Slevin and Covin[25] argue that having effective HRM practices– planning, staffing, appraisal, compensation, and training and development – is essential to the competitive performance of a business venture.
3. **Intra-business unit communications**. Burns and Stalker[26] argued for businesses to develop 'organic' rather than 'mechanistic' organizational structures so that they might respond flexibly and effectively in turbulent and hostile business environments. Covin and Slevin (amongst many

Figure **13.2** A model of total competitiveness factors

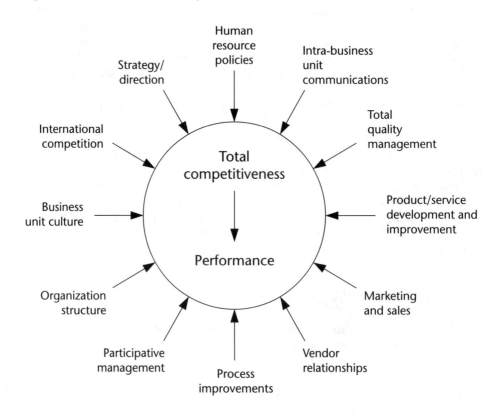

Source: Slevin and Covin 1995 (see note 23)

other distinguished authors, e.g. Miller) continue this tradition.[27] 'Organicity' means free flow information internally with cross functional sharing of information.

4. **Total quality management.**[28] The quality movement of the past two decades has given the business community a new and complete vocabulary of how to raise quality standards of both process and product within a business. Porter[29] has also pointed out that the firm is more likely to be effective if it is to pursue tactics that give it higher-order advantages – ones which are difficult for competitors to imitate.

5. **Product/service development and improvement.** Continuous improvement of products and services to customers is critically important if the business is to maintain a competitive edge. Customers have views and may be involved in this process.

6. **Marketing and sales.** The question of whether a firm is market-led or product-led is still pertinent despite all the energies that have been devoted to realizing 'market economies'. Market-led companies are responsive to customer needs and produce what the customer wants. Clearly, building up customer and brand loyalty are part of the competitiveness tactics that may be deployed.

7. **Vendor relationships**. How are customers regarded? Is the relationship remote? What kind of attention is paid to particular customer needs? Is the response standardized or tailored? How are customers involved in the business and its development? These are just some of the questions the owner-manager needs to address if they are to have an effective sales department.

8. **Process improvements**. These can achieve efficiencies and cost savings and they are not solely about increased quality control. Improved performance can be passed on to the customer – for example through shorter delivery times – and to the business through increased margins. This helps the company compete effectively by helping maintain good customer relations. But is this aspect of the management process sufficiently valued?

9. **Participative management**. Participative management is probably a non-obvious competitive tactic. It involves the adoption of a particular management style. Douglas McGregor suggested the Theory Y style.[30] More recent examples have stressed the importance of not only involvement, but also empowerment.[31] Empowerment can be achieved through training and personal development of employees and facilitated by sharing information and power. The strategic benefit for the company is the involvement of employees in performance, engendering a belief that the company's performance and image matter.

10. **Organization structure**. Organizational structure implies and also constrains strategic options and behaviour. The emphasis is on more flexible and responsive structures, small spans of control, networked and virtual structures which enable the firm to be more effective and sensitive to its environment.[32]

11. **Culture**.[33] Culture is underpinned by deep-seated values and beliefs, often untested. It results in shared norms (rules of behaviour: 'how we do things round here') and gives both energy and direction to people's behaviour. It gives 'character' to a company. For the new company, shaping this character is all important in developing reputation and presenting a positive external image.

12. **International competition**. The horizons of the owner-manager can be near or distant. The extent to which that individual and their firm recognizes they must operate in a global world affects their competitiveness.[34]

By adopting the Slevin and Covin model companies can carry out their own competitiveness audit. When associated with a consideration of, for example, Kuhn's creative entrepreneurial strategies, the firm can also get to grips with its present strategic position, consider where it might like to position the business and bench mark against its various, known competitors.

Strategies and tactics for different occasions

In chapter 6 the idea of 'defender' and 'prospector' strategies was introduced and it was shown how such strategies related to particular types of decision and organizational mission. There are, of course, many more strategies than this. When Porter's 'generic strategies' are included it becomes clear that they are of a 'higher order', they require considerably more strategic thought if they are to be realized in practice. However, few owner-managers or chief executives have time to dwell on strategies as a theoretical exercise. They want to know what is possible and might work for their particular enterprise. Box 13.3 comprises a list of some key strategies that may be adopted to meet particular goals and contingencies.

Box 13.3: Strategies in practice[35]

Functional

Strategic management of your suppliers

Strategic alliances

Strategies for stagnant businesses

Strategies for small firm shares in mature markets

Entry strategies in emerging markets

Strategies for business turnarounds

Diversification

Aggressive strategies – frontal, flanking, encirclement, by-pass, guerrilla

Functional strategies

The firm needs to position itself correctly within its industry. Part of this process[36] is the correct analysis of one's competitors. In effect this means understanding the competitor's strategy in each of the nine key functional areas – product research and development (R&D), process R&D, purchasing, manufacturing, marketing, wholesale distribution and sales, retail distribution, service and finance/administration. In high technology companies, where R&D expenditure is high and speculative, at the early stages of development the company needs to keep track of its own expenditure relative to that of the competition, whereas in the mature market R&D strategies will be more subtle. They may include product redesign, extending the technology to serve new markets or 'tinkering' with product features to stay marginally ahead of the competition.[37]

Strategic management of your suppliers

There are two basic alternative strategies which may be adopted: the **adversarial recipe** or the **partnership approach**.[38] The adversarial strategy comprises reducing the supplier's bargaining power and thus minimizing costs. The tactics that may be adopted to achieve this particular end are: locate and exploit alternative sources of supply; seek substitutes and the suppliers thereof, for example, plastic instead of glass; make some of the supplies yourself; design products to ensure there are multiple sources of supply of component parts; select suppliers that are small relative to your business.

The alternative partnership strategy is one which was strongly advocated by Deming[39] as part of his philosophy of total quality management. The essence of this arrangement is stability, consistency of quality and the maintenance of a long term, flexible relationship. Tactics that may be adopted to assure a cooperative partnership are: the development of a long term contractual relationship; the involvement of the supplier in developing their knowledge of the customers' needs; the development of a close working relationship with suppliers to improve their manufacturing practices, reduce their costs and improve quality. Such tactics result in what Deming[40] termed a 'win-win' situation.

Strategic alliance

These are contractual agreements which firms enter into with each other. They may take different forms including mergers, joint ventures, licensing arrangements, acquisitions or shared R&D projects. The objective is to achieve a specific strategic goal such as expansion of technology, access to certain markets or the acquisition of skills and capabilities that the firm does not possess.[41] Considerable planning and analysis usually precedes the alliance. The well-known examples are between large companies with household names but alliances do occur between SMEs.

Strategies or stagnant business

In a study carried out in 1991 the stagnant businesses were referred to as 'plateaued'.[42] Basically, the stagnant business shows slow growth and low returns, in other words an unspectacular, lack lustre performance. Controlling expenditure in order to cut costs is only a short term expedient which in the medium to long term may actually accelerate the rate of decline (for example because the company loses and ceases to be able to recruit, the best people). It is likely to be more effective to reduce the product portfolio and to refocus the business.[43] This results in higher growth and profits by focusing resources on fewer areas where the chances of success are highest. Another more daring strategy for the management of a stagnant business is 'dis-integration'. The company may have followed a path of vertical integration (forwards or backwards) in the past, for very good reasons which no longer hold. Dis-integration means the company divesting itself of unprofitable elements of the

Box 13.4: Jonathan's story

Jonathan comes from a family of restaurateurs. He trained as a chef and worked for some time in London before returning to his home country and setting up in business for himself. He has had two restaurants, a food manufacturing and a catering business. Jonathan found that he could not keep all four businesses in profit so he divested himself of all except the manufacturing business. This was a critical decision. The strategy was to develop this business further into chilled fresh food and to target supermarket chains. To achieve this the business would need distribution and marketing skills. He hadn't the resources to go it alone. He judged that an effective way of achieving his ends was by means of a joint venture. He described this decision as 'an absolute risk'. But the gamble came off. It took a year to set up the joint venture and in that time Jonathan's small manufacturing enterprise almost went out of business. He has had some frustrations though – working with a large organization which moved so slowly! A major concern of course was to ensure that he was not simply taken over!

business. However it is a strategy that should be pursued in a controlled and careful manner.

Strategies for small share firms in mature markets

Few people like to feel themselves to be beaten into second place, but for a firm to have a small share in a mature market is to be just that. There are two basic strategies that may be adopted to strengthen the firm's competitive position: invest in fast growth segments and/or seek and develop a niche with a highly differentiated product.[44] Tactics for increasing its market share include creating strong brand identity, as was the case with Perrier; introducing a new product form, making existing products appear obsolete (for example, the development the disposable razor) and by changing the rules of the game, for instance, by moving away from traditional marketing practices for that particular commodity. Other tactics include attempts to minimize the competitor's response by being first into a new growth segment and entering it whilst it is small and not yet significant, taking sales away from a number of competitors such that each loses only a small market share and is unlikely to set up a counterattack, competing with established competitors in such a way that direct competition by them would affect their existing products market share. The small share firm can also compete effectively by strengthening the distribution of its product by providing a full product range to the distributor in order to maximize their returns, and/or by distributing the product directly. A combination of some of these tactics will enable the firm to attain a larger share in a growth segment and enable it to defend its position in its chosen market niche.

Entry strategies in emerging markets

Moving into emerging markets involves high risk, with the potential for reaping high rewards. Emerging markets may be home-based or overseas (for example the current emergence of far eastern markets in the Republic of

China). The risks are high because of the lack of information and potentially very different environmental forces influencing the market. Assessing the competition is difficult due to the lack of information, and so developing a relationship with customers, distributors, suppliers and/or industry experts may give the marketeer access to valuable sources of information.[45] Arguably the most critical issue facing the company is whether its resource base is such that it can exploit the emerging market it has identified. Does it have or can it develop the necessary competencies? Does it have the right people with the right abilities, entrepreneurial flair and flexibility? Furthermore, once the entrepreneur has assessed the opportunity and decided that there are benefits to be had by entering this particular market, they also need to address the question of an appropriate entry strategy. This may be achieved by any one of the following: (a) founding a wholly owned new business; (b) acquiring a local established firm; (c) pursuing a joint venture strategy in order to share the risks; (d) contracting the new business to another firm; or, (e) franchising the new business. Clearly, strategy (a) contains the higher risk but the firm will reap all the rewards. The other strategies listed, (b)-(e), are means whereby the firm can attempt to reduce conceivable risks though it may lose some element of direct control.

Strategies for business turnarounds

A turnaround strategy is one of the least of three unpalatable options when a company is in a situation of decline; the other two are continued marginal performance or liquidation.[46] The formal process of company turnround includes five stages.

1. Stage 1: **the management of change**. One of the more traumatic changes includes honing the workforce. For example, if early recognition of the problem has not happened within the top management team then their replacement may be inevitable.
2. Stage 2: **situation diagnosis and strategy selection**. This is likely to be focused, simple and drastic and is likely to include further 'pruning'.
3. Stage 3: **emergency action**. This may be summarized as the 'stop the bleeding' stage. In effect, it means management must take control of cash flows and slough off the fat.
4. Stage 4: **stabilization**. By putting in place a longer term strategy, for example to protect the company's key assets, improve existing operations, and re-position the business in the industry a process of stabilization is commenced.
5. Stage 5: **'return to normal'**. A positive experience of 'take off' should now be evident.

In Box 13.5 a case is presented of how 'Joe' turned round a small bakery. His strategy was based on 25 years' experience in the industry. Consider to what extent his methods conform to the formal prescription of a turnround strategy presented in this text.

Aggressive strategies: frontal attack

The pure frontal attack is the 'me-too' approach. The firm matches its competitor on product (or service) characteristics and price. This is risky as the

---

Box 13.5: The Bakery Co Ltd

Joe has spent all his working life (some 25 years) as an employee in the baking industry. He now wished to do something for himself. He spotted a business he knew and took a managerial job there for six months before deciding that he wanted a share in the company. He was keen to turn the business round and bought a two thirds share plus an understanding with his new business partner that he would be in control of the changes he deemed necessary and that his partner's role was to stand by the decisions that he, Joe, made. Joe's turnround strategy was: to reduce the number of product lines from 30 to 4; to change the name of the business; and to increase the quality of the product. In addition, he restructured product distribution and kept a tight rein on costs. He has now started to export and develop new more profitable lines.

---

customer has no reason to buy from one firm rather than another. There are risks in this strategy associated with competitor response and so many firms would rather adopt a modified frontal attack. This may be to try and win a particular customer away from a competitor, to match the competition on all aspects but offer a much lower price (for example, textiles) or to add value to a product for the same price (for example, Japanese cars). Such tactics absorb plenty of resources and they may intensify the competition, resulting in depressed profits.[47]

Flanking strategies[48]

This is a niche strategy, avoiding direct competition where competitors are likely to be entrenched and identifying those areas where competition is thin. The market segment may involve a different type of customer, require the use of different distribution channels or even different geographical areas. Flanking strategies can only work where there are enough market segments, the industry is growing, entrenched competitors are complacent and a firm does not have the resources to embark on a frontal attack. Adopting a flanking strategy is a useful learning experience, however there are some risks. The identified segment may not turn out to be sufficiently lucrative, the time scale for harvesting may be too long and, finally, the competition may retaliate.

Encirclement strategies

The tactics are eventually to surround the competitor on all sides thus weakening their potential response. Product encirclement involves putting more types, sizes and styles of product on the market with the effect of swamping the competitor's product line. Marketing encirclement means offering product in all possible market segments thus leaving none open for the competition. Encirclement has been a very effective strategy of Japanese industries such as motor cycles, watches, audio and stereo equipment, televisions, radios and hand-held calculators (Fahey, see note 35).

Bypass strategy

This is adopted by firms who do not wish to engage in direct competition but instead compete by getting ahead of their rivals. They do this by developing new products, diversifying into unrelated products or diversifying into new geographical markets. Bypass strategies abound, for example, in the watch industry: mechanical watches were superseded by electronic and now by digital watches. Clearly, to adopt a bypass strategy successfully the firm must expend substantial resources on R&D. It must be highly committed to its product development or market diversification strategy and it must be prepared to wait to realize its anticipated performance. Risks associated with this strategy are having the skills and knowledge base to carry the strategy through successfully, and being able to avoid losing ground on its existing products and markets to competitors, thereby strengthening the competition for a possible attack on the bypass firm (Fahey, see note 35).

Guerrilla strategy

This takes two possible forms – market focused and non-market focused attacks. The market focused guerrilla strategy involves short, intermittent attacks on the competitor's territory, for example the use of targeted price reductions, special promotions, distribution channel pressure, brief bursts of advertising or supply interference by offering higher prices to a supplier. Non-market attacks include legal actions to delay or interrupt the plans of a competitor, executive raids, taking control of distributors by buying an exclusive arrangement and/or intelligence gathering activities. The aim of such tactics is to harass, demoralize and undermine the competitor in the short run. The risks are those of awakening the competition and thereby risking retaliation, making low returns, and losing sight of the big picture – the company's main business goals.

Diversification

The acquisitive company needs to maintain its existing business whilst entering a new industry. This means being able to cope with an entirely new set of strategic concerns (Hofer and Chrisman, 1986).[49] It raises a number of learning and development requirements on the part of the top management team: essentially it must be able to learn how to manage a multi-industry firm. Having said this, new research[50] shows that multiple business ownership amongst SMEs is not unusual. An interesting question therefore is how this process is managed at this level. It is certainly clear that such firms are not engaging in integration strategies. To what extent does chance or serendipity play a part in this process? There are many interesting questions still to be addressed in respect of knowing and understanding the portfolio entrepreneur.

Conclusions

In this chapter an underlying theme has been the importance of character in shaping strategy and strategic decisions. The term 'strategy' has been borrowed from military usage and even now is unfamiliar to many business men and women. In the business world therefore there are different senses of 'strategy' and the *post hoc* rationalization is not uncommon! Much of the thinking about 'strategy' has been concerned with *corporate* strategy. This suggests the large business. But the basic thinking is the same whatever the size of the concern. It is arguably the difference in entrepreneurial behaviour and intentions that makes the difference as to how strategies are developed and implemented. Certainly there is no lack of advice for the business intent on development and growth.

However, it is not possible to think of strategy in a vacuum divorced from the competitive forces that shape the business environment. But having all these at the back or even the forefront of the mind is only the backdrop for the very important decision of what strategy should be adopted on this occasion. There are many such strategies and any business owner who has a tacit understanding of the business they are in, knows the competitive environment and has a clear focus on where they want to take the business, will be able to develop the right strategy for their business.

Exercise
Using the information contained in this chapter, carry out a strategic audit of a company (large or small) with which you are familiar. Consider why the particular company has adopted such a strategy and set of tactics. How might you go about evaluating its effectiveness?

CHAPTER 14

Human resource management and the small- to medium-sized enterprise

In management or any other academic discipline it is not unusual to spend considerable time and space in discussion of a definition of terms. Human resource management is no exception to this rule; in fact there has been a considerable degree of 'navel gazing' over its essence, scope and level (in organizational terms). Whether this debate has any relevance for the majority of firms which are in fact small firms is a moot point. It is one issue which will be considered and returned to in this chapter.

Human resource management (HRM) may have no precise definition in theory or in practice. However there are some characteristics of HRM that will emerge in the course of this chapter. A core characteristic includes the strategic focus of HRM, which enables a link to be made between employee resource management issues and the achievement of business objectives. A further feature of HRM appears to be winning employee commitment, creating in effect a unitarist view of the firm. Assuming such features, it is argued that the training and development function is fundamental not only to HRM but also to the successful growth and development of the small- to medium-sized enterprise.

In this chapter HRM theory and practice is set against a backdrop of industrial relations in small firms of an earlier period. This case study of industrial relations in the UK not only highlights some key changes which have taken place, particularly in the role played by the trades unions, but also shows the importance of the heterogeneity of the small- to medium-sized enterprise (SME) population in structuring management options. Product market characteristics combined with business intentions on the part of an owner-manager create differences in context. Added to this are differences in the conditions under which firms are managed and situations that may need to be faced. The chapter continues to consider HRM and human resource (HR) development of SMEs against such a context.

The chapter commences with a discussion of the nature of HRM.

What is human resource management?

Human resource management (HRM) concerns **the deployment of human resources to achieve organizational objectives.** This definition seems straightforward enough. 'Unpacked' it suggests that a human resource manager is an individual who normally acts in an advisory capacity engaging in the dialogue of business strategy and its implications for the human 'capital' of the enterprise. Such a definition represents a shift from the concept of the 'personnel manager', who traditionally dealt with selection, recruitment and welfare issues but who was excluded from any involvement in the strategic level of discourse in the firm and as such had no 'automatic' seat on the board of directors.

However, perspectives expressed on the nature of HRM have raised a number of issues:[1]

- The management of change and innovation, the need for companies to be more competitive and entrepreneurial suggests that the people factor may be critical in the successful management of this process.
- Renewed interest in 'individual' rather than 'collective' relations.
- An increase in the utilization of direct forms of involvement and communication with employees (for example, team briefings, quality circles etc).
- Attempts to link remuneration/reward with performance.
- A restructuring of organizations to create new ways of working, with a view to increasing flexibility and harmony.
- A change in terminology from industrial relations to employee relations, and from personnel management to HRM.
- Differences nationally in work contexts.
- Whether HRM presents a threat or opportunity to personnel management.

These perspectives on the changing nature of employee relations suggest a further undermining of the trades unions, a reassertion of the 'managerial prerogative' and increased demands on individuals/groups to respond to new ways of working. The latter results in labour intensification practices and increased stress levels. Beneath the veneer of 'soft' managerial practice (increased participation and empowerment etc) there is a cynical managerial philosophy. Additionally, questions arise as to how central human resource management is to the concerns of the business. Is there really a distinction in theory and in practice between HRM and personnel management? Storey argues that HRM is key on two counts: operationally, as it shifts from 'securing compliance' to 'winning commitment'[2] and at a strategic level it concerns the deployment of human capital consonant with the achievement of the company's goals. This means the effective utilization of the workforce and suggests that a firm may operate within a coherent business plan as suggested in Figure 14.1.

What has been so evidently lacking is evidence that firms – large or small – work with such an HRM schema in mind.[3] Were HRM to be evident in practice there is no one way in which it may be managed. Reminiscent of McGregor's Theory X and Theory Y[4] approaches to employee management,

Figure **14.1** A model of the strategic human resource management of employers in the entrepreneurial firm

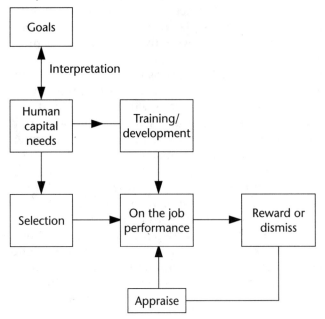

Source: Storey 1989 (see note 1)

Storey distinguishes between 'hard' and 'soft' versions of HRM. The former is said to be rational and calculative while the latter is facilitative, stressing the participative and motivational elements of the job of management. Presumably it is through the latter that commitment is achieved.

A further feature of HRM is that it is unitarist or corporatist, that is, there is little room for the classical approach to industrial relations in which labour was jointly regulated by means of negotiated and agreed procedures between management and the trade union. In the US HRM tends to be associated with non-unionism.

Such a picture of HRM suggests an affinity with the approach of the small firm owner-manager who is said to cherish his or her independence and identify with the business.[5] Trades unions may therefore be seen as an external interference constraining the owner-manager's say-so. A non-unionised plant would enable the owner-manager if he or she so wished to exploit the labour resource more fully.

Guest[6] looks specifically at the relationship between HRM and traditional industrial relations (in the UK). He points out that HRM policies are intended to produce strategic integration, high commitment, high quality of the managerial process and functional flexibility. He suggests that the problems for trade unionism are most likely to be felt in relation to employee commitment and functional flexibility. This is in addition to the threat to collective bargaining. A dual commitment to the firm and the trade union is more likely to work where there are cooperative industrial relations. However, the whole tenor of HRM is likely to undermine that cooperation. For example, management uses its own channels of communication, thus bypassing the union, improves its management capability and provides individual incentive schemes which reward well thus reducing the need for the protective mantle of the trade union. New managerial practices to cope with increased competitive pressures would emphasize greater employee involvement and a more flexible and adaptable workforce.

Legge[7] points to a number of logical contradictions inherent in the meaning of HRM. Crucially she considers the ambiguity in the term 'integration'. In terms of its external focus HRM is said to 'integrate with business strategy'. Internally, HRM seeks to integrate employee policies with a mutuality that generates employee commitment, flexibility, quality and the like. The former, external approach is surely contingent and responsive to competitive pressure, market opportunities etc whereas the latter seeks to be internally consistent; absolutist irrespective of external market and competitive conditions. With such an inherent contradiction is HRM not unworkable in practice?

This problem of integration of business strategy and HRM policy is exemplified in Miles and Snow's (1984) analysis of 'defender', 'prospector' and 'analyser' strategic behaviour (see chapter 13 in this volume). **Defenders** tend to be operating in a stable product market environment. Their HRM policy concerns selection and development and comprises weeding out the low performing employees whilst developing those with potential. **Prospectors**, on the other hand, have a strong recruitment policy, attempting to identify and 'buy in' talent with little need for training or development. **Analysers** tend to operate in a wider diversity of product-markets and their HRM policies will differ accordingly. Put succinctly 'defenders' *build* human resources, 'prospectors' *acquire* human resources whilst 'analysers' *allocate* human resources.

In a single company, single plant operation such consistency may be envisaged. But is it possible in a large diversified corporation to have HRM policies which match a wide range of product-market strategic requirements? The suggested way to achieve this is through strong sub-units that develop their own HRM policy. Only where there was a requirement to merge sub-units would a problem arise. Further, is it possible that some strategies would lead to policies that failed to emphasize employee commitment, flexibility and quality? Certainly in situations such as acquisition, asset stripping or divestment tough policies that, on the surface, contradicted the 'soft' HRM approach would prevail. The cutting out of 'dead wood' in the interests of the many, and the creation of opportunities for employees to develop their competencies and rise to the challenge of an altogether tougher working environment has been one attempt to reconcile the apparent contradiction. Moreover, after achieving cost efficiency, organizations also need to gain competitive advantage through quality – of product or service. Again this is a rather convoluted way of attempting to reconcile external business strategy with internal HRM policy.

However, perhaps one should not assume internal consistency within the elements of the 'soft' HRM model. What, for example, is the employee being asked to commit to? The higher the commitment to a set of skills (for example as in a profession) the less flexible the employee may be to respond to organizational requirements. Second, there is a contradiction between emphasis on individualism and collectivism, rewarding individual performance, for example, whilst operating quality circles and/or attempting to develop cooperative teams. Third, strong company cultures subtly socialize individuals and hence develop collective attitudes and ways of working. This has the advantage of promoting speed of response but only within certain parameters. Any radical departure is likely to be ruled out and may lock employees into a narrow set of behavioural responses that fail to identify and respond to changes in product-market demands.

In Western capitalist systems, there is a dependency on the employment and rational organization of free labour. Employers buy the right to control employees' work while recognizing the employees' calculative involvement in the effort-reward bargain. But employers cannot prescribe tasks in detail and so must rely to some extent on employees' cooperation, to exercise their discretion for rather than against employers' interests. This results in a situation of managerial control by consent. Management, in a sense, 'walks a tightrope' between exercising too tight a control and provoking resistance and the creation of commitment, which carries with it the danger of employee inflexibility and conservatism. Also, increased efficiency and cohesiveness is more likely to generate a collective solidarity which employees may use against their employers' interests. Soft HRM policies have attempted to respond to this dilemma by developing attitudes of 'responsible autonomy' through emphasizing the importance of skills, commitment and flexibility. Further, by developing a sense of a strong organizational culture HRM is also able to mediate the potential difficulty of dysfunctional solidarity. Employees can be united behind managerial (owner-management) values thus assuming an identity between employee and employer interests. In buoyant circumstances, soft HRM policies may well succeed in achieving employee dependability. However, in lean times it is difficult to see how such policies can ride the tide and contradictions inherent in the notion of the business strategies that require HRM policies compatible with the disposable employee.

The above discussion about the nature of HRM signals a change in the management of employee relations in firms, both conceptually and in practice. However, is HRM really only applicable to the large corporation – the conglomerate or the multinational? Is it relevant to the small enterprise? In order to begin to answer this question we need to take a step back in time and examine how employment relations were managed in the small firm. The British case is discussed below.

Industrial relations and the small firm: the British case

In 1969 the British government commissioned an Inquiry into the nature of small firms in the UK economy, chaired by John Bolton. Eighteen studies were commissioned and the final report was published in 1971.[8] The report is rightly considered as a landmark in highlighting the small firms sector of the British economy. It identified many of the burdens and problems facing the small firm, but unfortunately presented a 'rosy' portrait of employment relations in small firms, which was both uncritical and probably inaccurate even at the time. The following much cited paragraph gives a flavour of the view held:

> In many aspects the small firm provides a better environment for the employee than is possible in most large firms. Although physical working conditions may sometimes be inferior in small firms, most people prefer to work in a small group where communication presents few problems: the employee in a small firm can more easily see the relation between what he is doing and the objectives, and performance of the firm as a whole. Where management is more direct and flexible, working rules can be varied to suit the individual. Each employee is also likely to have a more varied role with a chance to participate in several kinds of work ... No doubt mainly as a result ... turnover of staff in small firms is very low and strikes and other kinds of industrial dispute are relatively infrequent. The fact that small firms offer lower earnings than larger firms suggests that the convenience of location and generally the non-material satisfactions of working in them more than outweigh any financial sacrifices involved.[9]

Several attempts have been made over the years to 'correct' this view, providing a more critical, analytical and empirically based understanding of employment relations in small firms. What industrial relations is, can only be understood in terms of related activities which are cast in the social and cultural mould of the time. The extent to which the industrial relations context has changed may be a moot point.[10] However, what has changed is the nature of our knowledge of employment relations in small firms.

The Bolton view and indeed that of Schumacher[11] that 'small is beautiful' assumed the happy family view of small firm employment relations. It failed to consider that the same economic forces structure these relations in small as in large firms.[12] Indeed, Curran and Stanworth argue that the industrial sub-culture was far more influential than size of firm in affecting social relations in small firms. Further, it was important to consider the capitalistic basis governing owner-manager-employee relations as it influenced the different interests and orientations of the parties concerned. Such contradictions of interest, they argue, 'inevitably' (my emphasis) affected the vertical relationship and 'patterns of interaction and involvement'.[13]

Moreover these researchers could find no evidence to suggest that workers employed in a small firm had a different orientation (which affected their decision to work in a small firm) to those who were employed in large firms.[14]

This setting of the industrial relations climate in the small firm was coloured by another set of issues: (i) the extent to which the owner-manager was viewed as socially distinct; (ii) their autocratic attitude and reluctance to delegate; (iii) the closeness of relations within the enterprise affected by the fact that there were likely to be fewer people of similar age, taste and outlook compared with the larger firm; (iv) the satisfaction with and success of employee-supervisor relations, industrial sub-culture and relative technical expertise of the supervisor; (v) social distance between owner-manager and employee.[15] Hence, far from there being an inevitable cosy, tight knit set of employee relationships within the small firm, there were forces which could fragment relationships, create distance between people and fan the flames of discontent, dissatisfaction and conflict.

There was a further socio-political issue which began its ascendancy in the mid 1970s, reinforcing the small is beautiful thesis: this concerned the then 'strike-prone' Britain. The argument being propounded was that there was a relative absence of collective expression of dissatisfaction through organized industrial action in the small firm.[16] However, whilst trades unions have found it difficult to organize small firms, and whilst owner-managers have been shown to dislike trades unions, this does not demonstrate that employee relations in small firms were (or indeed are) harmonious. Further, industrial relations issues in small firms tended to be problematized as personal relations problems arising from the odd or occasional employee who did not 'fit in'.[17] The unitary frame of reference of owner-managers meant that employers failed to recognize as legitimate any view other than their own. They thus identified individual employees as 'troublemakers' who deigned to entertain an alternative perspective. Not only this but they were likely to have 'an unsettling effect upon other workers'.[18] These particularistic relations became 'industrial relations' issues *through process*. So, what requires attention is how these relations are structured and the process by which they are handled. This issue will be addressed later in the chapter.

However, in the 1980s the issue of unemployment loomed very large. Small firms tended to be viewed as the panacea. Yet it could be argued that small firms have the capacity both to create and destroy jobs. They are not necessarily a solution to unemployment, but by pursuing niche strategies many are able to fill the interstices within a varied market economy. Interestingly, particularly in this decade, by processes of demerger, decentralization and the setting up of semi-autonomous business units, large firms not only discovered but were able to capitalize on the merits of smallness. 'Smallness' has primarily spelt 'flexibility'. Through functional, numerical and financial flexibility it has been possible both to lower wage levels and demands, and to weaken the trades unions.[19] For the small firm in a 'dependent' relationship such as a subcontractor or supplier (e.g. subcontractors to the car industry and suppliers to High Street multiples such as Marks and Spencer), this 'dependency', (of what Bechhofer and Elliott[20] have termed the *petite bourgeoisie*), has a two-fold effect on the small firm-large firm relationship.

1. It increases profitability on average (by depressing costs through lower wage levels in small firms).
2. It ensures a transfer of surplus revenue from the small to the large enterprise (through the imposition of lower prices by the large on the small firm).[21]

Subcontracting as a strategy has, if anything, been on the increase.[22] The effects of 'downsizing' and becoming 'leaner and fitter' has meant that many large firms have shed non-core activities. Hence ACAS reported that 77 per cent of all respondents used outside contractors and 90 per cent of manufacturers subcontract.[23] Services such as maintenance, cleaning and transportation were the most frequently subcontracted out. This situation may well have presented opportunities for small firm start up, growth and development, but one might ask, at what cost for the casualized, flexible labour force?[24]

However, not all small firms find themselves in such a dependent relationship. The small firms sector is highly heterogeneous and there are other structuring aspects of the socio-economy (see Table 14.1). They include the **competitive independent** firm, which survives by 'hyper-exploitation either of labour or of fixed capital' as a consequence of the dictation of terms ('the rules') by larger competitors, the **old independent** firm operating in niches that tend to be outside the competitive purview of the large firm, and the **new independent** firm developing specialist markets such as in R&D and high technology.[25] Rainnie uses this framework to point out the importance of structure in enabling the development of a finer-grained understanding of the locale, the pressures and forces that may be brought to bear on the small firm. For example, there is a lack of small firms in 'Silicon Fen', thus ensuring that small high technology new businesses around Cambridge do not suffer from local dependencies, in contrast with the Scottish electronics industry. Indeed, Oakey found that localities with ageing industrial structures are poor seedbeds for new small businesses.[26] The former tends to produce the subcontracting rather than the innovating firm. However, in terms of industrial relations process, the trades unions failed to recognize the changing employment and socio-economic situation and develop a strategy for organizing labour in small firms (in the UK – this was not so in, for example, Scandinavia). Hence the upshot is that there is little control over wages and conditions in small firms and Rainnie argues the need for a more extensive and detailed regulatory framework. The setting of a minimum wage perhaps comes some way towards meeting this criticism.

Context is also defined by the political economy. In this regard the context for trades unions was at its most hostile in the 1980s in the UK. This included weakening the trades unions through legislation and changing the institution of collective bargaining, pursuit of an enterprise economy and the privatization of public sector establishments. In sum, not only have the trades unions failed to organize the small firms sector, they have become generally weakened:

> Unlike their western European counterparts, UK unions lack the framework of national multi-employer bargaining to establish and develop standards for entire sectors. The ability of trades unions to mount industry-wide campaigns has been further undermined by the prohibition on secondary picketing; in 1989–90 the engineering unions, for example, were obliged to wage their campaign for reduction in the working week workplace by workplace rather than across the industry. The decentralization of negotiations within organizations is also putting unions at a disadvan-

Table **14.1** A typology of SMEs based on the owner manager's growth intentions for the business and product – market characteristics

		PRODUCT – MARKET			
	Firm	Dependent	Competitive independent	Old independent	New independent
Entrepreneurial intentions of owner-manager with respect to business performance	Realized entrepreneurial	High growth	High growth	High growth	High growth
	Unrealized entrepreneurial	No growth	No growth	No growth	No growth
	Emergent entrepreneurial	Unexpected growth	Unexpected growth	Unexpected growth	Unexpected growth
	Realized non-entrepreneurial	No/Low growth	No/Low growth	No/Low growth	No/Low growth

Key

Dependent	– subtractors, few customers
Competitive independent	– compete with large firms internationally
	– intensive use of capital and/or technology
Old/Independent	– operate/compete in niche markets
	– unlikely to be touched by large firms
New independent	– operate within/develop specialized markets e.g. high tech.
Realized entrepreneurial	– growth aspirations/goals which are successfully achieved through business performance/outcomes
Unrealized entrepreneurial	– growth aspirations, goals not yet achieved through business performance outcomes
Emergent entrepreneurial	– no growth aspirations, despite this achieves growth as measured through business performance/outcomes
Realized non-entrepreneurial	– no growth aspirations, for the business, these are realized through stable/no growth business performance/outcomes

tage. Management finds it relatively easy to coordinate the outcome. Trades unions, by contrast, have found coordination more difficult because they lack effective company (as opposed to workplace) organization. Decentralized negotiations, moreover, exaggerate the focus on workplace issues at the expense of occupational comparisons or notions of 'going rate'.[27]

The demise of trade union organization at plant level during the 1980s left a hiatus which management were only too willing to fill. Although, as we have seen, trade union organization varied between industrial sectors, the overall weakening of the trades unions reinforced the 'anti-union' attitude which prevailed amongst owner-managers of small firms. The tendency towards incorporation could thus be extended and legitimated. But where did this leave employees? Did the development of human resource management bridge the 'gap', and if so, how? In the next section human resource development applied to small to medium-sized enterprises will be considered.

Human resource development

The watchword of the 1990s must surely be 'strategy' and not least in respect of human resource management. However, the strategy process in the SME is highly contingent. It is not formally and rationally designed (as we are told occurs in the large corporation) but arises out of necessity. Hendry *et al.*[28] note that the strategy process is intimately linked to the activities of people who influence and implement the firm's unfolding strategy. Based on an earlier study of SMEs,[29] Hendry and his colleagues observed that SMEs experiencing high growth were vulnerable to crises, which ultimately signalled the necessity of change. The crises facing these firms varied: from financial difficulty, takeover, loss of internal control, loss of key employees, succession problems, loss of key customers, to product obsolescence. Essentially these problems, they suggest, fall into one of two types: a crisis of control arising from low internal efficiency and dealing in limited markets resulting in dependence on too few customers.

A crisis of control arises from an over reliance on the one individual – the owner-manager – his/her reluctance to delegate and reduce his/her involvement in day to day activities. Whilst this implies a need for training – bringing other people on to assume responsibilities which had hitherto been dealt with exclusively by the owner-manager – it is nevertheless a double edged problem. On the one hand, the owner-manager often has difficulty relinquishing power – this was found to be the case – yet, on the other hand, employees often shy away from assuming any mantle of responsibility, having had little preparation to enable them to feel confident of matching the owner-manager's power and assumed capabilities. If one adds to this a general reluctance on the part of the owner-manager to pay for training (ostensibly because employees may be poached) then human resource development tends (prior to the crisis) to lag behind business growth and development.

A crisis of customer dependence occurs as a consequence of the business outgrowing the owner-manager's original vision for business development. Consequently markets tend to be too narrowly focused, the firm ceases to meet customer needs as they change and develop, and the first signs of the impending crisis are often a loss of key customers. Such customers are often fundamental to the firm's survival and without them leave it in a vulnerable position. The solution is obvious when pointed out, but realization and action may occur after the fact!

Of course in reality crises do not necessarily occur singly or sequentially. Generation problems of the family concern may yield up succession problems, an unwillingness to step down or give the younger generation credence or scope to effect changes to what has become a narrowness of market and overreliance on the original vision. This can result in demoralizing squabbling and faltering direction. Only by recognizing and dealing effectively with such problems can the company's fortunes be turned around.

Hendry *et al.* separate crises from the problems of adaptation. Successful adaptation involves the same process of developing markets and building an efficient and appropriate internal resource base. This process involves the opportunistic (learning process) of exploring the market whilst defending the business' existing niche. Seven ways in which markets were found to be exploited and developed were identified.[30]

- **Capitalizing on environmental beneficence.** For example, a change in legislation will enable already established firms to exploit new opportunities.
- **Niche-based adventurism.** This involves incremental opportunistic steps to develop markets through, for example, customer requests.
- **Developing a related package of services and products.** Such 'packages' may be set up as related companies in order to manage risk. For example construction firms may develop various services such as equipment hire out.
- **Actively seeking and targeting additional niches.** Rather than having a related package of products or service which may leave the firm vulnerable in a downturn, the firm may choose to diversify its product/service portfolio. Such a strategy spreads risk.
- **Building a flexible resource base.** Although the small firm may start with a small customer base, this has the advantage of facilitating specialization; skills which are honed to particular customer needs. However, once this resource base has been built up it can be developed further in order to reduce dependence and serve a wider set of customer requirements.
- **Applying expertise in related product areas.** For example, where a firm has developed its own design capability such expertise can be extended to a new range of products.
- **Testing markets and boundaries.** Learning and discovery are central to this process. A firm may experiment at the boundaries and learn about the subtleties of existing markets as well as learning about new ones. Examples include entering into joint ventures or other synergistic arrangements and internationalizing by launching products overseas.

Getting the product-market strategy right goes hand in hand with human resource management issues. This may include recruiting and/or training new people and acquiring new specialist skills. There may also be equipment, systems and other requirements to be met. All the related decisions need to be carefully thought through otherwise problems can ensue. Thus it is essential that human resource and related investment decisions are anticipated. Occasionally this may mean challenging the old culture and values, heralding a change in top management. Alternatively it may mean bringing in new blood and developing a team that 'fits' the new strategic direction. Yet again the requirement of anticipating expansion and building up knowledge and resource skills is evident in developing businesses. However, to anticipate is to plan, and Hendry and his colleagues found, much to their surprise it would seem, that over half their sample of firms planned two to three years ahead. Planning 12 months ahead was not unusual in these smaller firms. Hence they conclude: 'Adaptation ... requires an outline vision, a strategy which is gradually fleshed out, and an investment in skills and capacity often in advance of the need to draw upon them. This is "strategic HRM".'[31]

Skills supply strategies

Skills supply strategies of SMEs vary considerably due to differences in industrial sectors and their labour markets. A skills supply strategy comprises the sources of recruitment, the additional training and development requirement for new recruits and policies for managing, retaining, promoting and shedding employees. Labour markets are complex. They comprise local, national and sectoral components. Major determinants of the supply of skilled labour comprise:

- the competitive environment
- conditions for the successful operation of the business, including technological
- autonomous nature of external labour markets
- regulatory industry-specific infrastructure e.g. systems of training and pay
- government intervention.

Other modifying factors tend to include the age of the firm where younger firms have evolving skills requirements and size of firm where smallness restricts recruitment and promotion opportunities. HRM therefore has a critical strategic role to play in managing these influences on skills supply (see Figure 14.2)

Figure **14.2** HRM in the management of skill supply

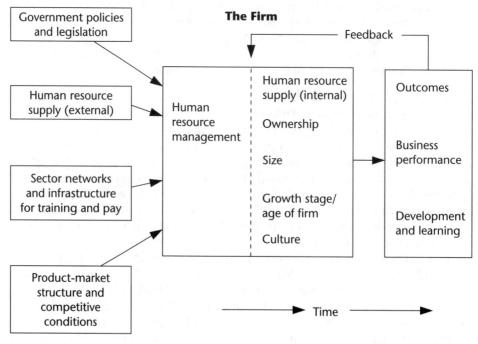

Source: Hendry *et al.* 1991 (see note 34)

Hendry *et al.* identified seven skills supply patterns.

1. Specialized skills

This was exemplified in a 'high skill' workshop, where products and their designs tend to be customized. Such workshops were illustrative of the fact of the complexity and variety of skills required by even the very small company. SMEs were also seen to operate with a variety of skills groupings, which meant that they drew upon a number of different labour markets. Hence recruitment and training tends in this type of firm to be highly focused and specific. Labour markets can be very tight for the more specialized skills and recruitment is often by word of mouth. Recruitment problems are evident due to the need to work through a 'cohort gap' and simply finding people with the right mix of skills. Consequently in such firms there tends to be a focus on training and poaching is often used as a competitive weapon. Industrial sectors where this skills supply pattern predominates are engineering, electronics, aerospace and defence. A culture of knowledge acquisition through external training, the development of team working and the raising of standards through the development of quality consciousness is evident.

2. Technical process

Some industries are dominated by the technical process that characterizes their product, for example fibre optics or glass. The skills requirement is complex, varied and technical within the specific sector. The remainder of the labour force tends to be un- or semi-skilled. The internal labour market is split between the technical grades recruited regionally or nationally – with promotion and good pay prospects – and the remainder of the workforce recruited locally – with modest pay levels and few prospects. This creates a tension within the pay structure. It is exacerbated by the fact that technical grades are critical and that strategically a stable labour force is desirable and so every attempt is made to tie technical grade employees to the company.

3. Flexible service

The rise of the service sector business has been evident over the past two decades. Service businesses are people intensive and customer-oriented. They tend to be youthful, demonstrate rising educational standards and employ more women in mainline jobs. Entry comes from a broad range of jobs. Employers tend to look for flexibility and interpersonal skills. Credentials tend to be externally acquired, such as language training, which is increasingly important in travel and tourism. The type of people attracted to this sector are mobile, require a job which is intrinsically interesting and are looking for high pay and prospects. From the employer's side, there is an expectation of high commitment and employees are allowed considerable discretion in their work. The organization structure tends to be flat and employees grow with the job. There is a philosophy of continuous individual improvement and a training culture that includes off-site professional and knowledge-based education, *ad hoc* training and 'learning by doing'.

4. Unskilled mass

Work is unskilled, monotonous and takes place in a relatively unpleasant environment. Training comprises a brief induction, pay is incentivized and there is direct discipline. Recruitment is almost exclusively local. Money is the main motivator and so there is little loyalty to the firm. This results in a high turnover of labour as employees move around seeking better pay. There is a narrow spectrum of skills at the apex of the firm. There is little inclination towards training. Industry examples are bakery (such as bread), garment manufacture and moulding.

5. Professional market

Professional firms in areas such as business services, consultancy, architecture and law typify this category. Architecture, law and accountancy (in that order) are highly regulated by external bodies, which accredit qualifications and sector standards though allow for flexibility over pay. There tends to be mobility between firms and less mobility within the firm. Architects, for example, tend to be recruited from a national labour market, the architect having spent their final year of training in full-time professional practice. In most professional firms the quality of recruitment is critical for the firm's image and reputation. Training is focused on the front end of people's careers. There is no formal continuing development, although changes in particular professions (such as law) do necessitate updating.

6. Flexible casualization

Flexible casualization typifies the construction industry, where subcontracting and casualization practices have operated traditionally over a very long period. Typically a construction firm will operate with a core staff of up to 20 per cent, with the remainder being self-employed or subcontracted workers. Pay and labour productivity are regulated through piecework. Attempts have been made to improve teamwork, although this is clearly difficult where there is little stability in the labour force. However, this requirement plus increased quality standards have meant that there is a need to recruit capable site managers. Some changes have worked against the industry such as reduction in the length of an apprenticeship (from five down to three and a half years). This has meant insufficient basic training and falling standards. It has assured the need for an industry training board to counterbalance the effects of such a highly fragmented industry structure.

7. Unstable market

A highly unstable labour market is evident in the hospitality industry, in particular in hotels. In this industrial sector labour turnover is particularly high amongst chefs and waiters. The sector struggles to meet the demand for high quality service where teamworking and people knowing precisely what to do are critical for effective on the job performance. Stability of employment is desirable in order to achieve such a goal but remains elusive. Hotels operate like total institutions in that a very high proportion of employees live in. However, even this characteristic is being eroded as the industry attempts to cope with the problems of unsocial hours, low pay and low status work. Annual turnover of employees can be as high as 85 per cent. Training tends to be acquired externally or experientially. The economic need to reduce staff has exacerbated the problems of work pressure, lack of time for training and increased instances of crisis management and labour turnover. Due to the high energy levels required, the work tends to favour the younger employee. Some attempts are made at technological solutions, whilst poaching is rife.

This analysis raises a number of issues in respect of strategic human resource management. It is abundantly clear that differences in context, influenced in particular in the above cases by sectoral variation, affect internal business process, organizational culture and work practices. Such contextual factors structure and indeed delimit what is possible. Hence they shape business policy (firm options) and business strategy on the one hand, and human resource management strategy on the other. From this combined set of forces the content of employee relations and managerial practice emerges.[32]

The nature of skills and the SME

Whilst it is clear that at certain strategic junctures the growing SME requires additional skills to take it to the next level, it is also clear that skill supply strategies vary considerably. By thinking in terms of jobs to be performed, it is very easy to miss one very important dimension of skill: that it is socially constructed and relational.[33] Skills' content is relative; some tasks being viewed as having a higher skills content than other tasks. The variation between supply and demand for a particular skill affect how it is valued. Those people in jobs with high skills content are viewed differently from those who are excluded – there is an imbalance in power. However, once acquired skills tend to be taken for granted; they become invisible. They are also assumed to be requisite for the performance of a particular kind of role or task. Hence this more fluid, social constructionist view of skills raises some interesting issues for skills analysis in the SME. When this is coupled with the predominant flexible orientation of the SME then it is clear that a 'check-lists' approach to skills needs is probably inadequate, indeed inappropriate.

An entrepreneurially-led business, for example, is largely under the control of the owner-manager who can dictate the way the business develops and the formation of its skills base and skills requirement. The owner-manager's vision shapes policies, such as the need for flexible skilling, multi-skilling or indeed deskilling. A person having certain generic skills (acquired through education and training) may be necessary in *some* sectors, but it is more likely to be the specific skills that are sought and valued. In areas such as engineering, catering and architectural practice, the education system provides a basic set of qualifications – core, generic skills. However, specific skills are often required where the craft is not defined by a qualification nor by formal vocational training. Catering falls into a grey area where on the job training may act as a substitute for formal training. Indeed, where the craft element of catering has been removed, the job becomes much more process oriented, for example heating up prepared meals. In general, the less craft dependent and more process oriented the job, the less the reliance on generic skills and the more the need for specific skills. Specific skills assume the acquisition of product/process knowledge and are influenced by quality standards also specific to the particular enterprise.

Jobs vary to the extent to which they can be considered to be routine. For the person who takes on a job with a high routine content, the skills content becomes invisible. Non-routine tasks demand some artistry from the incumbent if they are to be seen to perform a job competently. They will have developed tacit knowledge and understanding of what is required; they will need sound judgement in order to do the right thing in a timely fashion; they will have the confidence to use their discretion and enjoy the responsibility that this bestows. In the very small firm it is usually the owner-manager who behaves in this way. However, as the firm develops, the need to delegate and rely on others becomes essential. An owner-manager with foresight will recognize this turn of events and begin to identify the employee with the potential, the capability and the desire for greater responsibility. At such a stage the owner-manager will be managing the human resource development aspect of the enterprise.

The question of valuing the employee and the specific skills they have developed through the job also has HRM implications for retention of that individual. In the small firm such individuals may be critical, exhibiting specific competences which confer competitive advantage. It is essential that the owner-manager recognizes and values such employees. To retain them they need to be aware of pay relatives, offer some form of progression, and/or manage the culture so that it is an attractive place to work. Successful firms, especially leaders in their field, will help create job satisfaction and keep labour turnover low. Policies towards the acquisition of new technology affect the skills complement of the firm. This often results in bringing in young qualified people who gradually assume responsibility for key functional areas.

It has been argued that skills in the SME environment are overwhelmingly contingent on the sector, stage of development, size, technology, strategy and job to be performed. Job performance is affected by context (for example, location), conditions (such as time pressure and physical conditions) and situations (unexpected crises, for instance). In the smaller firm where a flexible skills policy predominates it is likely that the job incumbent will have to perform across a wide range of situations and engage with a wide variety of people. Understanding job performance requirements is therefore fundamental to understanding skill needs in the small firm.

Also, in the small firm, each individual employee is vital in the sense that a poorly performing individual and their effects will be only too apparent. However, on the positive side it is clear that the owner-manager can develop key individuals to a level of proficiency that enables them to contribute to the business through the execution of activities above and beyond the specific job requirement. Having to cope with crises is not unusual in the small firm context. Such situations demand extra capability primarily from the owner-manager who must be able to act under pressure, problem solve and think strategically in order to manage the crisis effectively.[34] Of course crises may arise due to a basic lack of competence. For example, a failure to manage the firm's resources shows a lack of competence in planning and control. However, to be able to deal effectively with a crisis and turn it round so that the potential threat becomes an opportunity requires personal attributes of flair and imagination. Such an individual will be operating proficiently. To have developed a 'right-hand-person' to whom the owner-manager can turn in such situations means that the strategic apex of the SME is operating proficiently.[35]

Human resource management and national policies

HRM has a clear business need and a nurturing, unitarist, integrative feel. It has placed flexibility of approach and quality as central to industrial regeneration. This resonates very much with the owner-managed enterprise, prizing its independence and shunning traditional industrial relations practices. Hence the goals of HRM summarized in the 'four Cs': **competence** and **commitment** of employees, **congruence** between the goals of employees and those of the organization and **cost effectiveness** of HRM practices;[36] add a humanistic perspective to HRM which, on the face of it, appears to be entirely compatible with the aims and objectives of the owner-manager and the view that owner-managers tend to be, if not paternalistic then certainly unitarist.

In the UK a government initiative to provide a nationally consistent training framework linking training provision directly to work based skills and to standardized accreditation has taken the form of National Vocational Qualifications (NVQs). Underlying the NVQs is the competencies approach to training. Competency is defined as the ability to perform the activities within an occupational area to levels of performance expected in employment. Hence NVQs are linked to required performance, making a more direct connection with business need. However, the NVQ approach has been criticized on the grounds that it does not assess an employee's competence in relation to the whole job, only to discrete bits of it.[37] Clearly, as has been argued in the preceding section, training in the SME requires not only an understanding of specific skills but also the contingent factors likely to affect performance of the job as a whole.[38]

A further initiative of the 1990s is Investors in People (IiP). This scheme, administered through Training and Enterprise Councils (TECs) explicitly links training, development and business strategy. It provides a planning framework to enable firms to develop systematically their own training provision to a standard that is nationally recognized. Such an initiative encourages firms to assess their own training provision in the light of their business needs and strategy. To gain IiP recognition, an organization has first to audit its existing training provision and then to take appropriate action to meet the standards where it has fallen short. When this is achieved it may apply to its local TEC for recognition. Although this initiative is compatible with HRM principles, it has been criticized on the grounds of the costs of assessment and its overly bureaucratic approach.[39] Certainly small firms may find such an approach intrusive as well as expensive and time consuming to put in place.

Conclusions

This chapter has argued that, whilst there is considerable debate amongst theoreticians regarding the nature of HRM, empirical work has shown that there are some features of HRM which the owner-manager of the SME may comfortably espouse in practice. Developments in HRM, away from the old industrial relations system, point to a unitary perspective, a diminution of trades unions' power to organize and represent and a reassertion of the managerial prerogative. This has enabled management to make more coherent the strategic goals of the business and HRM strategy (for example, in terms of recruitment and training policies) HRM practice is thus highly contingent; it reflects the heterogeneity of the SME sectors, skills requirement and labour market structures. Training on the whole tends to be highly specific, with employees learning on the job and adapting their know-how to the contingencies of situations encountered. This requires a breadth of capability. There appears to be a low demand for generic skills training. The NVQ system meets this need by, on the one hand, purporting to supply training of 'generic skills', whilst on the other hand, assessing the employee's ability to perform a range of tasks on the job to a specified standard. Such NVQ training meets the needs of the firm, but makes the skills *less* transferable!

Finally, it should be noted that this chapter has been limited to a UK perspective on human resource management/human resource development. This approach ensured a degree of depth of understanding at the expense of breadth and cross country comparisons. However, HRM practice in continental Europe varies between countries.[40] Further, there is an even wider categorical difference between HRM as practised in the USA and in Europe. Confining attention towards the British case of HRM practice in relation to the SME has suggested that the 'ideal set' of HRM characteristics may be close to those characteristics that the growth-oriented owner-manager or entrepreneur might espouse. The following table of such characteristics provides not so much a conclusion but, rather, food for further thought [see Table 14.3 below].

Exercise

Table 14.3 identifies the contrasting styles of Howard Stevenson's entrepreneurial 'promoter' and his more managerial 'trustee'. Consider how these different types of owner-manager might respond to the features listed in Table 14.2 below. Are there many – or indeed any – points of overlap?

Table **14.2** Contrasting features between personnel management/industial relations (IR) and human resource management (HRM)

Dimension	Personnel and IR	HRM
Beliefs and assumptions		
1 Contract	Careful delineation of written contracts	Aim to go 'beyond contract'
2 Rules	Importance of devising clear rules/mutuality	'Can-do' outlook: impatience with 'rules'
3 Guide to management action	Procedures	'Business-need'
4 Behaviour referent	Norms/custom and practice	Values/mission
5 Managerial task *vis-a-vis* labour	Monitoring	Nurturing
6 Nature of relations	Pluralist	Unitarist
7 Conflict	Institutionalized	De-emphasized
Strategic aspects		
8 Key relations	Labour-management	Customer
9 Initiatives	Piecemeal	Integrated
10 Corporate plan	Marginal to	Central to
11 Speed of decision	Slow	Fast
Line management		
12 Management role	Transactional	Transformational leadership
13 Key managers	Personnel/IR specialists	General/business/line managers
14 Communication	Indirect	Direct
15 Standardization	High (e.g. 'parity' an issue)	Low (e.g. 'parity' not seen as relevant)
16 Prized management skills	Negotiation	Facilitation
Key levers		
17 Selection	Separate, marginal task	Integrated, key task
18 Pay	Job evaluation (fixed grades)	Performance-related
19 Conditions	Separately negotiated	Harmonization
20 Labour – management	Collective bargaining contracts	Towards individual contracts
21 Thrust of relations with stewards	Regularized through facilities and training	Marginalized (with exception of some bargaining for change models)
22 Job categories and grades	Many	Few
23 Communication	Restricted flow	Increased flow
24 Job design	Division of labour	Teamwork
25 Conflict handling	Reach temporary truces	Manage client and culture
26 Training and development	Controlled access to courses	Learning companies
27 Focus of attention for interventions	Personnel procedures	Wide-ranging cultural, structural and personnel strategies

Source: Storey 1992[41]: p.37

Table **14.3** Enpreneurial versus administrative management styles

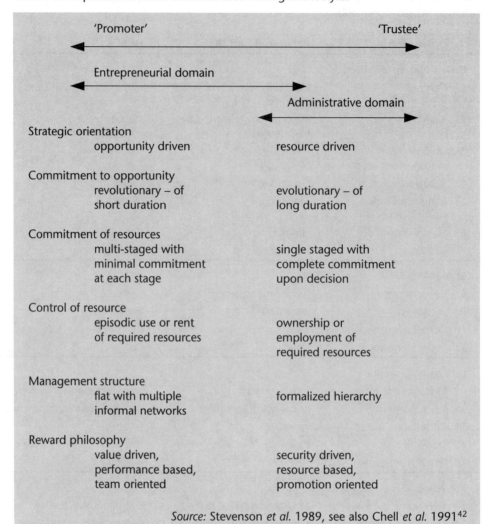

'Promoter'   'Trustee'

Entrepreneurial domain

Administrative domain

Strategic orientation
    opportunity driven   resource driven

Commitment to opportunity
    revolutionary – of   evolutionary – of
    short duration   long duration

Commitment of resources
    multi-staged with   single staged with
    minimal commitment   complete commitment
    at each stage   upon decision

Control of resource
    episodic use or rent   ownership or
    of required resources   employment of
                       required resources

Management structure
    flat with multiple   formalized hierarchy
    informal networks

Reward philosophy
    value driven,   security driven,
    performance based,   resource based,
    team oriented   promotion oriented

Source: Stevenson *et al.* 1989, see also Chell *et al.* 1991[42]

CHAPTER 15

Developing and managing quality

The 'quality movement' developed post the Second World War in Japan. One of the prime instigators was the late W. Edwards Deming, an American who was invited to Japan to help with post war restoration. The West began to be conscious of the 'movement' in the late 1970s, and in the 1980s 'total quality management' (TQM) became the 'flavour' of the decade. It was at this time that the author was carrying out field work in small firms. One project in particular aimed to identify and distinguish entrepreneurs (i.e. owner-managers intent on wealth creation and capital accumulation) from other owner-managers who were more likely to view the business as an alternative lifestyle, a source of income or a job.[1] One observation made was that the entrepreneurial type expressed a wish that his business become the 'best in the world'.[2] This same observation was made with entrepreneurially-led firms in a study carried out in New Zealand in 1994.[3] Was the intuitive sense of the entrepreneur shown by picking up a trend and making it their own strategic 'weapon' or was the quest 'to be the best' an expression of the entrepreneurial persona?[4] The question may reflect two sides of the same coin, but is still unresolved in any rigorous sense.[5]

In this chapter the relevant current literature on the concept of quality will be examined critically. The focus initially is on the 'quality gurus' – those individuals who have espoused particular philosophies of total quality management (TQM) and who largely came into prominence in the 1980s. By way of illustration, and also because it has arguably been the most influential TQM philosophy worldwide – the Deming approach will be elucidated. However, espousing TQM (whatever its origins) is not the only strategy open to an organization's management. Hence the next section will explore different strategies that firms may adopt, from the informal illustrated here by the case of quality management in a sushi bar to the adoption of formal external quality control measures. This is illustrated by an empirical study of the adoption (and reasons for non-adoption) of the BS5750/ISO9000 standard in small UK based enterprises. The discussion returns to the strategy of introducing TQM systems in small firms, with particular emphasis on the introduction of quality control circles (QCCs) and just-in-time (JIT) systems in western economies. This critical evaluation highlights the difficulties of successfully introducing formal, externally conceived quality management systems into organizations. The penultimate section draws many of the threads together by considering some of the difficult issues with respect to developing a quality culture especially in the small to medium-sized enterprise. The chapter concludes with a case study of quality management in Malaysia by way of contextualizing in a particular cultural setting many of the issues with respect to quality management that are raised throughout the chapter.

What is quality?

In the context of quality management 'quality' is usually understood to mean **an essential or distinctive characteristic that signifies fineness or a grade of excellence in a process, product or service.** Various writers have reviewed various definitions of quality (e.g. Garvin, 1988; Hardie, 1993; Smith, 1993).[6] Table 15.1 below summarizes a selection of these definitions.[7]

North, Blackburn and Curran[8] argue that definitions of 'quality' are vague; they tend to be used in a 'universalistic sense' and ignore crucial market economic issues of cost and price. Whilst quality systems such as BS5750 are designed to assure quality requirements and customer needs are met, there is an implicit assumption that customer requirements are known. However, such vagueness is insufficient to assure quality, customer requirements need to be *explicitly* defined. Does this objection, and others aimed at TQM that suggest it lacks realism hold true? What are the issues?

Fundamental objections appears to rest on the following premises:

- Quality systems such as BS5750 address procedures but do not ensure quality of product or service.
- Quality philosophies (for example those of Deming and Crosby) aim to change the culture of the organization totally in order to instil full quality consciousness, as such it is argued they cannot fulfil their espoused aim.
- Both quality systems and quality philosophies are prescriptive in a general way. They do not provide the tools or practical help to enable owner-managers and other senior executives to implement quality objectives. Further, being generic they lack context-specific advice of a 'how-to-do-it' kind. Owner-managers and others are obliged to seek advice from consultants, thus adding to the overall costs of implementation.

However, to satisfy customer needs is not an easy task as Deming (paraphrasing Shewart, 1931) points out:

> The difficulty with defining quality is to translate future needs of the user into measurable characteristics, so that a product can be designed and turned out to give satisfaction at a price that the user will pay. This is not easy, as soon as one feels fairly successful in the endeavour, he finds that the needs of the consumer have changed, competitors have moved in, there are new materials to work with, some better than the old ones, some worse; some cheaper than the old ones, some dearer ...[9]

Table **15.1** Some definitions of quality

Source	Quality Definitions
Webster's New Collegiate Dictionary, 1977	'quality, *n*.1) peculiar and essential character; an inherent feature;...2) degree of excellence; superiority in kind;...3) social status; an acquired skill... 4) a special or distinguishing attribute.'
Deming, 1986; p168	'Quality can be defined only in terms of the agent. ... In the mind of the production worker, he produces quality if he can take pride in his work ... [and] quality to the plant manager means to get the numbers out and to meet specifications.'
Juran, 1988a; p.5	'... quality is "fitness for use."'
Crosby, 1984; p.60	'Quality has to be defined as conformance to requirements.'
Adam, Hershauer and Ruch, 1986; p.9	'Quality is the degree to which a product or service conforms to a set of predetermined standards related to the characteristics that determine its value in the market place and its performance of the function for which it was designed.'
Groocock, 1986; p.27	'The quality of a product is the degree of conformance of all of the relevant features and characteristics of the product to all of the aspects of a customer's need, limited by the price and delivery he or she will accept.'
Thurston, 1985; p.31	'Quality is the index that reflects the extent to which the customer feels that his need, the product, and his expectations for the product overlap. The relevant measure of quality does not reside in the product. It resides between the customer's ears.'
Ross, 1988; p.1	'The quality of a product is measured in terms of these characteristics [of performance relative to customers or expectations]. Quality is related to the loss to society caused by a product during its life cycle [i.e. Taguchi Loss Function].'
Gitlow, Gitlow, Oppenheim and Oppenhiem, 1989; p.3	'Quality is a judgement by customers or users of a product or service; it is the extent to which the customers or users believe the product or service surpasses their needs and expectations.'
Hanan and Karp, 1989	'Quality is an assessment of the general goodness of a product. It is the sum total of all the ingredients or components that compose the product and that contribute to the value it adds.'
Collier, 1990; p.239	'Quality is the distinctive tangible and intangible properties of a product and/or service that are perceived by the customer as being better than the competition.'
Senior and Akehrust, 1991; p.102	'... a word used by an individual to describe whether his or her perception of a product or service has reached a satisfactory level of excellence.'

Source: Mat Hassan 1996 (see note 7): p.16

In fact, Deming's philosophy is based on a very practical managerial tool – **statistical process control** (SPC). Statistical control does not imply the absence of defective items. Rather it assumes a state of random variation in which the limits of that variability are predictable. Such methods enable management to identify the causes of poor quality and so reduce variation. This results in 'continuous improvement'. Such an approach can be applied in all areas, not just conformance to product or service specifications. According to Deming the notion of 'zero defects' (an exhortation made by one of the other quality gurus, namely Crosby) cannot be achieved, it is fallacious. It fails to acknowledge that in any system there will be random variation around the mean, arising from 'common causes' (for example human fatigue, the need to meet quotas, machinery needing maintenance). Consequently Deming advises managers to develop a deep understanding of their organizations as systems or networks of processes and of the types of problems that can arise and to learn the effects of such different but common causes of variation on that system. Thus, such 'common causes' can be reduced by diligent management. Importantly also everyone is involved in developing an understanding of this process, and being able to recognize the difference between such 'common causes' and 'special causes'. The latter arise, for example when a particular event occurs, for example a piece of equipment falters and ceases to function correctly. This process of reducing the 'common causes' of variation also implies (he claims) increased productivity: it is costless – 'same workforce, same burden, no investment in new machinery'.[10] What is the alternative? It is possible to obtain a high quality product from a low quality process – thorough inspection and checking of output at all stages – but this involves extra costs in overheads, rejects and reworking. If the quality of the process is improved, however, then overheads will be reduced and there will be less wasted effort.

Gaining a 'profound knowledge' of how one's organization works is a necessary but not sufficient condition for achieving total quality consciousness. Deming combines this with the necessity of being 'obsessed with quality' manifested through 'delighting the customer', the achievement of this objective through teamwork – i.e. the necessity of carrying one's workforce with one and a philosophy of management encapsulated in Deming's '14 points'. These points require considerable interpretation and thinking through before they are capable of implementation within a particular organization.[11] They comprise a set of prescriptions (see Table 15.2).

A number of Deming's prescriptions are counterintuitive, or at least run counter to 'received wisdom'. Accepted practice in most industries would recommend that a firm does not adopt a single source of supply, but in the TQM system envisaged by Deming this dependent relationship is not a problem but an advantage. For example, the supplier needs to understand the use to which supplies are to be put if they are to perform to the required standard. Further, using a single source helps assure consistency of that which is supplied. Third, dealing with a single source reduces administrative overheads. Philosophies such as Deming's are not intended to be 'quick fixes', they require a change of management style and organizational culture, and a commitment from the top. Certainly Deming's is what one might term, the 'thinking person's man-

Table **15.2** Deming's 'fourteen points'

1.	To create constancy of purpose toward improvement of product or service.
2.	To adopt the new philosophy.
3.	To cease dependence on inspection to achieve quality.
4.	To move towards a single supplier relationship.
5.	To improve the system for increased quality and productivity constantly and to decrease costs.
6.	To institute on-the-job training.
7.	To institute leadership.
8.	To drive out fear.
9.	To break down barriers between departments.
10.	To eliminate slogans, exhortations and targets asking the workforce to achieve 'zero defects' and/or new levels of productivity.
11.	To eliminate work standards that set quotas and management by objectives (MBO).
12.	To remove barriers to a pride in workmanship.
13.	To institute a vigorous programme of education and self-improvement.
14.	To involve all employees in the process of transformation.

Source: Deming 1986 (see note 9): pp.199–203

agerial philosophy'. It results in organizational learning as the owner-manager and the team reflect on changes in procedures, processes, techniques and actions that have been implemented and their effects observed.

Far from TQM philosophies being inappropriate for the small firm, it is clear that for internal managerial purposes they could be effective. However, it is undoubtedly the case, as North *et al.* point out, that few small firms have formally implemented TQM. A practical danger, as Legge has identified for firms regardless of size (but the smaller firm presumably is more vulnerable) arises from the role and powerful position of the external stakeholder, the taken-for-granted nature of quality achievements, and the external pressures that customers can place on their suppliers.[12]

Indeed, satisfying the customer – the one and only criterion of the achievement of quality – narrowly meets the market economics requirement but fails to meet wider social considerations. From a broader stakeholder perspective and a view of quality as negotiated,[13] this broader perspective takes account of conflicts of interest that may arise between any stakeholder body – workforce, shareholders, the community, etc – and managerial practice aimed at customer satisfaction. Indeed on occasions the 'customer satisfaction' may be dubiously served, as when poor quality materials are used (built-in obsolescence), frequent changes are made to the product (for example software packages, football strips), or a product is produced that runs counter to the consumers' health, and consequently may have wider social costs (e.g. cigarette smoking, the marketing of baby milk as a substitute for mother's milk).

Finally, there is a social perception which assumes that when quality is considered it is quality in an *absolute* sense. However, the concept of quality is unstable and subject to many influences: changes in technology, changing tastes, strategies and budgets over time (for example the impact of entry strategies of new firms), a general awareness of how others in the market are behaving, the effects of recession, of war and the availability of materials. There is also the negotiated relationship between quality of product or service and price. Considerations such as 'value for money' or offering the customer a 'good deal' may be competitive tactics adopted which change over time. For example, Marks and Spencer plc has gradually increased its sourcing of supplies from abroad (low cost producers) in order to maintain precisely this market objective of giving its customers value for money.

The conclusion from the above discussion is that achieving quality in practice is overwhelmingly contingent. Of course, to achieve a competitive edge through enhanced quality of service or product is highly desirable, but whether one is considering quality management systems or philosophies there is no off-the-shelf package that will neatly fit the particular firm. The system or philosophy have to be moulded to the specifities of the firm's context. Management needs time to do this. However, for it to work effectively involvement of employees at all levels is necessary. Discussion of how to tackle problems can be highly motivating, but of course there is also the issue of the distribution of the bottom line benefits. Or, put more succinctly, who benefits?

Strategies for delivering quality standards

Discussion has tended to revolve around the notion of formal methods of quality control, however it is also worth considering informal methods of assuring quality.[14]

Simple informal strategies include *proactive* methods of quality assurance, strategies that affect the quality of the product or service before it reaches the consumer, for example, close supervision of staff and 100 per cent inspection of product at all stages. Also, an owner-manager, in anticipating the need to achieve a quality standard will recruit skilled staff and/or offer additional training. The importance of employing the right people goes as far as selecting people with the 'right attitudes' and various personal qualities, the assumption being that further technical expertise can be developed either on the job and/or through further training. This tactic underscores the importance of the team (and not simply the owner-manager) in delivering quality to the standard the owner-manager requires.

Reactive informal strategies occur after production and delivery to the customer. In the small firm they are often predicated on personalized relations with the customer – a form of 'relationship marketing' and show the extent to which small firm owner-managers understand the importance of their customers to them. Other tactics deployed may be the use of 'dummy customers' to provide feedback on how the service 'feels' from the recipient's perspective, telephoning competitors and posing as a customer,[15] visiting competitors and sharing intelligence, carrying out simple customer surveys. A wide variety of organizations fall into the service sector: banks, hotels, hospitals, consultancy firms, estate agents, solicitors, veterinary practices, hairdressers, restaurants, retail outlets, etc. In all cases, the relative proportions of the delivery of service to production interface is large and contrasts with that of the manufacturing firm. Special features[16] are shown in Box 15.1 in relation to the case of service quality in a sushi bar.

Box 15.1: Quality in the service sector

Managing service delivery
In the sushi bar, meals are delivered by a novel conveyor belt system, and drinks by a robotic 'waiter'. Quality of service is important to retain customers; reliance on good food is necessary but not sufficient to retain the customer.

Perishability
Reducing instances of perishability relies on matching capacity with demand. Opening a new sushi bar (or other restaurant) presents problems of estimating capacity and dealing with over-demand. Restaurants generally use bar waiting areas and may have more than one sitting on busy evenings. The sushi bar, however, is closer to the 'fast-food' concept and any over-capacity may be handled by the robotic waiter offering drinks and developing a slick service in billing customers to ensure fast turnround.

Interaction between the service operator and consumer
Interaction is kept to a minimum in the sushi bar (in contrast with the restaurant), again in order to provide novelty and produce a slick operation. Nevertheless it can be reassuring to new customers in particular if there is a service manager around whose job clearly is to orient customers, seat them, respond to their questions and generally keep them enchanted by the novelty of the experience.

The intangible nature of quality of service
A customer's perceptions of quality may be idiosyncratic and have little to do with the product or manner of delivery. This means that there are some aspects of quality over which the restaurant can have little control.

Anticipating what matters most to the targeted market segment of customers is important intelligence. The sushi bar caters for a young, active and often professional class of customer. Whilst the technical aspects of the experience are important – good quality, delicious food, well presented in terms of design, balance of colours, shapes etc – it is not the most important aspect. Functional aspects associated with staff behaviour in delivering the service are particularly important. Young people often want to impress their friends – their self image is bound up with who they hang out with and where they wish to be seen – and professional people want to create a good impression with their client. Therefore the following ten aspects of service quality are crucial:

● **Reliability**. When a customer returns with friends or another client they want to be sure of the same quality of experience. Hence staff must maintain standards day in day out and generally 'get things right first time'.
● **Responsiveness**. The service manager is fronting the operation but relies on the back up of the rest of the team. Key aspects of responsiveness include timeliness, taking

Box 15.1: Continued

pleasure in providing a service and showing a willingness to please.
● **Competence**. This is revealed by the fact that the staff have the skills and knowledge to perform the service.
● **Access**. Staff do not appear to be 'rushed off their feet' however busy the sushi bar/restaurant is. Contact can easily be made, people are not kept waiting for bills, drinks or other aspects of service. Staff are approachable. Again, in the sushi bar the service manager's role of acting very much as 'mine host', is pivotal in these respects.
● **Courtesy**. Staff are considerate and respectful to customers and their property at all times; they are personally well presented.
● **Communication**. The sushi bar relies less on verbal communication, but there is a system of colour coding to indicate prices, types of dish, etc. Customers may wish to experience a sense of adventure and be educated, however cursorily, in Japanese cuisine. Such information is best conveyed in plain and succinct language. Leaving the sushi bar with a few Japanese words or a better developed understanding of the concept of Japanese cuisine may be important for some customers. Also, it must never be forgotten that communication is a two-way process and that it is important to listen to, and hear, what customers are saying.
● **Credibility**. The experience of the sushi bar must be believable, convincing and satisfying. Staff must convey this through the service they offer, showing customer care through service delivery and providing the experience the customer desires.
● **Security**. The customer must feel physically and psychologically safe. Pristinely clean work surfaces, etc help assure a sense of food hygiene, and a brisk but professional manner gives a dynamic which gels with the customer.
● **Understanding**. Staff make an effort to understand customer needs and concerns – modifications may be made to restaurant menus and other aspects of the service. Regular customers may be given that extra attention and recognition that boosts the ego and mutual feelings of confidence and also adds to the psychological sense of security.
● **Tangibles**. A designer restaurant conveying a particular concept must sport the kind of facilities and equipment that reinforce the concept; it must be well designed and maintained. The personal appearance of the staff and also the behaviour of other customers are also important.

The key issue from the customer's perspective, in respect of whether they believe that they are receiving a quality service, is confidence; all the points made in the case of the sushi bar restaurant suggest that an owner-manager should be able to assure the customer and build up their confidence in the service on offer. In managing quality, further considerations include how much energy is being expended in order to add value to the service and what aspects of the process need to be addressed if they are being made to look laboured.

From the edicts of the 'quality gurus' there are both prescriptions and implications. For example if customer satisfaction is the ultimate objective, then fulfilling customer expectations is crucial. Analysis would suggest that the owner-manager must:

● find out what matters most to the customer and concentrate on providing it
● manage customer expectation, because pleasure is a sublime, ephemeral experience and disappointment is to be avoided

- manage impressions of service and delivery by anticipating 'customer psychology'
- educate the customer as to how they can gain maximum benefit from the use of the service
- develop reliable support systems
- solicit reliable feedback.[17]

The provision of a quality service must be well integrated across the firm. For example, in a small franchised business known to the author, quality was the owner-manager's watchword. 'InstantoPrint'[18] is a franchised business producing instant print and photocopying services. Whilst the quality of the product delivered to the customer was of paramount importance, the owner-manager realized after a number of incidents at the customer-interface that the front line staff played a crucial role in delivering a quality service (or not, as the case may be). He concluded that they must be 'mature and professional' in their dealings with all over the counter customers. This highlighted the importance of their appearance, self-presentation and interpersonal skills – but not only those aspects. It was also clear that the front line staff needed to be trained to be able to deal with technical queries, otherwise staff with the requisite technical expertise had to be called in from the backroom to deal with specific queries. This took the technical staff away from their work and proved to be inefficient. Further, and more importantly, it created a poor impression with the customer who was kept waiting (albeit only a short while) for a response to their queries.

Undoubtedly this case illustrates the need for well trained staff to be employed in a firm that intends achieving and maintaining high quality products and service delivery. InstantoPrint also pointed up the need for firms – especially small firms – to have excellent selection and recruitment practices in place. This became apparent after InstantoPrint had employed young, immature staff in the 'front of shop' positions: an incident with a valued (by the owner-manager) customer showed their lack of professionalism. Whilst small firm owner-managers often use 'word-of-mouth' and personal recommendations as their chief methods of selection, increasingly there is a need to back this up with a further set of clear criteria that enables them to sort out job applicants. Such criteria need to identify whether the candidate has:

- received basic skills training
- the ability to do the job in practice
- appropriate on-the-job training
- relevant experience
- a need for some retraining.

Complex informal strategies occurs as the firm grows and the ability of the owner-manager directly to control quality decreases. The owner-manager then has to decide how to continue to deal with the quality-control issue. There are several options, including delegation and devolving responsibility to another – perhaps newly developed – layer of management. However, owner-managers in general have difficulty in practising delegation. An alternative method therefore is to use a paper-based system such as a 'job card' which follows the product or service through the various stages until it finally reaches the customer; at each stage the employee responsible adds their initials to the card before it moves on. Other examples include the supply of an 'operating manual' by a franchiser where the recommendations in the manual are voluntarily applied; the use of customer surveys in order to obtain feedback on the quality of the service; and aborted preparation for BS5750 where the manual is retained and implemented but the firm never reaches the stage of registration.

Second party controlled strategies are utilized in a routine and bureaucratic way by a second party – usually the firm's customers or suppliers – in an attempt to assure quality of service or product received. The second party may insist that the supplier adopts their quality control methods or indeed becomes BS5750-registered. Examples include the control of their suppliers by High Street retailers such as Marks and Spencer in the UK. Comparable practices are exercised by the Ministry of Defence and Health Service Trusts with their suppliers. The extent of second party control strategies is unknown. North *et al.* report a low incidence – two of their sample of 150 firms, with only one reported in any detail. This firm, 'Meditron', produced 'high qual-

---

Box 15.2: Adoption of BS5750: what is the evidence?

There are few empirical studies of the adoption of the quality standard BS5750 in small firms; one of the more recent is that of North *et al.* referred to above. Some of the results of this study are worthy of further attention because the researchers take careful cognisance of sectoral differences (and not simply firm size) and other factors such as history, organizational characteristics, the relative routiness by which the product or service is produced and the processes utilized in production and customer behaviour. This fine grained analysis goes a long way to explaining variations between sectors that cannot be attributed to size alone.

They found a very high level of awareness of BS5750 amongst their 150 responding owner-managers; the lowest levels of awareness were amongst the microbusinesses (one to four employees) but they were still high at 89 per cent whereas amongst the larger small firms (ten plus employees) awareness was total. Perhaps surprisingly, the biggest source of information was the mass media and not local economic development agencies such as the training and enterprise councils (TECs). Only a minority of the firms they surveyed had actually adopted formal methods of quality control. This amounted to 19 firms or 13 per cent of the sample and for those that had completed the full BS5750 certification process it was as low as six firms (four per cent of the sample). Whilst it was the case that the smaller the firm the less likely were their intentions to implement BS5750, the results could not solely be explained by size. For example, of the microbusinesses, 39 firms (85 per cent) had no intention of implementing BS5750 and only one firm (two per cent) was actually implementing the standard. Of firms in the 10–19 employee size bracket, 13 (42 per cent) had no intention of implementing BS5750, whereas eight firms (26 per cent) were in the process of implementation. These figures can be compared with those for firms with 20 or more employees, where 11 firms (55 per cent) had no intention of implementing BS5750, while six (30 per cent) were in the process of doing so. Clearly the size effect is not strong enough to explain the decision to implement or not.

Table **15.3** Small firm owners' intentions towards implementing BS5750, by sector

	Printing	%	Garages	%	Advertising, marketing, design	%	Plant and equipment hire	%	Computer services	%	Electronics	%	Employment agencies	%	Totals	%
No intention/unaware	13	(82)	27	(79)	13	(76)	17	(71)	15	(58)	9	(50)	5	(33)	99	(66)
Thinking/intending	1	(6)	7	(21)	3	(18)	5	(21)	6	(23)	5	(28)	8	(53)	35	(22)
Implementing/registered	2	(12)	0	(0)	1	(6)	2	(8)	5	(19)	4	(22)	2	(13)	16	(12)
N =	16		34		17		24		26		18		15		150	(100)
Rank Order	1		2		3		4		5		6		7			

Ranked according to their intentions towards implementing BS5750: 1 = least likely, 7 = most likely.

Source: North *et al.* 1998 (see note 8): p.73

ity, technically specific products for the medical and health care sectors'. Given the nature of the products 'there is little scope for errors where reliability and performance of, for example, a pacemaker is at stake' (North *et al.* p. 194).

Third party control strategies are fully bureaucratized procedures externally dictated and controlled by a third party and include BS5750/ISO9000. One of the drawbacks of this standard is that it is generic and firms often require a version specific to their needs. However there are benefits:

- provision of a framework to enable the firm to improve its operating procedures
- increased provision of employee training
- reductions in operating costs through increased efficiency
- improved understanding of management processes, systems and capability.

Table 15.3 shows one set of results based on North *et al.*'s survey.

The actual numbers for any given sector are quite small and in each cell, even smaller so it is not possible to run tests of significance. I have therefore rank ordered the sectors according to their intentions towards adoption of the standard. The first clear observation that may be made is that there is no clear difference between manufacturing and service sector firms in terms of their attitude towards adoption. This contradicts rather more simplistic analyses, which have suggested that BS5750 is more suitable for the manufacturing firm and therefore more likely to be found there. The next observation that may be made is that the printing industry appears to be the least likely to adopt BS5750, whereas employment agencies are the most likely adopters.[19] How might this be explained?

The low adoption of BS5750 by general printers is significant and probably explained by the history of that industry. Historically, printing was a craft industry with strong trades unions controlling both the labour supply and work standards. Presently, printers tend to use simple inspection methods to control the standards of workmanship. Such management strategies are underpinned externally by well defined skills training standards and internalized quality norms. This combination has reduced the need for, and therefore the likelihood of, adoption of formal quality standards such as BS5750.

Garages or small vehicle repairers compare with general printing in respect of historical influences that may be affecting their attitude towards adoption of BS5750. Maintenance and repair work was regarded as a craft skill and garage mechanics would serve their time as apprentices. Such training was supported through the provision of courses in technical and further education colleges. However, unlike printing the quality of service is much less apparent and whilst there may be an argument for adoption of a formal quality assurance standard like BS5750, there has been no customer pressure for such a development.

Advertising, marketing and design firms are related to print in so far as they use print products. However, according to North *et al.* they are also unlikely to adopt BS5750 – they are more likely to use complex informal methods of quality control. Characteristically in this sector, each customer requires something different, tailored to their requirements. This militates against the adoption of standardized approaches to quality assurance. Firms in this industry know that they must compete on quality, as price undercutting tends to put firms out of business (because overheads are not properly costed in). They attempt to find novel ways of attracting new customers and once a tender is won, they develop close relations with the customer. Mock ups will be composed and delivered to the customer and changes will be made until the customer agrees that what has been created closely reflects their wishes. Only when the 'nod' of approval has been given will the final version be produced. In this industry, the customer may be the final arbiter of quality.

Owner-managers of plant and equipment hire firms still do not show a keenness to adopt BS5750 – they tend to use complex informal methods of quality control. This is due to the different ways equipment is used and the need to ensure for health and safety reasons that it is well maintained and perfectly reliable. They are often aided in this through membership of relevant trade associations. In effect health and safety legislation controls and assures quality in this sector.

Computer services is amongst the top three sectors to have adopted formal quality procedures such as BS5750. Nonetheless the actual proportion is not especially high (less than one in five). One explanation for this is that this sector includes a high non-manufacturing element of software design, software applications and hardware-software packages tailored to customers' requirements. Establishing formal quality standards in these areas is much more difficult and customers are likely to have a low awareness of formal quality standards.

Electronics firms appear to have a higher propensity to adopt formal quality standards. This may be explained by the nature of the industry which, over its development, has been specifically concerned with quality standards. Furthermore, production within the industry tends to take the form of a chain of sub-contracting relationships and as such is highly conducive to the adoption of formal standards. In effect there are significant external pressures on small electronics firms to adopt formal methods, though not necessarily BS5750. As North *et al.* point out, such pressures have developed historically. One of the reasons for opting for the adoption of BS5750 is its use competitively and as a marketing tool. However, BS5750 does not guarantee quality of the product and so some firms prefer to use other available formal quality assurance methods.

Finally, North *et al.* comment that 'BS5750 was very much a live issue' in the sub-sector of business services, namely employment agencies. The table shows that only a third had no intention of adopting the standard. With rapid growth of this sector, employment agencies appear to have been resorting to BS5750 as a competitive/marketing weapon. While some large clients may have made BS5750 a criterion for doing business, this explanation was thought to be less likely as a reason for adoption.

Total quality management (TQM) strategies comprise holistic approaches to achieving quality in product and processes through the full commitment from staff and employees at all levels, thus affecting the firm's entire culture. Few small firms appear to have adopted a TQM philosophy although it is suggested that rather more have developed their own philosophies. Criticisms of the formal TQM systems have centred on the adoption of Quality Circles (QCs), which appear to have been an abject failure in western economies such as the US and the UK. The aim of the QC is to identify a problem/quality failure at group or section level and to identify ways to redress this problem as a group. 'Solutions' are put to management for their approval; the approved solution is adopted and the group moves on to address a further problem. A clear difficulty has arisen where savings accrue from implementation of the quality solution: who is to benefit from this? How are the savings to be distributed, to whom and for how long? What happens to the QC when it runs out of problems?[20]

Legge suggests that a major issue arises with TQM when it is (logically and inextricably) linked with a Just-in-time (JIT) system. The system is designed in such a way to optimize efficiency, making the firm price competitive, giving value for money but also flexibility in responding to customer requirements. The advantages of JIT are reduction in machine set up times, batch sizes and lead times, and increased responsiveness to the customer. The system assumes the elimination of waste – waste of time and resources, waste through reworking or overproduction, waste through unnecessary movement, idle time and double handling. However, such a system is extremely fragile so much can go wrong such as work scheduling, equipment reliability and employees' commitment and responsiveness. But whilst there are clearly benefits to be had from the implementation of such a system, there is also a down side. According to Legge, JIT can result in the following disadvantages.

- A reduction in employee autonomy and control of the system.
- The reduction of waste, which implies labour intensification.
- The possible oppressiveness of team working through peer surveillance.
- The marginalisation of the trades unions.
- The sheer difficulty of effectively managing a just-in-time system.

These criticisms are based on a critical management analysis of JIT in the car manufacturing industry, primarily in the UK.[21] However, certainly criticism of work intensification practices can be extended to the garment manufacturing industry, where machinists may also be required to work flat out all of the time. Hence as with any system, problems can arise when its management is taken to extremes. Certainly there are some efficiencies to be gained from the appropriate application of JIT that an owner-manager will find beneficial.[22] For example, the experience of delays due to unnecessary handling, overcontrol, routing of jobs and paperwork can be addressed without oppressive interaction. However, the actual practice of this or any other management system is contingent; the owner-manager needs to work through what will work most effectively in their business.

Developing a quality culture

In this chapter there is a marked contrast between, on the one hand, the apparently idealistic total quality management systems and, on the other, the more realistic practices of small business owner-managers who adopt a variety of informal/formal systems (usually falling short of the implementation of formal systems like BS5750) honed to their business needs. How can these apparent differences be reconciled? Indeed should they be? Are TQM – the sublime object – and the means – the adoption of quality control circles – discredited? Or are there some real practical messages in Statistical Process Control, Deming's 14 points, etc, which, when thought through, may be applied to any business whatever its size? Indeed, why this obsession with 'quality'?

The rationale for focusing on 'quality' is the lack of competitiveness of many western economies relative to the 'Five Tigers of the Far East'. Whilst this bald assertion has come under question by academicians,[23] there still remains the concern over the quality of management practice. In particular it has been argued that in the UK small business owners on the whole lack management training and consequently have poor management skills. Further, people are crucial for the delivery of quality. If there is a lack of management skills for delivering quality, then there is a need to introduce a formal system of quality assurance to substitute and make good this inadequacy. North *et al.*'s study has challenged this view on a number of counts. They argue that their evidence suggests that owner-managers are concerned with quality and that they are well aware that having the right people in place is crucial. A second strand of their argument is that the concept of 'quality' is vague whilst in practice it is dynamic and contextually meaningful. Introducing a rigid formal quality management system is not the best way to deliver quality. Furthermore, standards such as BS5750 do not guarantee delivery of a quality product or service. Finally their evidence showed that informal systems for managing quality in small firms were often as, if not more, effective than a formal system. Dismissing 'zero fault quality strategies' as 'idealizations', they point out:

> Owner-managers are committed seriously to quality as the findings from the study demonstrated and they seek to ensure staff help realize this commitment. But the everyday reality of running a business in a market economy means that many other kinds of requirements intrude. Production is always at a price, customers are sometimes vague, inconsistent or insist on difficult-to-deliver conditions, employees have varying skills, experience and commitment levels, owner-managers have many demands on their time besides maintaining quality and, where the firm is larger, quality management will frequently be shared with others or bureaucratized to some extent. In some firms, quality management will be easier to achieve than in others because some of the above conditions are more favourable but a quality management strategy always has to cope with adverse conditions. (North *et al.*, see note 8: p.165

It would seem that the wholesale introduction of any particular formal quality management philosophy into a small enterprise has no place. However, studying the principles that these philosophies espouse can be a valuable learning exercise for the management and organization development of such enterprises. Owner-managers often feel isolated. They often complain that there is no one with whom they can discuss their problems (especially if their business partner is the problem!). TQM philosophies offer some guidelines but if viewed as a start point they can be developed appropriately to meet the needs of the particular enterprise. This requires second order changes to the system – double loop learning (see chapter 4) ' ...we can change our thinking from "the problem" of managing people to "the potential" of people managing.'[24]

Quality management in practice *is* dependent on good human resource management practice and a sustainable view of enterprise development. In practice, it means having the right person with the right attitudes in jobs that can be developed together as the business grows. This means that owner-managers must be able to manage and develop resourceful employees, and resourceful employees must be given scope to do the managing. Some of the difficulties facing the owner-manager are clear – the ability to attract, nurture and develop a mature trusting relationship with their employees is fundamental. Further, such development needs to be sustainable; change enhances capability and so generates resources for further development. The management system thus comes under scrutiny. In order for control to be exercised effectively there must be consistency between the firm's stated purposes and what is done in practice. Whilst it is so easy to espouse the sentiment that employees are the firm's most valuable asset, deeds must be consonant with such sentiments otherwise they will be seen for what they are – empty words.

Developing quality management in Malaysia[25]

Background

Examination of a case study of a developing eastern economy reminds us of the importance of national cultural and religious values that imbue philosophical underpinnings of social systems and mores. Malaysia, unlike western developed economies such as the UK, has embraced the principles of total quality management at a political level. It has been developed as a significant part of the socio-economic policies of the government for social restructuring and integration, economic prosperity and moral exactitude. This has involved a movement to disseminate greater national awareness of quality since 1989 and has involved stimulating awareness amongst commerce, manufacturers, distributors, consumers and the general public.

Institutional structures

There are four main bodies that play a key role in this awareness raising and standards setting process. The Standards and Industrial Research Institute of Malaysia (SIRIM) – a body similar to the British Standards Institute – is responsible for developing and implementing national standards and their certification. It has conducted an aggressive marketing and promotions effort to encourage companies to implement ISO9000. This promotional effort has been backed by seminars for business leaders explaining the need for quality systems. The National Productivity Corporation (NPC) is mandated to carry out the promotion of total quality management. Its declared strategy is the development of human resources and enterprise towards excellence, advice to government and other bodies on quality issues and the creation of local sources of expertise on quality, productivity, management and entrepreneurship. It promotes the use of quality control circles (QCCs) and offers an award for the best QCC. The National Institute of Public Administration is a third public body whose focus on quality is confined to the improvement in the human resource of the civil service. Measures undertaken include the introduction of total quality management (TQM) and QCCs into the service. Apart from behavioural changes, fostering team work and establishing performance measurement, training has also attempted to engender a set of core values, including moral values. A fourth government quango – the Malaysian Administrative and Management Planning Unit (MAMPU) – is also directed at the civil service and the country's administrative systems. Its primary role is to bring about change in public service.

Smaller organizations include the Institute for Quality Control Malaysia (IQCM), which has around 150 individual and corporate members. It runs courses and seminars on quality control, quality auditing and documentation, the Quality and Reliability Society of Penang, which promotes quality in the electronics/electrical engineering sector in the Penang area and the Centre for Instructor and Advanced Skill Training – a vocational training centre specializing in training in the basics of quality control. It is financed partly with Japanese aid and uses Japanese specialists as trainers. Finally, the Quality Management Institute set up in 1993 is based in the Northern University of Malaysia and offers academic courses and research in quality management. It is intended to be the country's main reference centre in quality management.

Reinforcing the message: quality awards

Clearly Malaysia has embraced quality management, at least at a policy level. In an attempt to ensure that this happens on the ground the government has instigated several awards. The Prime Minister's Quality Award is intended to be a highly prestigious and therefore much sought after award. Competing companies have to meet five criteria, which assess quality culture, the management of quality towards the improvement of skills, productivity and information, human resource development and management, quality assurance of support services and corporate responsibility. Information must be supplied and there is also on-site inspection. The winning company is able to sport the

'Q' symbol for publicity purposes for three years; it also receives a cash prize and certificate of achievement.

A second prestigious award is the Quality Management Excellence Award (QMEA), which is offered competitively to four size bands of company, ranging from small local companies to the very large, possibly foreign owned companies. The criteria are extensive and include the policy and strategic areas of management as well as the behavioural and functional ones. Such toughness on standards has tended to deter many companies from applying (indeed they are usually invited to participate). This is said to be because the country introduced the quality movement relatively recently and many organizations are struggling to introduce quality management techniques and philosophy.

Reinforcing the message: religious values

Underpinning economic reform are social, moral and religious values, which are being explicitly and deliberately inculcated. The aim is not simply to have a well developed economy by 2020 but also a society imbued with moral and spiritual values. The intention is that these principles embrace both Muslims and non-Muslims and help towards the integration of Muslim society. The idea is to develop an ethic which is uniquely Malay and is independent of western values. It is suggested, for example, that decisions and choices may not always follow the profit motive and should enable an organization to take a long term development view of its human resource. The underpinning belief is that quality of organizational products and services in the long term is affected by the level of human skills, innovation and moral development. Further it is intended that 'motivational tools would be based on religious teachings' and 'would normally be used to reinforce belief and behaviour or organizational members'.[26]

The general picture that emerged from fieldwork

Several of Malaysia's top companies adopted their own tailored versions of total quality management systems in the early 1990s. This was true of recently privatized governmental quangos. Moreover, in mid-1993 there was 'a lot of enthusiasm for quality'.[27] At this time the 'obsession' was with implementation of the 'hard' side – that is, the introduction of total quality control tools into the work environment. By 1995/6, the enthusiasm had stabilized and there was more concern with the cultivation of values that were perceived to bring positive and long term effects to the organization. This strategy was underpinned by a growing belief that employees needed to possess such values if a company was to sustain its continuous improvement process, although there was some evidence to suggest that even in some of the top companies there was not a total grasp of the quality concept amongst employees.

Privatized government quangos were heavily influenced by government policy statements on the subject of quality. In addition, government aspirations seemed to have a pervasive effect amongst local, Malay-dominated organizations both strategically and in respect of the need to make efforts towards achieving the aspiration of continuous improvement. Furthermore, there appeared to be a general belief and enthusiasm amongst Malay managers of the need to link religious and moral values to the quality improvement process. This emerged across the board in certain key concerns – company performance, human development, competency and the achievement of national objectives.

Hence, as a national strategy, targeting the country's large organizations, whether government-influenced or private sector corporations, appeared to be effective. A question remains however, as to what extent that influence has (or was intended to) trickle down to the country's smaller enterprises. Certainly there was scope for dissemination of the message through the normal processes of employee mobility.

'AirCon' – an example of total quality management in practice

AirCon is one of Malaysia's larger, successful, private sector companies. It is in fact a subsidiary of an American parent, and its principal business is the manufacture of air conditioners. It exports about 70 per cent of its product across the world.

AirCon embraced the total quality management concept. In the early 1990s it charted its business processes with a view to 'fostering understanding among managers of the various relationships existing within it'. This enabled managers to review and improve the business process by introducing better quality control mechanisms. Further, 'AirCon' renewed its policies and practice towards 'quality' by adopting the rhetoric of the TQM gurus such as 'meeting customer satisfaction' and delivering 'continuous improvement'. This was to be supported by the introduction of the ISO9000 international standard to quality assurance and extensive and appropriate employee training.

The evaluation of the effectiveness of AirCon's total quality structure and process did not rest solely on the achievement of customer satisfaction. Organizational performance criteria were to be met in respect of the improved quality of products, business growth measured by expanded market share and additional profitability.

The policy was championed by a senior Singaporean quality manager who had previously been employed by a Japanese company for some 18 years and was fluent in that language. It is perhaps not surprising therefore that 'the activities and initiatives for quality in [AirCon] closely resemble the typical Japanese company – suggestion schemes, quality control circles, the **5Ss (seiri, seiton, seiso, seiketsu, shitsuke)** housekeeping habits, quality slogans and campaigns ...'.[28] This management of the organizational culture is supported by formal monthly quality management meetings chaired by the company's managing director.

Exercise

Consider the following questions based on the case and this chapter's analysis and readings.

1. Identify cultural differences in the Malaysian approach to quality. Are there any similarities to that of your own nation?

2. Are there any additional measures that the Malaysian government might have taken to influence further the adoption of its policies toward quality? What are they? And how effective do you think they might have been?

3. Prepare a case study of your country's approach to quality based on the insights gained from this chapter. Illustrate with company examples and other hard evidence to support your statements.

4. Debate whether the concept of quality is appropriate for the smaller organizations. Use evidence from actual company cases and secondary sources to back your point of view.

5. To what extent do you believe that national economic policies and/or the rhetoric of management gurus shape the aspirations of entrepreneurs' attitudes towards quality?

Conclusions

It is apparent from this chapter that 'quality' is an important but fluid concept which has, over the past 20 years, been hijacked by the total quality management (TQM) 'gurus' and given different meanings according to the philosophy espoused. However, other approaches, such as quality management (assurance) systems do not, it seems, guarantee the quality of the product or service being delivered, rather they assure the customer that a management system or process has been put in place that reaches specified standards.

In this chapter a wide range of approaches to quality has been discussed. The underlying question integrating the disparate material was: 'is such knowledge of value to the small firm owner-manager?' The answer is tentatively affirmative: knowledge and critical judgement furnish the manager with decision making capability. Certainly the chapter covers different strategic approaches which may be taken as a means by which quality considerations may be introduced into a firm, the variety of forms appropriate for different business contexts and the kinds of criteria that are taken into account when attempting to attain or assure the attainment of, a quality standard.

However, in further considering the nature of quality its status as a relative (not absolute) concept became apparent. This was explored further when considering the adoption of formal second or third party assurance systems. Several illustrations were given but the adoption of BS5750/ISO9000 by small firms in the UK was discussed at length. This discussion highlighted the fact that only a small proportion of small firms had adopted this quality standard and that adoption was patchy when sector was considered.

The benefits of introducing a TQM system were shown to be put in the balance if this was linked to a just-in-time (JIT) system. Certainly enthusiasm for such systems has waned over recent years. But surely this is not because of the potentially oppressive or exploitative nature of JIT? Rather for a linked TQM-JIT system to work effectively it is necessary that they are embedded in an appropriate organizational culture. This is not a 'one off' process but must be sustainable. Given the fragility of JIT and the potential disillusionment with a TQM system that fails to deliver clear incentives to employees across an organization, the ability to develop a workable TQM-JIT self-generating system is open to question. Still, attempts have been made throughout the world to do just that: the chapter ends with an example of an attempt to create a quality culture in a developing economy – Malaysia. What is extraordinary in this case is the level of government intervention in the process. Perhaps even more so is the declared intention to mould quality management to the indigenous Malay culture, inclusive of its religious and ethical values. This case opens up many questions, not least of which is how far might the quality management philosophy have pervaded the economy and reached the small privately owned enterprise in Malaysia? This question, at present rhetorical, requires an answer.

Part 5
The New Economy

CHAPTER 16

The future of enterprise?

From [the] ingenuity [of those in a position to manipulate rising and falling expectations], and from the impatience of the small punter to see his fortune magically transformed, there arose the great speculative manias of the seventeenth and early eighteenth centuries ... The most spectacular, and certainly the most alarming of these speculative breakouts, was the great tulip mania of 1636–37. Only a deeply bourgeois culture ... could possibly have selected the humble tulip – rather than say, emeralds or Arabian stallions – as a speculative trophy. But there was nothing suburban about tulips in the seventeenth century. They were, at least to begin with, exotic, alluring and even dangerous. It was precisely at the point that their rarity seemed capable of domestication for a mass market that the potential for runaway demand could be realized. ... The key was reproducibility. Highly prized varieties ... were jealously guarded from casual imitation. But what would otherwise have been a practice not unlike the careful preservation of buffer stocks to preserve price differentials was continually subverted by trade in outgrowths and the efforts of growers themselves to produce new and more handsome varieties. [They experimented] with unlimited combinations of hues, petal shapes and sizes, created a huge range of varieties, destined to attract not just the wealthy connoisseur but thousands of small buyers.

Schama 1987 (see note 1): pp. 350–51.

E-mania

There were a number of conditions that gave rise to tulip mania in an international seaport like Amsterdam; one was a glut of capital. People were looking for things to do with their money. Gossip and rumour fuelled speculation. The idea that the market in bulbs could be opened up to a mass market sparked the runaway demand. Anyone with a little specialized knowledge could 'make their way among the bulbmen'. A prize of some form was within reach of the common man. But such speculation, like gambling, became addictive. Growers became tempted into satisfying increasing demand by selling outgrowths – which could only be supplied after a period – and thus created a 'futures market'. By 1637 paper deals were being made without the specimen having been seen. Seasonality tended to inflate the prices of the bulbs. Such prices were staggering. One farmer is said to have paid 2500 florins for a single 'Viceroy' in the form of 'two last of wheat and four of rye, four fat oxen, eight pigs, a dozen sheep, two oxheads of wine, four tons of butter, a thousand pounds of cheese, a bed, some clothing and a silver beaker'.[1] Trading houses, tracts of land, gold and silver vessels and fine furniture were typical items in the feverish transactions for prized and highly sought after bulbs.

But like all bubbles it eventually burst. Growers became concerned that a crash would leave them with worthless stock. Government intervention was rumoured. And unfounded 'advice' was circulating in 1637 suggesting that people should stop buying bulbs. Panic began. Bulb prices started dropping by the hour and the tulip 'futures' had become worthless.

The past, given the wisdom of hindsight, is clear, but what is the future for enterprise and enterprising behaviour? The turn of the millennium has seen both the rise and fall of the e-commerce businesses. Flotations of dot.com businesses were oversubscribed and their valuations by the market soared. Now there is a winnowing out, values are falling and the feverish excitement that surrounded them has all but dissipated. For those wedded to the idea of the internet revolution the eventual success of the e-commerce business seems assured. People simply have to be more patient. But will that future be quite what has recently been predicted? Will the dot.com be the small emergent global business of the future? Or will the more successful be swallowed up by large corporations who see trading via the internet as an essential attribute of any leading edge company? 'Essential' does not necessarily mean highly 'profitable': the dot-commerce company may continue to be very hard to value for many years to come.

This suggests that the information technology revolution has not yet played itself out. Some of the obvious reasons for this are that the infrastructure for IT operations are still being developed and laid down.

The IT Revolution

Like the Industrial Revolution, the Information Technology Revolution started in particular areas of the world. A critical ingredient in IT is not the newness of institutional and cultural settings but its ability to create synergy on the basis of knowledge and information directly related to industrial production and commercial applications. This creates a 'privileged environment', hence innovation in the information age is not placeless.

The entrepreneurial model of innovative genius, opportunistic flair and great courage in the face of uncertainty has to be put in the context of the role of states, their defence and technology policies. This is the case for Japan, South Korea, Taiwan, India and China. In the US military contracts played a key role in the formative stages of the IT revolution. As too did the space programme, creating essential markets for the electronics industry. Indeed, Castells goes so far as to suggest that innovators could not have survived without the generous funding and protected markets of the US government.[2]

It is indeed by this interface between macro-research pro-grammes and large markets developed by the state, on the one hand, and decentralized innovation stimulated by a culture of technological creativity and role models of fast personal success, on the other hand, that new information technologies came to blossom.[3]

Key features of the 'IT paradigm' are:

- **information** – the raw material
- the **pervasiveness of the effects of new technologies** – they impact all human activity
- the **networking logic** – it can cope with increasing complexity and unpre-dictability of patterns of development
- its **flexibility** – the ability to reconfigure, alter and modify
- **technological convergence** of specific technologies into a highly inte-grated system – telecommunications, microelectronics, optoelectronics and computers.

The impetus for firms to engage in technological innovation is to improve their competitive position and enhance their profitability. IT therefore has been used to reduce production costs and accelerate capital investment. Increased production (and productivity) necessitated finding new markets in order to absorb the increased capacity. Once again, IT has played an essential part in enabling the linking of market segments through a global network facilitated by the mobility of capital and enhanced communication tech-nologies. Clearly the global integration of financial markets has been a criti-cal development effectively disassociating capital flows from national economies. A further direct beneficiary has been high technology firms involved in the development of the communications infrastructure such as telecommunications, microelectronics and microcomputer industries. Firms in these industries became highly productive and profitable on a global scale. This contrasted markedly with firms within industries struggling with obso-lescence. However, competition within these high growth sectors was also on a global scale, including Japan, the Asian 'Tigers' and China. This interna-tional scene confirmed that, when faced with strong competition, firms must improve their performance.

The architectural geometry of the global, information economy is that of an asymmetric interdependent world in which there are three major eco-nomic regions – Europe, North America and the Asian Pacific. Polarization occurs along an axis between the productive, information-rich and affluent countries and the impoverished, economically devalued and socially excluded. This has given rise to a new pattern of international division of labour constructed around:

- producers of high value goods based on information labour
- producers of high volume goods based on lower-cost labour
- producers of raw materials based on natural endowments
- redundant producers reduced to devalued labour.

Labour is organized in networks and flows using the technological infrastructure of the information economy. There are geographical concentrations of particular kinds of labour, although all countries possess all four to some degree. Changes within countries are due to the actions of governments and entrepreneurs.

The global information economy has, as argued in chapter 2, given rise to new organizational forms. The reasons for this arise from four fundamental changes: the separation of production facilities from markets; the diffusion of IT; enhanced flexibility; the automation of jobs. Whilst 'Fordism' spelt *mass* production, post-Fordism has meant *flexible* production. Moreover, the bureaucratic, mechanistic form of Fordism showed its limitations in a turbulent, highly competitive global environment. Advanced western economies such as the US lost their international competitive edge during the 1980s due to sluggishness of their corporate giants. SMEs, however, showed themselves to be more resilient as agents of both innovation and job creation. Other important changes crept in, in particular new methods of management. 'Just-in-time' and 'total-quality-control' were introduced as methods of increasing efficiency, standards of process production and flexibility. They relied on the minimum of disruption and had clear implications for industrial relations practice.[4]

The introduction of IT has also had implications for organizational learning. Nonaka introduced the idea of the 'knowledge creating company' based on the interaction between 'explicit and 'tacit' knowledge as the source of innovation. Experiential or tacit knowledge is pervasive within a company and may be harnessed as a source of innovation *if* management can bridge the gap between tacit and explicit knowledge. This has been enabled by the use of computers to record and store information.

Undoubtedly one of the most fundamental and far reaching changes that has resulted from IT is that of 'networking'.[5] Networking between firms has taken on two predominant forms – the multidirectional model of interlinked SMEs and the subcontracting model. Other networking forms might more properly be termed 'corporate strategic alliances'. Here the firm recognizes that it is not self-sufficient but needs to cooperate with another firm to share vital information and/or technological expertise. In all other respects the firms may compete. Networking has also meant that corporations have been able to pursue a strategy of horizontal spread through the development of their global business networks. Characteristically, they have become organized around processes not tasks developed a flat hierarchy, developed team management, measured their performance by customer satisfaction, rewarded team performance, maximized their contacts with suppliers and customers and emphasized training or retraining at all levels. Hence, IT has increased the corporations' internal flexibility and responsiveness, producing, arguably, more effective management. Externally the corporation has adopted a strategy for globalization that has taken the form of a multidomestic, global market or cross border network strategy. The role of IT in this process has been the retrieval of on-the-spot information from the various markets around the world and its integration into a flexible, strategy making system. Hence, under conditions of fast technological change, networks, not firms, have emerged as the actual operating unit. The networked form is able to change its goals and reshape the means by which it can achieve its goals. This contrasts sharply with the traditional bureaucracy whose main goal is to reproduce its systems. The networked enterprise is the organizational form of the global information economy, to be effective it depends on its interconnectedness and the consistency of goals between its 'nodes'.

It is clear that culturally western economies lent themselves to individually competitive, bureaucratic corporations. East Asian business systems, however, are traditionally based on business groups, which more readily fit into the network enterprise model. Arguably this gives these economies a comparative advantage. Certainly East Asian economic organization has been the most successful over the past 30 years. There are, however, subtle cultural differences amongst these business networks, although they do share some key characteristics:

- religious values based on Confucianism and Buddhism
- a social unit based on the family
- highly valued education
- valued trust and reputation, fundamental to the operation of business networks.

How then do multinational corporations (MNCs) and transnational corporations (TNCs) shape up relative to the networked enterprise? The reality is that increasingly economic activity is organized around (international) networks of firms such as supplier, producer and customer. Additionally there are global standard setters in industries such as electronics and computing, and technology cooperation networks. Where the MNC and the TNC score is their oligopolistic concentration: there is, at least in some industries, a need for considerable resources to be a truly global player. Moreover the MNC/TNC has the capacity to transform itself into a truly international networked enterprise. It can become internally differentiated by forming decentralized networks which form external dependencies in a complex changing structure of cross border interconnections. In this way the logic of the network can become more powerful than the powers within the network. However it will only be effective if it can simultaneously manage its overall global strategy and the nationally or regionally rooted interests of its component firms.

The New Economy

The information revolution, combined with globalization, are key to the development of the 'New Economy'. The New Economy is a distinctive socio-economic system distinguished by the critical role played by information and knowledge. Fundamentally, knowledge and information are embodied in all processes of material production and distribution. Moreover the New Economy is global; it is an economy with the capacity to work as a unit in real time on a planetary scale.[6] This manifests itself in an information infrastructure which enables capital to be managed around the clock, labour to be utilized as a global resource and science and technology to be concentrated in centres of excellence. The organizational form which works effectively in the New Economy is the network enterprise, which constitutes a web of multiple networks in a multiplicity of institutional environments. The 'spirit of informationalism', which underpins the New Economy, comprises an organizational paradigm of:

- **business networks** – primarily entrepreneurial networks that have emerged from technological seedbeds (e.g. Silicon Valley, California, the M4 Corridor, the UK);
- **technological tools** – such as new telecom, desktop PCs, adaptive software, mobile communication systems.

The network within the New Economy is:

> Made of many cultures, many values, many projects, that cross through the minds, and inform the strategies of the various participants in the networks, changing at the same pace as the network's members, and following the organizational and cultural transformations of the units of the network. It is a culture ... of the ephemeral, a culture of each strategic decision, a patchwork of experiences and interests, rather than a charter of rights and obligations. It is a *multifaceted, virtual culture,* as in the visual experiences created by computers in cyberspace by rearranging reality. It is not a fantasy, it is a material force because it informs, and enforces, powerful economic decisions at every moment in the life of the network. But it does not stay long ... the network enterprise learns to live within this virtual culture. Any attempt at crystallizing the position in the network as a cultural code in a particular time and space sentences the network to obsolescence, since it becomes too rigid for the variable geometry required by informationalism. The 'spirit of informationalism' is the culture of 'creative destruction' ... Schumpeter meets Weber in the cyberspace of the network enterprise.[7]

The development of informationalism based on the integration of various modes of communication into an interactive network has clear implications for the ways businesses operate. Already with the emergence of the internet and of multimedia systems a new culture is emerging. Its structure includes the multiplication of television channels, its customization to a segmented society and the emergence of computer mediated communications systems. One effect is the increasing commercialization of the internet through the development of the World Wide Web (www). This has facilitated the co-existence of various interests (not solely business interest groups) within a flexible network where institutions, firms and individuals can create their own website. The website has greatly enabled meaningful interaction, for example, on a business to business, customer to producer/supplier or individual to institution basis.

This computer-mediated communications system has users with particular characteristics – primarily they are educated and affluent, and located in the industrialized world. Uses include: telebanking, teleshopping, business to business interaction (e.g. producer supplier networks) and e-mail. Businesses rather than governments are now shaping the multimedia by developing new markets, forming global regional consortia and communicating effectively across vast distances. The strategy for a profitable worldwide communications system is for telecom, cable TV and satellite TV to create a giant electronic entertainment system. Such a system is, ironically, being created when leisure time for a vast number of people is decreasing! The success of the system is also at risk due to the lack of good content. However, from this multimedia system a socio-cultural pattern is emerging which includes the following characteristics.

- Wide segmentation of markets, the formation of virtual communities according to their interests.
- Increasing stratification amongst users. The constraints include having sufficient time and money and regions with enough market potential.
- The integration of messages in a common cognitive pattern that resembles the action movie.
- The ability to capture the diversity of cultural expression.

Another phenomenon of the system is its ability to generate **real virtuality**, that is, a system in which reality is captured in a virtual image. The experience is communicated through the image on the screen and becomes the experience!

The new industrial space

The networked society has spatial dimensions. One crucial nodal aspect of the network is the **global city**. Global cities are the crux of knowledge generation and information flows and are scattered around the globe. Pivotal global cities are New York, Tokyo and London. The New Economy has in effect created a new role for the major cities around the world. They have become concentrated command points, key locations of finance and specialized services, sites for the production of innovation, markets for products and services. In line with the New Economy, such cities and business districts are information based, value production complexes where headquarters and advanced financial institutions locate suppliers and source highly skilled, specialized labour. Once such urban nodes are created heavy investment follows in 'real estate'. Moreover, they become the locus of opportunities for status, prestige, and personal enhancement.

The creation of high technology manufacturing based on microelectronics and computerization has led to the development of four different kinds of space:

- R&D innovation in core areas with a good quality of life (e.g. Cambridge, UK)
- skilled fabrication in branch plants (e.g. the North East of England)

- semi-skilled, large scale assembly and testing in off-shore locations (such as some Far East economies)
- after sales service and maintenance in regional centres around the globe.

Such milieux of innovation have had the effect of developing a work culture for generating new knowledge, new processes and new production. Spatial proximity appears to have been a necessary precondition. Such high technology-led industrial milieux have been labelled 'technopoles'.[8] Leading technopoles include Tokyo, Paris-Sud, the London-M4 corridor, Seoul-Inchon, Silicon Valley, California and Boston Route 128. Factors that have facilitated their development include the generation of new knowledge in strategically important fields of application (such as biotech/bioscience) and the concentrated location of highly skilled scientists and engineers.

A further important feature of the new industrial system is that there is an interplay between the need to have a global and local focus.[9] The flexibility of the information system is such that firms can be locally adapted whilst competing on a global scale. Scale is another key concept, for the SME can also compete alongside the global giant. The 'electronic cottage' is one example of the global networked enterprise, which markets its services over the internet and uses outworkers and home workers as its skilled labour force. Combined with the image of the idyllic location the electronic cottage selling on specialist produce, for example, combines the benefits of entrepreneurship with home-centredness and lifestyle.

Technological innovation and the challenge to the science community

It has been suggested that governments have played a major role in stimulating innovation. This has been through pursuing a national competitiveness agenda in defence and space programmes in particular. More recently the need to introduce digital technologies in order to expand the use and availability of a computerized multi-media communications system is being funded by the private sector with a view to providing a global entertainment system. Furthermore, the British government, for example, is currently pursuing an explicit competitiveness strategy aimed at the development of an enterprise culture and stimulating innovation to the point of commercial exploitation of scientific ideas. The problem is made quite explicit:

> The UK has a world-class science, engineering and design base, which provides a pool of talented people to work in and with business. We win more major science prizes than any country apart from the US. But university R&D is too rarely translated into UK commercial success.[10]

The White Paper went on to signal government's intention to provide funds to set up eight enterprise centres at leading UK universities. This Science Enterprise Challenge, as it was termed, is underway and the centres have been selected and established. But what are some of the ingredients that

Box 16.1: The Silicon Valley story

Silicon Valley had a significant research tradition in electronics going back to the turn of the 20th century. The crucial individual in the story was Frederick Terman, a Stanford professor who for health reasons stayed in Palo Alto. Terman's vision was of the need to forge closer links between the university and industry. He therefore encouraged his best graduates to start up electronics firms. His best known students of that period were William Hewlett and David Packard. After the Second World War Terman built up a major programme in electrical engineering, supported by local industry. The idea was to diffuse innovations into industry. In 1951 he set up the Stanford Industrial Park and several Stanford spin offs including Hewlett-Packard, moved into the Park.

In 1955, Nobel Prize winner William Shockley founded Shockley Semiconductors Laboratory in Palo Alto. He recruited eight electronics graduates. There ensued a dispute between the young scientists and Shockley over the direction the research – into silicon transistors – should take and the graduates left to found their own company Fairchild Semiconductors. Through the work of Robert Noyce, Fairchild was credited with inventing the integrated circuit. It was able to attract the best talent in microelectronics and by 1965 ten new firms were spun off by Fairchild engineers. When Fairchild was taken over by an East Coast corporation, its founders left the firm. By 1976 about 40 semi-conductor firms had been spun off from Fairchild and were located in Silicon Valley.

Important underlying factors that fostered the success of Silicon Valley were: the military demand for electronics devices and the aerospace programme; military contracts that formed a substantial proportion of the market for semiconductors; the Defence Department's and NASA's roles in effectively underwriting some of the riskiest R&D ventures; and the Defence Department's requirement for public diffusion of the innovations. A second set of factors included the social networking and culture that fostered innovation in the Valley. Part of this culture included the ability to move around, share information and create a virtuous spiral of innovation. Also, the scientists were well rewarded; they achieved both wealth and fame from their endeavours. This culture then attracted a fourth ingredient – the venture capitalist – who appeared on the scene in the 1980s.

By the mid 1970s Silicon Valley had in fact developed an innovative milieu, which facilitated technological spin offs into the market place. However, the development of a personal computer by Ed Roberts in 1974 marked another turning point in the development of Silicon Valley. It led to the development of a computer hobbyist club – the Home Brew Computer Club – whose members included Steve Wozniak, Bill Gates and Steve Jobs. The Wozniak-Jobs partnership led to the creation of the multi-million dollar personal computer company Apple, and Gates, of course, founded the renowned Microsoft global software corporation. There were an additional 20 founders emanating from this computer club.

In the mid-1980s there was considerable competition from Japan and a global decline in the computer industry. Silicon Valley has now refocused and specialized in R&D, design and advanced manufacturing. Other automated manufacturing plant has tended to be relocated in cheaper areas of the US. The role which the universities have played in the area has been to provide a labour market of well-trained scientists and engineers.

will enable the commercialization of scientific ideas? To help answer this question it is instructive to look abroad at established centres of technological innovation. Silicon Valley is perhaps the most well known and best documented.[11] It is where the story begins.

The case of Silicon Valley highlights the importance of 'critical mass', of visionary leadership and support for the innovation process. Formal scientific knowledge was clearly necessary but not a sufficient condition for the development of commercial applications. This required depth of understanding – tacit knowledge – and a variety of skills.[12] Initially the scientific community was effectively backing itself – making the ultimate entrepreneurial judgement – before the venture capitalists moved into the area. The sharing of information, the 'hobbyist' culture suggests that innovation was something people enjoyed and could enthuse about. It is difficult to see how 'becoming seriously wealthy' could have been a prime motivator in the very early days. But the seeking of rich rewards and the belief that they are in (nearly) everyone's reach is clearly embedded in the Valley culture.

Castells and Hall[13] have suggested a set of factors which they believe are critical dimensions of the Silicon Valley culture.

- **The centrality of work.** Work is more important than leisure, and being a successful entrepreneur requires considerable hard work.
- **The professional ethic of the innovator** – the importance of being on the cutting edge of innovation.
- **Entrepreneurialism** – the spirit of enterprise combines audacious attempts to create new firms, innovative capability and wealth creation.
- **Aggressive competition** – characterized by personal drive, cut-throat ambition and loose ethical standards.
- **Extreme individualism** – this included the proportion of the population who were single (i.e. unmarried or divorced).
- **The affluence of the area** – the majority of the population has a high standard of living. This has led to high expectations of being able to make a good living whilst still young and a degree of intolerance of people who do not make it.
- **Technostress** – the toll of technological drive and innovation is that of social and psychological stress in relation to the job, alcohol and drugs abuse and family disruption.
- **Corporate subcultures** – including strong feelings of company loyalty, informality and flexibility, teamwork, interpersonal cooperation and psychological support.
- **Compensatory consumption** – the affluent relieve some of their stress through status-oriented conspicuous consumption.

In sum, the initial government push which was a necessary condition to the establishment of microelectronics in Silicon Valley was not a sufficient explanation of the entrepreneurial successes emanating from this particular locale. To sustain its development over decades, there has been technological excellence and scientific knowledge stimulated by social networks amongst scientists, entrepreneurs and managers, creating a synergy for innovation. High-risk capital and a work-oriented culture that valued technological genius and entrepreneurialism were also critical conditions. This was supported by a territorialism of values and interests that embraced the social and economic successes of the innovators and marginalised or excluded the rest.

What lessons can be learnt from the above case study by a government intent on stimulating innovation? Are cultural ingredients replicable? To what extent can observed necessary conditions be adapted to suit particular cultures?

There are issues of regional infrastructure – industrial, communications and housing developments – which sit alongside the development of an innovation milieu, making it an attractive place to live and work. Silicon Valley became densely populated, creating traffic problems, environmental pollution and so on. This is a critically important area for government policy because an **innovative cluster** is fundamental to the creation of synergy, technology transfer and commercial exploitation. A culture of **excellence** that promotes the identification and retention of the best scientists and technologists is another fundamental but replicable ingredient. By grading its scholarship by academic department, the UK has in place a system for the identification of centres of excellence in science, engineering and business management. The third critical issue is that of an infrastructure of enabling **support**. This support needs to include a thriving business community that has an interest in engaging with the universities in promoting and supporting through investment, the commercialization of science and technology. Venture capitalists need to understand the scientific ideas so that investment can be made at earlier stages in the development of those ideas. Risk can then be managed more effectively. Fourth, from cumulative knowledge of the venture founding process, it is generally the case that the fostering of ideas comes from the development of **informal, social networks** by the entrepreneur and that these informal networks are particularly important at the early stages of founding. This was demonstrated in the case of Silicon Valley; it can be and has been replicated elsewhere.[14]

There is a sense that this innovative milieu is all that matters; however, it is people who embody principles and ideas, who make decisions, pursue particular interests and value certain phenomena over others. Furthermore, what – if any – is the role for entrepreneurship in this process of technological innovation? Is it not a redundant idea? On the contrary, from the technological cluster the opportunity arose to create something new, which was highly prized. This led to the rewards for risk taking and innovation: the creation of wealth. What the technological milieu also did was to bring together in close proximity all those resources (capital, scientific expertise, skills and capability and physical infrastructure) necessary prerequisites for enterprise.

But can entrepreneurship be taught or is it sufficient simply to create technological spaces with the above ingredients? Certainly alongside the existence of business incubation units for science graduates, specialist courses in leading edge scientific knowledge, technical knowledge of business planning, intellectual property and technology transfer issues there is much that can be achieved through an enterprise/entrepreneurship curriculum. The learning style in entrepreneurship appears to be from role models and concrete examples, so gaining an understanding of, and insights from, live case studies is one prerequisite. This enables the young scientist to understand the process that technological entrepreneurs have experienced and managed.

From such cases critical issues in the process of business development may be identified and wisdom distilled. Getting one's fingers burnt by an unhappy engagement with a large corporation wanting to form an advantageous alliance is one way of learning from another's unfortunate experience. The lesson is not to be distrustful of large scale industry, rather to recognize the importance of negotiating skills in managing any kind of partnership and realizing the importance of the multi-skilled entrepreneurial team. Therefore an important part of the support process is the team member who can broker relationships with potential sponsors and investors in the commercialization process whilst protecting the technological entrepreneur's intellectual capital. Testing and developing ideas that may be industrially sensitive is necessary but difficult and so building up effective business and commercial relationships over time is essential. The informal, social networking and the use of business and hobbyist clubs are ways in which this process may be facilitated. Thus, the teaching process will be ineffective if it does not follow less than conventional lines. The medical model of the teaching hospital is one aspect of this; another is to create clubs and spaces for informal interaction and sharing of ideas and information. Blocking opportunities is the antithesis of entrepreneurialism.

Entrepreneurship and the establishment of an enterprise is a process, so the enterprise curriculum should reflect this. Budding technological entrepreneurs may 'need to know' about the immediate but they also need to develop an insight into the future. They need to know what business enterprises are like from the inside out and how a fledgling enterprise may be transformed into a large thriving, professionally managed corporation. They need to know how to develop strategies to manage any contingencies, whether that be survival when cash flow may be causing problems or maintenance when building up capability for the next stage of development and growth – managing the pace of growth and not overtrading, for example. Insight enables the technological entrepreneur to be able to anticipate problems that will occur in the real world of business venturing and to be able to manage successes and avoid, as far as possible, failures.

Summary and conclusions

In earlier chapters it has been established that:

- a critical part of any firm's environment is other firms
- the vast majority of firms – even transnational corporations – are not global, although they are international, on the grounds that a high proportion of the company's assets are home-based
- firms are highly heterogeneous on many dimensions such as size, structure, industrial sector, legal form and so on
- national, local and organizational culture are influences on firm behaviour.

Given such variation, each chapter has sought a way through the complexity and aimed to pose the question: 'what does such diversity mean for entrepreneurial behaviour?' It is observed that there are some environmental and structural dimensions which 'map' onto entrepreneurial behaviour rather more than others. So what knowledge might be extracted that will enable people to create more effective entrepreneurially-led businesses?

It has become apparent that entrepreneuring is a mind*ful* activity. Within the entrepreneurially-led business, the leadership has clear intentions and a strategy for developing the business, accumulating capital and creating wealth. This observation applies as much to the internet company as it does the franchised business, science-based spin off company or global conglomerate. Further, there is considerable evidence to underscore the prescription that such a firm must understand its competitive environment and have within the team the technical knowledge to compete effectively – and on a global stage – with a flexible, open-minded approach to future possibilities. This is indicative of the need to take a 'team approach' to business development. Other than in the case of the sole trader, firms are never 'one person bands'. Thus, to enable development and effective performance, the correct skills' mix and balance of talents is critical.

Depth of experience brings with it tacit knowledge and understanding. In this way, experience and enthusiasm make good bedfellows, positive and open to new possibilities. Hence, the entrepreneurially-led firm is an enlightened firm. It creates **profound knowledge** (= depth of understanding born out of experience) and **foresight** (= the ability to think through and envision possible futures) and is **energized** by 'youthful' enthusiasm, drive and a sound sense of direction.

Shortened timeframes for making decisions encourages decision making 'on the hoof'. In uncertain or turbulent environments, such apparently hasty decision making may suggest **riskiness** or even **recklessness**. To manage this inevitable reality of the business environment, directors and managers of entrepreneurial firms need to bolster their intuitive sense by establishing the habit of being proactive. Proactivity in this context means, colloquially, 'having one's finger on the pulse', in other words, being able diagnose situations accurately in order to anticipate the future. To 'have one's finger on the pulse' requires work. It means relentlessly seeking out information. But information alone is not enough, it must be contextualized and its implications worked through. This analytical approach usefully counterbalances the need to be intuitive and make fast but informed judgements.

Further, for information to become useful intelligence, that information needs to be shared and debated within the firm. This sharpens the critical capacity and refines judgement. Moreover, it creates an organizational culture that embraces open debate where people are not afraid to play 'devil's advocate', where obstacles are anticipated and problems resolved. This organizational culture appears to have one vital ingredient, which has been summed up in the term **learning organization**. The directorial team may not have set out to create a learning culture but by encouraging debate and openness, assumptions are exposed, considered and, where appropriate, changed or adapted. This frees up thinking to aid the corporate resolution of problems, lateral thinking, the identification of strategic options and the emergence of plausible innovative scenarios. This facilitates an engagement by staff in the realistic possibility of change and development.

The external milieu that appears to be conducive to entrepreneuring encourages interdependency and cooperation. This finding exposes one myth – the idea that entrepreneurially-led businesses might be highly independent and autonomous – 'fortress enterprise' as it has been metaphorically termed. On the contrary, effective enterprises are interlinked and located in a web of interdependencies which are likely to include suppliers, producers, service providers and consumers, among others. They form structural interdependencies that affect interfirm or business to business behaviour. The slightly overworked word 'trust' is, at best, a contingent effect. Firms have achieved a negotiated position within their particular network of interdependent relations. Any defaulting behaviour would very likely mean a loss of one's position and probably (in the case of the small venture) put its longevity at risk. The value of the structure is security, reliability (for example of supply), and the ability to negotiate within an understood framework, thus ensuring a high degree of cooperation. The outcome appears to create a 'virtuous spiral' of effective business dealings as a consequence of **mutual self-interest**.

Hence the idea of the entrepreneur as a 'lone' or even 'local', 'hero' needs careful qualification. There are a number of issues, to which some have already been alluded. Not all cultures espouse individualism. The idea of making heroes of entrepreneurs certainly fits the North American culture but it does not sit easily with certain national cultures, for example in the Far East, Africa and South America. Furthermore, the entrepreneur as leader needs interpersonal and communications skills that will enable him or her to excite and motivate others to support, invest in and develop his or her vision. Moreover, good ideas can come from anywhere – and certainly not always from the entrepreneur or lead figure. This suggests a different image of the entrepreneur, possibly as a catalyst, a distiller of ideas that can be galvanized through the efforts of the managerial team into an actionable plan. It is therefore evident that relationships within the firm are fundamental to the effective performance of the whole enterprise.

Finally, it is worth returning to the issue addressed in previous chapters as to whether the 'glocal/global' business is possible. The notion of 'globalization' appears to rest on an ambiguity: one interpretation emphasizes the worldwide distribution of assets, combined with the ability of the company to provide its products and/or services regionally or locally; alternatively, there is an interpretation that places less emphasis on the physical, worldwide location of the company, but instead emphasizes the importance of the firm's ability to achieve world-class standards in whatever it does, and to be able to provide those products or services in local markets globally. With developments in the New Economy, the increasing importance of IT and the development of the networked organizational form, it is the second sense of the 'global company' that is likely to emerge as the more meaningful and prevalent. However, at present the developed world is in the throes of an information revolution. This heralds change and vast opportunities for entrepreneurialism and enterprise.

Notes

Chapter 1

1. Storey, D.J. (1994) *Understanding the Small Business Sector*, London: Routledge.
2. Mintzberg, H. (1983) *Structure in Fives: Designing Effective Organizations*, Englewood Cliffs, New Jersey: Prentice-Hall.
3. These issues are discussed further in chapter 12 of this volume.
4. The issue of growth is discussed further in a number of chapters, notably chapters 12 and 13.
5. See chapter 15 of this volume.
6. See Burns, T. and Stalker, G.M. (1961) *The Management of Innovation*, London: Tavistock; quoted in Chell, E. (1993) *The Psychology of Behaviour in Organizations*, 2nd edn Houndsmills and London: Macmillan, pp. 86–7.
7. Mintzberg *op. cit.*, p. 168.
8. See, for example, Kanter, R.M. (1983) *The Change Masters*, London: Unwin.
9. See Chell, E. *et al.* (1991) *The Entrepreneurial Personality: Concepts, Cases and Categories*, London: Routledge, pp. 115–120. Also refer to Box 11.1, chapter 11 of this volume.
10. The topic of team organization, development and management is discussed more fully in chapter 10 of this volume.
11. Tsosvold, D. (1991) *Team Organization: An Enduring Competitive Advantage*, Chichester: Wiley.
12. Kanter *op. cit.*, esp. p. 166 (note 8).
13. Bobbe, L. (2000) 'The rise of she-commerce', *Telegraph Magazine* 18 March: p.40.
14. Morgan, G. (1980) 'Paradigms, metaphors and puzzle solving in organization theory', *Administrative Science Quarterly* 25: 605–22.
15. Morgan, G. (1993) *Imaginization*, London: Sage, in which Morgan invites us to make up our own metaphors.
16. Carnall, C.A. (1990) *Managing Change in Organizations*, Hemel Hempstead: Prentice-Hall; Clegg, S. (1990) *Modern Organizations: Organization Studies in the Post Modern World*, London: Sage; also see discussion in Chell, E. (1993) *The Psychology of Behaviour in Organizations*, London: Macmillan, ch. 7 esp. pp. 162–8.
17. Morgan, G. (1996) *Images of Organization*, London: Sage, p. 225.
18. Kets de Vries, M. and Miller, D. (1985) *The Neurotic Organization*, San Francisco: Jossey-Bass; also, compare Kets de Vries, M. (1995) *Organizational Paradoxes: Clinical Approaches to Management*, 2nd edn London and New York: Routledge.
19. I am indebted to Dr Paul Tracey for collecting this case study which I have anonymised and modified for illustrative purposes.
20. Kets de Vries, *op. cit.*, esp. pp. 22–3.
21. Ajiferuke, M. and Boddewyn, J. (1970) '"Culture" and other explanatory

variables in comparative management studies', *Academy of Management Journal*, June: 153–63.

22. Smircich, L. (1983) 'Concepts of culture and organizational analysis', *Administrative Science Quarterly*, 28: 339–58; Allaire, Y. and Firsirotu, M.E. (1984) 'Theories of organizational culture', *Organization Studies*, 5 (3): 193–226. For a useful summary of these issues, see Chell, E. and Adam, E. (1994), 'Exploring the cultural orientation of entrepreneurship: conceptual and methodological issues', School of Business Management Discussion Paper No. 94–7, University of Newcastle upon Tyne, UK.

23. Harvey-Jones, J. (1988) *Making it Happen*, Glasgow: Fontana/Collins.

24. Hofstede, G. (1991) *Cultures and Organizations – Software of the Mind*, Maidenhead: McGraw-Hill Europe, p. 4.

25. Hofstede, G. (1980) *Culture's Consequences: International Differences in Work Related Values*, Newbury Park, Calif.: Sage.

26. Hofstede (1991) *op. cit.*; Hofstede, G. and Bond, M.H. (1988), 'The Confucius connection: from cultural roots to economic performance', *Organization Dynamics*, (Spring): 4–21.

27. Hofstede (1991) *op. cit.*, esp. pp. 164–6.

28. Allaire and Firsirotu, *op. cit.*

29. Hofstede, G., Neuijen, B., Ohayv, D.D. and Sanders, G. (1990) 'Measuring organizational cultures: a qualitative and quantitative study across twenty cases', *Administrative Science Quarterly*, 35: 286–316.

30. Schneider, S.C. and Barsoux, J-L. (1997) *Managing Across Cultures*, London: Prentice-Hall, esp. ch. 3.

31. Bartlett, C.A and Ghoshal, S. (2000) 'Going global', *Harvard Business Review* (March-April), esp. pp. 138–9.

32. Enriquez, J. and Goldberg, R.A. (2000) 'Transforming life, transforming business: the life-science revolution', *Harvard Business Review* (March-April): 96–104.

33. See earlier discussion and reference.

34. See chapter 12 of this volume; Chell, E. *et al.* (1991) *The Entrepreneurial Personality*, London: Routledge.

35. Schneider and Barsoux *op. cit.*

36. Trompenaars, F. (1993) *Riding the Waves of Culture*, London: Nicholas Brealey.

37. *Ibid.* p. 6.

38. *Ibid.* p. 19.

39. Deal, T. and Kennedy, A. (1982) *Corporate Cultures – the Rites and Rituals of Corporate Life*, Addison-Wesley.

40. Newman, J. (1995) 'Gender and cultural change', in Itzen, C. and Newman, J. (eds) *Gender, Culture and Organizational Change*, London: Routledge, pp. 11–29.

41. See chapter 8 of this volume.

42. Morgan, G. (1986) *Images of Organization*, Beverley Hills: Sage, p. 200.

43. Cameron, K.S. and Quinn, R.E. (1999) *Diagnosing and Changing Organizational Culture*, Reading, Massachusetts: Addison-Wesley, p. 4.

Chapter 2

1. 'Firm' is used here in the layman's sense – a place where business is transacted – rather than the economist's purely theoretical notion of 'the firm'. See, Penrose, E.T. (1959) *The Theory of the Growth of the Firm*, London: Basil Blackwell, esp. ch. 2 for a discussion.

2. Dicken, P. (1998) *Global Shift*, London: Paul Chapman, p. 82; this point relates in particular to the effects of national culture on 'ways of doing' – see ch. 1 and especially references to the work of Hofstede.

3. For example they do not have a 'bottom line', they cannot 'go out of business'.

4. See for example Dicken *op. cit*, esp. pp. 88–90.

5. Scase, R. (1997) 'The role of small businesses in the economic transformation of Eastern Europe: real but relatively unimportant?', *International Small Business Journal*, 16 (1):13–21.

6. As discussed in ch. 1 of this volume.

7. The 'social chapter' of the Treaty of the EU was negotiated and largely agreed in 1991 at Maastricht.

8. Canada-United States Free Trade Agreement.

9. Dicken *op. cit.*, p. 177.

10. *Ibid.* esp pp. 183–8.

11. *Ibid.* pp. 193–6.

12. *Ibid.* p. 196.

13. Smith, K.G., Curtis, C.M. and Gannon, M.J. (1992) *Dynamics of Competitive Strategy*, Newbury Park: Sage, p. 123.

14. *Ibid.*

15. See for example the government White Paper *Our Competitive Future: Building the Knowledge Driven Economy*, Cm 4176, December 1998, London: The Stationery Office Ltd.

16. Obloj, K. and Kolvereid , L. 'Entrepreneurs in different environments and cultures in Britain, Norway and Poland: towards a comparative framework', in Joynt, P. and Warner, M. (eds) (1996) *Managing Across Culture: Issues and Perspectives,* London: International Business Press, pp. 338–359.

17. Storey, D. (1994) *Understanding the Small Business Sector*, London: Routledge.

18. Barclays National Entrepreneurial Index; source *Barclays Small Business Bulletin*, Issue 2, 1999;
www.smallbusiness.barclays.co.uk/news/press_rel_07.htm

19. Perrow, C. 'Small-firm networks', in Nohria, N. and Eccles, R.G. (eds) (1992) *Networks and Organizations: Structure, Form and Action*, Boston, Mass.: Harvard Business School Press, ch. 17, pp. 445–470.

20. See, for example Piore, M. and Sabel, C. (1984) *The Second Industrial Divide*, New York: Basic Books; Sabel, C. 'Flexible specialization and the re-emergence of regional economies, in Hirst, P. and Zeitlin, J. (eds) *Reversing Industrial Decline*, New York: St. Martin's, pp. 17–70.

21. A British example of a franchised business is The Body Shop. See, for example specially prepared case 'The Body Shop International' in

Mintzberg, H., Quinn, B. and Ghoshal, S. (1998) *The Strategy Process*, London: Prentice-Hall, pp. 447–466 and Roddick, A. (1991) *Body and Soul*, New York: Crown.
22. Best, B. (1991) *The New Competition*, Cambridge: Harvard University Press.
23. See also ch. 15 of this volume.
24. Perrow *op. cit* (note 19).
25. See additional discussion in ch. 7 of this volume.
26. Porter, M.E. (1980) *Competitive Strategy – Techniques for Analysing Industries and Competitors*, New York: The Free Press.
27. Porter, M.E. (1990) *The Competitive Advantage of Nations*, London: Macmillan. See also earlier discussion.
28. Kanter, R.M. (1983) *The Change Masters – Corporate Entrepreneurs at Work*, London: Unwin.
29. The theme of innovation is developed further in ch. 9 of this volume.
30. The broader issue of innovation is discussed fully in ch. 11 of this volume.
31. Kanter *op. cit.*, p. 29.
32. Based on Kanter *op. cit.*, p. 101.
33. Kanter *op. cit.*, p. 147.
34. Kanter *op. cit.*, p. 148.
35. Kanter, R.M. (1989) *When Giants Learn to Dance*, London: Routledge, p. 201.
36. Kanter, R. M. (1995) *World Class – Thriving Locally in the Global Economy*, New York: Simon and Schuster, pp. 12–13.
37. Hofstede, G (1991) *Cultures and Organizations*, London: McGraw-Hill, p. 11.
38. *Ibid.*
39. *Ibid.* p. 89.
40. Castells, M. (1996) *The Rise of the Networked Society*, Malden, Massachusetts & Oxford, UK: Blackwell.

Chapter 3

1. Johannsen, H. and Page, T.G. (1995) *International Dictionary of Management*, 5th edn. London: Kogan Page, p. 288.
2. *Ibid.*, p. 231.
3. Chell, E., Haworth, J. and Brearley, S. (1991) *The Entrepreneurial Personality: Concepts, Cases and Categories*, London: Routledge, p. 99.
4. Drummond, H. and Chell, E., (1993) 'Training needs and sole practitioner solicitors.' *Industrial and Commercial Training*, 25 (1): 3–5; Drummond, H. and Chell, E. (1994) 'Crisis management in a small business: a tale of two solicitors', *Management Decision*, 32 (1): 37–40.
5. Roddick, A. (1992) *Body and Soul*, London: Vermillion, p. 71 *et seq.*
6. Dewhurst J. and Burns, P. (1993) *Small Business Management*, Houndsmills: Macmillan p. 135.
7. Roddick *op. cit.*
8. *Ibid.* pp. 85–6.
9. Chell *et al op. cit.* pp. 107–114 (note 3).

10. Based on actual cases investigated by the author in the UK and New Zealand.
11. See also discussion in chapter 12 of this volume.
12. See Bolton, W. (1997) *The University Handbook on Enterprise Development*, Paris Cedex: Columbus, especially pp. 100–161.
13. Kanter, R.M. (1984) *The Change Masters*, London: George Allen & Unwin.
14. Dewhurst and Burns *op. cit.*
15. Bolton, W. (1997) *The University Handbook on Enterprise Development*, Paris Cedex: Columbus, pp. 152–166, 170 *et seq.*
16. See also chapter 12 in this volume.
17. Bolton *op. cit.*
18. Quoted from *The Times Higher* (2000) February 18: 4.
19. Block, Z. and MacMillan, I.C. (1993) *Corporate Venturing*, Boston, Mass.: Harvard Business School Press.
20. Kanter, R.M. (1984) *The Change Masters*, London: Unwin Hyman.
21. Block and Macmillan *op. cit.* p. 20.
22. Block and MacMillan *op. cit.* pp. 34–5.
23. Quoted in Block and MacMillan *op. cit.* pp. 59–60.

Chapter 4

1. Bill Gates *et al.* (1995) *The Road Ahead* (revised edn), London: Penguin Books, pp. 19–20.
2. Chell, E. (1993) *The Psychology of Behaviour in Organizations* 2nd edn, London: Macmillan, esp. ch.7; Chell, E. (1985) 'The entrepreneurial personality: a few ghosts laid to rest?' *International Small Business Journal*, 3 (3):43–54.
3. Smith, N.R. (1967) *The Entrepreneur and His Firm: The Relationship Between Type of Man and Type of Company*, East Lansing, Michigan: Michigan State University Press.
4. Miller, D. (1983) 'The correlates of entrepreneurship in three types of firm', *Management Science*, 29 (7): 770–91.
5. Chell, E. and Baines, S. (1998) 'Does gender affect business performance? A study of microbusinesses in business services in the UK', *International Journal Of Entrepreneurship and Regional Development*, 10 (4):117–135.
6. **Characteristics of the franchised system**
   On the **positive** side: risk reduction; the benefits of the accumulated experience of the franchiser and other members of the system; standardization of the product or service, company image, style and presentation; formalization e.g. of training; financial assistance; proven marketing methods; quick start up conditions. On the **negative** side: costs of operating a franchise, including fees and royalties; loss of independence; restrictions on growth and sources of supply; the terms of the contract, for example termination and renewal clauses.
   How many characteristics did you identify?
7. Boyatzis, R.E. (1982) *The Competent Manager: A Model for Effective Performance*, London & New York: Wiley.
8. Chell, E., Lau T., Chan K.F. and Man T.W.Y. (1999) 'Entrepreneurial com-

petencies and firm performance: some data from small business owner-managers based in Hong Kong', *Discussion Paper No.: 99–5*. Newcastle, UK: Newcastle School of Management.

9. Roddick, A. (1992) *Body and Soul*, London: Vermillion.
10. Smith, N.R. (1967) *The Entrepreneur and His Firm: The Relationship between Type of Man and Type of Company*, East Lansing, Michigan: Michigan State University Press; Stanworth, J. and Curran, J. (1973) *Management Motivation in the Small Firm*, London: Gower; Tuck, P. and Hamilton, R. (1993) 'Intra-industry differences in founder-controlled firms', *International Small Business Journal*, 12 (1): 12–22.
11. Chell, E., Haworth, J. and Brearley, S. (1991) *The Entrepreneurial Personality: Concepts, Cases and Categories*, London: Routledge; Chell, E. and Haworth, J. (1992) 'A typology of business owners and their orientation towards growth', in Caley, K., Chell, E., Chittenden, F. and Mason, C. (eds), *Small Enterprise Development: Policy and Practice in Action*, London: Paul Chapman; Chell, E. and Haworth, J. (1993) 'Profiling entrepreneurs: multiple perspectives and consequent methodological problems', in Klandt, H. (ed.) *Entrepreneurship and Business Development*, Aldershot: Avbury, pp. 251–260.
12. Berger, P.L. and Luckmann, T. (1966) *The Social Construction of Reality*, London: Penguin.
13. *Ibid.*
14. Rosa, P. and Scott, M. (1999) 'Entrepreneurial diversification, business-cluster formation and growth', *Environment and Planning C: Government and Policy* 17 (5):527–548.
15. Bechhofer, F. and Elliott, B. (1976) 'Persistence and change: the petite bourgeoisie in industrial society', *European Journal of Sociology*, 17 (2):74–99.
16. Birley, S. and Westhead, P. (1993) A comparison of new businesses established by 'novice' and 'habitual' founders in Great Britain', *International Small Business Journal*, 12 (1):38–60.
17. Chell, E. (1985) *op. cit.*; Gartner, W.B. (1989) '"Who is an Entrepreneur?" is the Wrong Question', *Entrepreneurship Theory and Practice*, 14 (1): 27–37; Stevenson, H.H. and Sahlman, W.A. (1989) 'The entrepreneurial process', in Burns P. and Dewhurst J. (eds) *Small Business and Entrepreneurship*, Houndmills and London: Macmillan, ch. 5, pp. 94–157.
18. See Chell, E. and Burrows, R. (1991) 'The small business owner-manager', in Stanworth, J. and Gray, C. (eds) *Bolton 20 Years On: The Small Firm in the 1990s*, London: Paul Chapman, ch.7, pp. 151–177.
19. Chell, E. (1999) 'The entrepreneurial personality; past, present and future', *The Occupational Psychologist*, 38: 5–12.
20. McClelland, D.C. (1987) 'Characteristics of successful entrepreneurs', *Journal of Creative Behavior*, 21 (3): 219–33.
21. Chell E. *et al.* (1991) *op. cit.*
22. Chell, E. (2000) 'Towards researching the "Opportunistic entrepreneur": a social constructionist approach and research agenda', *European Journal of Work and Organizational Psychology*, 9 (2) (forthcoming)
23. Kirzner, I.M. (1982) 'The theory of entrepreneurship in economic growth',

in Kent, C.A., Sexton, D.L. and Vesper, K.H. (eds) *Encyclopaedia of Entrepreneurship*, Englewood Cliffs, New Jersey: Prentice Hall.

24. Johnnisson, B., Chell, E. and Baines, S. (2000) 'Networking, entrepreneurship and microbusiness performance', *Entrepreneurship and Regional Development*, 12 (1): 1–21.

25. Penrose, E.T. (1959) *The Theory of the Growth of the Firm*, Oxford: Blackwell; Shackle, G.L.S. (1967) *The Years of High Theory*, Cambridge University Press; Filion, L. J. (1991) 'Vision and relations: elements for an entrepreneurial metamodel', *International Small Business Journal*, 9 (2): 26–40.

26. Casson, M. (1982) *The Entrepreneur – an Economic Theory*, Oxford: Martin Robertson.

27. Hart, M.M., Stevenson, H.H. and Dial, J. (1995) 'Entrepreneurship: a definition revisited', in Bygrave, W.D. *et al. Frontiers of Entrepreneurship Research* (1995), Centre for Entrepreneurial Studies, Babson College: MA, pp. 75–89.

28. Excerpt based on Brown, M. (1992) *Richard Branson The Inside Story*, London: Headline, pp. 87–98.

29. Chell, E. (1985) *op. cit.*; Bird, B. (1988) 'Implementing entrepreneurial ideas: the case for intention', *Academy of Management Review*, 13 (3): 442–453.

30. West, M. A. and Farr, J.L. (eds) (1990) *Innovation and Creativity at Work: Psychological and Organizational Strategies*, Chichester: Wiley.

31. Schumpeter, J.A. (1934) *The Theory of Economic Development*, Cambridge, Mass.: Harvard University Press.

32. Chell, E., Haworth, J. and Brearley S. (1991) *The Entrepreneurial Personality: Concepts, Cases and Categories*, London: Routledge.

33. Shackle, G.L.S. (1979) *Imagination and the Nature of Choice*, Edinburgh: University of Edinburgh Press.

34. Schultz, T.W. (1980) 'Investment in entrepreneurial ability', *Scandinavian Journal of Economics*, 82: 437–48; Shackle, G.L.S. (1967) *The Years of High Theory*, Cambridge University Press; Kirzner, I.M. (1982) 'The theory of entrepreneurship in economic growth', in C.A. Kent *et al.*, *Encyclopedia of Entrepreneurship*, Englewood Cliffs, N.J.: Prentice Hall; Casson, M. (1982) *The Entrepreneur: An Economic Theory*, Oxford: Martin Robertson.

35. Bird, B. (1988) 'Implementing entrepreneurial ideas: the case for intention', *Academy of Management Review*, 13 (3): 442–453; Allison, C.W., Chell, E. and Hayes, J. (2000) 'Cognitive style and entrepreneurial behaviour,' *European Journal of Work and Organizational Psychology*, 9 (1):31–43.

36. Chell, E. (1985) *op. cit.*; Bird, B *op. cit.*; Low, M.B. and Macmillan, I.C. (1988) 'Entrepreneurship: past research and future challenges', *Journal of Management*, 14 (2): 139–161.

37. Boyd, N.G. and Vozikis, G.S. (1994) 'The influence of self-efficacy on the development of entrepreneurial intentions and actions', *Entrepreneurship Theory and Practice*, (Summer): 63–77; Learned, K.E. (1992) 'What happened before the organization? a model of organization formation', *Entrepreneurship Theory and Practice*, (Fall): 39–48.

38. Busenitz, L.W. (1996) 'Research on entrepreneurial alertness', *Journal of Small Business Management*, 34 (4): 35–44.

39. Chell, E., Haworth, J. and Brearley S. (1991) *The Entrepreneurial Personality: Concepts, Cases and Categories*, London: Routledge.

40. Crant, J.M. (1996) 'The proactive personality scale as a predictor of entrepreneurial intentions', *Journal of Small Business Management*, 34 (3):42–49.

41. Adam, E. and Chell, E. (1993) 'The successful international entrepreneur: a profile', paper presented to the 23rd European Small Business Seminar, Belfast; Baum, J.R. (1995) 'The relationship of traits, competencies, motivation, strategy and structure to venture growth', *Frontiers of Entrepreneurship Research*, Wellesley, Mass.: Babson College, Center for Entrepreneurial Studies; Chell, E., Lau, T., Chan, K.F. and Man, T.W.Y. (1999) 'Entrepreneurial competencies and firm performance: some data from small business owner-managers based in Hong Kong', *discussion paper no. 99–5*. Newcastle upon Tyne, UK: Newcastle School of Management; Hood, J.N. and Young, J.E. (1993) 'Entrepreneurship's requisite areas of development: a survey of top executives in successful entrepreneurial firms', *Journal of Business Venturing*, 8:115–135; Huck, J.F. and McEwen, T. (1991) 'Competencies needed for small business success: perceptions of Jamaican entrepreneurs', *Journal of Small Business Management*, 29 (4): 90–93; McClelland, D.C. (1987) 'Characteristics of successful entrepreneurs', *Journal of Creative Behaviour*, 21 (l): 18–21; Mitton, D.G. (1989) 'The compleat entrepreneur', *Entrepreneurship Theory and Practice*, 13 (3): 9–19.

42. Chell, E. (1985) *op. cit.*; Chell, E. (2000) *op. cit.*; Harre, R. (1979) *Social Being*, Oxford: Blackwell.

43. Bouchikhi, H. (1993) 'A constructivist framework for understanding entrepreneurship performance', *Organization Studies*, 14 (4): 549–570; Martin, J. and Sugarman, J. (1996) 'Bridging social constructionism and cognitive constructivism: a psychology of human possibility and constraint', *The Journal of Mind and Behaviour*, 17 (4): 291–320; Chell, E. and Rhodes, H. (1999) 'Exploring vertical relationships in SMEs: a social constructionist approach,' paper presented at the British Academy of Management Annual Conference, Manchester, UK, 1–3 September.

44. Fischer, E., Reuber, A.R., Hababou, M., Johnson, W. and Lee, S. (1997) 'The role of socially constructed temporal perspectives in the emergence of rapid-growth firms', *Entrepreneurship Theory and Practice*, 22 (2): 13–30.

45. Chell, E. (1997) 'The social construction of the entrepreneurial personality', paper presented at the British Academy of Management Conference, London, UK, 8–10 September.

46. Crant (1996) *op. cit.*

Chapter 5

1. Burgoyne, J. (1998) 'Learning: conceptual, practical and theoretical issues', paper presented at the British Academy of Management Conference, Nottingham, September.

2. Pavlov, I.P. (1972) *Conditioned Reflexes*, Oxford: Oxford University Press;

Skinner, B.F. (1953) *Science and Human Behaviour*, New York: The Macmillan Press.

3. Boyatzis, R.E. (1982) *The Competent Manager: A Model for Effective Performance*, New York: Wiley.

4. Morgan, G. (1989) *Images of Organization*, Beverley Hills, California: Sage.

5. Beer, S. (1972) *The Brain of the Firm*, Harmondsworth: Penguin; Senge, P. (1990) *The Fifth Discipline – The Art and Practice of the Learning Organization*, New York: Doubleday.

6. Davis, T.R.V. and Luthans, F. (1983) 'A social learning theory approach to organizational behaviour', in Steers, R.M. and Porter, L.W. (eds) *Motivation and Work Behaviour*, 3rd edn New York: McGraw-Hill.

7. Bandura, A. (1969) *Principles of Behaviour Modification*, New York: Holt, Rinehart and Winston; Bandura, A. (1977) *Social Learning Theory*, Englewood Cliffs, New Jersey: Prentice-Hall.

8. Miller, G.A., Galanter, E. and Pribram, K.H. (1960) *Plans and the Structure of Behaviour*, New York: Holt, Rinehart & Winston; Bannister, D. and Mair, J.M.M. (1968) *The Evaluation of Personal Constructs*, London: Academic Press.

9. Rogers, C. (1969) *Freedom to Learn*, Ohio: Bobs Merrill; Kohlberg, L. (1981) *Essays on Moral Development, vol.1: The Philosophy of Moral Development*, New York: Harper & Row.

10. Bion, W. (1961) *Experiences in Groups*, London: Tavistock.

11. Hofstede, G. (1991) *Cultures and Organizations – Software of the Mind*, Maidenhead: McGraw-Hill.

12. Sartre, J-P. (1970) *Existentialism and Humanism*, London: Methuen.

13. Lave, J. and Wenger, E. (1991) *Situated Learning: Legitimate Peripheral Participation*, Cambridge: Cambridge University Press.

14. Polanyi, M. (1967) *The Tacit Dimension*, London: Routledge.

15. See Kolb, D.A. (1984) *Experiential Learning*, Englewood Cliffs, New Jersey: Prentice-Hall, chapter 1.

16. Mead, G.H. (1934) *Mind, Self and Society*, Chicago: University of Chicago Press.

17. Weick, K.E. (1995) *Sense Making in Organizations*, Thousand Oaks: Sage.

18. *Ibid.* p. 107.

19. Pedler, M., Burgoyne, J. and Boydell, T. (1978) *A Manager's Guide to Self Development*, London: McGraw-Hill.

20. Easterby-Smith, M. (1997) Disciplines of organizational learning: contributions and critiques, *Human Relations*, 50 (9): 1085–1113.

21. Revans, R. (1980) *Action Learning: New Techniques for Managers*, London: Blond and Briggs.

22. Hayes, J. and Allinson C.W. (1994) Cognitive style and its relevance for management practice, *British Journal of Management*, 5:54.

23. De Bello, T.C. (1989) *Comparison of Eleven Major Learning Style Models; Variables; Appropriate Populations; Validity of Instrumentation; and the Research Behind Them.* National Conference of the Association for Supervision and Curriculum Development, Orlando, Fl. (quoted in Hayes and Allinson, *op. cit.*)

24. Allinson, C.W. and Hayes, J. (1996) 'The cognitive style index: a measure

of intuition-analysis for organization research', *Journal Of Management Studies*, 33 (1): 119–135.

25. Allinson, C.W., Chell, E. and Hayes, J. (2000) 'Intuition and entrepreneurial behaviour', *European Journal of Work and Organizational Psychology*, 9 (1): 33–46.

26. Argyris, C. and Schön, D.A. (1978) *Organizational Learning*, Reading: Addison-Wesley; Argyris, C. (1986) 'Reinforcing organizational defensive routines: an unintended human resources activity', *Human Resource Management* 25 (4): 541–555.

27. See chapters 1 and 2 of this volume.

28. Hedlund, G. and Nonaka, I. (1993) Models of knowledge management in the West and Japan. In Lorange P. (ed.) *Implementing Strategic Processes*, Oxford: Blackwell, pp. 117–144.

29. Argyris C. and Schön, D. A. (1978) *Organizational Learning: A Theory of Action Perspective*, Reading, Massachusetts: Addison-Wesley, ch. 1.

30. Sackmann, S.A. (1991, 1992) *Cultural Knowledge in Organizations – Exploring the Collective Mind*, Newbury Park, California: Sage.

31. *Ibid.* p. 18.

32. See in particular, chapters 1 and 2 of this volume.

33. See for example Drummond, H. (1992) *The Quality Movement*, London: Kogan Page.

34. See chapter 11 of this volume.

35. Easterby-Smith *op. cit.*, esp. p. 1103.

36. Senge, P. M. (1990) *The Fifth Discipline: the Art and Practice of the Learning Organization*, London: Century Business.

37. See Kolb, *op. cit.*

38. Argyris and Schön *op. cit.*

39. Easterby-Smith *op. cit.* esp. p. 1106.

40. Burgoyne, J., Pedler, M. and Boydell, T. (1994) *Towards the Learning Company*, London: McGraw-Hill.

41. *Ibid.*

42. Pedler, M., Burgoyne, J.G. and Boydell, T. (1991) *The Learning Company: A Strategy for Sustainable Development*, London: McGraw-Hill.

Chapter 6

1. March, J.G. (1988) *Decisions and Organizations*, Oxford: Blackwell.

2. Notably Simon, H.A. (1957) *Models of Man*, New York: Wiley.

3. See chapter 11 of this volume.

4. Jenkins, M. and Johnson, G. (1997) 'Entrepreneurial intentions and outcomes: a comparative causal mapping study', *Journal of Management Studies*, 34 (6): 895–920.

5. Fishbein, M. and Ajzen, I. (1975) *Belief, Attitude, Intention and Behaviour: An Introduction to Theory and Research*, Reading, Mass.: Addison-Wesley. See, also Chell, E. (1985) *Participation and Organization: A Social Psychological Approach*, London: Macmillan pp. 93–102.

6. Fishbein and Ajzen *Ibid.* use the term 'subjective norm', which I have interpreted as 'personal preference'.

7. Greenberger, D.B. and Sexton, D.L. (1988) 'An interactive model of new venture initiation', *Journal of Small Business Management* (July): 1–7.
8. Learned, K.E. (1992) 'What happened before the organization? a model of organization formation', *Entrepreneurship Theory and Practice* (Fall): 39–48.
9. Bird, B. (1988) 'Implementing entrepreneurial ideas: the case for intention', *Academy of Management Review*, 13 (3): 442–453.
10. *Ibid.*
11. Boyd, N.G. and Vozikis, G.S. (1994) 'The influence of self-efficacy on the development of entrepreneurial intention and actions', *Entrepreneurship Theory and Practice* (summer): 63–77.
12. Naffziger, D.W., Hornsby, J.S. and Kuratko, D.F. (1994) 'A proposed research model of entrepreneurial motivation', *Entrepreneurship Theory and Practice* (spring): 29–42.
13. Ornstein, R.E. (1977) *The Psychology of Consciousness*, New York: Harcourt Brace Jovanvich; Hayes. J. and Allinson, C.W. (1994) 'Cognitive style and its relevance for management practice', *British Journal of Management*, 5: 53–71.
14. Leonard, D. and Straus, S. (1997) 'Putting your company's whole brain to work', *Harvard Business Review* 75 (4):110–119.
15. Allinson, C.W., Chell, E. and Hayes, J. (2000) 'Intuition and entrepreneurial behaviour', *European Journal of Work and Organizational Psychology*, 9 (1): 33–46.
16. Chell, E. *et al.* (1991) *The Entrepreneurial Personality: Concepts, Cases and Categories*, London: Routledge, esp. pp. 107–115.
17. Agor, W.H. (1986) 'How top executives make important decisions', *Organization Dynamics* (winter); Agor, W.H. (1986) *The Logic of Intuitive Decision Making: A Research Based Approach for Top Management*, Westport, CT: Greenwood Press.
18. Chell, E. (2000) 'Towards researching the "opportunistic entrepreneur": a social constructionist approach and research agenda', *European Journal of Work and Organizational Psychology*, 9 (1): 65–82.
19. Mintzberg, H. (1987) 'Five Ps for strategy', *California Management Review*, (fall).
20. Miles, R.E., Snow, C.C., Meyer, A.D. and Coleman, H.J. (1978) 'Organizational strategy, structure and process', *The Academy of Management Review*, 3 (3).
21. Stevenson, H.H., Roberts, M.J. and Grousbeck, H.I. (1989) *New Business Ventures and the Entrepreneur*, 3rd. edn, Homewood Illinois: Irwin, quoted in Chell, E. *et al.* (1991) *The Entrepreneurial Personality: Concepts, Cases and Categories*, London: Routledge pp. 58–9.
22. See chapter 13 for a more extensive discussion of this point.
23. Pennings, J.M. (1977) 'Structural correlates of the environment', in Thorelli, H.B. (ed.) *Strategy + Structure = Performance*, Indiana University Press.
24. Burns, T. and Stalker, G.M. (1961) *The Management of Innovation*. London: Tavistock.
25. March, J.M. and Shapira, Z. (1987) 'Managerial perspectives on risk and

risk taking', *Management Science*, 33; reprinted in March, J.G. (1988) *Decisions and Organizations*, Oxford: Basil Blackwell, ch.4, pp. 76–97.

26. March, J.G. (1994) *A Primer on Decision Making: How Decisions Happen*, New York: The Free Press; March, J.G. (1997) 'Understanding how decisions happen in organizations', in Z. Shapira (ed.) *Organizational Decision Making*, Cambridge University Press, ch. 2, pp. 9–32.

27. March, *Ibid*. p. 16.

28. See chapter 5 in this volume.

29. *cf*. earlier section of this chapter and note 8.

30. Berger, P. and Luckmann, T. (1966) *The Social Construction of Reality: A Treatise in the Sociology of Knowledge*, New York: Doubleday; Weick, K.E. (1979) *The Social Psychology of Organizing*, 2nd edn, Reading Mass.: Addison-Wesley; Weick, K.E. (1995) *Sensemaking in Organizations*, Thousand Oaks, Calif.: Sage.

31. March *op. cit.* p. 23 (note 26).

32. Staw, B.M. 'The escalation of commitment: an update and appraisal', in Z. Shapira (ed.) *Organizational Decision Making*, Cambridge University Press, 1997, chapter 9, pp. 191–215.

33. *Ibid.*

34. Drummond, H. (1996) *Escalation in Decision Making*, Oxford University Press.

35. *Ibid.* p. 182.

36. *Ibid.* p. 184.

37. *Ibid.* p. 189.

38. Boyd, N.G. and Vozikis, G.S. (1994) 'The influence of self-efficacy on the development of entrepreneurial intentions and actions', *Entrepreneurship Theory and Practice* (summer): 63–77.

Chapter 7

1. Chell, E. (1993) *The Psychology of Behaviour in Organizations*, London: Macmillan, ch. 3.

2. Gartner, W.B., Bird, B. and Starr, J.A. (1992) 'Acting as if: differentiating entrepreneurial from organizational behavior', *Entrepreneurship Theory and Practice*, 16, (spring): 13–31.

3. This is based on a published case study written by Aleke Dondo and Mwangi Ngumo in Morrison, A. (ed.) (1998) *Entrepreneurship: An International Perspective*, Oxford: Butterworth-Heinemann, pp 23–5.

4. McClelland, D.C. (1961) *The Achieving Society*, Princeton, New Jersey: Van Nostrand.

5. Collins, O.F. and Moore, D.G. (1970) *The Organization Makers*, New York: Appleton-Century-Crofts; Dunkelberg, W.C. and Cooper, A.C. (1982) 'Entrepreneurial typologies: an empirical study', in Vesper, K.H. (ed.) *Frontiers of Entrepreneurial Research*, Wellesley, Mass.: Babson College, Center for Entrepreneurial Studies: 1–15; Kets de Vries, M.F.R. (1977) 'The entrepreneurial personality: a person at the crossroads', *Journal Of Management Studies*, (Feb): 34–57.

6. Greenberger, D.B. and Sexton, D.L. (1988) 'An interactive model of new venture initiation, *Journal of Small Business Management* (July): 1–7.

7. Brockhaus, R.H. (1982) 'The psychology of the entrepreneur', in Kent, C.A., Sexton, D.L. and Vesper K.H. (eds) *Encyclopedia of Entrepreneurship*, Englewood Cliffs, New Jersey: Prentice-Hall; Hull, D.L., Bosley, J.J. and Udell, G.G. (1980) 'Renewing the hunt for the heffalump: identifying potential entrepreneurs by personality characteristics', *Journal of Small Business*, 18 (1): 11–18.

8. Bolton Report (1971) *Report of the Committee of Enquiry on Small Firms*, chaired by J.E. Bolton, Cmnd. 4811, London: HMSO.

9. Kets de Vries, M.R.F. *op. cit.*

10. Curran, J. (1986) *Bolton Fifteen Years On: A Review and Analysis of Small Business Research in Britain 1971–1986*, London: Small Business Research Trust.

11. Curran, J. and Blackburn, R. (1994) *Small Firms and Local Economic Networks: the Death Of the Local Economy?* London: Paul Chapman esp. p. 113.

12. Bechhofer, F. and Elliott, B. (eds), (1981) *The Petite Bourgeoisie, Comparative Studies of an Uneasy Stratum*, London: Macmillan.

13. Carland, J.W., Hoy, F. Boulton, W.R. and Carland, J.A.C. (1984) Differentiating entrepreneurs from small business owners: a conceptualization', *Academy of Management Review*, 9 (2): 354–9.

14. Scase, R. (1997) 'The role of small businesses in the economic transformation of eastern europe: real but relatively unimportant? *International Small Business Journal*, 16 (1):13–21.

15. *Ibid.* p. 14.

16. McClelland, D. (1975) *Power: The Inner Experience*, New York: Irving.

17. Rotter, J.B. (1966) 'Generalised expectancies for internal versus external control of reinforcement, *Psychological Monographs, Whole No. 609* (80): 1.

18. Begley, T.M. and Boyd, D.P. (1986) 'Psychological characteristics associated with entrepreneurial performance', in Ronstadt, R., Hornaday, J.A., Peterson, R. and Vesper, K.H. (eds) *Frontiers of Entrepreneurship Research*, Wellesley, Mass.: Babson College, Center for Entrepreneurial Studies, pp. 146–165. See also, Chell and Burrows, R. (1991) 'The small business owner-manager', in Stanworth, J. and Grey, C. *Bolton 20 Years On*, London: Paul Chapman, esp. pp. 159–160.

19. Birley, S. and Westhead, P. (1994) 'A taxonomy of business start up reasons and their impact on firm growth and size, *Journal of Business Venturing*, 9 (1): 7–31.

20. Kolvereid, L. (1996) 'Organizational employment versus self-employment: reasons for career choice intentions'. *Entrepreneurship Theory and Practice* (spring): 23–31.

21. Maslow, A.H. (1943) 'A theory of human motivation', *Psychological Review*, 50 (4): 370–96. Maslow's work was in fact pre-dated by that of Murray.

22. Hofstede, G. (1980) 'Motivation, leadership and organization: do american theories apply abroad? *Organization Dynamics*, 9 (1): 42–63.

23. Porter, L.W. and Lawler, E.E. (1968) *Managerial Attitudes and Performance,*

Homewood, Ill.: Irwin-Dorsey. See also, Chell, E. (1993) *The Psychology of Behaviour in Organizations*, 2nd edn, London: Macmillan, pp. 73–77.

24. Adams, J.S. (1965) 'Inequity in social exchange', In Berkowitz, L. (ed) *Advances in Experimental Social Psychology*, vol. 2. New York: Academic Press. pp. 267–300.

25. This specific point of comparison with another is an important part of Adams' equity theory which is not picked up by Naffziger, D.W, Hornsby, J.S. and Kuratko, D. F 'A proposed research model of entrepreneurial motivation', *Entrepreneurship, Theory and Practice* (spring): 37–8.

26. Mintzberg, H. (1973) *The Nature of Managerial Work*, New York: Harper & Row. Mintzberg suggests the types of role are interpersonal, informational and decisional.

27. Miner, J.B. (1993) *Role Motivation Theories*, London & New York: Routledge.

28. *Ibid.* p. 4.

29. Chell, E, H., J. and Brearley, S. (1991) *The Entrepreneurial Personality: Concepts, Cases and Categories*, London: Routledge, esp ch. 5; Stevenson, H. *et al.* (1989) *New Business Ventures and the Entrepreneur*, 3rd edn Homewood, Ill.: Irwin.

30. McClelland, D.C. (1961) *The Achieving Society*, Princeton, N.J.: Van Nostrand.

31. Smith, N.R. and Miner, J.B. (1983) 'Type of entrepreneur, type of firm and managerial motivation, *Strategic Management Journal*, 4: 325–340.

32. Smith, N.R., Bracker, J.S. and Miner, J.B. (1987) 'Correlates of firm and entrepreneur success in technologically innovative companies, *Frontiers of Entrepreneurship Research*, 7: 337–353.

33. Bellu, R.R. (1993) 'Task role motivation and attributional style as predictors of entrepreneurial performance: female sample findings, *Entrepreneurship and Regional Development*, 5 (4): 331–344.

34. Hofstede *op. cit.*

35. Illman, P. E. (1980) 'Motivating the overseas workforce', in *Developing Overseas Managers and Managers Overseas*, New York: AMACOM, 83–106; Adler, N.J. (1997) *International Dimensions of Organizational Behavior*, 3rd edn, Cincinnati, Ohio: South Western College Publishing, esp. p. 166.

36. Welsch, H. (1998) 'America: North', in Morrison, A. (ed) *Entrepreneurship: An International Perspective*, Oxford: Butterworth-Heinemann, ch. 5, pp. 58–75.

37. Miner, J.B. (1986) *Scoring Guide for Miner Sentence Completion Scale-Form T*, Buffalo, New York: Organizational Measurement Systems Press.

38. McClelland, D. (1961) *The Achieving Society*, Princeton, New Jersey: Van Nostrand.

39. This case is inspired by a case study in Morrison *op. cit.* pp 88–90.

40. McGregor, D.M. (1960) *The Human Side of Enterprise*, New York: McGraw-Hill.

41. Herzberg, F. Mausner, B. and Snyderman, B. (1959) *The Motivation to Work*, New York: Wiley.

42. Locke, E. and Latham G.P. (1990) *A Theory of Goal Setting and Task Performance*, Englewood Cliffs, New Jersey: Prentice-Hall.

43. Granovetter, M. (1973) 'The strength of "weak ties"', *American Journal of Sociology*, 78: 1360–1380.
44. Chell, E. (1985) 'The entrepreneurial personality: a few ghosts laid to rest?' *International Small Business Journal*, 3 (30):43–54.
45. Perrow, C. (1992) 'Small Firm Networks', in Nohria, N. and Eccles, G. (eds) *Networks and Organizations: Structure, Form and Action*, Boston: Harvard Business School Press.
46. Dubini, P. and Aldrich, H. (1991) 'Personal and extended networks are central to the entrepreneurial process', *Journal of Business Venturing*, 6: 305–313; Birley, S., Cromie, S. and Myers, A. (1991) 'Entrepreneurial networks: their emergence in Northern Ireland and overseas', *International Small Business Journal*, 9 (4): 56–74; Johanisson, B. (1986) 'Network strategies: management technology for entrepreneurship and change', *International Small Business Journal*, 5 (1): 19–30.
47. Curran, J., Jarvis, R., Blackburn, R.A. and Black, S. (1991) 'Networks and small firms: constructs, methodological strategies and some findings', *International Small Business Journal*, 11, 2, 13–25; Curran, J. and Blackburn, R.A. (1994) *Small Firms and Local Economic Networks: The Death of the Local Economy?* London: Paul Chapman; Gray, C. (1997) 'Managing entrepreneurial growth: a question of control?' in Deakins, D., Jennings, P. and Mason, C. (eds) *Small Firms: Entrepreneurship in the Nineties*, London: Paul Chapman.
48. Chell, E. and Baines, S. (2000) 'Networking, entrepreneurship and microbusiness behaviour', *Entrepreneurship and Regional Development*, 12: 195–215.
49. Granovetter *op. cit.*
50. Dubini and Aldrich *op. cit.*

Chapter 8

1. Mackie, L. and Pattullo, P. (1977) *Women at Work*, London: Tavistock.
2. Pennington, S. and Westover, B. (1989) *A Hidden Workforce, Homeworkers in England, 1850–1985*, Houndsmills: Macmillan.
3. Oakley, A. (1974, 1985) *The Sociology of Housework*, Oxford: Blackwell; Oakley, A. (1976) *Housewife*, Harmondsworth: Penguin.
4. Pennington and Westover, *op. cit.*
5. Rees, T. (1992) *Women and the Labour Market*, London & New York: Routledge.
6. Rees, T. *Ibid.* reviews critically a number of theories, for example Parsons' functionalist interpretation of gender and family roles and a variety of feminist theoretical perspectives, including Marxist feminism, in which Engels argues the need for the abolition of the family in order to achieve equality between the sexes. Patriarchy is seen as an important element in the ideology of the family. Dual systems theory goes one step further by distinguishing between a sex-gender system (patriarchy) and an economic system (capitalism) and the interaction between them. Patriarchy is the dynamic driving force, which can exist in other economic systems. It is a system of male domination and exploitation. However, as a system it has

changed and it is this dynamic nature that enables an explanation to be given of the fact that 'not every individual man is in a dominant position and every single woman in a subordinate one' p.32

7. Burrows, R. (ed) (1991) *Deciphering the Enterprise Culture: Entrepreneurship, Petty Capitalism and the Restructuring of Business*, London: Routledge; Gray, C. (1998) *Enterprise and Culture,* London and New York: Routledge, esp. ch.2.
8. Rees, T. (1992) *Women and the Labour Market*, London & New York: Routledge, esp. ch.8.
9. Curran, J. and Roberts, L. (1989), 'Why single-minded operators reap rewarding benefits', *Guardian* 28 March.
10. Williams, S. (2000) 'The rise of she-commerce', *Telegraph Magazine*, 18 March pp. 39–43.
11. Gracie, S. (1998) 'In the company of women', *Management Today*, June pp. 66–70.
12. Cm 4176 (1998) *Our Competitive Future: Building the Knowledge Driven Economy*, London, Department of Trade and Industry: The Stationery Office Ltd.
13. Smith, N.R. (1967) *The Entrpreneur and his Firm: The Relationship between Type of Man and Type of Company*, East Lansing, Michigan: Michigan State University Press; Carland, J.W., Hoy, F., Boulton, W.R. and Carland, J.A.C. (1984) 'Differentiating entrepreneurs from small business owners: a conceptualization', *Academy of Management Review* 9 (2): 354–9; Hornaday, R.W. (1990) 'Dropping the E-words from small business research', *Journal of Small Business Management*, 28 pp. 22–33.
14. Goffee, R. and Scase, R. (1985) *Women in Charge*, London: George Allen and Unwin.
15. Carter, S. and Cannon, T. (1992) *Female Entrepreneurs,* research paper no. 65., Department of Employment, London: HMSO.
16. Dyer, W. Gibb and Handler, W. (1994) 'Entrepreneurship and family business: exploring the connections', *Entrepreneurship, Theory and Practice*, 19, 1 (fall): 71–83.
17. Chell, E. and Baines, S. (1998) 'Does gender affect business "performance"? a study of microbusinesses in business services in the UK', *Entrepreneurship and Regional Development*, 10:117–135.
18. *Ibid.* p.121.
19. *Ibid.* p.125.
20. *Ibid.* p. 126.
21. Hofstede, G. (1991) *Cultures and Organizations*, London: McGraw-Hill.
22. Carter and Cannon, (1992) *op. cit.*
23. See discussion in previous section. See Goffee, R. and Scase, R. (1985) *Women in Charge*, London: Allen & Unwin; Carland, J. W., Hoy, F. Boulton, W.R. and Carland, J.A.C. (1984) 'Differentiating entrepreneurs from small business owners: a conceptualisation', *Academy of Management Review*, 9: 354–9.
24. Perrow, C. (1972) *Complex Organizations: a Critical Essay*, Glenview, Ill.: Scott, Foresman; Dyer, W.G. (1994) 'Potential contributions of organiza-

tional behaviour to the study of family owned businesses', *Family Business Review*, 7 (2): 109–131.

25. Foley, S. and Powell, G.N. (1997) 'Reconceptualizing work-family conflict for business/marriage partnerships: a theoretical model', *Journal of Small Business Management*, 35 (4): 36–47.

26. *Ibid*. p. 37.

27. Foley and Powell *op. cit.*; Marshack, K.J. (1994) 'Co-preneurs and dual-career couples: are they different? *Entrepreneurship, Theory and Practice*, 19 (fall): 49–69.

28. Dyer, W.G. and Handler, W. (1994) 'Entrepreneurship and family business: exploring the connections', *Entrepreneurship Theory and Practice*. 19 (1): 71–83.

29. In chapter 4 the case of Anita Roddick and her attempts to attract a bank loan are discussed.

Chapter 9

1. Taylor, F.W. (1947) *Scientific Management*, New York: Harper.

2. Ritzer, G. (1996) *The McDonaldization of Society*, Thousand Oaks, Calif.: Pine Forge Press, rev edn, p.1.

3. Fayol, H. (1930) *Industrial and General Administration*, Geneva International Management Institute.

4. Weber, M. (1947) *Economy and Society*, New York: Bedminster.

5. Burns, T. and Stalker, G.M. (1961) *The Management of Innovation*, London: Tavistock.

6. Parker Follett, M. (1941) *Collected Works*, New York: Harper.

7. Mayo, E., Roethlisberger, F.J. and Dickson, W.J. (1939) *Management and the Worker*, Cambridge, Mass.: Harvard University Press.

8. Rice, A.K. *Productivity and Social Organization – The Ahmedabad Experiment*, London: Tavistock.

9. Katz, D. and Kahn, R.L. (1966) *The Social Psychology of Organizations*, New York: Wiley.

10. Child, J. (1984) *Organization: A Guide to Problems and Practice*, London: Harper and Row.

11. Drucker, P.F. (1979) *Management*, London: Pan Books.

12. Peters, T. (1987) *Thriving on Chaos*, London: Pan Books.

13. Ouchi, W.G. (1981) *Theory Z*, Reading, Mass.: Addison-Wesley; Peters, T.J. and Waterman, R.H. (1982) *In Search of Excellence*, New York: Harper & Row.

14. Handy, C. (1985) *Understanding Organizations*, 3rd edn, Harmondsworth: Penguin.

15. Stewart, R. (1967) *Managers and Their Jobs*, London: Macmillan (paperback edn Pan, 1970).

16 Mintzberg, H. (1973) *The Nature of Managerial Work*, New York: Harper & Row.

17. Chell, E. and Rhodes, H. (1998) *An Investigation of the Relationship Between Owner-Managers and the First Line Manager and its Effect on Business*

Performance In SMEs, Centre for the Study of Entrepreneurship, University of Newcastle.

18. Berger, P.L. and Luckmann, T. (1967) *The Social Construction of Reality*, London: Penguin; Weick, K.E. (1995) *Sensemaking in Organizations*, Thousand Oaks, Ca.: Sage. See also, Chell, E. (2000) 'Towards researching the "opportunistic entrepreneur": a social constructionist approach and research agenda', *European Journal of Work and Organizational Psychology*, 9 (1): 63–80.

19. Bird, B. (1988) 'Implementing entrepreneurial ideas: the case of intention', *Academy of Management Review*, 13 (3):442–453.

20. Chell, E., Haworth, J. and Brearley, S. (1991) *The Entrepreneurial Personality: Concepts, Cases and Categories*, London: Routledge; Shackle, G.L.S. (1975) *Imagination and the Nature of Choice*, Edinburgh: Edinburgh University Press.

21. Adair, J. (1989) *Great Leaders*, Guildford, Surrey: Talbot Adair Press.

22. Bales, R.F. (1950) 'A set of categories for the analysis of small group interaction', *American Sociological Review*, 15: 257–63. See also, Chell, E. (1985) *Participation and Organization A Social Psychological Approach*, London: Macmillan, esp. ch. 5.

23. Halpin, A.W. and Winer, B.J. (1957) 'A factorial study of the leader behaviour descriptions', in Stogdill, R.M. and Coons, A.E. (eds) *Leader Behaviour: its Description and Measurement*, Columbus: Ohio State University, Bureau of Business Research;. Hemphill, J.K. and Coons, A.E. (1957) 'Development of the leader behaviour description questionnaire', in Stogdill and Coons, *op. cit.*

24. Bryman, A. (1986) *Leadership and Organizations*, London: Routledge & Kegan Paul.

25. Blake R.R. and Mouton, J.S. (1964) *The Managerial Grid: Key Orientations for Achieving Production Through People*, Houston: Gulf.

26. Fiedler, F.E. (1967) *A Theory of Leadership Effectiveness*, New York: McGraw-Hill.

27. Smith, P.B. and Peterson, M.F. (1988) *Leadership, Organizations and Culture*. London: Sage.

28. House, R. J. (1971) A path-goal theory of leadership effectiveness. *Administrative Science Quarterly*, 16: 321–8.

29. Tannembaum, R. and Schmidt, W. (1973) 'How to choose a leadership pattern', *Harvard Business Review*, May-June.

30. Maier, N.R.F. (1963) *Problem-solving Discussions and Conferences: Leadership Methods and Skills*, New York: McGraw-Hill; Maier, N.R.F. (1970) *Problem-solving and Creativity in Individuals and Groups*, Belmont, Calif.: Brooks Cole.

31. Vroom, V.H. and Yetton, P.W. (1973) *'Leadership and Decision making'*. Pittsburgh, Pa.: University of Pittsburgh Press.

32. Vroom, V.H. (1984) 'Leadership and decision making', *Osaka University 50th Anniversary International Symposium on Democratization and Leadership in Industrial Organizations*, Osaka University: Japan.

33. Hersey, P. and Blanchard, K. (1982) *Management of Organizational Behaviour: Utilising Human Resources*, Englewood Cliffs, N.J: Prentice-Hall.

34. Weber, M. (1947) *The Theory of Social and Economic Organizations*, New York: The Free Press.
35. Burns, J.M. (1978) *Leadership*, New York: Harper & Row.
36. Adair, J. (1989) *Great Leaders*, Guildford: Talbot Adair Press.
37. Bass, B.M. (1985) *Leadership and Performance Beyond Expectations*, New York: The Free Press; Bass, B.M. (1998) *Transformational Leadership: Industrial, Military and Educational Impact*, Mahwah, N.J.: Lawrence Erlbaum Associates.
38. Handy, C. (1990) 'The language of leadership', reproduced in Syrett, M. and Hogg (eds) *Frontiers of Leadership – An Essential Reader*, Oxford: Blackwell, pp. 7–12.
39. Kotter, J. P. (1990) 'What leaders really do', *Harvard Business Review*, May-June, reproduced in Syrett, M and Hogg, C. *op. cit.*
40. Watson, C.M. (1983) 'Leadership, management and the seven keys', *Business Horizons*, March-April, reproduced in Syrett, M. and Hogg, C. (1990) *op. cit.*
41. Hunt, J.G. (1991) *Leadership: A New Synthesis*, Newbury Park: Sage.
42. Tichy, N.M. and Devanna, M.A. (1986) *The Transformational Leader*, New York: Wiley.
43. Chell, E. *et al.* (1991) *The Entrepreneurial Personality: Concepts, Cases and Categories*, London: Routledge, see esp. p.71.
44. Conger, J.A. (1989) *The Charismatic Leader: Behind the Mystique of Exceptional Leadership*, San Francisco: Jossey-Bass.
45. Chell, E. *et al.*, *op. cit.*; Chell, E. (2000) *op. cit.*
46. Sashkin, M. (1988) 'The visionary leader', in Konger, J.A. and Kanungo, R.N. (eds) *Charismatic Leadership*, San Francisco: Jossey-Bass, pp. 122–160.
47. Kotter, J.P. (1982) 'What effective general managers really do', *Harvard Business Review*, 60: 156–167.
48. Kotter, J.P. (1990) *A Force for Change: How Leadership Differs from Management*, New York: The Free Press.
49. Hunt, J. G. (1991) *Leadership: A New Synthesis*, Newbury Park: Sage.
50. Gouillart, F.J. and Kelly, J.N. (1995) *Transforming the Organization*, New York: McGraw-Hill.
51. Boyatzis, R.E. (1982) *The Competent Manager*, New York: Wiley.
52. Cosh, A., Duncan, J. and Hughes, A. (1998) *Investment in Training and Small Firm Growth and Survival: An Empirical Study for the UK 1987–95*, DfEE Research Report No. 36, London: HMSO.
53. Westhead, P. and Storey, D.J. (1996) 'Management training and small firm performance: why is the link so weak?', *International Small Business Journal*, 14: 13–24; Westhead, P. and Storey, D.J. (1997) *Training Provision and the Development of Small and Medium-sized Enterprises*, DfEE Research Report No. 26, London: HMSO.
54. Amos, E. (1998) 'Training and Development in the Middle Market – Can it Pay?', paper presented at the seminar Assessing the Impact of Training on the Performance of Small and Medium-sized Enterprises, Coventry, UK.: Warwick Business School, University of Warwick.
55. For example, Peters, T. and Waterman, R.H. Jr. (1987) *In Search of Excellence*, New York: Harper Row.

56. EFQM – European Foundation for Quality Management; http://www.efqm.org/htm

57. See, Syrett, M. and Hogg, C. (eds) *Frontiers of Leadership An Essential Reader*, Oxford: Blackwell, esp. chs. 12 & 13.

Chapter 10

1. Vyarkarnam, S., Jacobs, R. and Handelberg, J. (1999) 'Exploring the formation of entrepreneurial teams: the key to rapid growth businesses?', *Journal of Small Business and Enterprise Development*, 6 (2):153–165; Lechler, T. and Gemuenden, H.G. (1999), 'Social interaction: a determinant of entrepreneurial team venture success', awarded the 'best paper award' and presented at the RENT Conference, (IEASM/ECSB) London, November.

2. *Ibid.*

3. Baliga, B.R. and Hunt, J.G. (1988) 'An organization life cycle approach to leadership', in J.G. Hunt *et al.*, *Emerging Leadership Vistas*, Lexington: Mass.: D.C. Heath & Co. pp. 129–149.

4. Stewart, R. (1982) *Choices for the Manager*, Englewood Cliffs, N.J.: Prentice Hall.

5. Chell, E. (1993) *The Psychology of Behaviour in Organizations,* 2nd edn, London: Macmillan, esp. ch.5.

6. Mayo, E. (1949) *Hawthorne and the Western Electric Company: The Social Problems of an Industrial Civilisation*, London: Routledge.

7. Crouch, A. and Yetton, P. (1988) 'The management team: an equilibrium model of management performance and behavior, in J.G. Hunt *et al. Energising Leadership Vistas*, Lexington, Mass.: D.C. Heath & Co. 107–128.

8. Zander, A. (1982) *Making Groups Effective*, San Francisco: Jossey-Bass; Chell, E. (1993) *The Psychology of Behaviour in Organizations,* 2nd edn, London: Macmillan, pp. 89–90.

9. Janis, I.L. (1971) 'Groupthink', *Psychology Today* (November), reprinted in J.R. Hackman *et al.* (1977) *Perspectives on Behaviour in Organizations*, New York: McGraw-Hill; Janis, I.L. (1972) *Victims of Groupthink*, Boston, Mass.: Houghton Mifflin.

10. Peters, T. (1987) *Thriving on Chaos*, London: Pan Books.

11. Kanter, R.M. (1983) *The Change Masters*, London: Unwin.

12. McGregor, D.M. (1960) *The Human Side of Enterprise*, New York: McGraw-Hill; Zander, A. (1982) *Making Groups Effective*, San Francisco: Jossey-Bass; Chaudry-Lawton, R. *et al.* (1992) *Quality: Change Through Teamwork*, London: Century Business Books.

13. Tsosvold, D. (1991) *Team Organization: An Enduring Competitive Advantage*, Chichester: Wiley.

14. Chaudry-Lawton, R. *et al.* (1992) *Quality: Change through Teamwork*, London: Century Business Books, p. 267.

15. The reader should refer to chapter 15 of this volume for a more extensive discussion of quality issues and business performance.

16. Hutchins, D. (1985) *Quality Circles Handbook*, London: Pitman.

17. Hill, S. (1991) 'Why quality circles failed but total quality might succeed', *British Journal of Industrial Relations*, 29 (4): 541–568.

18. Weick, K.E. and Roberts, K.H. (1993) 'Collective mind in organizations: heedful interrelating on flight decks', *Administrative Science Quarterly*, 38: 357–381.
19. See earlier section, pp. 203–204.
20. McGrath, R.G., MacMillan, I.C. and Venkataraman, S. (1995) 'Defining and developing competence: a strategic process paradigm', *Strategic Management Journal*, 16: 251–275.
21. Adler, N. (1997) *International Dimensions of Organizational Behavior*, 3rd edn, Cincinnati, Ohio.: South Western College Publishing, esp. ch.5.
22. *Ibid.* p. 138.
23. Maznevski, M.L. and Peterson, M.K. (1997) 'Societal values, social interpretation and multinational teams', in Skromme Granrose, C. and Oskamp, S., (eds) *Cross-Cultural Work Groups*, Thousand Oaks, Calif.: Sage, pp 61–89.
24. Maznevski, M.L. (1994) 'Understanding our differences: performance in decision making groups with diverse members', *Human Relations*, 47 (5): 531–52.
25. Chell, E. (1993) *The Psychology of Behaviour in Organizations*, London: Macmillan, ch. 5. pp. 107–127.
26. Belbin, M. (1981) *Management Teams – Why they Succeed or Fail*, London: Heinemann; discussed in Chell, E. *The Psychology of Behaviour in Organizations*, London: Macmillan, pp. 115–123.
27. Belbin, M. (1993) *Team Roles at Work*, Oxford: Butterworth-Heinemann, p. 58.
28. See, Chell, E. *et al.* (1991) *The Entrepreneurial Personality: Concepts, Cases and Categories*, London: Routledge.

Chapter 11

1. Ford, C.M. (1995) 'Creativity is a mystery: clues from an investigator's notebooks' in Ford, C.M. and Gioia, D.A. (eds) *Creative Action in Organizations*, Thousand Oaks, Calif.: Sage, p. 17.
2. Research evidence is equivocal, however see Ford (1995) for a summary.
3. Gioia, D.A. (1995) 'Contrasts and convergences in creativity; themes in academic and practitioner views', in Ford and Gioia *op. cit.*, p. 325.
4. Ford, C.M. (1995) 'Striking inspirational sparks and fanning creative flames. A multi-domain model of creative action taking' in Ford and Gioia *op. cit.*, pp. 330–354.
5. Schumpeter, J.A. (1934) *The Theory of Economic Development*, Cambridge, Mass.: Harvard University Press.
6. *Ibid.*, p. 78.
7. Chell, E., Haworth, J.M. and Brearley, S.A. (1991) *The Entrepreneurial Personality: Concepts, Cases and Categories*, London: Routledge, esp. pp. 21–23.
8. Kanter, R.M. (1983) *The Change Masters*, London: Unwin.
9. West, M.A. (1997) *Developing Creativity in Organizations*, Leicester: BPS, p. 3.
10. Abernathy, W.J. and Clark, K.B. (1988) 'Innovation: mapping the winds of

creative destruction' in Tushman, M.L. and Moore, W.L. (eds) *Readings in the Management of Innovation,* 2nd edn, Cambridge, Mass.: Ballinger, pp. 55–78.

11. See Chell *et al. op. cit.,* esp. pp. 107–114.
12. Roddick, A. (1991) *Body and Soul*, London: Vermilion, esp. ch. 1.
13. Van de Ven, A.H. (1988) 'Central problems in the management of innovation', in Tushman and Moore *op. cit.,* pp. 103–122.
14. Galbraith, J.R. (1982) 'Designing the innovating organization', *Organizational Dynamics* (winter): 3–24.
15. Chell *et al. op. cit.,* p. 118.
16. Chell *et al. op. cit.,* p. 119.
17. West, M.A. (1990) 'The social psychology of innovation in groups', in West, M.A. and Farr, J.L. (eds) *Innovation and Creativity at Work,* Chichester: Wiley, pp. 309–330.
18. *Ibid.,* p. 310.
19. *Ibid.* p. 311.
20. *Ibid.* p. 315.
21. *Ibid.* p. 313.
22. West 1997 *op. cit.*
23. West 1997 *op. cit.,* esp. pp. 56–9.
24. Kuhn, R.L. (1989) *Creativity and Strategy in Mid-Sized Firms,* Englewood-Cliffs, New Jersey: Prentice-Hall.
25. *Ibid.,* p. 245.
26. Vroom, V. and Yetton, P.W. (1973) *Leadership and Decision making,* Pittsburgh: Pittsburgh University Press. See also, Chell, E. (1993) *The Psychology of Behaviour in Organizations,* 2nd edn, London: Macmillan, pp. 149–152.
27. Kuhn, R.L. (1989) *Creativity and Strategy in Mid-Sized Firms,* Englewood-Cliffs, N.J.: Prentice Hall, pp. 250–1.
28. Kanter *op. cit.*
29. Kanter R.M. (1988) 'Change-master skills: what it takes to be creative', in Kuhn, R.L. (ed) *Handbook for Creative Managers,* New York: McGraw-Hill.
30. Tushman, M.L., Anderson, P. C. and O'Reilly, C. (1997) 'Technology cycles, innovation streams and ambidextrous organizations: organizational renewal through innovation streams and strategic change', in Tushman, M.L. and Anderson, P.C. (eds) *Managing Strategic Innovation and Change,* Oxford: Oxford University Press.
31. Burns, T. and Stalker, G.M. (1961) *The Management of Innovation,* London: Tavistock.
32. Kim, W.C. and Mauborgne, R. (1999) 'Strategy, value innovation, and the knowledge economy', *Sloan Management Review,* 40 (3): 41–54.
33. *Ibid.* p. 45.
34. Kim and Mauborgne go on to argue that the concept of value innovation is consistent with the Schumpeterian notion of 'creative destruction', but suggest one fundamentally important difference, which is that ideas can come from anywhere, whereas for Schumpeter (1934) the entrepreneur is the major factor in creating innovation. This seems to be a spurious distinction. As discussed earlier in this chapter and illustrated in Box 11.1 –

VSW Scientific Instruments – entrepreneurs may be adept at combining other people's ideas in order to create something new. As such they act as catalysts. Further, it is named individuals such as Bill Gates, Anita Roddick, Richard Branson, Nicholas Hayek and Hasso Plattner who have developed an entrepreneurial strategy of value innovation in order to create wealth and give their business a dominant position in the marketplace. However, it may be conceded that the nature of the monopolies created through value innovation does show some different features from the traditional economic view of the monopoly/monopolist. This is a strong argument for suggesting that value innovation is a key entrepreneurial act and a major strategy in the process of successful entrepreneurship.

35. DTI (1998) *Our Competitive Future: Building the Knowledge Driven Economy*, Cm 4176, London: The Stationery Office.
36. Gates B. (1995) *The Road Ahead*, London: Penguin Books.

Chapter 12

1. Handy, C. (1995), *Beyond Certainty: The Changing World of Organizations*, London: Hutchinson.
2. Burns, T. and Stalker, G.M. (1961) *The Management of Innovation*, London: Tavistock.
3. Mintzberg, H. (1983) *Structure in Fives: Designing Effective Organizations*, Englewood Cliffs, New Jersey: Prentice-Hall.
4. Kanter, R.M. (1983) *The Change Masters: Corporate Entrepreneurs at Work*, London: Unwin.
5. Snow, C.S., Miles, R.E. and Coleman, H.J. (1992) 'Managing 21st Century network organizations', *Organization Dynamics*, 20: 5–16.
6. Franke, U.J. (1999) 'The virtual web as a new entrepreneurial approach to network organizations', *Entrepreneurship and Regional Development*, 11 (3): 203–229.
7. Quoted in Franke *Ibid.*, p. 213.
8. *cf.* the case study of VSW in Chell, E. *et al.* (1991) *The Entrepreneurial Personality: Concepts, Cases and Categories*, London: Routledge, pp. 115–121.
9. Barnatt, C. (1997) 'Virtual organization in the small business centre: the case of Cavendish Management Resources', *International Small Business Journal*, 15 (4): 36–47.
10. *Ibid.*, p. 37.
11. See Barnatt *op. cit.*
12. Storey. D.J. (1994) *Understanding the Small Business Sector*, London and New York: Routledge.
13. *Ibid.*, pp. 119–20.
14. Cooper, A.C. (1982) 'The entrepreneurship-small business interface' in C.A. Kent, D.L. Sexton and K.H. Vesper (eds) *Encyclopedia of Entrepreneurship*, Englewood Cliffs, New Jersey: Prentice-Hall, 10: 193–208.
15. Greiner, L.E. (1972) 'Evolution and revolution as organizations grow', *Harvard Business Review*, July/August; Scott, M. and Bruce, R. (1987) 'Five

stages of growth in small business', *Long Range Planning*, 20 (3): 45–52; Churchill, N. and Lewis, V.L. (1983) 'The five stages of small business growth', *Harvard Business Review* (May-June).

16. Churchill, N.C. (1983) 'Entrepreneurs and their enterprises: a stage model', in Hornaday, J.A., Timmons, J.A. and Vesper, K.H. (eds) *Frontiers of Entrepreneurship Research*, Wellesley, Mass.: Babson College, Centre for Entrepreneurial Studies, pp. 1–22.

17. Churchill, N. (1997) 'The six key phases of company growth', in Birley. S. and Muzyka, D.F. *Mastering Enterprise*, London: FT Pitman Publishing, pp. 213–219.

18. *Ibid.*, p. 214.

19. Flamholtz, E.G. (1986) *How to Make the Transition from an Entrepreneurship to a Professionally Managed Firm*, San Francisco: Jossey-Bass, p. 35.

20. Kazanjian, R.K. (1984) 'Operationalising stage of growth: an empirical assessment of dominant problems', in Hornaday, J.A., Tarperley, F., Timmons, J.A., and Vesper, K.H. (eds) *Frontiers of Entrepreneurship Research*, Wellesley, Mass.: Babson College, Centre for Entrepreneurial Studies, pp. 144–58.

21. Bolton, W. (1997) *The University Handbook on Enterprise Development*, Paris Cedex: Columbus.

22. Greiner, L.E. (1972), 'Evolution and revolution as organizations grow', *Harvard Business Review* July/August.

23. Scott and Bruce (1987) *op. cit.* 20 (3): 47.

24. Hendry, C. *et al.* (1991) *Human Resource Development in Small and Medium Sized Enterprises*, London: Department for Employment Research Paper No. 88; Chell, E. (1998) 'The critical incidence technique', in Cassell, C. and Symon, G. (eds) *Qualitative Methods and Analysis in Organisational Research*, London: Sage ch.4.

25. Storey, D.J. (1994) *Understanding the Small Business Sector*, London: Routledge, p. 122.

26. Chell, E., Haworth, J.M. and Brearley, S. (1991) *The Entrepreneurial Personality: Concepts, Cases and Categories*, London: Routledge.

27. *Ibid.*, p. 72.

28. *Ibid.*, esp. pp. 71–74.

29. Perren, L. (2000) 'Factors in the growth of micro-enterprises (part 1): developing a framework', *Journal of Small Business and Enterprise Development*, 6 (4):366–385.

30. *Ibid.*, p. 376.

31. Dubini, P. and Aldrich, H. 1991 'Personal and extended networks are central to the entrepreneurial process', *Journal of Business Venturing*, 6:305–313; Chell, E. and Baines, S. (2000) 'Networking, entrepreneurship and microbusiness behaviour', *Entrepreneurship and Regional Development*, 12 (1): 1–21.

32. See, Chell, E. (2000) 'Towards researching the "opportunistic entrepreneur": a social constructionist approach and research agenda', *European Journal of Work and Organizational Psychology*, 9 (1): 65–82.

33. *Ibid.*

34. *op. cit.* p. 382.

Chapter 13

1. Shackle, G.L.S. (1967) *The Years of High Theory*, Cambridge, UK: Cambridge University Press.
2. Quinn, J.B. (1980) *Strategies for Change: Logical Incrementalism*, Homewood, Illinois: Irwin.
3. *Ibid.*
4. Mintzberg, H. and Walters, J. A. (1985) 'Of strategies, deliberate and emergent', *Strategic Management Journal*, 6: 257–72.
5. Schneider, S.C. and Barsoux, J-L (1997) *Managing Across Cultures*, Hemel Hempstead: Prentice Hall, pp. 106–127; Schneider, S.C. (1989) 'Strategy formulation: the impact of national culture', *Organization Studies*, 10 (2): 149–68.
6. Pascale, R.T. (1984) 'Perspectives on strategy: the real story behind Honda's success', *California Management Review*, 26 (3): 47–72.
7. See Schneider and Barsoux *op. cit.*, who refer to 'defender' and 'prospector' types in Miles, R.E. and Snow, C.C. (1987) *Organizational Strategy, Structure and Process*, New York: McGraw-Hill; Miles, R.E. and Snow, C.C. (1984), 'Designing strategic human resource systems', *Organization Dynamics*, (summer); see, also, chapter 6 in this volume.
8. Houlden, B. (1990) *Understanding Company Strategy – an Introduction to Thinking and Acting Strategically*, Oxford: Blackwell, p. 43.
9. See chapter 2.
10. Stevenson, H.H., Roberts, M.J. and Grousebeck, H.I. (1989) *New Business Ventures and the Entrepreneur*, 3rd edn, Homewood Ill.: Irwin.
11. Porter, M.E. (1980) *Competitive Strategy: Techniques for Analysing Industries and Competitors*, New York: The Free Press, p. 4.
12. Porter, M.E. (1990) *The Competitive Advantage of Nations*, London: Macmillan.
13. Houlden *op. cit.*, p. 46.
14. Bird, B. (1988) 'Implementing entrepreneurial ideas: the case for intention', *Academy of Management Review*, 13 (3): 442–453.
15. Mintzberg, H. (1987) 'Five Ps for strategy', *California Management Review* (Fall); Jenkins, M. and Johnson, G. (1997) 'Entrepreneurial intentions and outcomes: a comparative causal mapping study', *Journal of Management Studies*, 34 (6): 895–920.
16. Stevenson *et al. op. cit.*, p. 7.
17. Kuhn, R.L. (1989) *Creativity and Strategy in Mid-Sized Firms*, Englewood Cliffs, New Jersey: Prentice-Hall.
18. Porter, M.E. (1980) *Competitive Strategy*, New York: The Free Press.
19. Chell, E., Haworth, J. and Brearley, S. (1991) *The Entrepreneurial Personality: Concepts, Cases and Categories*, London: Routledge.
20. *Ibid.* pp. 107–115.
21. Schumpeter, J.A. (1934) *The Theory of Economic Development*, Cambridge, Mass.: Harvard University Press.
22. See chapter 11 of this volume for a more detailed discussion of the concepts of 'creativity' and 'innovation'.

23. Slevin, D.P. and Covin, J.G. (1995) 'New ventures and total competitiveness: a conceptual model, empirical results and case study examples,' paper presented at the Babson College-Kauffman Foundation Entrepreneurship Research Conference, London Business School, UK, 9–12 April.
24. See chapter 14 of this volume.
25. Slevin and Covin *op. cit.*
26. Burns, T. and Stalker, G.M. (1961) *The Management of Innovation*, London: Tavistock.
27. Covin, J.G and Slevin, D.P. 'The strategic management of small firms in hostile and benign environments', *Strategic Management Journal*, 10: 75–87; Miller, D. and Friesen P. H. 'Innovation in conservative and entrepreneurial firms: two models of strategic momentum', *Strategic Management Journal*, 3: 1–25.
28. See chapter 15 of this volume.
29. Porter *op. cit.*
30. McGregor, D.M. (1960) *The Human Side of Enterprise*, New York: McGraw-Hill.
31. Tsosvold, T. (1991) *Team Organization: An Enduring Competitive Advantage.* Chichester: Wiley.
32. See chapter 12 of this volume.
33. See chapter 1 of this volume.
34. See also chapter 2 of this volume.
35. Based on Fahey, L. (1989) *The Strategic Planning Management Reader*, Englewood Cliffs, New Jersey: Prentice-Hall.
36. See also chapter 2 in this volume.
37. Fifer, R.M. (1985) 'Understanding your competitor's functional strategies', *Strategic Planning Management*, February, reproduced in Fahey *op. cit.*, pp. 68–72.
38. Isenman, A.W. (1986) 'Managing suppliers: the strategic implications', *Strategic Planning Management*, December, reproduced in Fahey *op. cit.*, pp. 90–95.
39. Deming. W. E. (1982) *Out of the Crisis*, Cambridge University Press.
40. *op. cit.*
41. Herring, J. (1986) 'Strategic alliances: a new competitive force,' *Strategic Planning Management*, May, reproduced in Fahey, *op. cit.*, pp. 102–108.
42. Chell, E., Haworth, J.M. and Brearley, S. (1991) *The Entrepreneurial Personality: Concepts, Cases and Categories*, London: Routledge.
43. Dysart, J.A. (1983) 'Strategies for stagnant businesses', *Strategic Planning Management*, January, reproduced in Fahey *op. cit.*, pp. 145–151.
44. Stasch, S.F. and Ward, J.L. (1984) 'Strategies for small-share firms in mature markets', *Strategic Planning Management*, July/August, reproduced in Fahey *op. cit.*, pp. 151–155.
45. Louden, T. (1984) 'Entry strategies in emerging markets', *Strategic Planning Management*, May/June, reproduced in Fahey *op. cit.*, pp. 156–164.
46. Hofer, C.W. (1983) 'Strategies for business turnarounds', *Strategic Planning Management*, July/August, reproduced in Fahey *op. cit.*, pp. 164–173.

47. Fahey, L. (1985) 'Frontal strategies: attacking competitors', *Strategic Planning Management*, August, reproduced in Fahey *op. cit.*, pp. 178–181.

48. Fahey, L. (1985) 'Flanking strategies: competition by avoidance', *Strategic Planning Management*, October, reproduced in. Fahey *op. cit.*, pp. 181–185.

49. Hofer, C.W. and Chrisman, J.J. (1986) 'The strategic management of first diversificiation: a new perspective', *Strategic Planning Management* (August).

50. Rosa, P. and Scott, M. (1999) 'Entrepreneurial diversification, business-cluster formation and growth', *Environment and Planning c: Government and Policy* 17 (5):527–548.

Chapter 14

1. Storey, J. (1989) 'Introduction: from personnel management to human resource management' in Storey, J. (ed), *New Perspectives in Human Resource Management,* London: Routledge, pp. 1–18.

2. *Ibid*. p.6.

3. See, however, Hendry, C. *et al.* (1991) *Human Resource Development in Small to Medium Sized Enterprises*, London: Employment Department Research Paper Series no. 88.

4. McGregor, D.M. (1960) *The Human Side of Enterprise*, New York: McGraw-Hill.

5. Curran, J. (1988) 'Employment and employment relations in the small enterprise: a review', *London Business School Small Business Bibliography*, London: London Business School Library; is Stanworth, J. and Gray, C. (1991) in *Bolton 20 Years On* London: Paul Chapman, pp. 190–208.

6. Guest, D.E. (1989) 'Human resource management: its implications for industrial relations and trades unions', in Storey *op. cit.* pp. 41–55.

7. Legge, K. (1989) 'HRM: a critical analysis', in Storey *op. cit.* pp. 19–40.

8. Bolton Report (1971) *Report of the Committee of Inquiry on Small Firms*, chaired by J.E. Bolton, Cmnd. 4811, London: HMSO.

9. *Ibid*. p.21.

10. Sisson, K. (1997), 'Change and continuity in British industrial relations: "Strategic Choice" or "Muddling Through"?', in Locke, R., Kochan, T. and Piore, M. (eds) *Employment Relations in a Changing World Economy*, Cambridge, Massachusetts, London, England: The MIT Press, pp.33–58.

11. Schumacher, E.F. (1973) *Small is Beautiful, a Study Of Economics As If People Mattered,* London: Blond and Briggs.

12. Curran, J. and Stanworth, J. (1979) 'Worker involvement and social relations in the small firm', *The Sociological Review*, 27 (2): 317–42.

13. *Ibid*. p.337.

14. Curran, J. and Stanworth, J. (1979) 'Self-selection and the small firm worker – a critique and an alternative view', *Sociology*, 13 (3): 427–44.

15. Curran, J. and Stanworth, J. (1979) 'Worker involvement and social relations in the small firm', *The Sociological Review*, 27 (2): 317–42.

16. Rainnie, A. and Scott, M. (1986) 'Industrial relations in the small firm', in Curran, J. *et al.* (eds) *The Survival of the Small Firm vol. 2*, Aldershot: Gower, pp. 42–60.

17. Mike Scott *et al.* (1989) *Management and Industrial Relations in Small Firms*, London: Department of Employment Research Paper no. 70.
18. *Ibid.* p.42.
19. Functional flexibility relates to multiple tasking/skilling to facilitate movement of personnel between different jobs; numerical flexibility concerns the ability to increase or decrease the headcount by means of devices such as short term contracts and removal of rights to redundancy payments and/or claims of unfair dismissal; financial flexibility reflects the ability to vary pay according to market forces (supply and demand). See, for example, Atkinson, J. (1984) 'Manpower strategies for flexible organizations', *Personnel Management*, 16 (8): 28–31. For a detailed review of the concept and the empirical evidence see Legge, K. (1995) *Human Resource Management Rhetorics and Realities*, Houndsmills, Basingstoke: Macmillan Press, esp. ch. 5. For a lively, debunking of the concept of flexibility see also Legge, K. (1998) 'Flexibility: the gift-wrapping of employment degradation?' in Sparrow, P. and Marchington, M. *Human Resource Management*, London: FT-Pitman Publishing, ch. 19, pp.286–295.
20. Bechhofer, F. and Elliott, B. (eds) (1981) *The Petit Bourgeoisie: Comparative Studies of an Uneasy Stratum*, London: Macmillan.
21. Rainnie, A. (1989) *Industrial Relations in Small Firms*, London & New York: Routledge.
22. Brewster, C. and Hegewisch, A. (1994) *Policy and Practice in European Human Resource Management*, London: Routledge; Brewster, C. (1998) 'Flexible working in Europe', in Sparrow, P. and Marchington, M. (eds) (1998) *Human Resource Management, The New Agenda*, London: Financial Times/Pitman Publishing, 245–258.
23. Advisory, Conciliation and Arbitration Service (1988), *Labour Flexibility in Britain*, ACAS Occasional Paper 41, London: ACAS.
24. Legge, K. (1998) 'Flexibility: the gift-wrapping of employment degradation?' in Sparrow, P. and Marchington, M. (eds) *Human Resource Management A New Agenda*, London: Financial Times/Pitman Publishing, pp.286–295.
25. Rainnie *op. cit.,* esp. p.85.
26. Oakey, R. (1984) *High Technology Small Firms*, London: Pinter.
27. Sissons, K. (1997), 'Change and continuity in British industrial relations', in Locke, R., Kochan, T. and Piore, M. (eds) *Employment Relations in a Changing World Economy*, Cambridge, Mass.: the MIT Press, p. 51.
28. Hendry, C., Arthur, M.B. and Jones, A.M. (1995) *Strategy through People Adaptation and Learning in the Small-Medium Enterprise*, London & New York: Routledge.
29. Hendry, C., Jones, A., Arthur, M. and Pettigrew, A. (1991) *Human Resource Development in Small to Medium Sized Enterprises*, London: Department for Employment, Research Paper No. 88.
30. *Ibid.* pp. 28–31.
31. *Ibid.* p. 36.
32. Hendry, C. and Pettigrew, A. (1990) 'Human resource management: an agenda for the 1990s', *International Journal of Human Resource Management*, 1 (1): 17–44; Hendry, C. and Pettigrew, A. (1992) 'Patterns of strategic

change in the development of human resource management', *British Journal of Management*, 3 (3):137–56.

33. Chell, E. and Rhodes, H. (1999) 'The development of a methodology for researching vertical relations in small to medium sized enterprises', Manchester: *British Academy of Management Proceedings*, pp. 170–186; Attewell, P. (1990) 'What is skill?' *Work and Occupations*, 17 (4): 422–448.

34. Hendry *et al.* (1991), *op. cit.*, p.60.

35. Chell and Rhodes *op. cit.*

36. Beer, M., Spector, B., Lawrence, P., Quinn Mills, D. and Walton, R. (eds) (1984) *Managing Human Assets*, New York: The Free Press.

37. Holmes, L. (1990) 'Trainer competences: turning back the clock', *Training and Development*, April:17–20.

38. Training Agency (1989) *Training in Britain: Employee Perspectives*, research report, London: HMSO.

39. Hilton, P. (1992), 'Shepherd defends training policy', *Personnel Management*, December.

40. For further reading on this issue consult, for example, Tyson, S. *et al.* (eds), (1993) *Human Resource Management in Europe*, London: Kogan Page; and Sparrow, P.R. and Marchington, M. (1998) *Human Resource Management The New Agenda*, London: FT Pitman, esp. chs 14, 16 and 17.

41. Storey, J. (1992) *Developments in the Management of Human Resources*, Oxford: Blackwell, p.37.

42. Stevenson, H.H. *et al.* (1989) *New Business Ventures and the Entrepreneur*, Homewood, Illinois: Irwin. See also, Chell, E. *et al.* (1991) *The Entrepreneurial Personality, Concepts, Cases and Categories*, London: Routledge, p.59.

Chapter 15

1. Chell, E., Haworth, J. and Brearley, S. (1991) *The Entrepreneurial Personality: Concepts, Cases and Categories*, London: Routledge.

2. *Ibid.*, see especially the case studies of Henri-Lloyd and VSW.

3. Chell, E., Hedberg-Jalonen, N. and Miettinen, A. (1997) 'Are types of business owner-managers universal? A cross-country study of the UK, New Zealand and Finland' in Donckels, R, and Miettinen, A, (eds) *Entrepreneurship and SME Research: On its Way to the Millennium*, Aldershot: Ashgate, pp. 3–18.

4. This is redolent of the work of David McClelland (1961) *The Achieving Society*, (Princeton, New Jersey: Van Nostrand), which suggested that entrepreneurs have a high need for achievement. However, in such small firms, the owner-manager is the firm, therefore the choice of strategy is likely to reflect the deep seated needs of the owner-manager.

5. Davies (1990) quoted in North *et al.*, (see note 8) argues that TQM for the small enterprise is irrelevant *because it already practises TQM*. North *et al.* believe this to be 'wishful thinking' on the part of the owner-managers. However, the fact that owner-managers of small firms '[rarely] make an explicit commitment to TQM in a formal sense ...' (*Ibid.*, p.41) appears to miss Davies' point!

6. Garvin, D.A. (1988) *Managing Quality: the Strategic and Competitive Edge*, New York: Free Press; Hardie, N. (1993) 'Using theories of quality from disciplines outside the quality movement' in Chan, J.F.L. (ed) *Quality and its Application*, Sunderland, UK: Penshaw Press; Smith, C.F. (1993) 'The meaning of quality', *Total Quality Management* 4 (3):235–244.

7. Mat Hassan, M.E. (1996) *Quality Management in Malaysian Organizations – the Relevance of Values in the Improvement Process*, Doctoral Thesis, School of Management, Newcastle University, UK; Deming (see note 9) p.168; Juran, J.M. (1988) 'The quality function (section 2),' in Juran, J.M. and Gryna, F.M. (eds) *Juran's Quality Control Handbook*, 4th edn, New York: McGraw-Hill, p. 5; Crosby, P.B. (1984) *Quality Without Tears*, Maidenhead: McGraw-Hill, p.60; Adam, E.E. Jr., Hershauer, J.C. and Ruch, W.A. (1986) *Productivity and Quality*, 2nd edn, Columbia, Missouri: University of Missouri-Columbia Press, p.9; Groocock, J.M. (1986) *The Chain of Quality*, Chichester: Wiley, p.27; Thurston, W.R. (1985) 'Quality is between the customer's ears', *Across the Board*, January: 29–32; Ross, P.J. (1985) *Taguchi Techniques for Quality Engineering*, New York: McGraw-Hill, p.1; Gitlow, H., Gitlow, S., Oppenheim, A. and Oppenheim, R. (1989) *Tools and Methods for the Improvement of Quality*, Homewood, Illinois: Irwin, p.3; Hanan, M. and Karp, P. (1989) *Customer Satisfaction*, New York: AMACON; Collier, D.A. (1990) 'Measuring and managing service quality', in Bowen, D.E., Chase R.B., Cummings, T.G. and associates (eds) *Service Management Effectiveness*, San Francisco: Jossey-Bass, pp. 234–265; Senior, M. and Akehurst, G. (1991) 'The development of budget/economy hotels in the United Kingdom: the consumers' perceptions of quality', in Brown, S.W., Gummesson, E., Edwardsson, B. and Gustavsson, B. (eds) *Service Quality: Multidisciplinary and Multinational Perspectives*, Lexington, Massachusetts: Lexington Books, pp. 94–107.

8. North, J., Blackburn, R.A. and Curran, J. (1998) *The Quality Business – Quality Issues and Smaller Firms*, London: Routledge, esp. pp. 24–5.

9. Deming, W.E (1982, 1986) *Out of the Crisis*, Cambridge: Cambridge University Press, p. 169.

10. *Ibid.*, p.8.

11. See Drummond, H. (1992) *The Quality Movement*, London: Kogan Page, ch. 2.

12. Legge, K. (1995) *Human Resource Management – Rhetorics and Realities*, London: Macmillan Business, ch. 7.

13. North *et al. op. cit.*, esp. pp. 28–30.

14. North *et al. op. cit.*, esp. pp. 33–43.

15. I rely on North *et al. op. cit.* as my source; I have not come across an example of this method of quality assurance.

16. This actual case is anonymised and the analysis aided by Drummond *op. cit.*, ch. 6

17. Drummond *op. cit.*, pp. 99–104.

18. 'InstantoPrint' is a pseudonym to protect the identity of the company.

19. This rank order clearly is not absolute, a larger survey might reveal something different. The researchers had attempted to represent the population of small firms according to size bands. They were not totally

successful in this (see, North *et al.*, *op. cit.*, p.49) However, the relevant parameter here is sector and there is no way of knowing whether their sample represents firms by this parameter.

20. For a detailed review see Chell, E. (1993) *The Psychology of Behaviour in Organizations, 2nd edn*, London: Macmillan pp. 221–225; Drummond, H. and Chell, E. (1991) 'Should organizations pay for quality?', *Personnel Review*, 21 (1): 46–54; Hill, S. (1991) 'Why quality circles failed but total quality might succeed', *British Journal of Industrial Relations*, 29 (4): 541–68; Legge, K. (1995) *Human Resource Management*, London: Macmillan pp. 208–46.
21. See especially Legge, K. *op. cit.* pp. 228–234.
22. Drummond, H. *op. cit.*, p. 108 *et seq.*
23. One of the objections of academicians relates to the religious verve with which followers of TQM 'gurus' espouse. Even the rhetoric underscores such religiosity. For example, Carla Lazzareschi notes of the late W. Edwards Deming: 'he is a man with a *mission*. Today the 93-year old Deming still *preaches the gospel* of listening to workers and customers' (my emphasis) *Los Angeles Business* (Sunday, December 5, 1993).

    However, the European Foundation for Quality Management (EFMQ) uses the language of 'excellence' in promoting the pursuit of total quality management, founded by presidents of 14 major European companies in 1988, the EFQM at the time of writing (December 1999) had a membership of 600 organizations 'ranging from major multinationals and important national companies to research institutes in prominent European universities.' However, close examination of the EFQM 'excellence model' reveals a concept of the key inter-linked management processes that enable an organization to be successful 'regardless of sector, size, structure or maturity'. The rhetoric is nevertheless aspirational, and there are still recognizable phrases from the so-called 'gurus' such as 'constancy of purpose', but there are also some new ideas – the stakeholder concept has crept in, there is equal emphasis on innovation and improvement and the notion of involvement and the need to realize people's potential are also given prominence. But perhaps most noticeable is the importance given to the notion of leadership in developing 'the mission, *vision* and values and ... (presenting) role models of a culture of excellence'. [http://www.efqm.org/].
24. Drummond *op. cit.*, p. 130.
25. This case material is based on work reported in Mat Hassan *op. cit.*
26. Mat Hassan *op. cit.*, p.78.
27. Mat Hassan *op. cit.*, p.180.
28. Mat Hassan *op. cit.*, p.140.

Chapter 16

1. Schama, S. (1987) *The Embarrassment of Riches*, London: Collins, p. 358.
2. Castells, M. (1996) *The Rise of the Network Society*, Malden, Mass. and Oxford, UK: Blackwell.
3. *Ibid.* p. 60.

4. See discussion in chapter 14 of this volume.
5. The networked form of organization is also discussed in chapters 2 and 7 of this volume.
6. Castells, *op. cit.* p. 92 *et seq.*
7. Castells, *op. cit.* p. 199.
8. Castells, M. and Hall, P. (1994) *Technopoles of the World: The Makings of 21st Century Industrial Complexes*, London: Routledge.
9. See also chapter 2 of this volume.
10. The government's White Paper (1998) *Our Competitiveness Future – Building the Knowledge Driven Economy*, Cm 4176, London: The Stationery Office.
11. Saxenian, A.L. (1993) *Regional Networks: Industrial Adaptation in Silicon Valley and Route 128*, Cambridge, Mass: Harvard University Press; Castells, M. and Hall, P. (1994) *Technopoles of the World*, London: Routledge esp. ch. 2, pp. 12–28.
12. For a discussion of the role of tacit knowledge in the process of innovation, see Senker, J. and Faulkner, W. (1996) 'Networks, tacit knowledge and innovation' in Coombs, R., Richards, A., Saviotti, P.P. and Walsh, V. (eds) *Technological Collaboration*, Cheltenham, UK, Brookfield, US: Edward Elgar, pp. 76–97.
13. Castells and Hall *op. cit.*, esp. pp. 21–24.
14. Tokyo, Japan and Cambridge, UK are two examples.

Index